CUMBRIAN MEMORIES

JOHN MARSH & JOHN GARBUTT

SUTTON PUBLISHING

First published in the United Kingdom in 2000 by
Sutton Publishing Limited · Phoenix Mill
Thrupp · Stroud · Gloucestershire · GL5 2BU

British Library Cataloguing in Publication Data
A catalogue record for this book is available from the British Library.

ISBN 0-7509-2365-2

Typeset in 11/14pt Photina.
Typesetting and origination by
Sutton Publishing Limited.
Printed in Great Britain by
Butler & Tanner, Frome, Somerset.

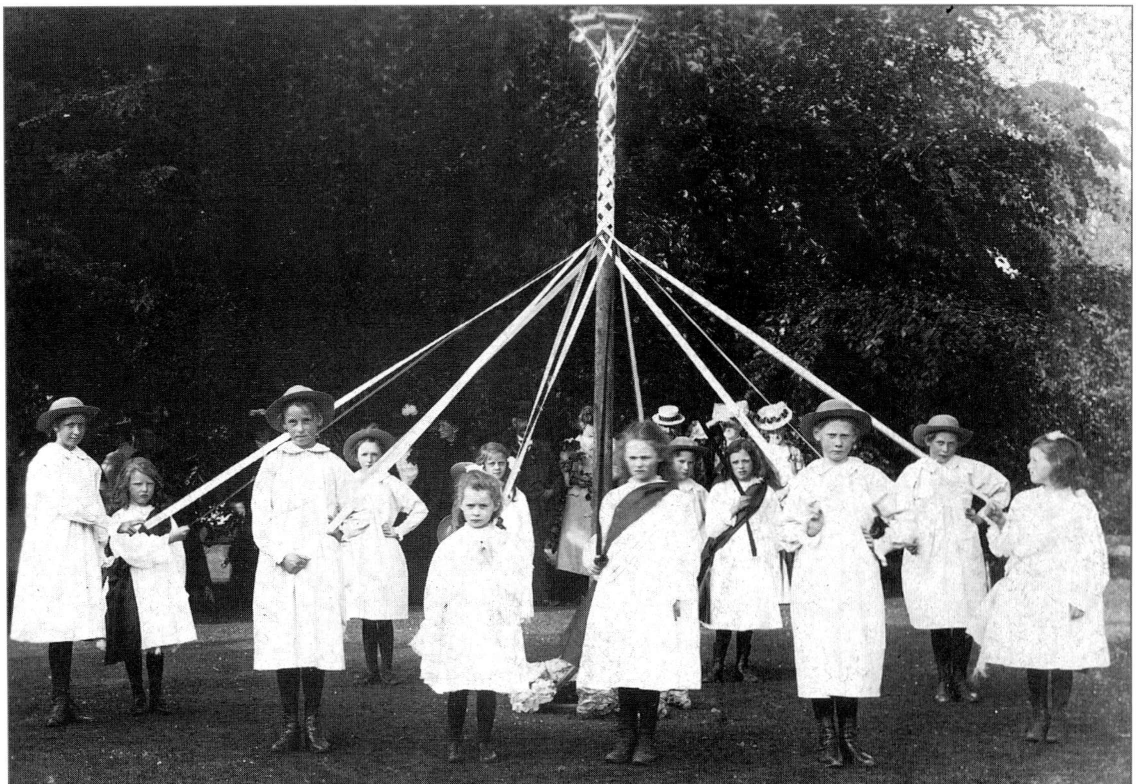

Maypole dancers at Beetham, near Milnthorpe, *c*. 1910. (*Mrs Sutcliffe, Burton*)

Contents

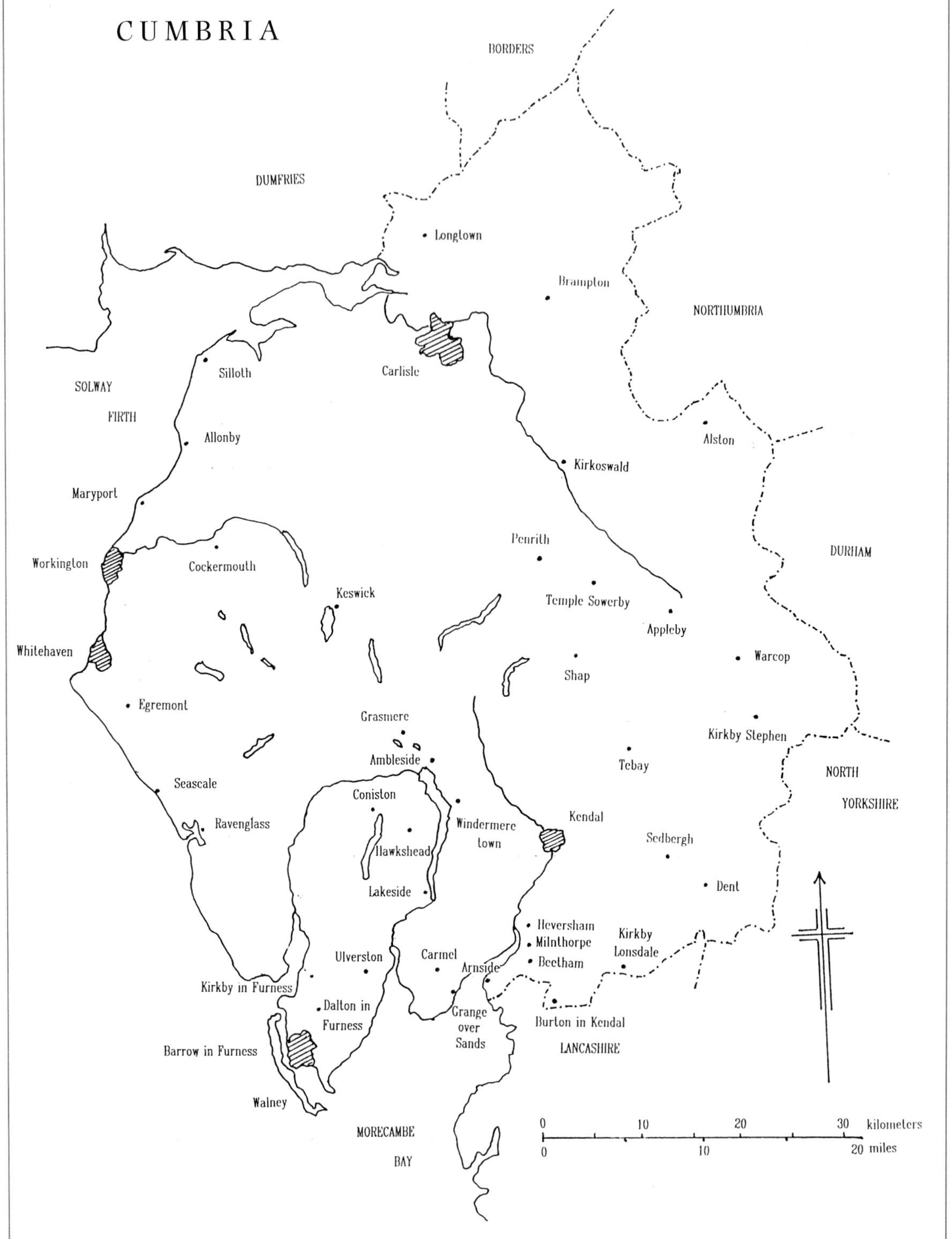
CUMBRIA
BORDERS
DUMFRIES
Longtown
Brampton
NORTHUMBRIA
Silloth
Carlisle
SOLWAY
FIRTH
Allonby
Alston
Kirkoswald
Maryport
Penrith
DURHAM
Workington
Cockermouth
Temple Sowerby
Keswick
Appleby
Whitehaven
Warcop
Shap
Egremont
Grasmere
Kirkby Stephen
Ambleside
Tebay
NORTH
YORKSHIRE
Seascale
Coniston
Ravenglass
Windermere
town
Kendal
Hawkshead
Sedbergh
Lakeside
Dent
Heversham
Milnthorpe
Beetham
Kirkby
Lonsdale
Ulverston
Carmel
Arnside
Kirkby in Furness
Dalton in
Furness
Grange
over
Sands
Burton in Kendal
LANCASHIRE
Barrow in Furness
Walney
MORECAMBE
BAY
0
10
20
30
kilometers
0
10
20
miles

Introduction

The authors have, in the past, published a number of books of photographs where the majority of pictures were just outside living memory. In *Cumbrian Memories* we trace life in a county that did not exist as an administrative unit in 1900 and illustrate events that many alive in the county today will remember or even took part in. This collection covers most decades of the last century, except the very recent, and attempts to include most parts of the huge area now called Cumbria. Probably the biggest event of the century has been the formation of 'Cumbria' on All Fools' Day 1974 (a point that the famous fell-walking writer Alfred Wainwright was keen to point out to readers of his books at the time).

oth of the authors have lived in Cumbria for over fifty years although at the start of our journey through life we would both have claimed to be Lancastrians as Ulverston, our home town, was in Furness when 'Lancashire North of the Sands' was part of Lancashire. 'Cumbria' came about as an administrative arrangement to suit the local authorities of the 1970s and proved a source of much annoyance to local romantics and those anxious to retain the status quo. The demise of Westmorland as an administrative unit along with Kendal as a royal chartered borough caused Wainwright to produce a map of the ancient county and books on both the county and on the ancient borough – all of which were new ventures for this author of fell-walking guides. The books were received with acclaim by residents and copies of all of them now change hands at greatly enhanced values, not through nostalgia for the old days but more out of the realisation that the author was a gifted genius of the twentieth century, and a chance to acquire anything such as a first edition of any of his works must not be missed.

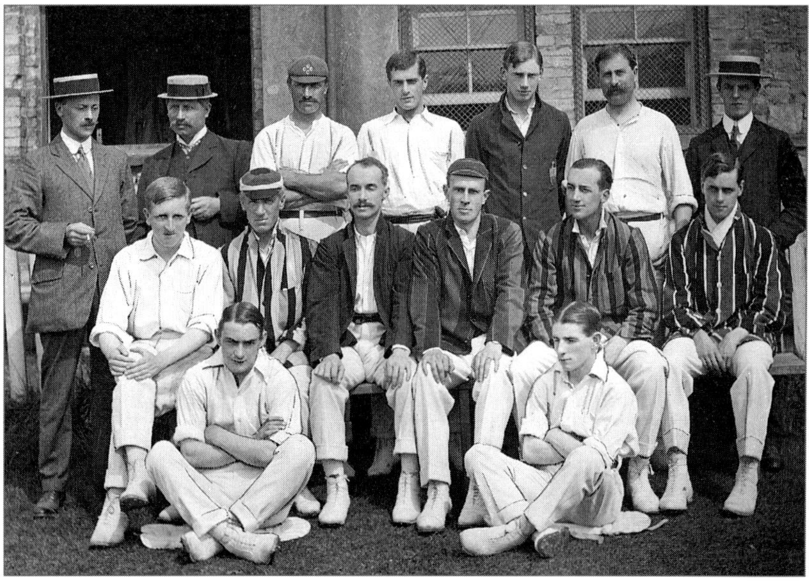

Kendal Cricket team pose for their photograph just before the First World War. The local Bateman shield competition was very serious as nearby Burneside Cricket Club kept winning it. (*Atkinson & Pollitt*)

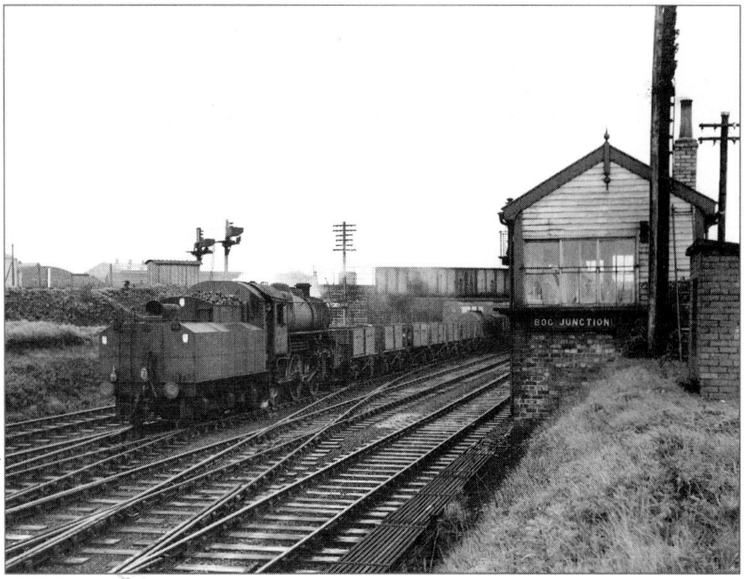

Bog Junction, Carlisle, with an express goods train on the main line. This was where the Maryport and Carlisle Railway used to join the main line into Carlisle Citadel station. (*Neville Stead*)

Cumberland and the Sedbergh area of the West Riding of Yorkshire (the Wapentake of Ewecross) received no epitaph from AW even though they were also absorbed into Cumbria. So Lancashire North of the Sands, the Sedbergh area of Yorkshire West Riding, Westmorland and Cumberland lost their unique identities to become part of Cumbria. Two large conurbations (by Cumbrian standards), Barrow-in-Furness and Carlisle, both somehow retained their borough status with enlarged areas to administer and the county of Cumbria found itself without a capital, while both boroughs (not part of the new county) vied for the position. The administration of the county, in many ways through expediency, crept into both towns, and thus Cumbria at the turn of the twentieth century is more than a bit of an administrative dogs' dinner, with services and offices in Barrow and Carlisle covering areas outside the administration in which they are situated. Add to this the mix-up with the National Parks (Dales and Lakes), the health services, the police and the arts organisations (North and North West), and the only conclusion that can be safely reached is that AW was probably right to draw attention to All Fools' Day.

Maybe the occupants of Cumbria prefer the mix-up. They were always individualistic in their approach to life (the geography of high fell and rivers until around the beginning of the twentieth century kept people in their place), and even after more than half a century of 'offcomers' moving into the various districts it is still possible to detect regional differences in the old Norse dialect that was used by most of the local families. Even if the dialect has been lost in modern speech the accent remains, and thus it is possible to detect where in Cumbria a person lives. It is strange to record that while Sedbergh, Furness, Cumberland and Westmorland were, from the eleventh century, divided by man-made boundaries, they all share a north country dialect based on the old Norse which crossed the boundaries as though they did not exist. It is unfortunate that modern education is killing this reminder of centuries past. The dialect is also likely to become just a memory, as have many of the events we record in these pages.

Using photographs ranging in date from the days of our grandparents through to only yesterday we attempt to offer Cumbrian Memories of the whole large area. Maybe the new race of Cumbrians born in the twenty-first century will look at these and wonder at what we consider, even now, as normal well-remembered events and styles. Our generation is unique in its ability to have photographic images of the previous generation and to be able to see how things really were. The photographers of the nineteenth century left a legacy which their pupils in the twentieth continued. By collecting and publishing their work we both hope, as custodians, to leave future generations an easy reference to life as lived by their parents and grandparents in the glorious hotch-potch of a county now called Cumbria.

It is now fashionable to call most of Cumbria 'The Lakes' or 'The English Lake District', but these are titles for the holiday industry and estate agents selling local housing to people from far away who find the area to their liking in spite of the weather and general lack of amenities. The weather cannot be easily changed but the lack of amenities, and the correction of that lack, is the subject of much debate in local planning committees. That many people depicted in our photographs took lack of amenities as a way of life is now a memory in itself. When we were young we walked almost everywhere and our parents walked even more. Wheeled transport, even the bicycle, was not generally available to all. Many in rural areas used the horse as transport or to pull a cart or carriage well into our lifetimes, as their forebears had done for many generations. There were no car parks as there were no cars, or lorries or buses that today seem to do as much harm to town and country as can possibly be compensated for by their usefulness. Our pictures contain few motor vehicles, as Cumbria, until the middle of the century, did not have many. The wonder of the steam railway was still causing excitement as the twentieth century began and not many communities were far from a railway station. The horse carriage and the stagecoach and charabanc continued in use into the first decades of the century to be replaced by motorised vehicles in the 1920s and '30s. Narrow roads were straightened and widened to accommodate the anticipated rush of motor vehicles. Many of our pictures show roads that were not straight, or wide, or even properly made, as that was the norm in the county until the middle of the twentieth century. Then the A6 through route from south to north was replaced by the M6 and many of the railways were closed. Traffic problems such as that at Ambleside, where a small market town found itself

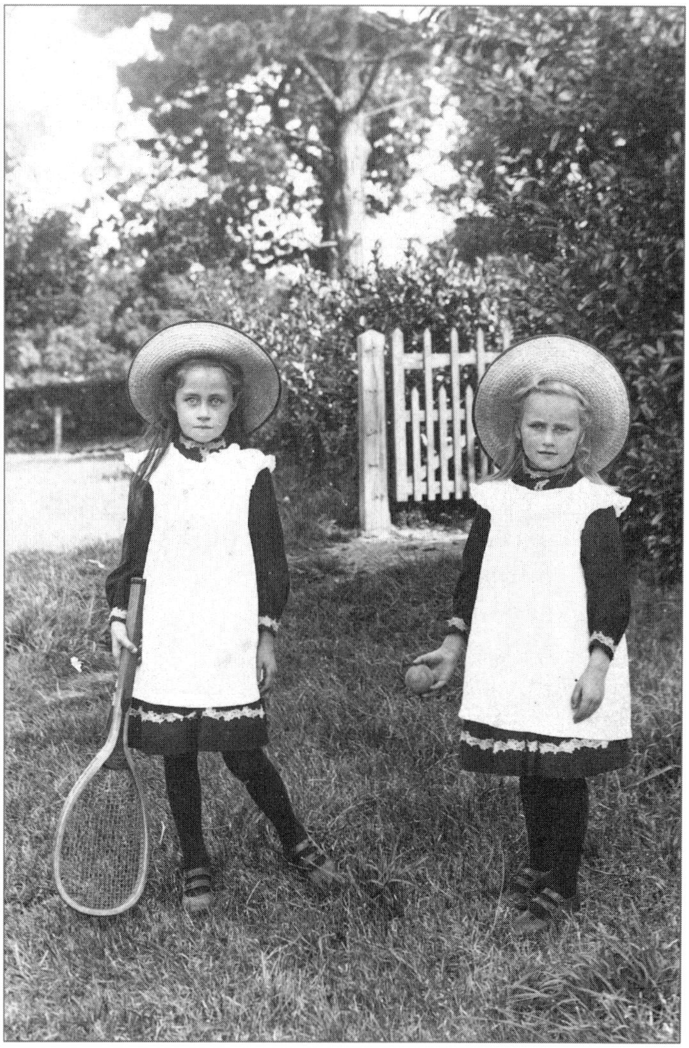

Twins Peggy and Connie Heath ready to play bat and ball, Burton-in-Kendal, 1905. (*John Marsh Collection*)

drowned by through traffic, created much debate without much result. The debates became political and thus were doomed to failure, and any 'offcomer' offering an opinion based on experiences from elsewhere was viewed with such suspicion that they need never have spoken. Most of the motorists to be found in our pictures knew nothing of such problems. Theirs was the joy of the open road (even if it twisted a bit and was unmade).

Our Cumbrian Memories are mostly from an age that has been so overtaken by modern times that the events depicted cannot be easily related to our present way of life – and yet the change was gradual, as will be found by careful examination of the pictures. Agriculture, once the main part of the local economy, changed as did the transport systems and much else. There seemed more hours to the day and more days in the week. Money was scarce to most Cumbrians and near-poverty, a memory that cannot be preserved photographically, was a fact of life for many to whom a photograph was a luxury. Maybe a poor diet can be detected even if it is hidden behind a smile.

A number of our pictures come from a photographic series of postcards published under the title *Atkinson & Pollitt* by the *Westmorland Gazette* from the 1920s through to the 1950s and we are grateful to the Editor for his kind permission to use these pictures. We have, as always, tried our best to trace copyright holders of pictures from the collection that carries no trace of a source. Many of the pictures are by local photographers, second and third generation picture-takers who have left a historical legacy of high importance to present and future historians of the fascinating county of Cumbria. Those we know we name against their work but it is unfortunate, we find, that when collecting old photographs in many cases there is nothing to indicate the source of the picture and, often, nothing to say where the picture was taken. Most collectors will have a number of images that give no clue of photographer or whereabouts. In sorting the pictures for this collection a number of first-class photographs were excluded for these very reasons.

Our collection of Cumbrian Memories depicts many things that have now gone and a way of life completely changed. We offer our record of life in the past century.

John Marsh & John Garbutt
Autumn 1999

Transport

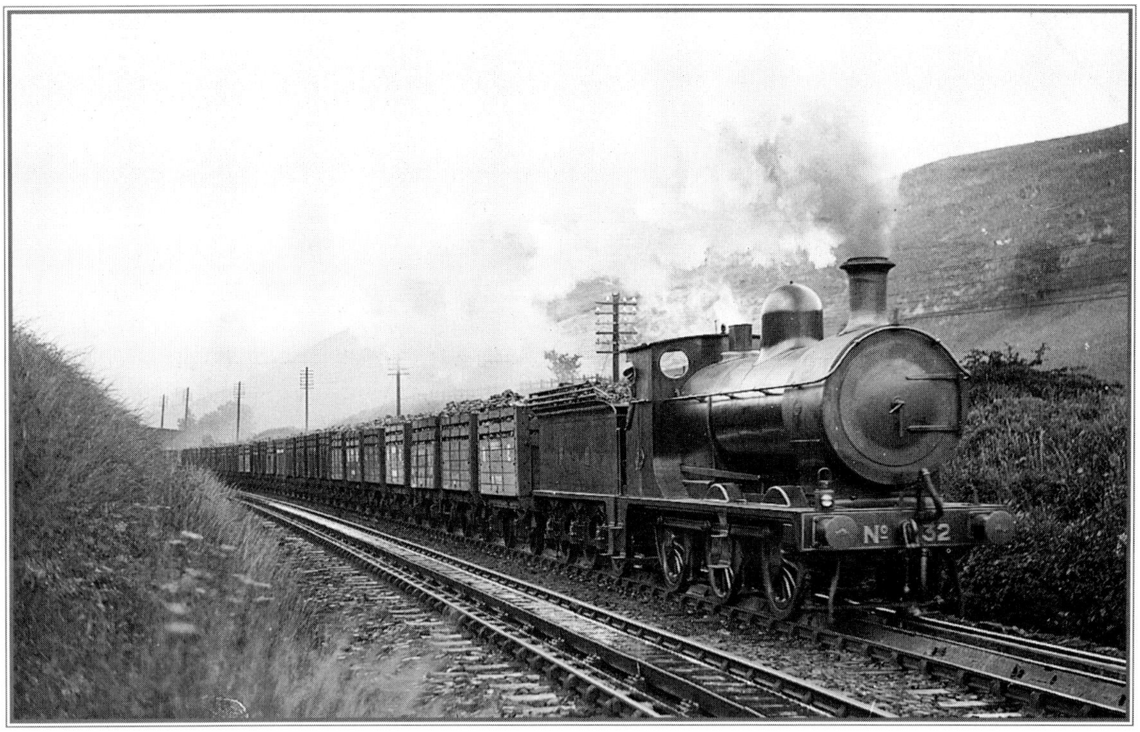

The Dillicar water troughs were situated in the Lune valley just south of the railway village of Tebay. By lowering a special feeder pipe the engines travelling on the main London and North Western, later London Midland and Scottish, Railway were able to refill their water tanks without stopping. Here can be seen a Furness railway engine class D.5 0–6–0 no. 32 taking a Barrow-bound train of full coke wagons from the coke ovens of the north-east coalfield to the furnaces of the Furness iron and steel industry, sometime before the 1924 take-over of the Furness railway by the LMS. The unknown photographer waited in vain for the usual splash when water was being picked up but this Furness engine did not use the facility. This trade, the Stainmore line, the Tebay to Kirkby Stephen branch line which carried it in Cumbria and the Dillicar troughs are now but a memory. The engine, built in 1920, was withdrawn by British Rail in 1956. The line at Dillicar now shares the Lune valley with the M6 and has been electrified since the 1970s (see also p. 25). *(John Marsh Collection)*

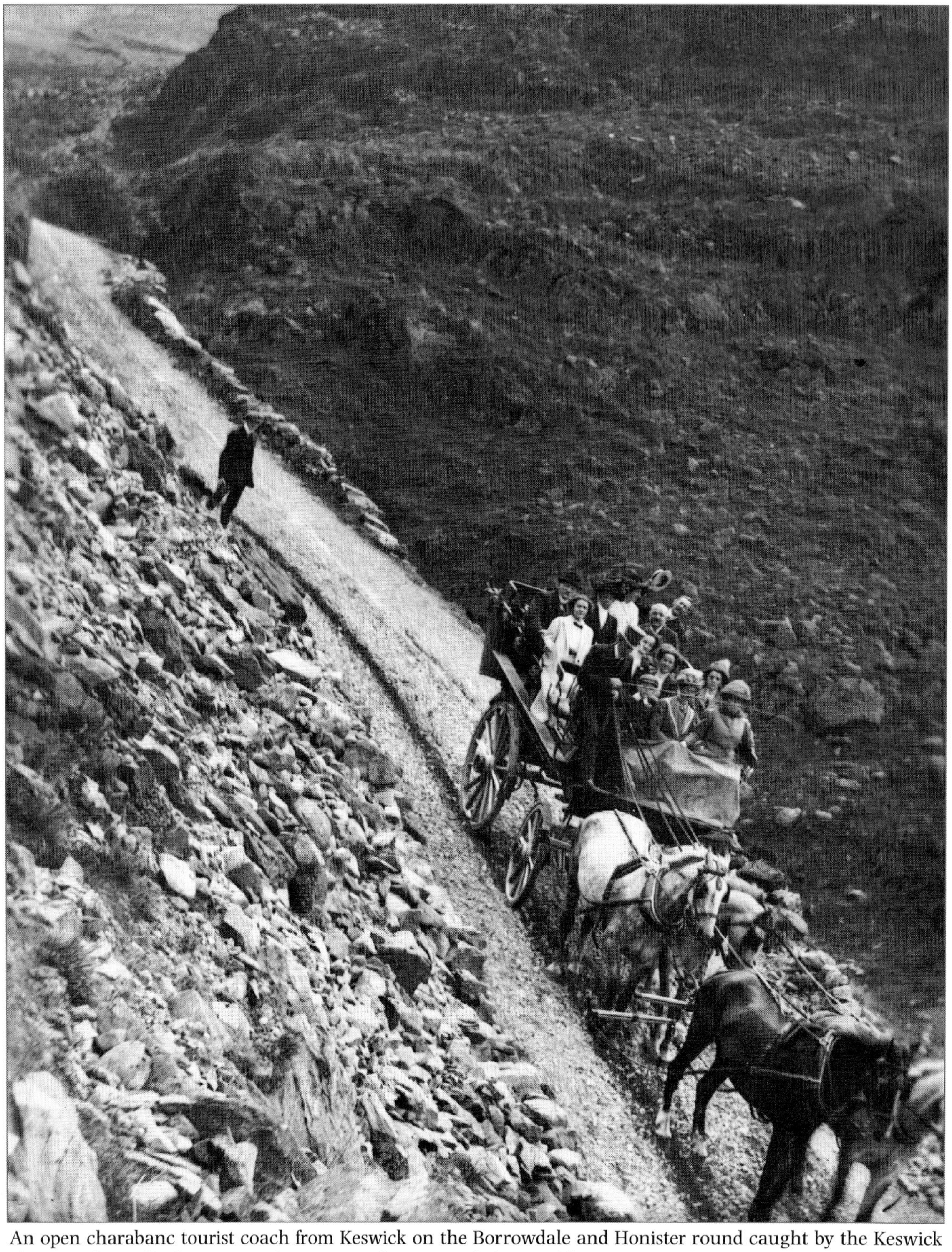

An open charabanc tourist coach from Keswick on the Borrowdale and Honister round caught by the Keswick photographer Alfred Pettitt in the 1920s. The postcard, from Hilda staying at the Grosvenor House Hotel in Blethcathra Street, Keswick, claims that she was riding on the very same coach 'yesterday' (3 September 1923). 'We mounted 1100 feet above sea level – we enjoyed it very much' she told Miss Muriel Jones of Pudsey, Yorkshire. The horses are seen drawing the fully laden coach downhill with the brakes full on – note the deep skid marks left in the unmade road. (*Alfred Pettitt, Keswick*)

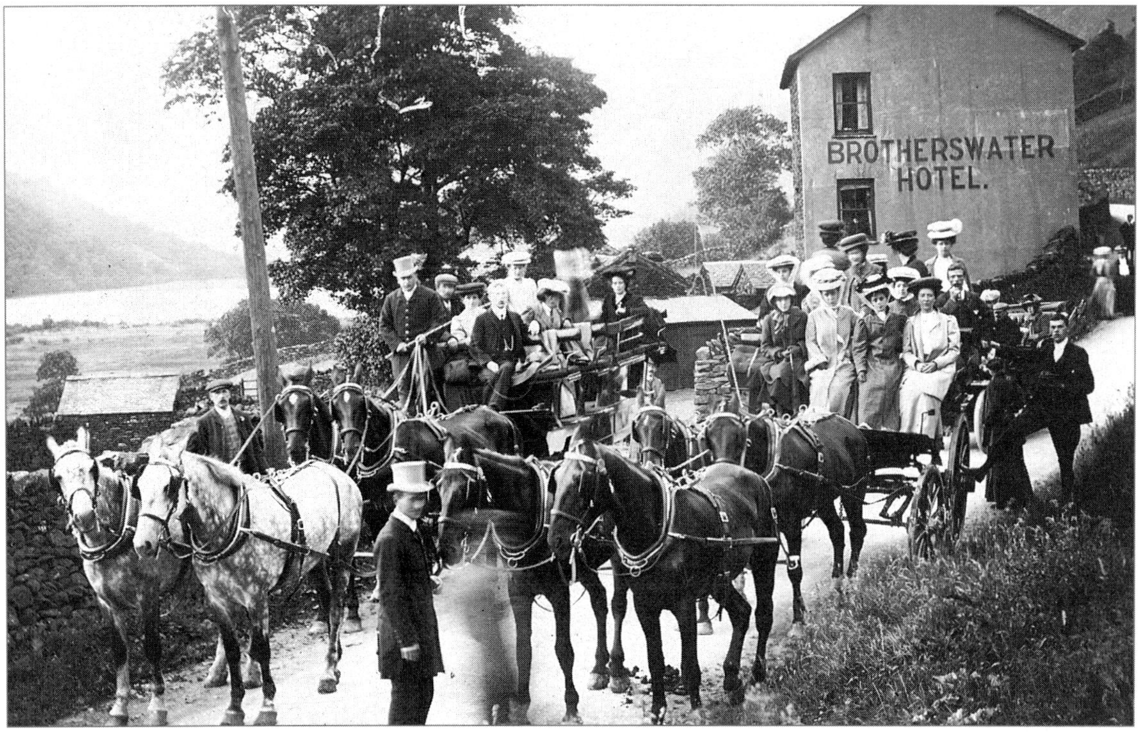

Brotherswater was in the old county of Westmorland until 1974 although it was on the Cumberland side of the Kirkstone Pass. On 5 August 1907 the Kendal Zion chapel choir hired two coaches with drivers from Riggs, the then famous Lakeland coaching firm with headquarters at Windermere railway station. Here they are seen outside the Brotherswater Hotel where, perhaps, a refreshment break was taken. (*John Marsh Collection*)

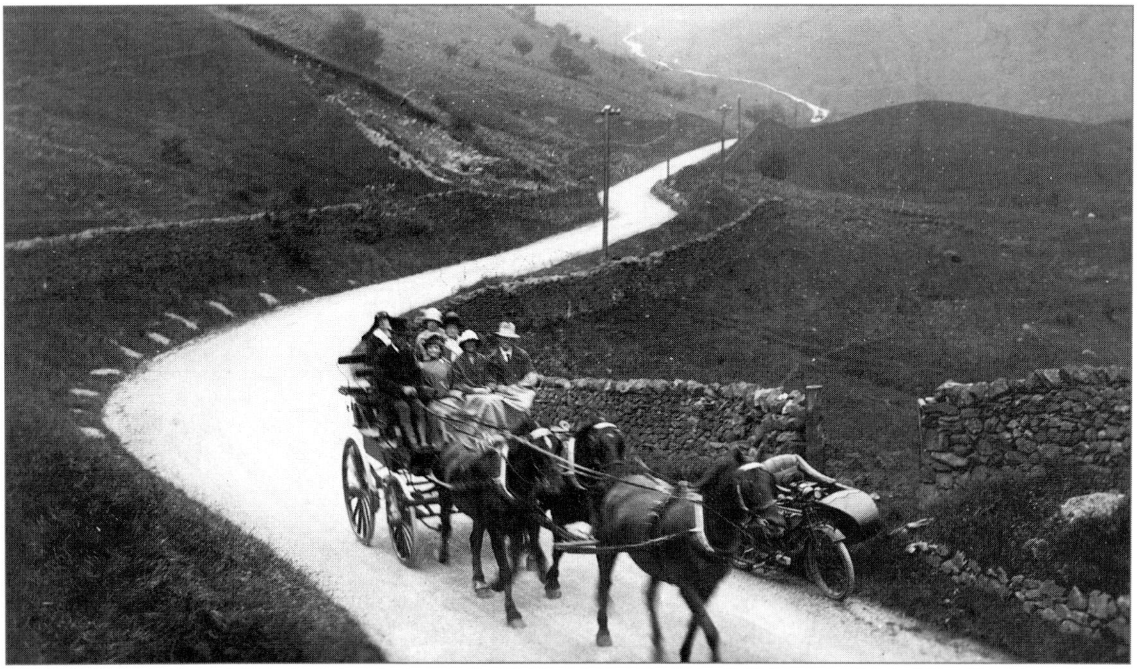

En route from Patterdale to Ambleside at the bottom of 'the Struggle' on Kirkstone Pass in the 1920s. The open touring charabanc with three horses in hand passes the Atkinson & Pollitt photographer's motorcycle and sidecar. The road surface shows signs of being in good condition, although it is not yet tarmacadamed. (*Atkinson & Pollitt*)

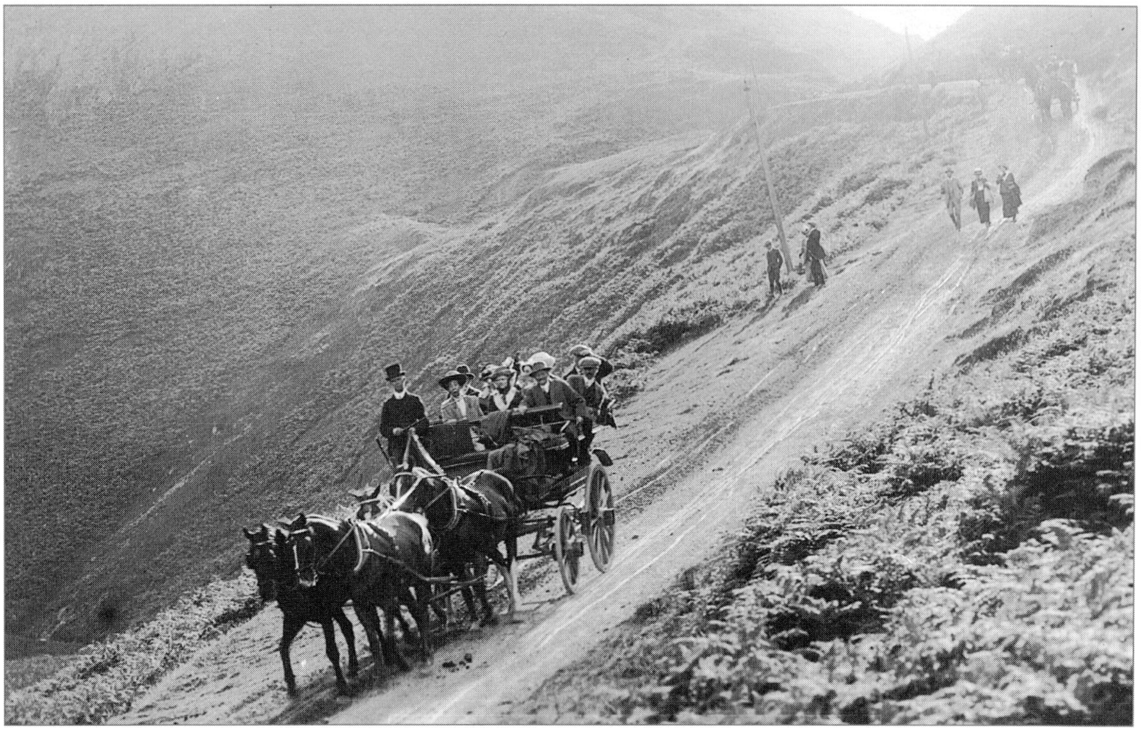

A four-in-hand charabanc on the lake side of Buttermere Hause. Alfred Pettitt of Keswick, one of the earliest Lakeland photographers, had obviously learned by 1910 how to exaggerate the precariousness of travel over a Lakeland pass. The rough nature of the unmade road needs no emphasis. (*Alfred Pettitt, Keswick*)

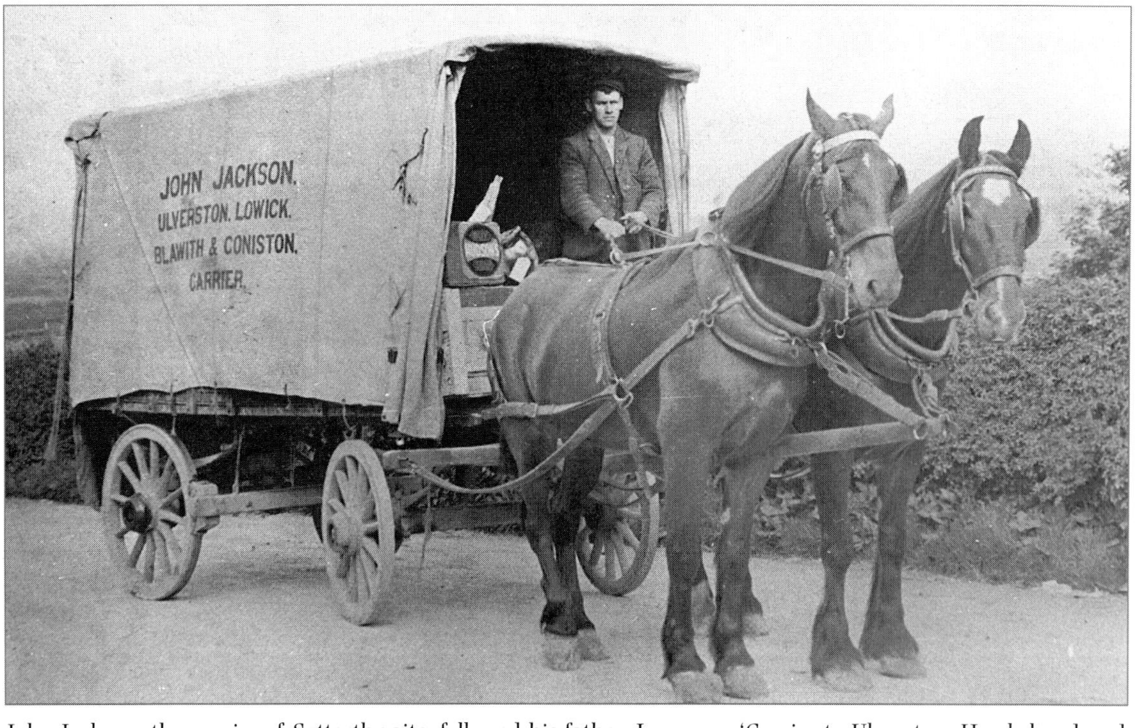

John Jackson, the carrier of Satterthwaite, followed his father, James, as 'Carrier to Ulverston, Hawkshead and Ambleside'. Father and son had one of many carrier businesses which provided an essential inter-community service in the days before motor transport. (*John Garbutt Collection*)

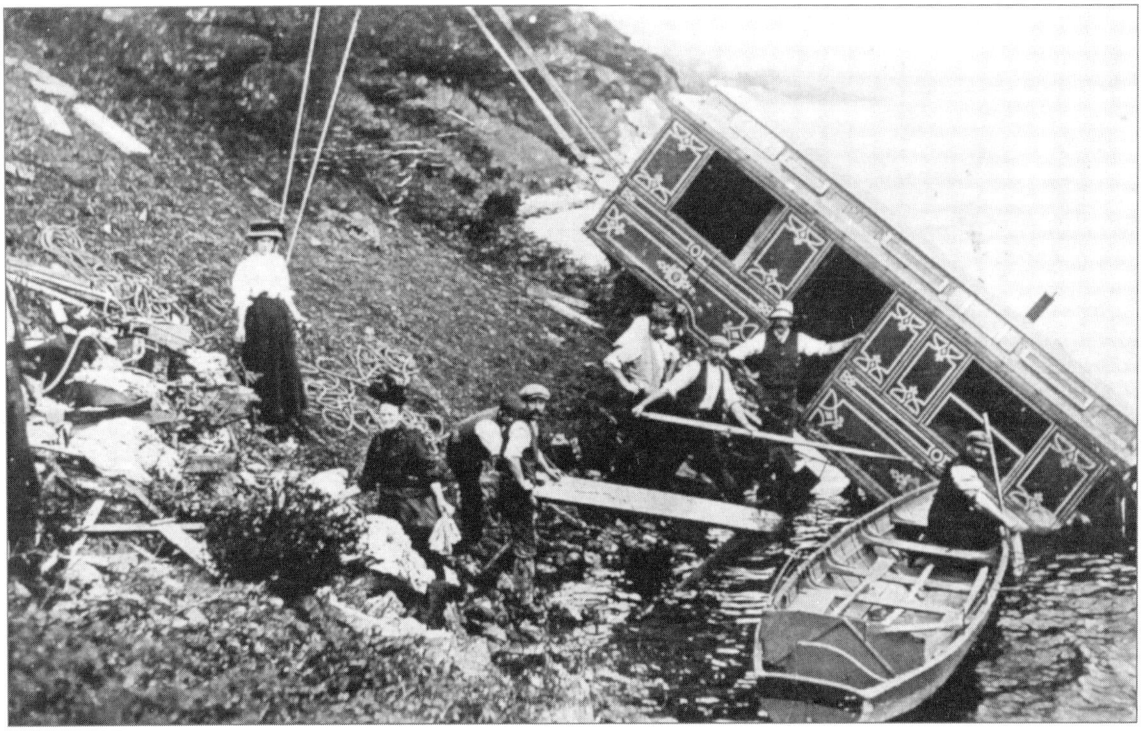

Burrell fairground steam engine 2979, pulling a series of showmen's vans, ran into Thirlmere on 2 June 1908 when the new lakeside road, built by Manchester Corporation only ten years before, subsided. Driver Francis Wood and steersman Thomas Hector Allen were killed. Damages and costs were awarded against the Corporation in a civil court case. (*John Marsh Collection*)

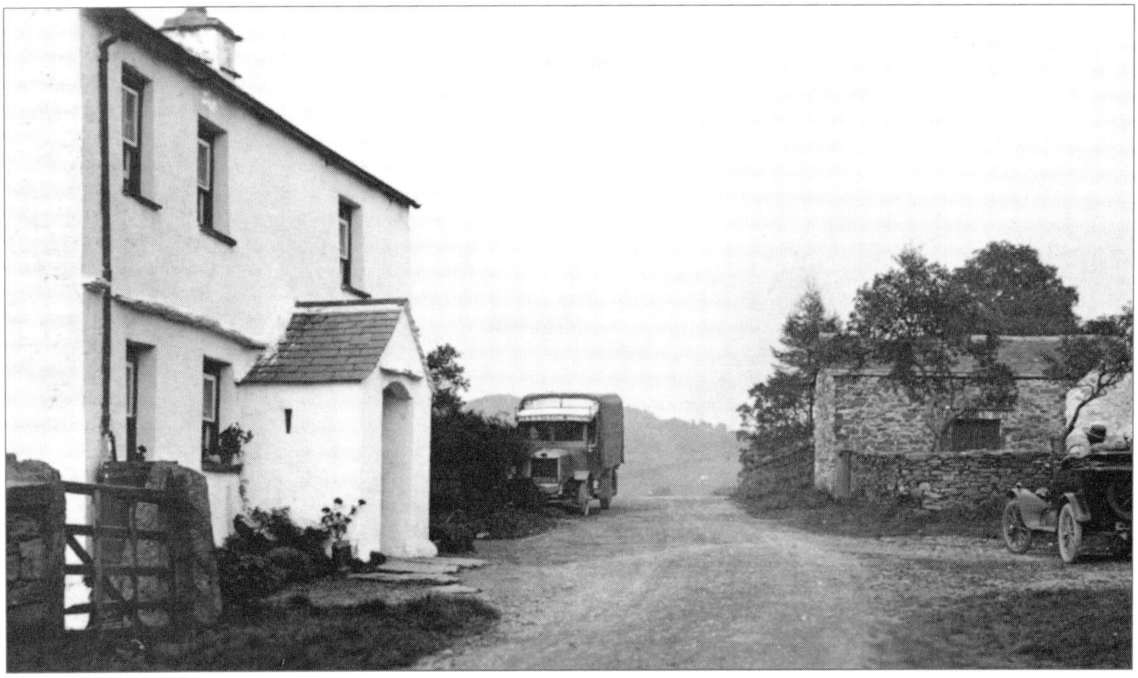

Bowland Bridge post office with Harrison Brothers carrier's lorry in the early 1930s when Atkinson & Pollitt's photographer (see p. 3) had acquired what appears to be a Model T Ford open tourer motor car. Note the unmade road. The neat whitewashed house has an air of prosperity. (*Atkinson & Pollitt*)

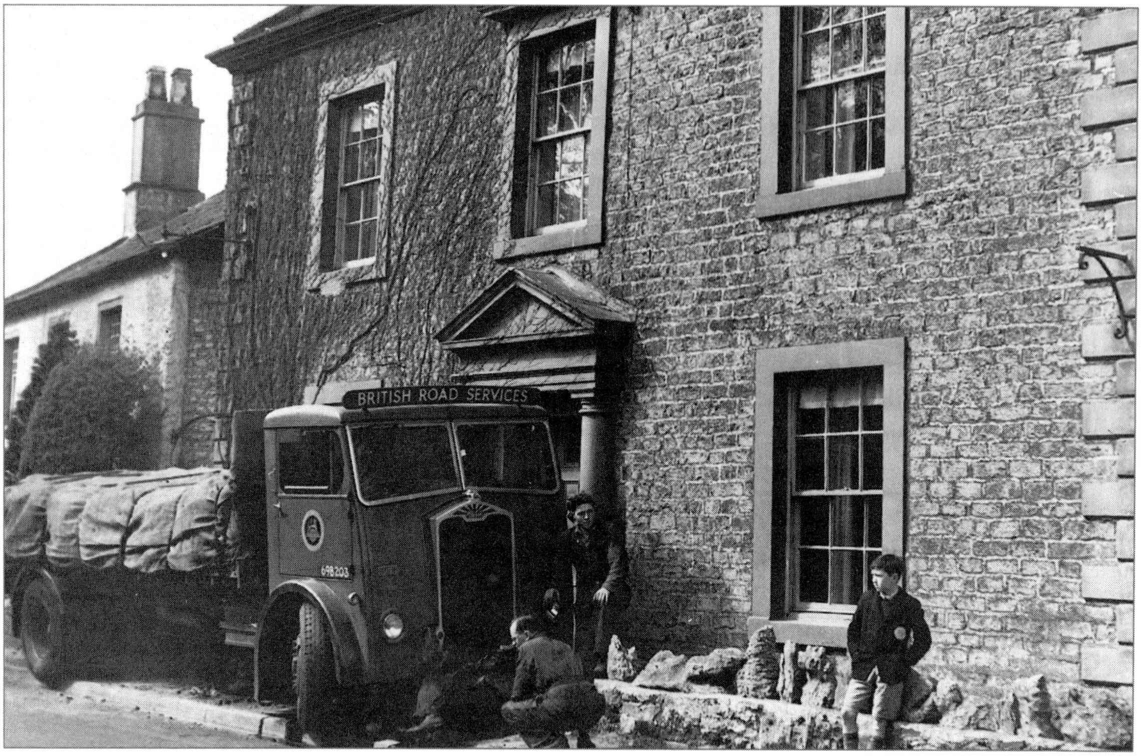

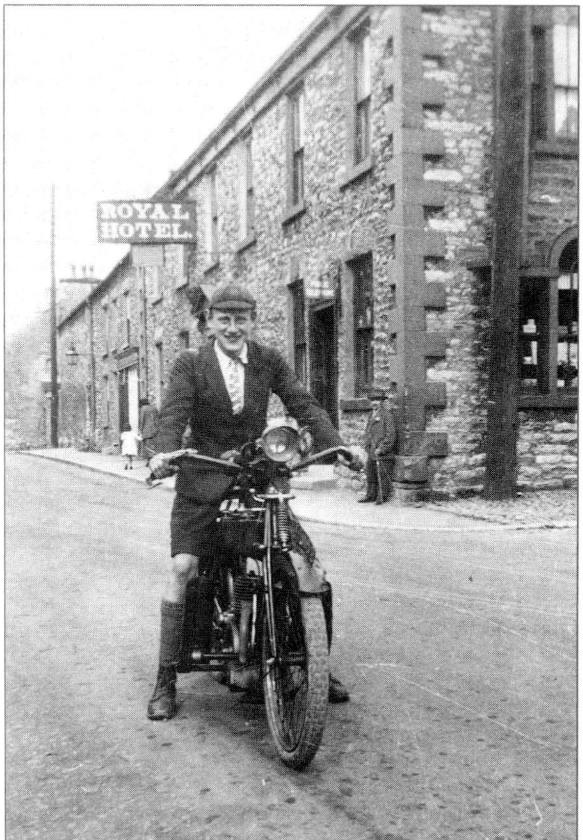

Burton-in-Kendal is sited on the old turnpike road to the north, which became the A6070 and a handy escape from the A6 used by many hauliers. In the top picture a 1950s mistake by a British Road Services driver left his lorry on the main gate to the Mansion House, and the recovery team is seen trying to rectify the situation. Left: outside the Royal Hotel in earlier times of light traffic a juvenile motor cyclist from the days before the 1930s motoring regulations proudly poses with his machine. *(John Marsh Collection)*

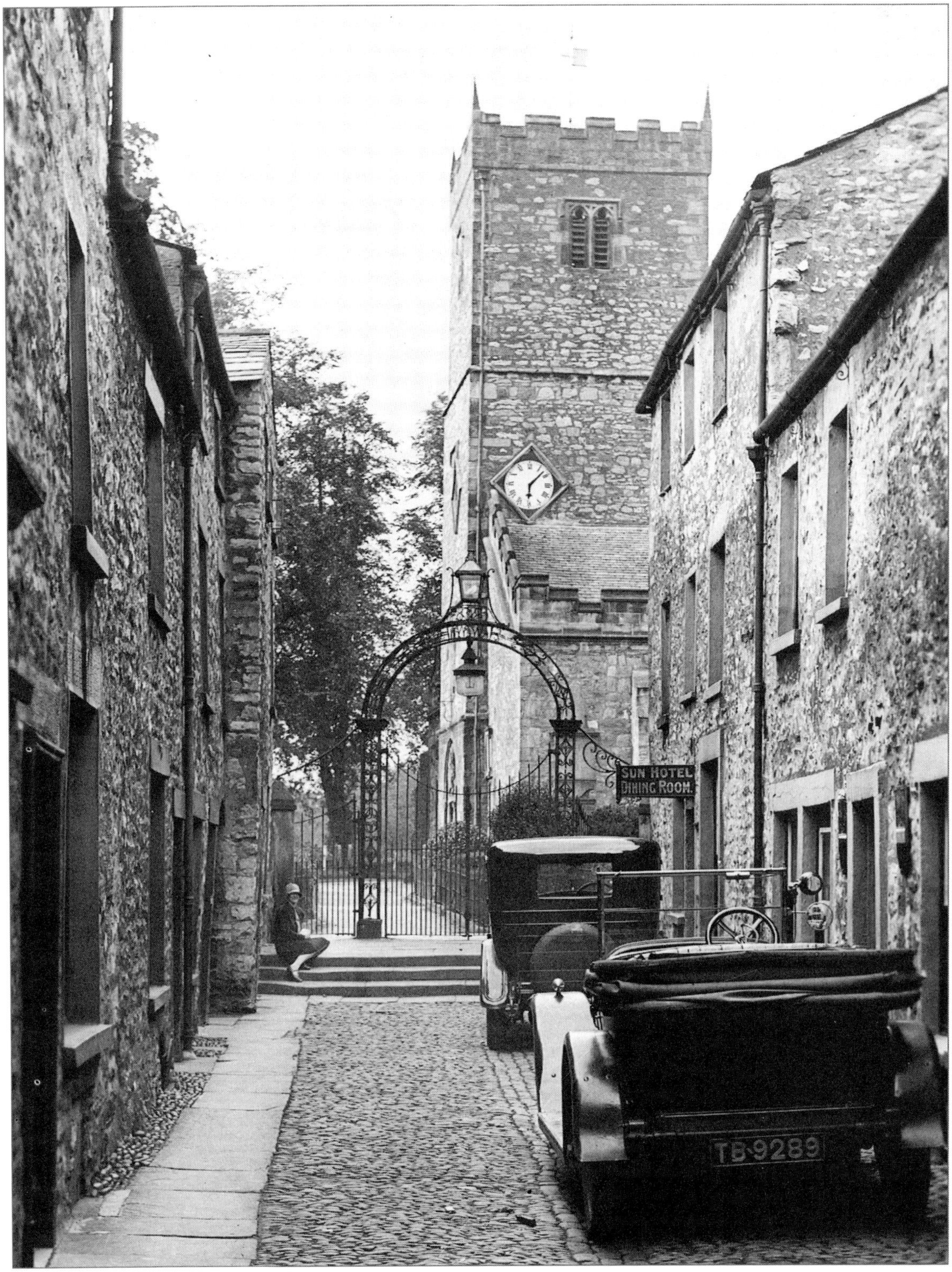

Kirkby Lonsdale parking problems in the 1920s with Church Street, leading to the ancient St Mary's church, obstructed by a saloon and an open tourer car. The Sun Hotel dining room could have been entered only with some difficulty. This was the portent of a much larger problem in the last seventy years of the century, as personal motorised transport changed Cumbrian life in many ways. (*Atkinson & Pollitt*)

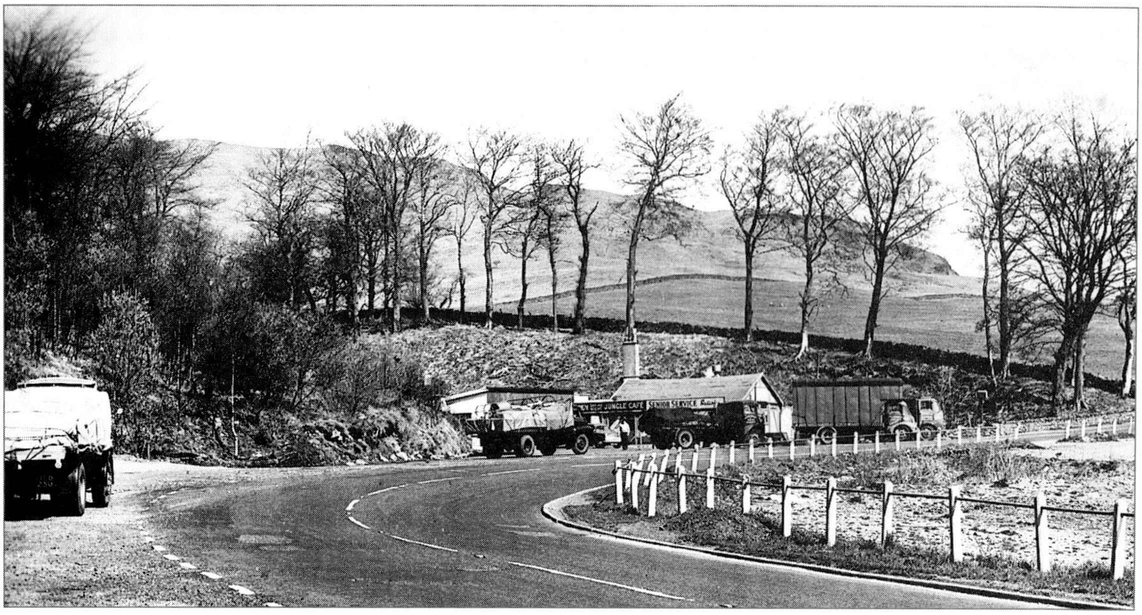

The Jungle Café, Selside, was built in a small quarry surrounded by a copse behind the main A6 road over Shap Fell. It offered all the services of a roadside transport café particularly during the harsh winters when many lorries were marooned by snowdrifts. It existed until the M6 was opened in 1970, when the site became a caravan sales park. (*Atkinson & Pollitt*)

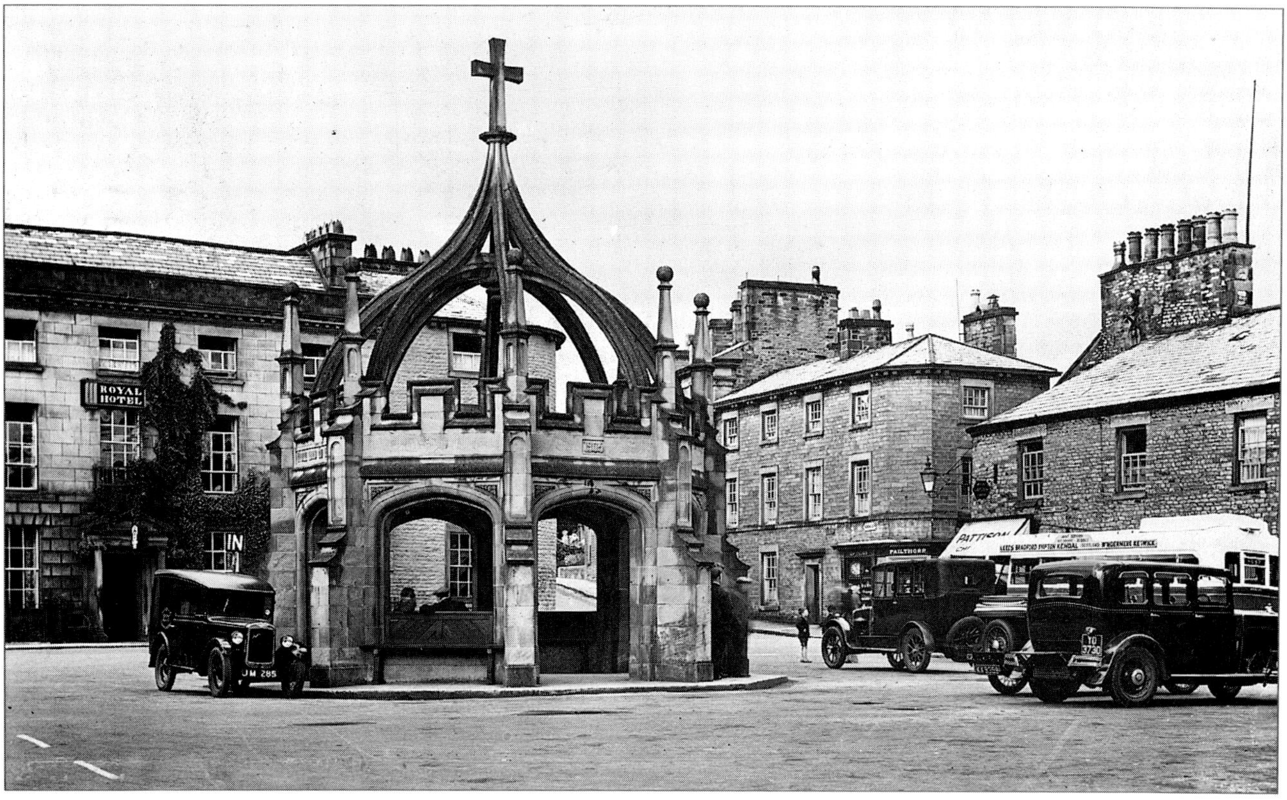

Kirkby Lonsdale's 'new' Market Square was also becoming nothing more than a car park well before the cross was taken off the 1905 Llewellyn Davies memorial in the 1920s. The local bus company was helping to turn the square into a bus stop. Transport was changing everything. (*Atkinson & Pollitt*)

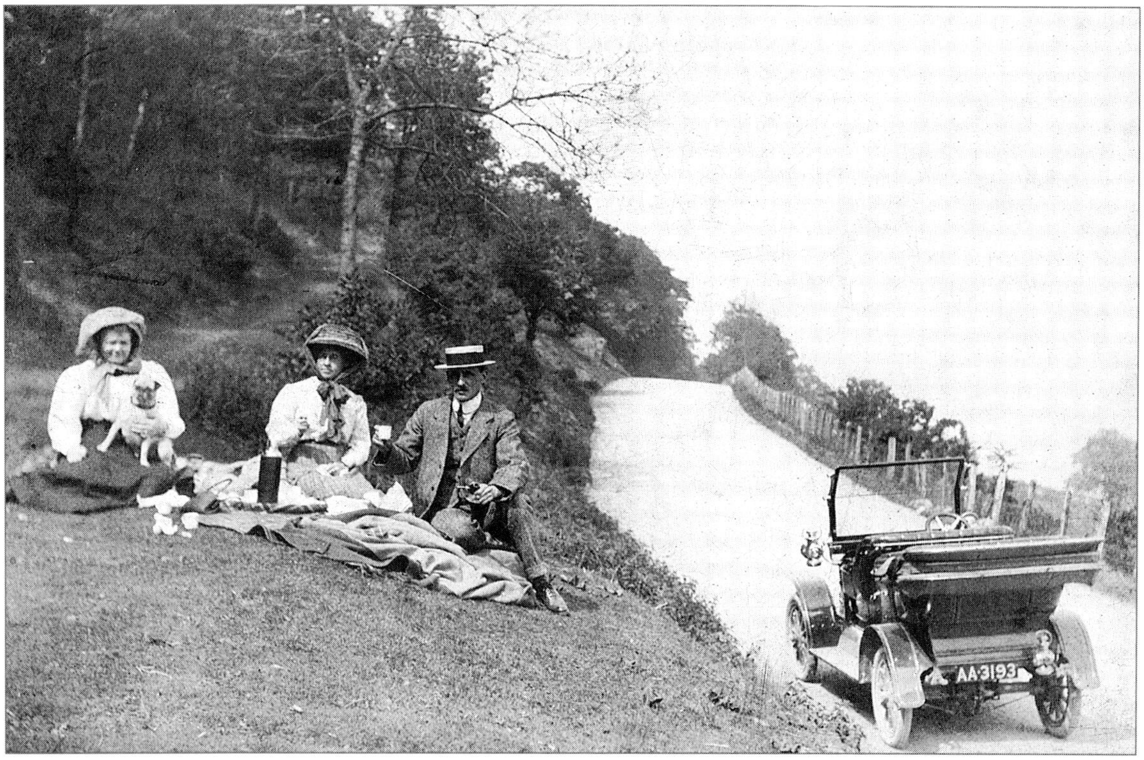

The Kirkstone Pass road in the Troutbeck valley when one could park one's Model T Ford by the roadside and disembark for a picnic. How times have changed! Nowadays the early numberplate AA3193 would cost more than the car did then. (*Brockbank of Windermere*)

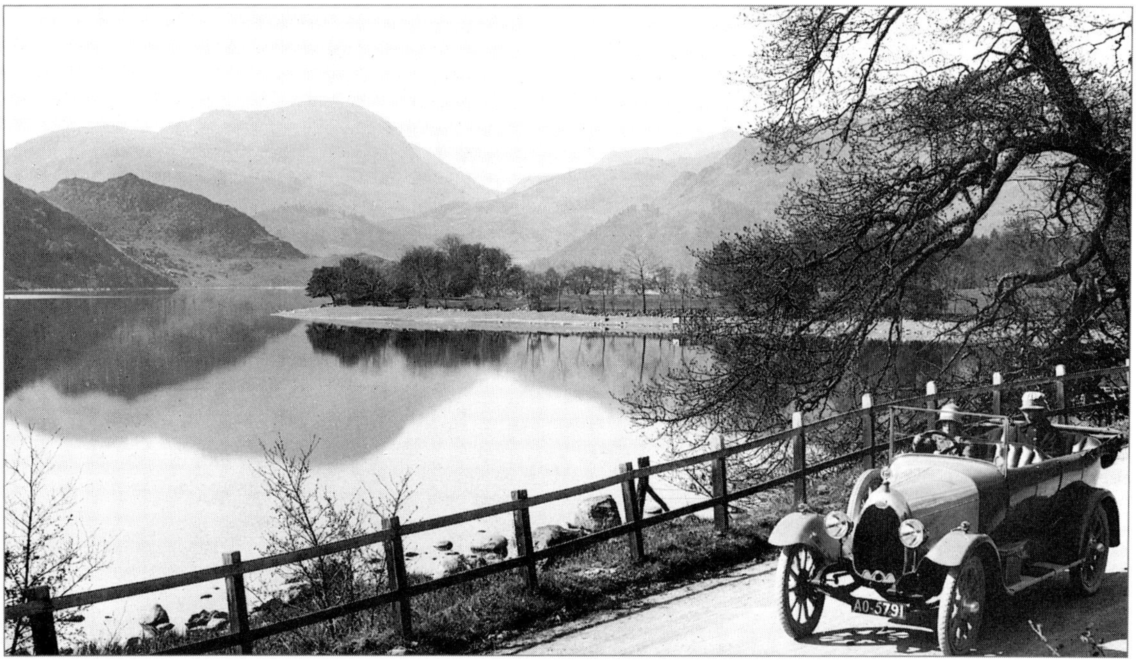

'Motoring along Ullswater' was the title G.P. Abraham gave this 1920s postcard photograph. The car, which has electric headlamps, may be a rare Angus Sanderson – and is being driven by a lady on the wrong side of the road.

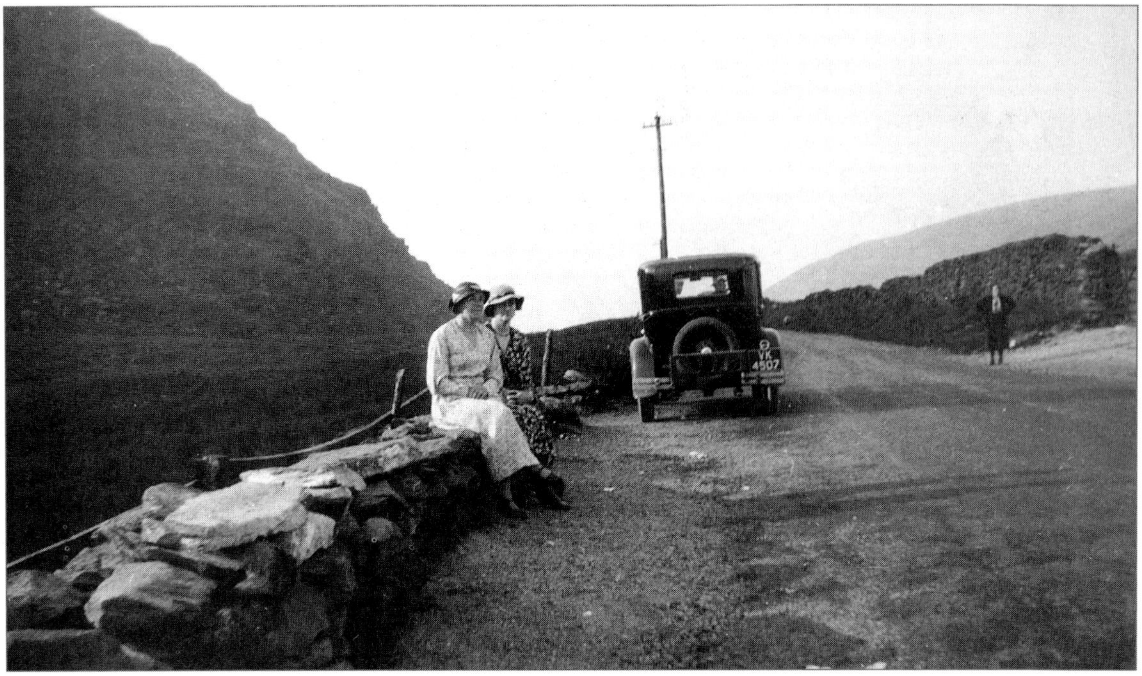

Kirkstone Pass summit layby was a narrow strip in the early 1930s when this Newcastle upon Tyne-registered saloon car used the opportunity to cool down after the climb. The radiators of some cars boiled on the way up and many didn't make it to the summit. In the lower picture we see the Kirkstone Pass Inn in the 1920s. The Blackpool-registered open tourer is having its radiator replenished. (*John Marsh Collection*)

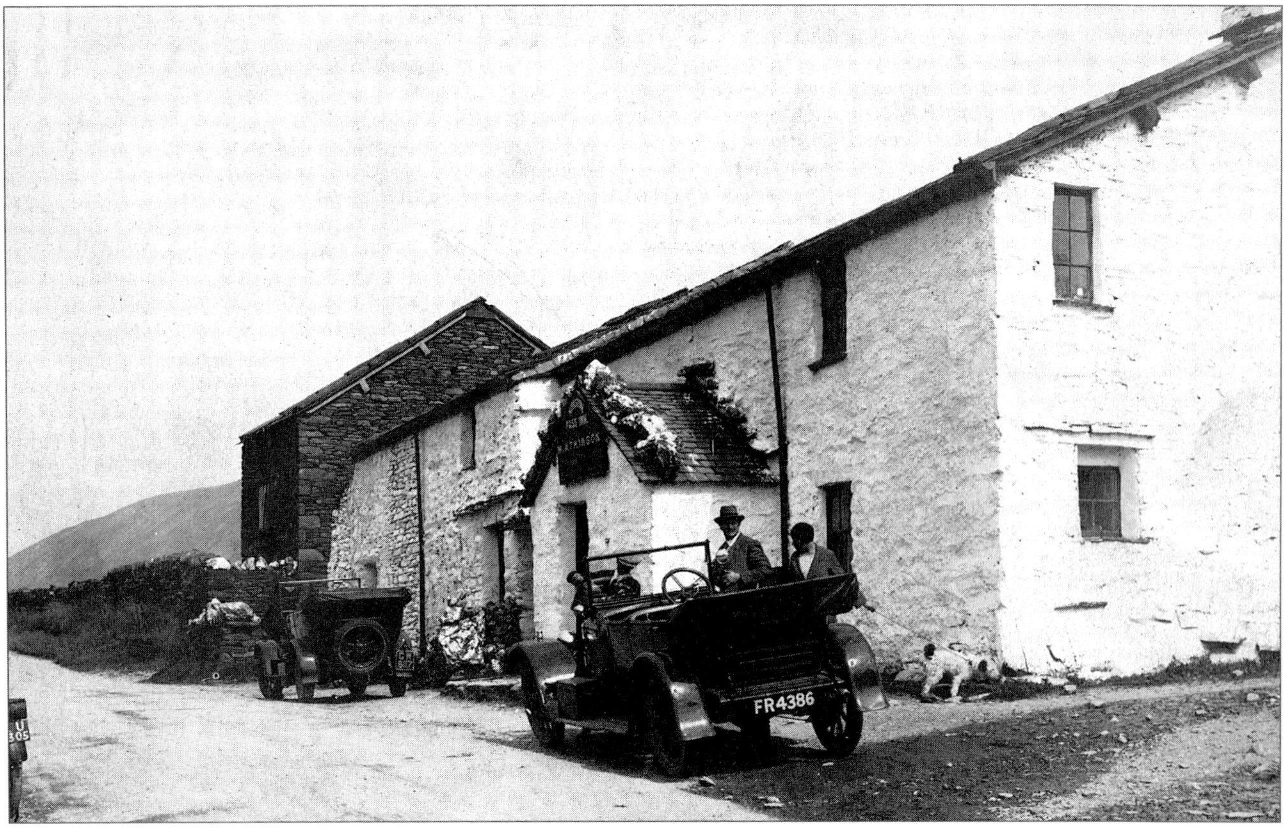

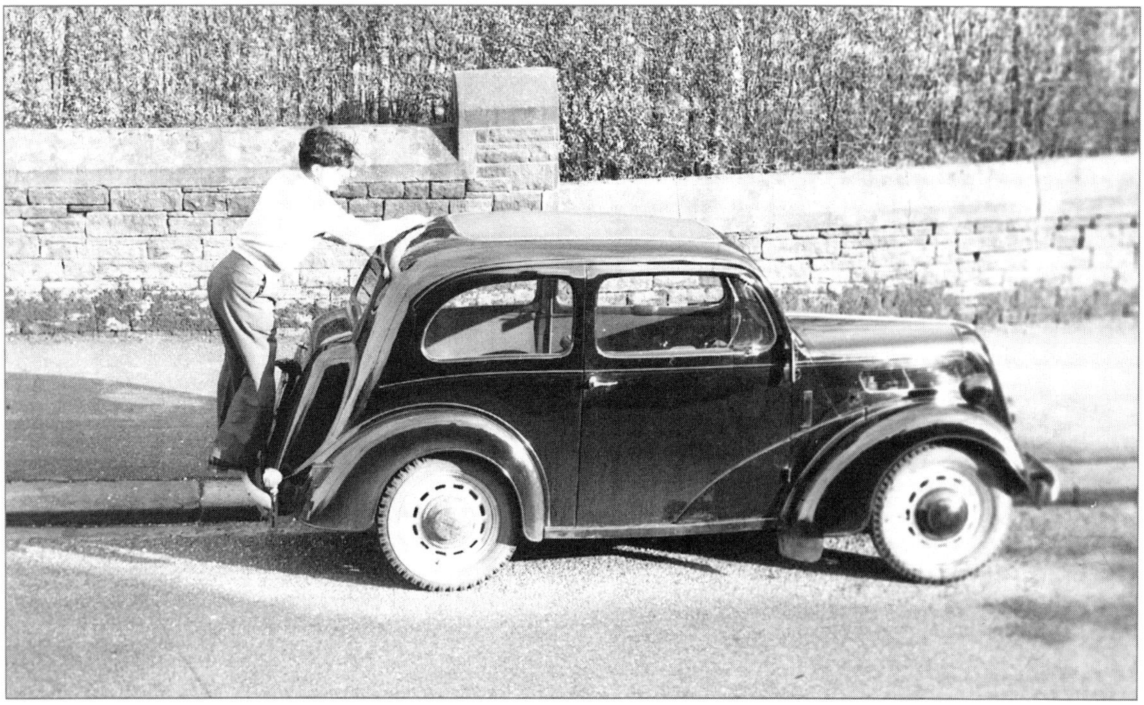

In Penrith in 1955 Colin Milligan, Manchester Water Works junior engineer, visited friends on Beacon Edge and gave his Ford Popular motor car a wash and polish while he was there. Climbing on the rear bumper was the way to get to the top of the car. (*John Marsh*)

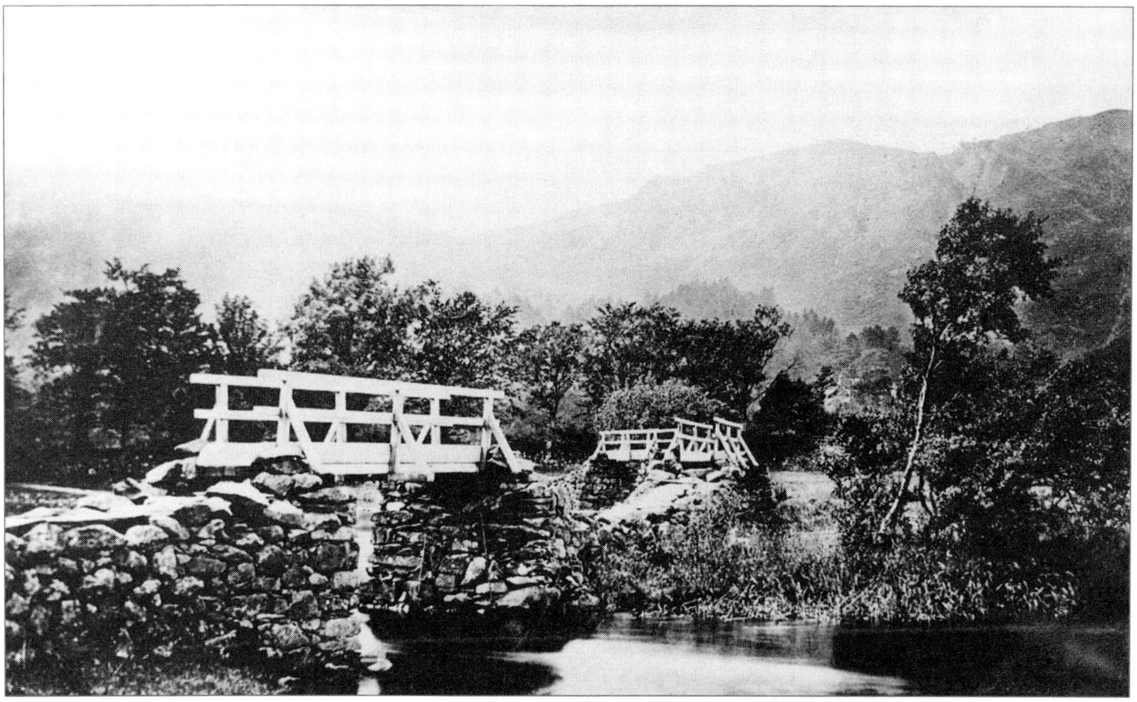

The footbridges at the north end of the Thirlmere valley are now but a distant memory. A late nineteenth-century guidebook said 'the shape of the lake is very curious, being contracted almost opposite Dalehead Hall to the width of a river by the delta of a beck from Fisher Gill and the strait thus formed is picturesquely spanned by a little wooden footbridge.' (*Kendal Library, Local Studies Collection*)

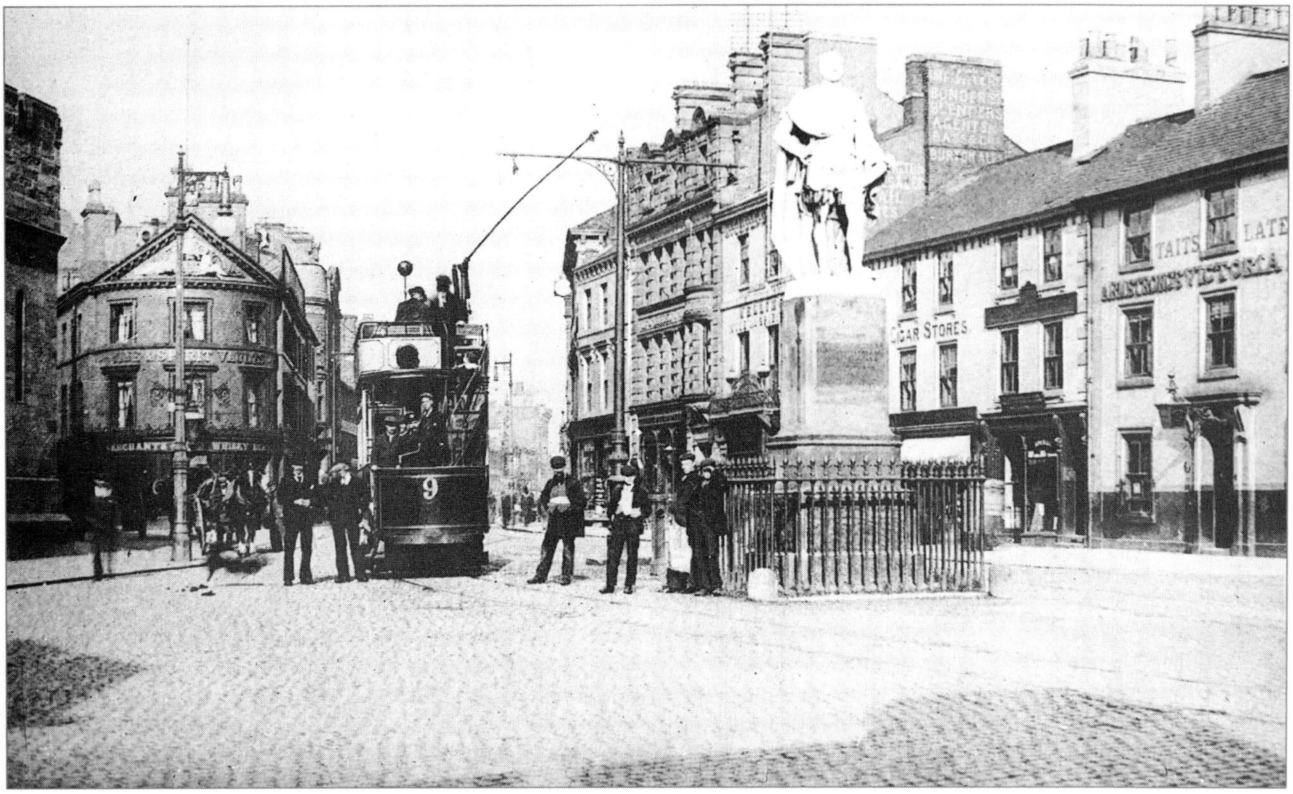

English Street, Carlisle, was cobbled when the Corporation's tramway ran along it, powered from the City Power Station in James Street. Electric tram no. 9 is seen opposite the Victoria Hotel. (*John Marsh Collection*) In the picture below can be seen the arrangement at Barrow-in-Furness, where the trams were towed by a steam-powered unit from 1884 to 1904 when that system, too, was electrified. (*John Garbutt Collection*)

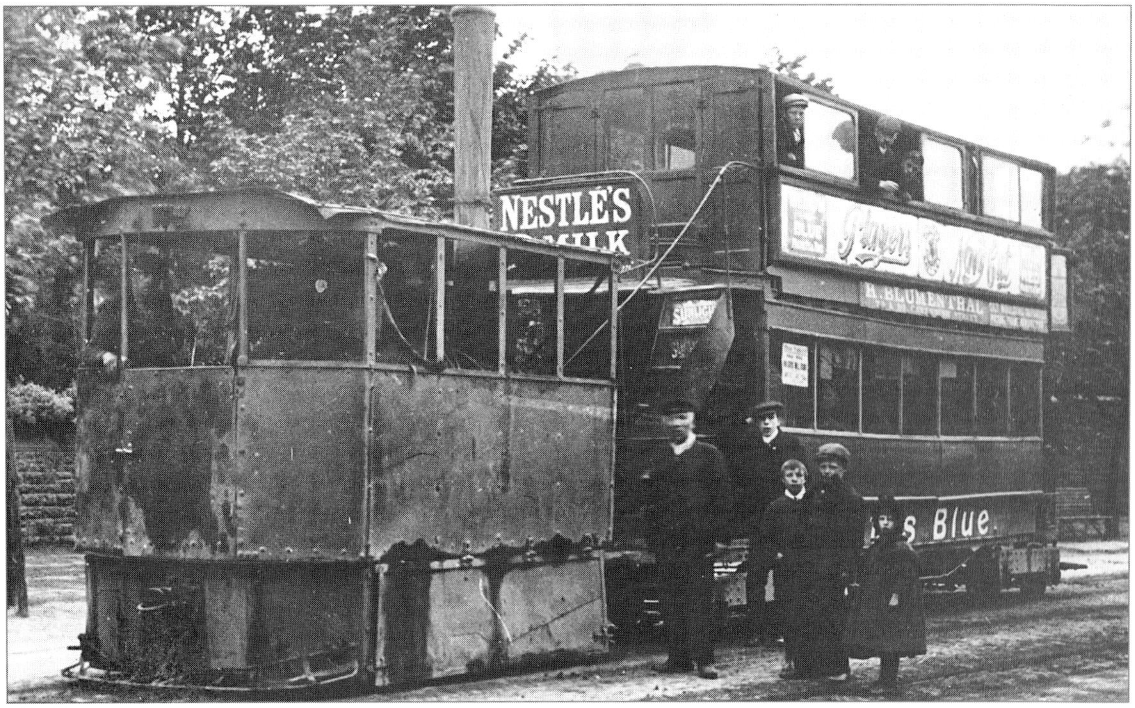

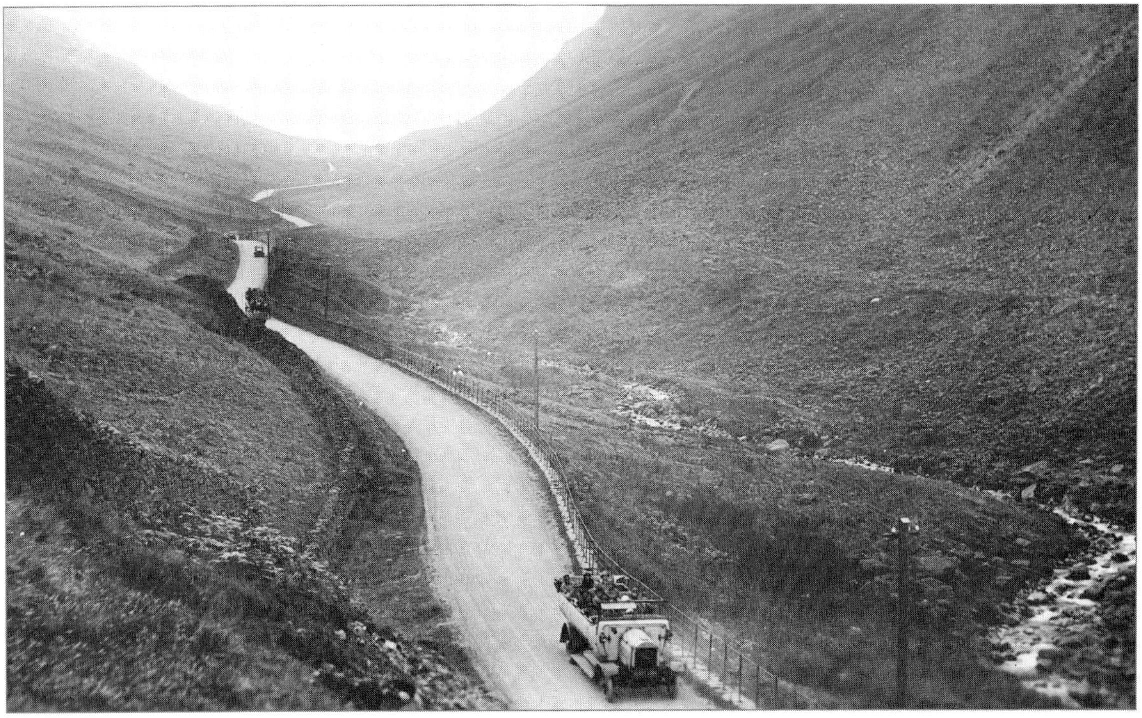

Open tourer motor charabancs had almost completely replaced horse-drawn carriages by the 1920s. Above: a Daimler is descending Kirkstone Pass towards Brotherswater. (*Atkinson & Pollitt*) *Below*: a Guy Motors vehicle is followed by the versatile Ford Model T charabanc through the new road cutting on the 'scenic route' along the side of Thirlmere at Hause Point cutting. (*G.P. Abraham*)

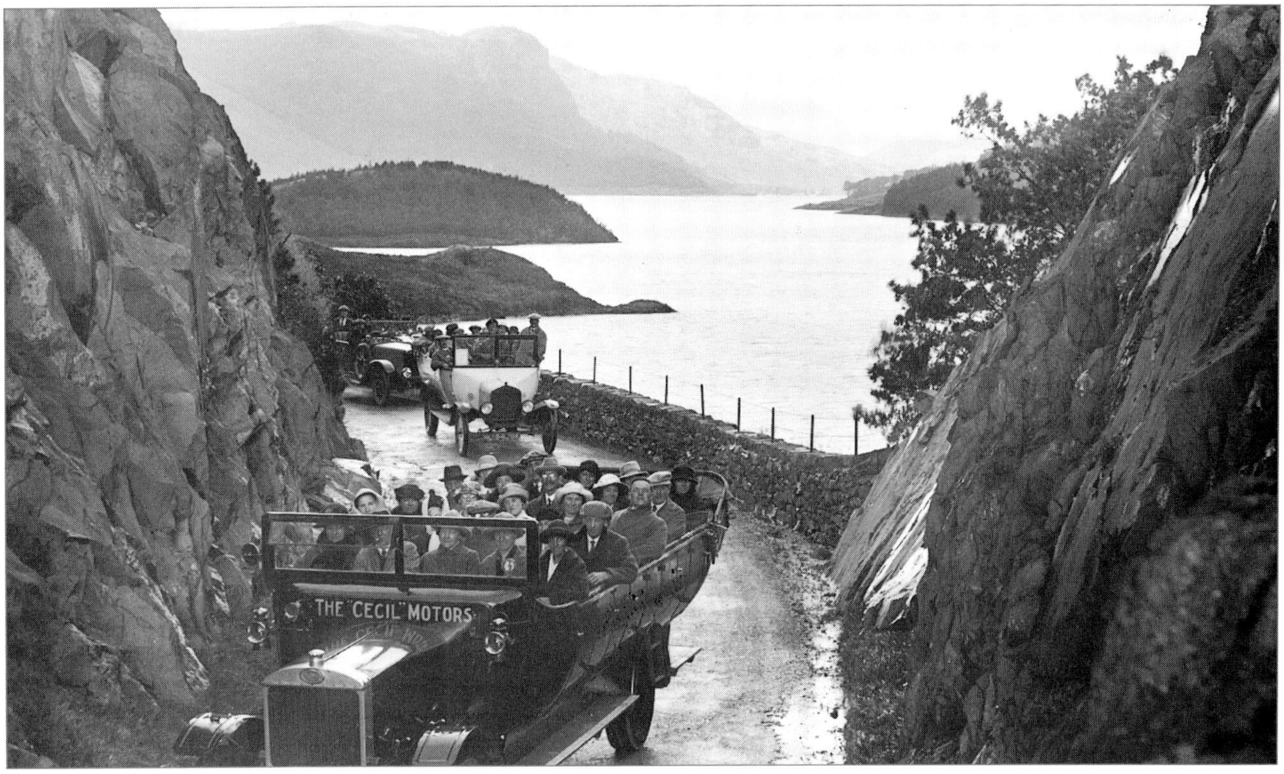

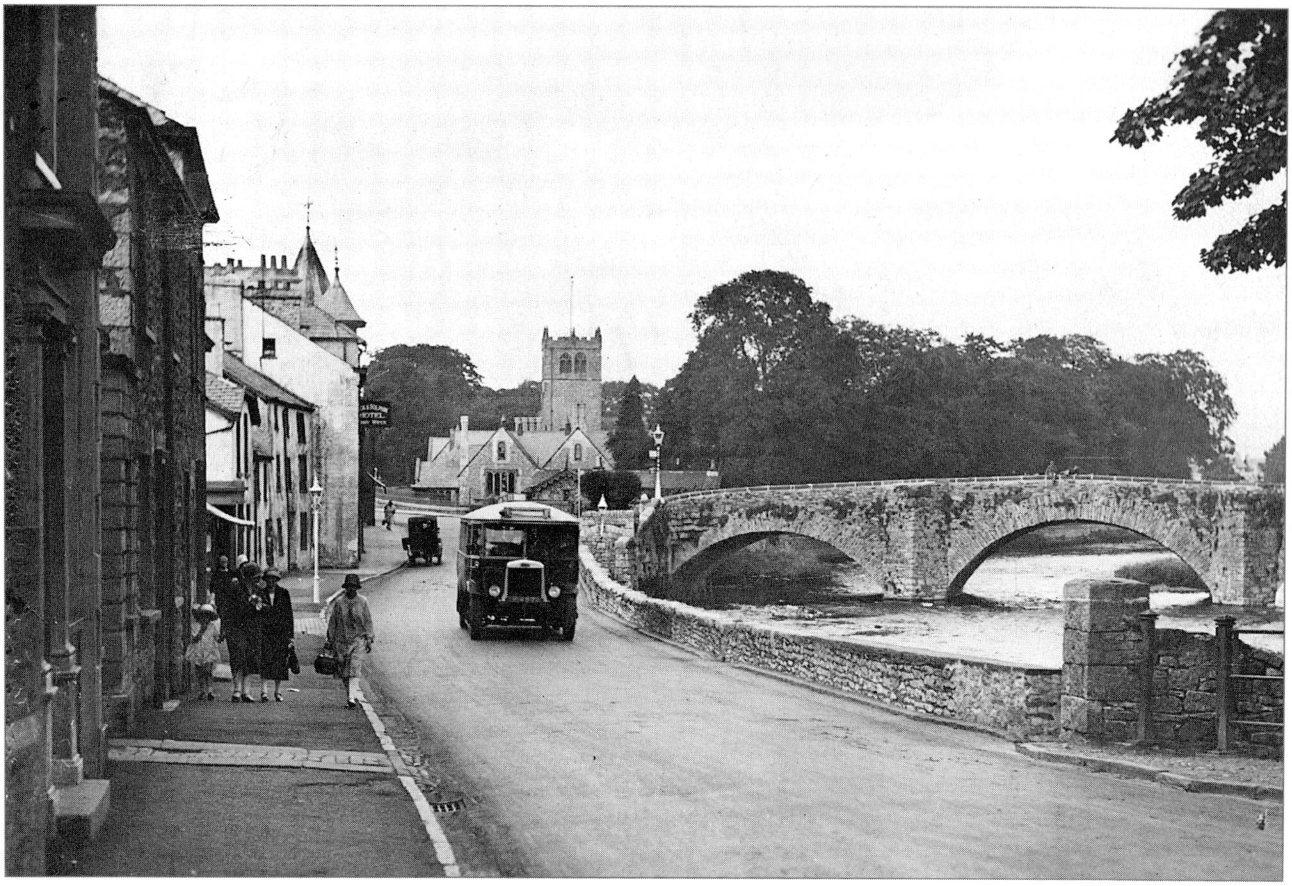

In less congested days, a service bus travels south on the Milnthorpe road, Kendal, in the 1930s, forty years before the infamous one-way system was introduced. The Netherfield bridge dates from medieval times, being constructed originally to carry the main London road out of Kendal. (*Atkinson & Pollitt*)

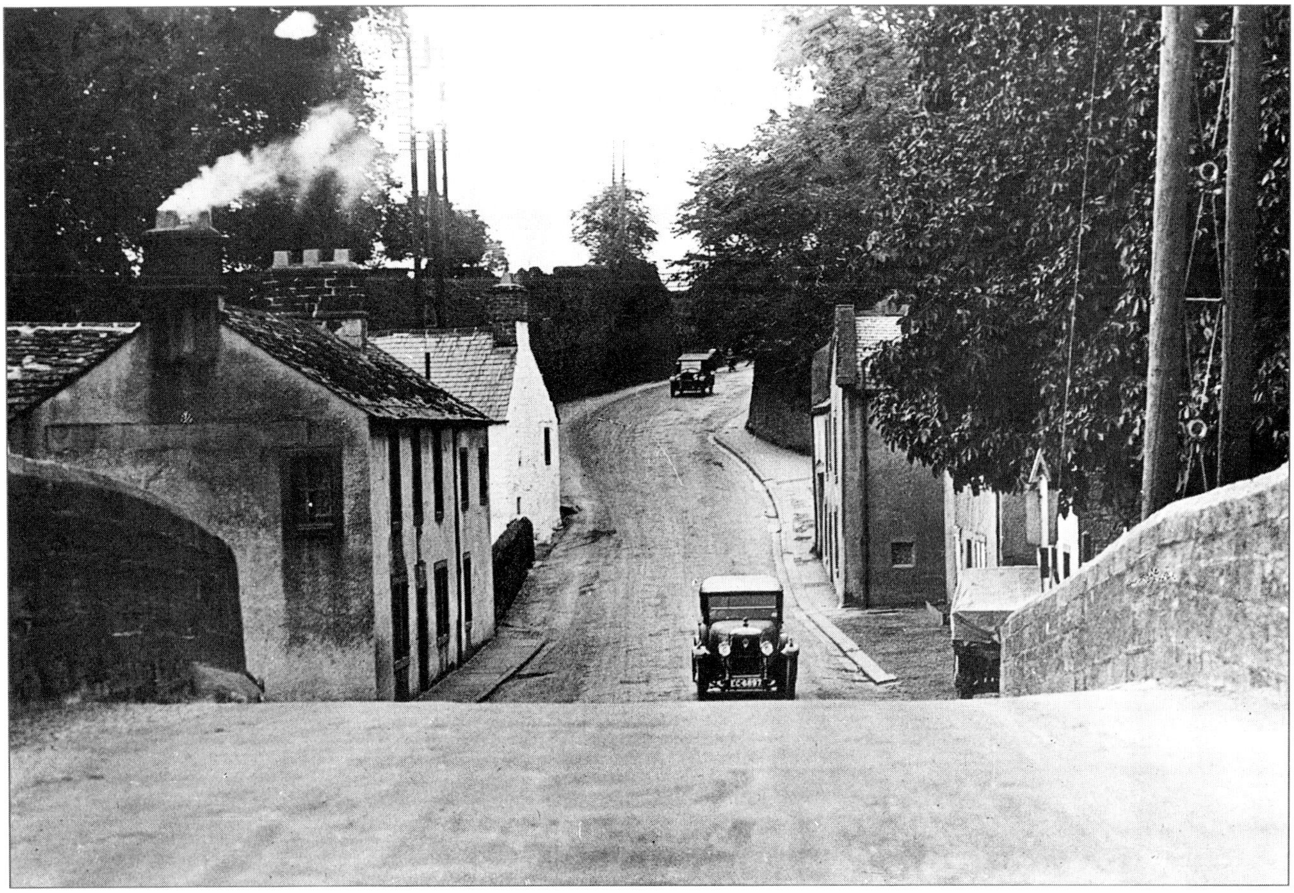

Eamont Bridge was visited by the Atkinson & Pollitt photographer in the early 1930s where he photographed a quiet A6 road from the centre of the bridge. This ancient route to Scotland here crosses the River Eamont which was once the border between England and Scotland. Many Cumbrians will remember the traffic queues here in the years before the M6 was opened. (*Atkinson & Pollitt*)

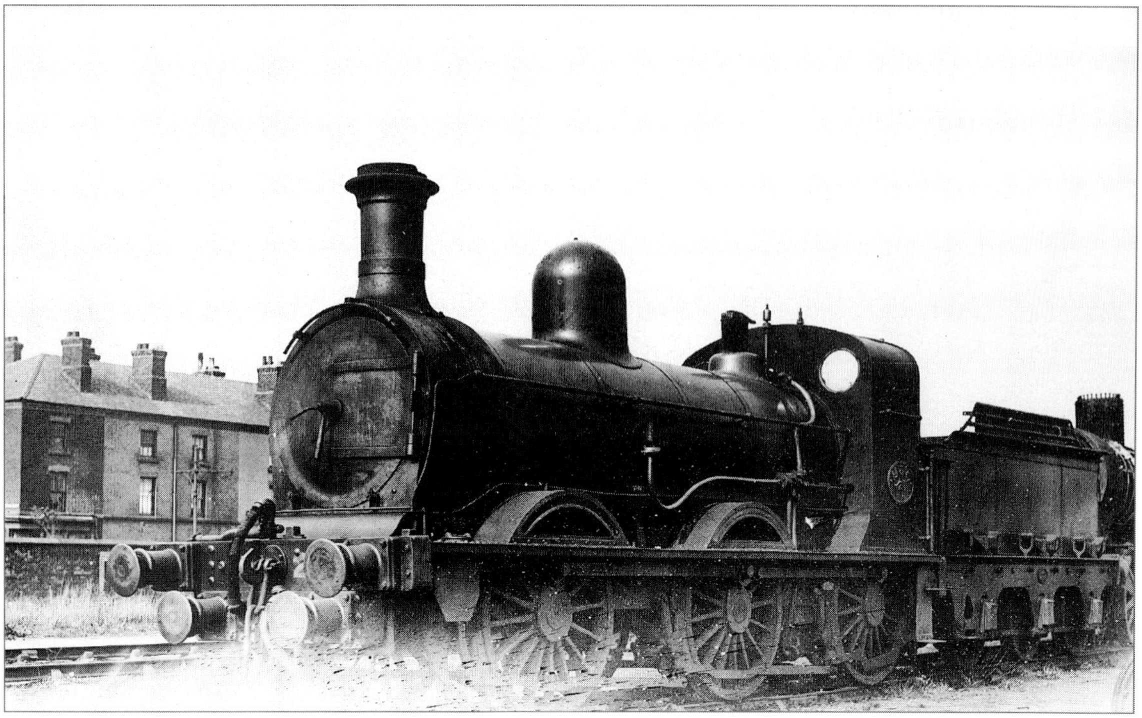

Barrow-in-Furness railway siding was where many engines from the Maryport and Carlisle Railway were scrapped in the years following the 1924 amalgamation with the LMS Railway. Here can be seen 0–6–0 engine no. 20 awaiting its fate with the engine behind already partially dismantled. (*John Marsh Collection*)

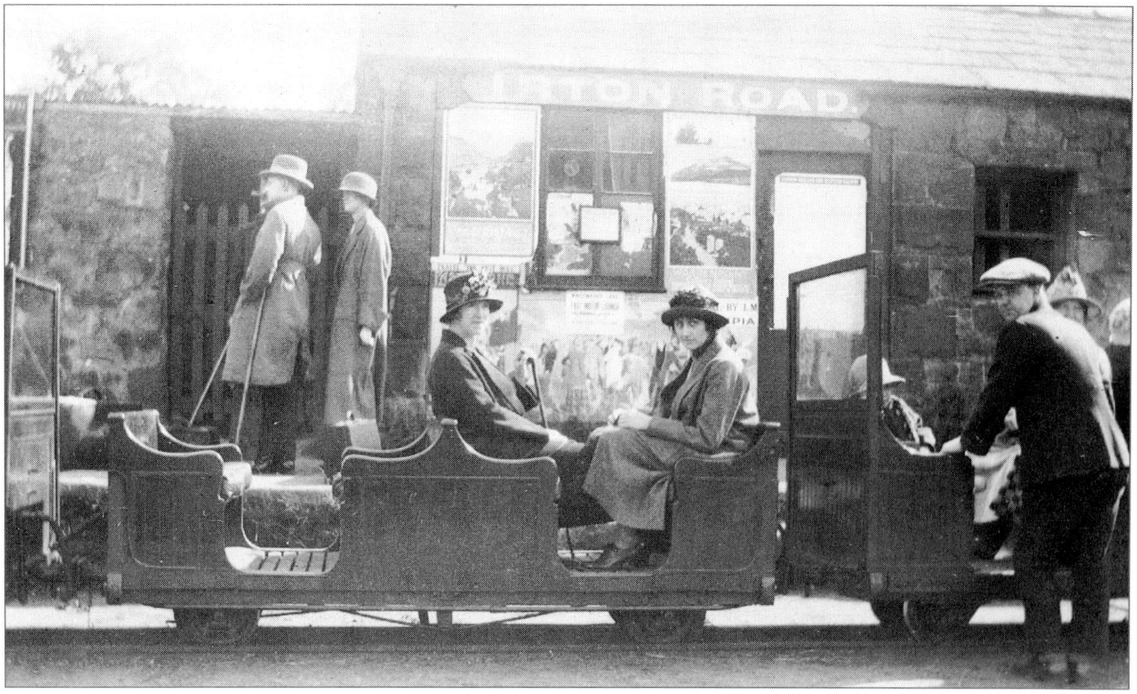

Burton-in-Kendal choir outing in 1931 was to the Eskdale Railway. The ladies attempt to sit sedately in the small carriages at Irton Road station. Next stop was Eskdale Green, then Beckfoot on the way to Boot at the east end where many would walk to see the Stanley Ghyll waterfall. This type of outing was the annual highlight of many groups, societies and choirs. (*John Marsh Collection*)

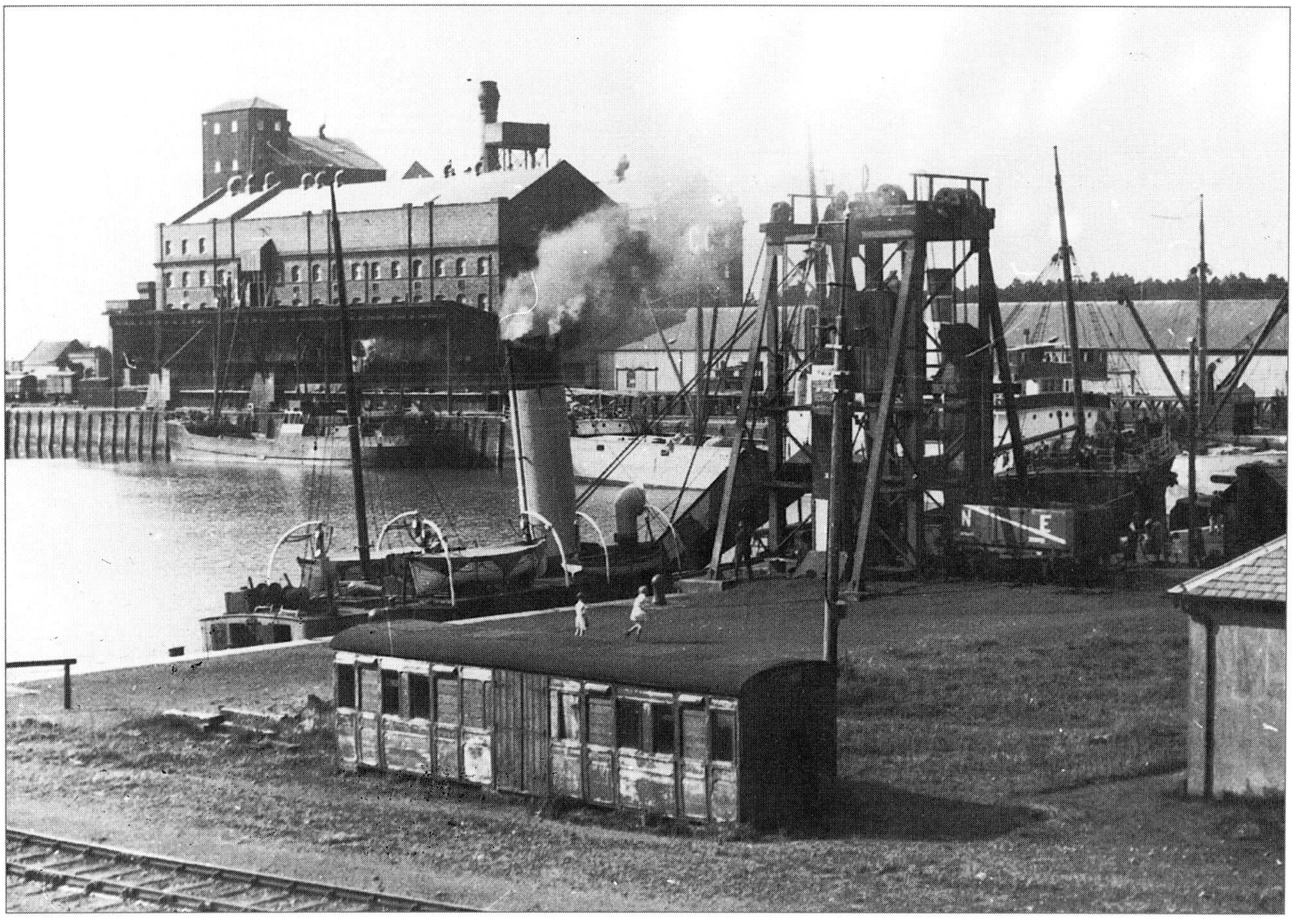

Silloth docks in more active days, 1930s. A coaster steamer is moored on the dockside, against the coal hoist, refilling its bunkers. An old railway carriage serves out its last days as a shed. The huge Carr's corn mill oversees the scene. Silloth has declined since the railway closed in September 1964. Many will remember that the closure was implemented so quickly that rolling stock was left at Silloth, cut off by the lifted track! (*George Dawson Collection*)

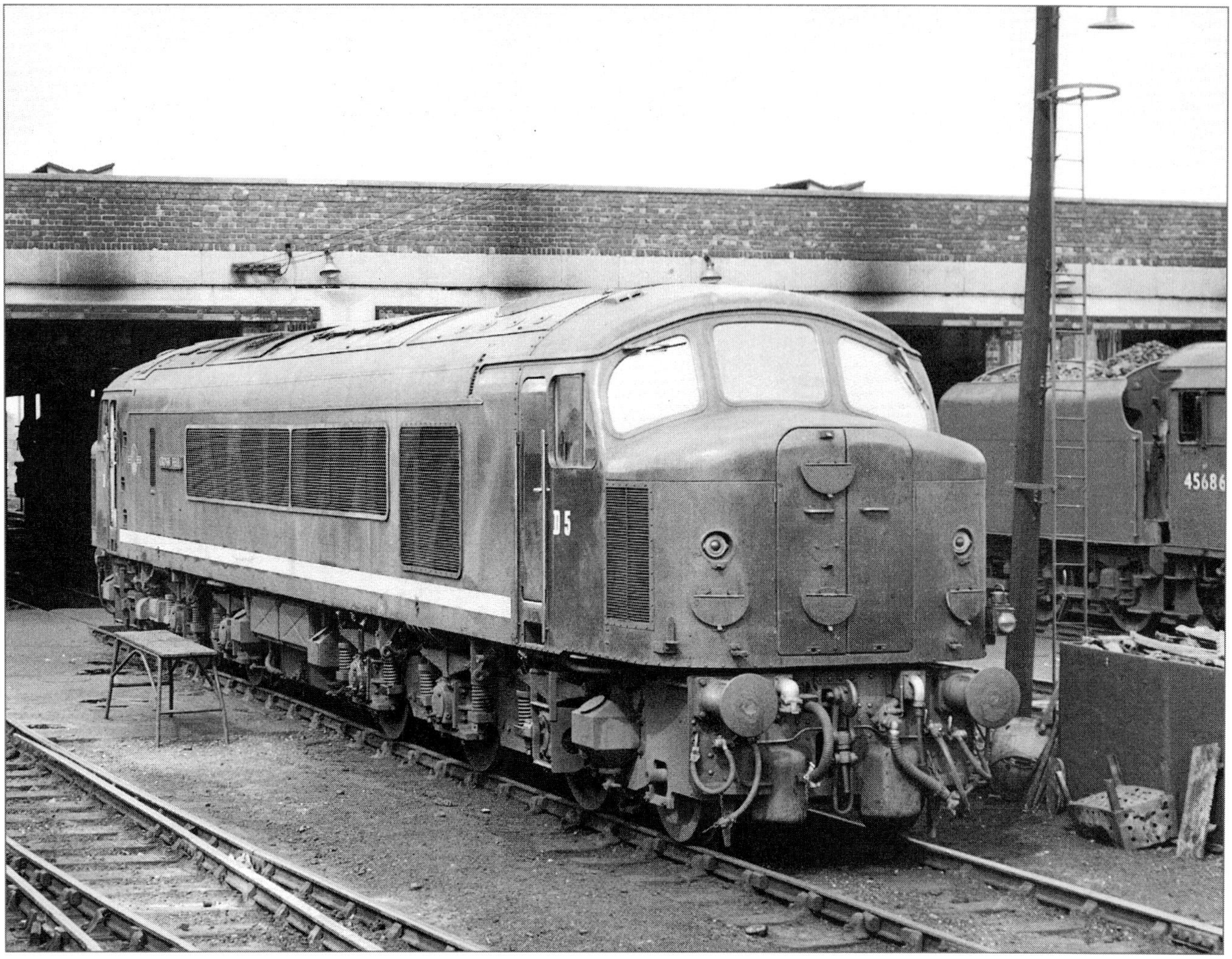

Carlisle railway sheds were visited by Preston Whiteley in August 1960 to record the changing scene as diesel engines took over from steam. Here British Rail type 4 diesel no. D5 *Crossfell* is seen with work in hand. It was very new at the time. The first ten of these engines were named after mountains in England and Wales. In the background the tender and cab of steam engine Royal Scot class 4–6–0 no. 45686 *St Vincent* can be seen – its days as a British Rail engine were numbered. (*Preston Whiteley*)

Opposite, above: In the cutting south of Oxenholme railway station, Black Five 4–6–0 locomotive no. 45315 pulls a goods train south towards Carnforth.

Below: An eight-coach passenger train is being pulled north over Shap Fell by Princess Royal class 4–6–0 no. 46206 *Princess Marie Louise* passing the line-side cabin at Shap Wells on 3 September 1960. Rail enthusiast Preston Whiteley of Kendal let us use these pictures from his record of the last days of steam engines in the area. (*Preston Whiteley*)

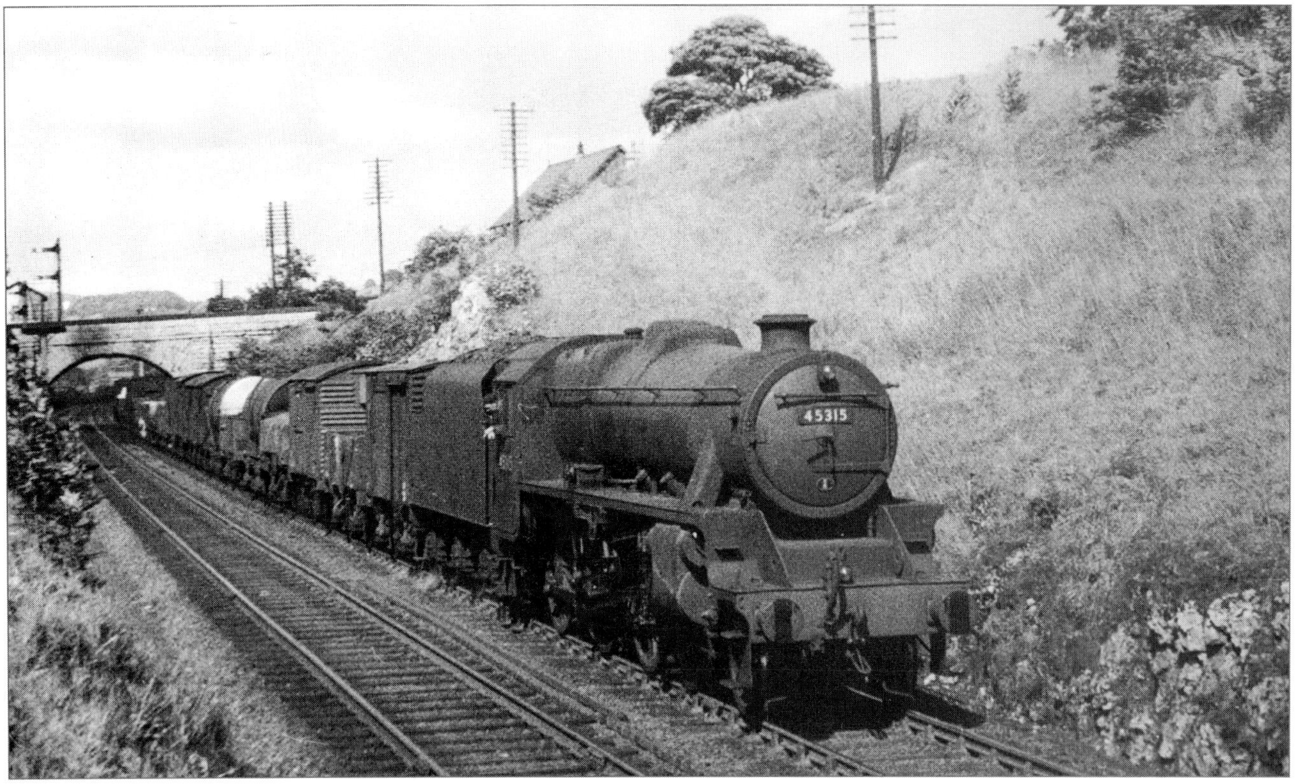
45315

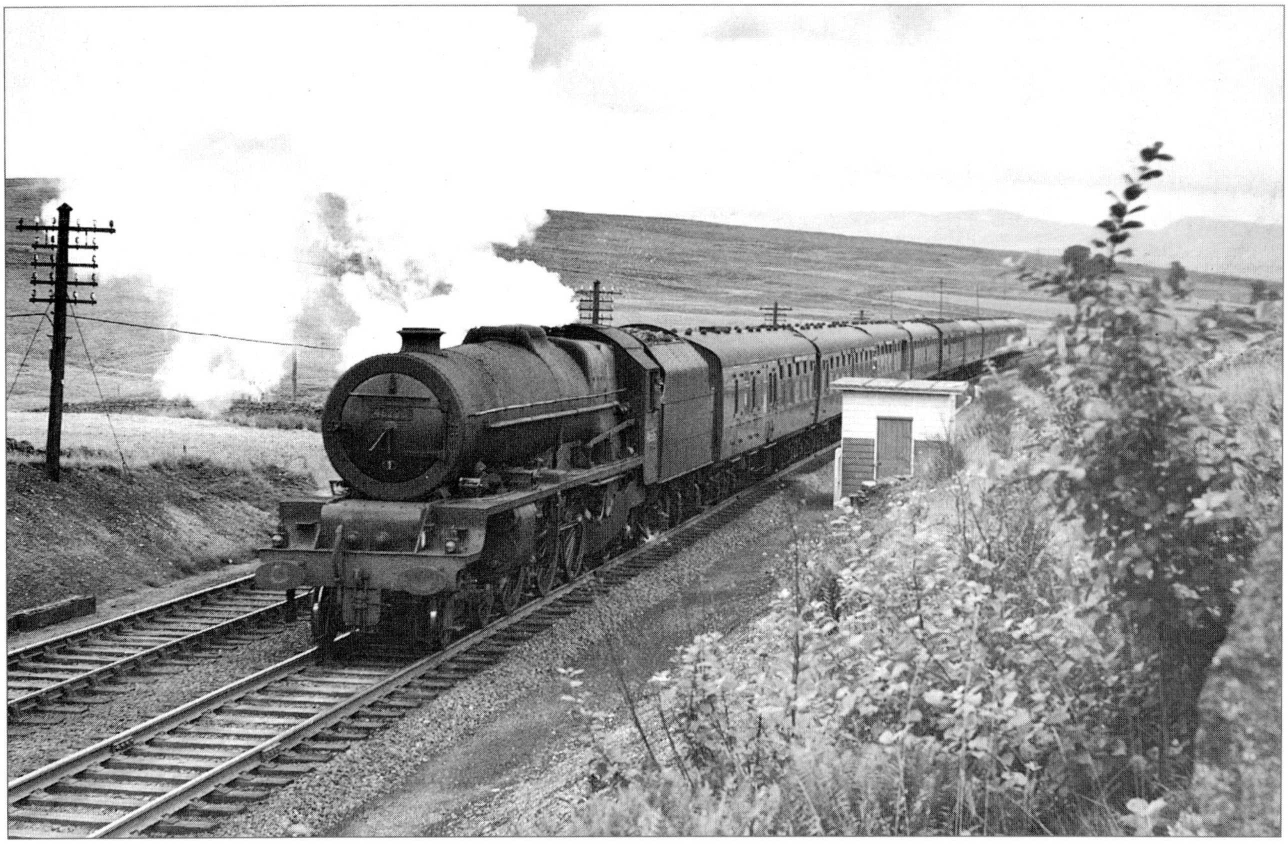

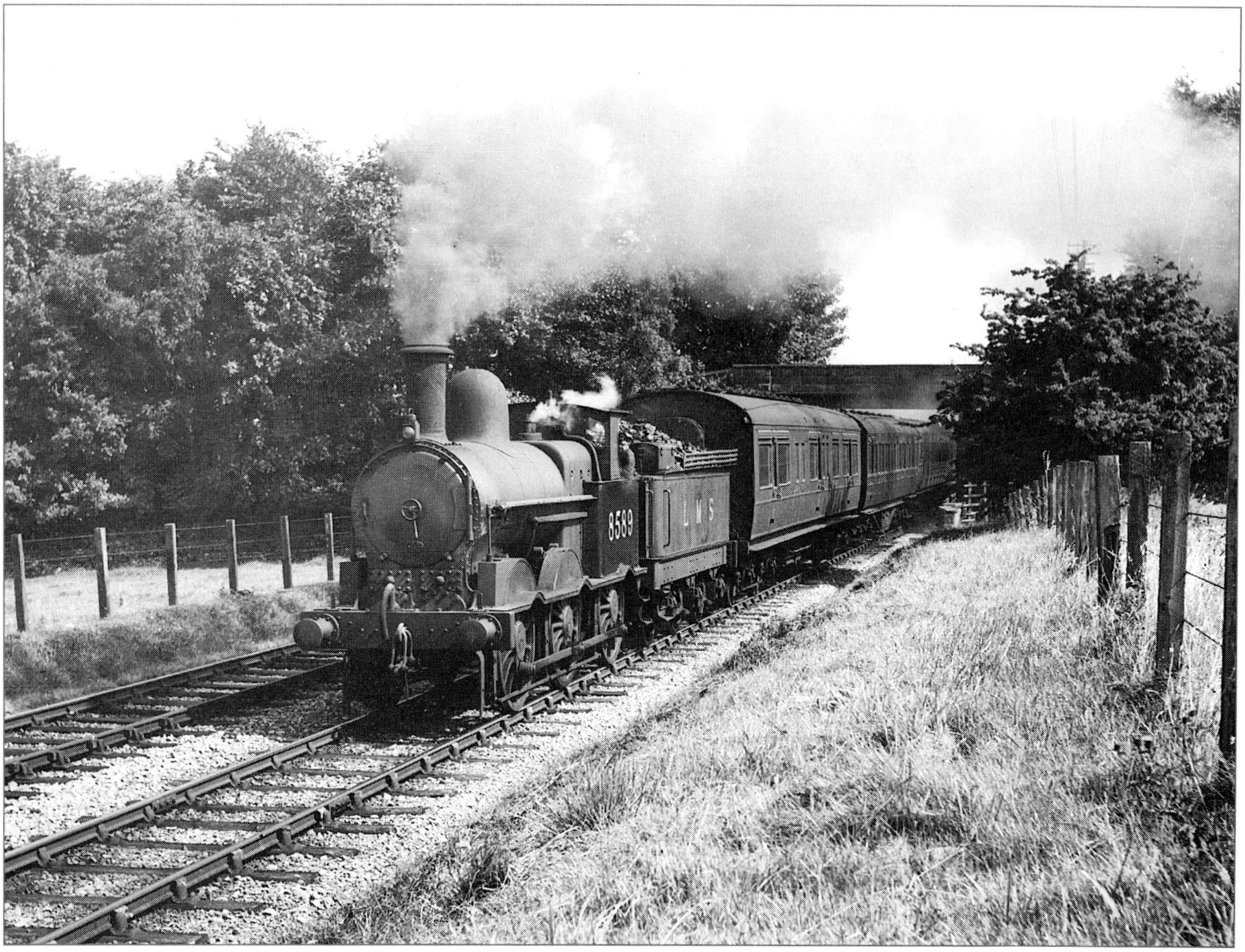

The closure of the railway from Penrith to Keswick was as short-sighted a transport policy as any that has been inflicted on the county. The line was closed all the way through to Workington and replaced with the ugly and dangerous A66 trunk road. The Keswick to Cockermouth and Workington railway closed in 1966 and the Keswick to Penrith section went in 1972. Here we see ex-LNWR Webb Cauliflower 0–6–0 no. 8589 on a passenger train near Troutbeck in LMS days before the Second World War. (*Neville Stead*)

Opposite, above: Memories of steam trains on the ex-Furness Railway lines at Grange-over-Sands. Class 5MT 4–6–0 no. 45371 takes a Carnforth-bound seven-coach passenger train along the front, south of Grange station in the 1960s. (*Preston Whiteley*)

Below: Arnside station is now an unmanned halt but many will remember the busy platforms of an earlier age. A Furness Railway goods train heads south in this photograph by J.D. Wilson of Arnside who, in his work as a local postcard photographer, has done so much to record memories of the delightful village he lived in for many years. (*J.D. Wilson of Arnside*)

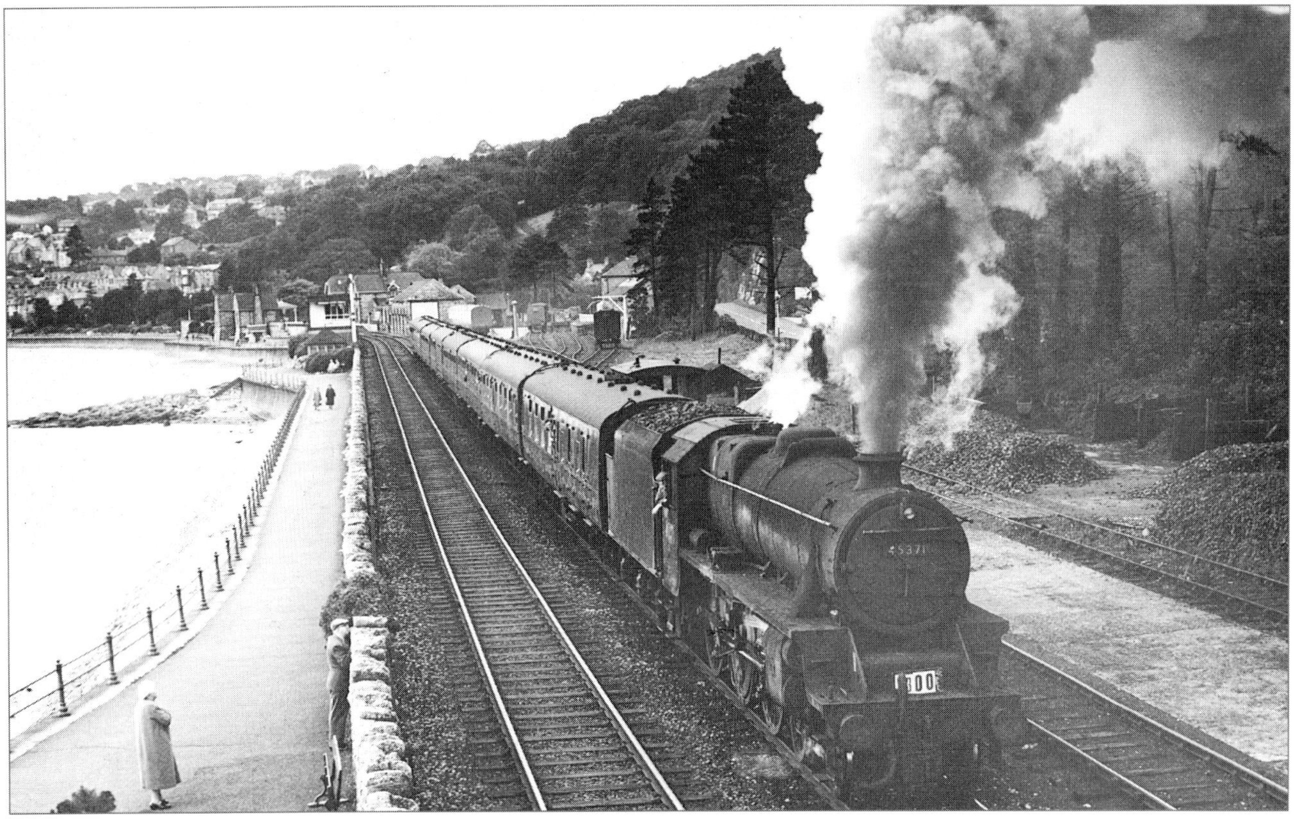

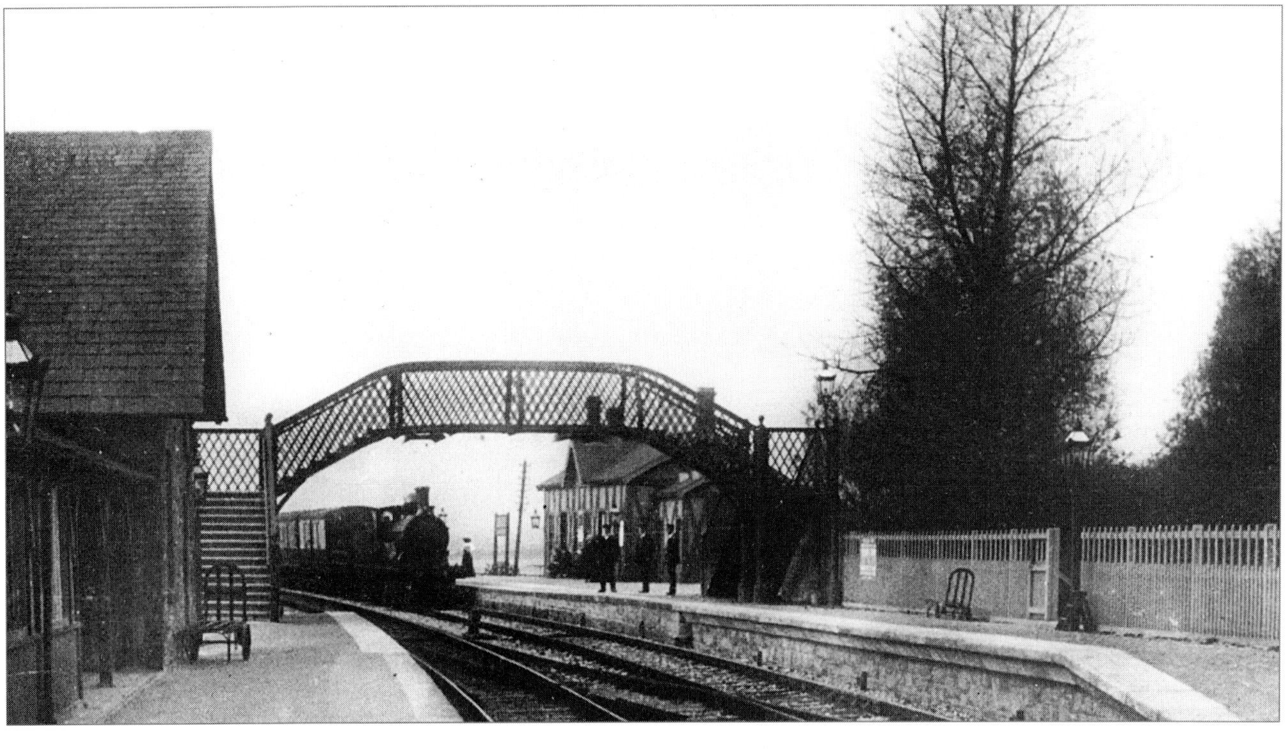

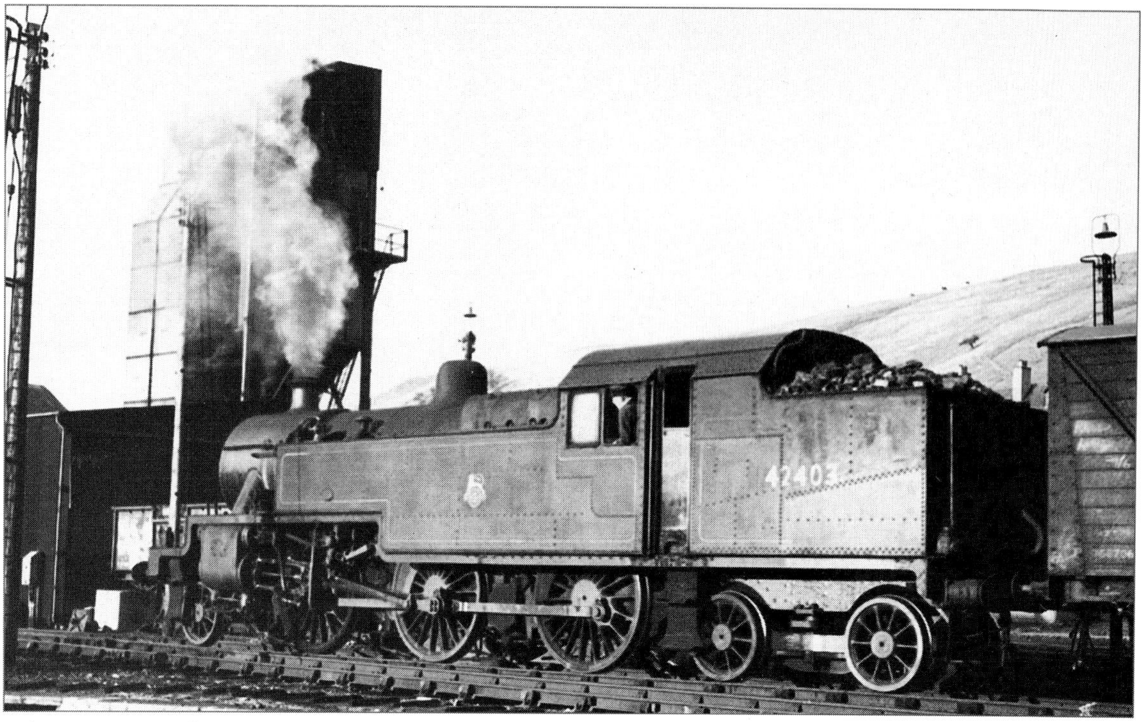

Tebay was a very busy junction on the west coast main line. It does not exist now. A large passenger station and busy railyard are illustrated in our book *Cumbrian Railways* (Sutton Publishing, 1999). Here a shunting scene was captured by Preston Whiteley on 15 July 1960, showing Fowler 4 MT 2–6–4 tank engine no. 42403 on yard duties in the decade that saw the end of steam and of Tebay Junction. (*Preston Whiteley*)

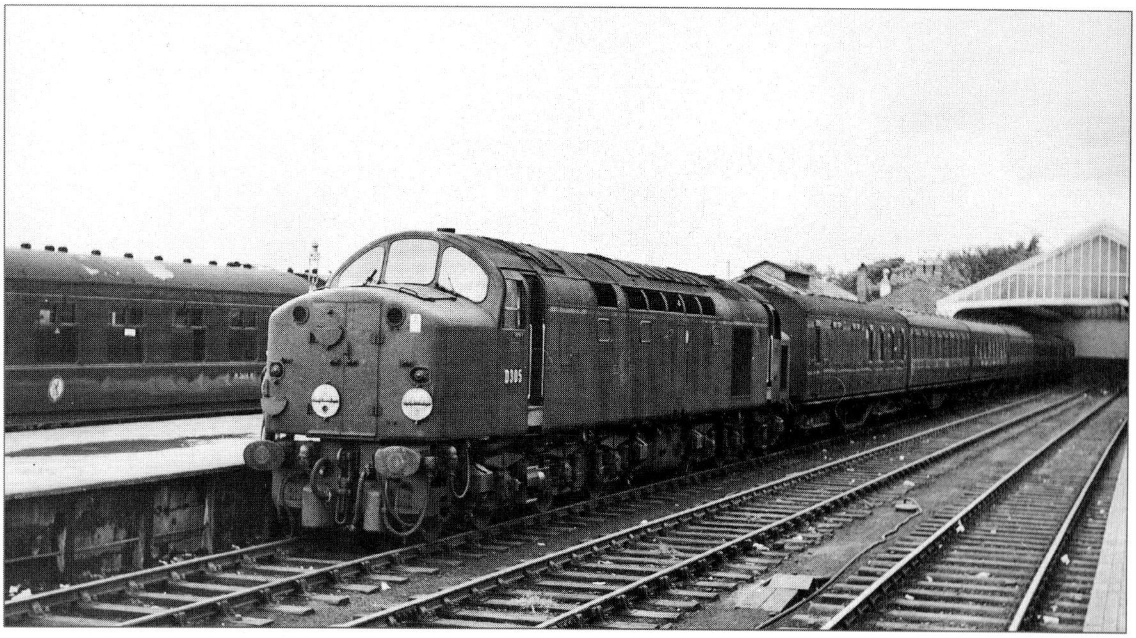

Windermere station platforms were large to accommodate the lengthy trains that brought thousands to this busy holiday resort. The line still exists from Windermere to Oxenholme but has been cut back to a single track with stations reduced to unmanned halts. The motor traffic problems this policy produced have polluted the holiday resorts of Windermere, Bowness and Ambleside ever since. To be seen in the picture is a type 4 Diesel locomotive no. D305 at one of the original platforms on 4 August 1962. (*Preston Whiteley*)

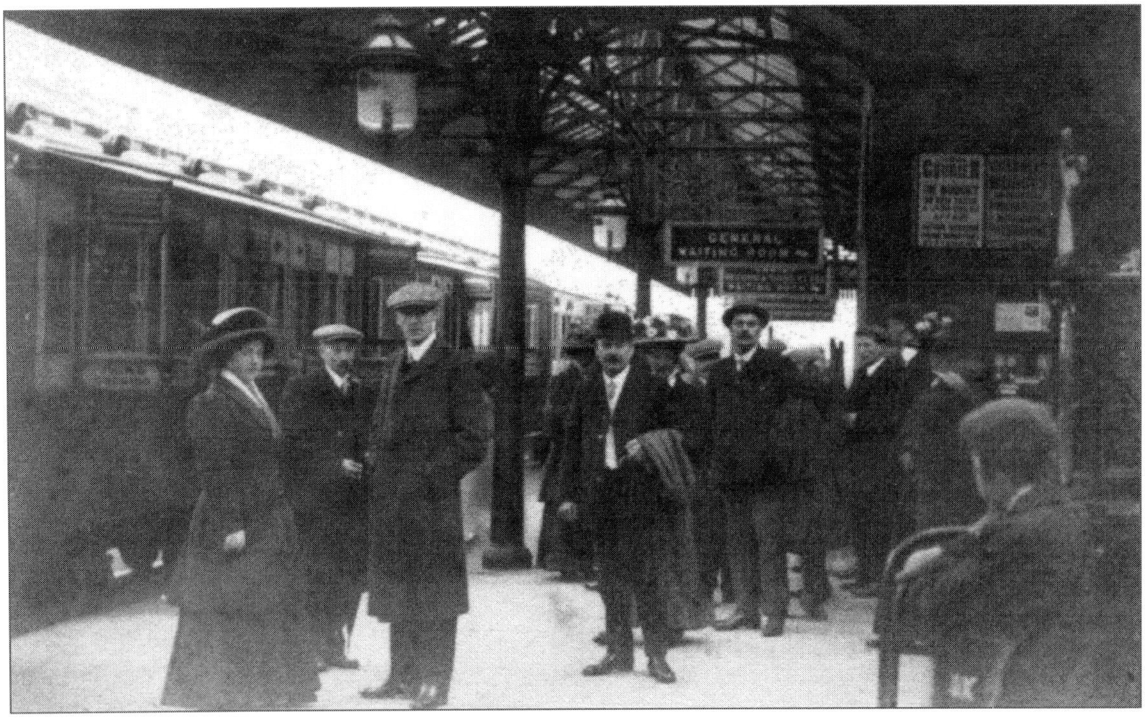

Kendal railway station in the days before the Windermere branch line, on which it stands, was cut back to the minimum. This view of a busy town station platform will evoke many memories for Kendal residents. (*Anne Bonnett Collection*)

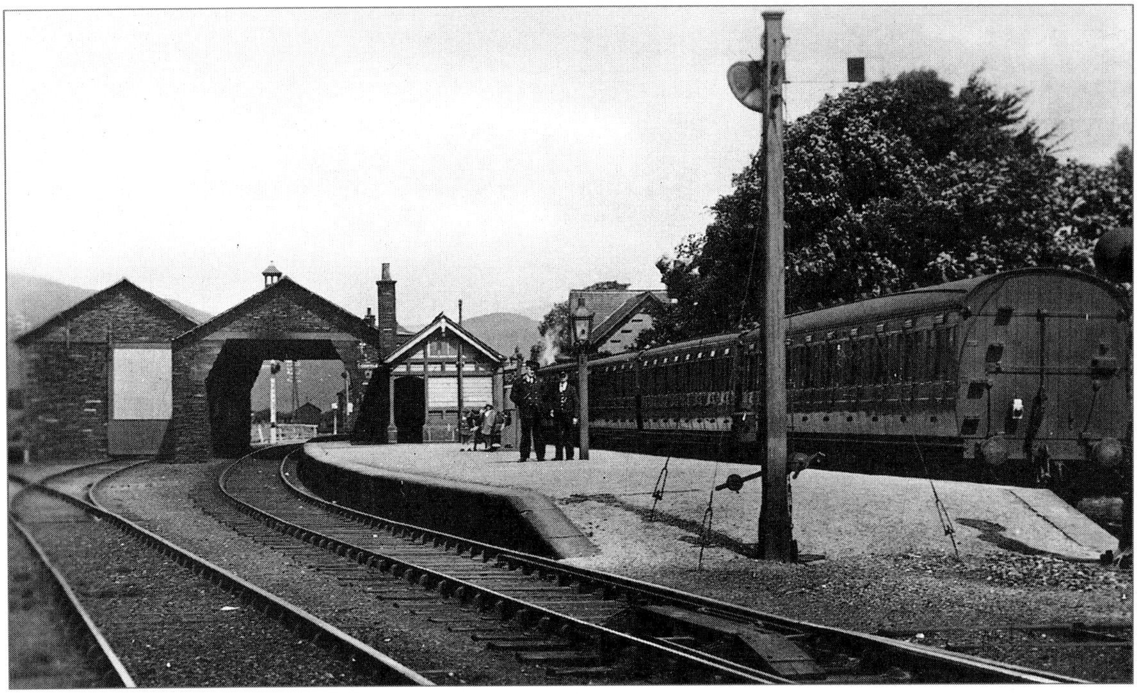

Foxfield station with a train at the Coniston platform. The branch line to Coniston closed in 1958 for passengers and 1962 for goods. This between-the-wars picture is by Lilywhite of Sowerby Bridge. Many will have happy memories of changing trains here to travel to the village of Coniston with its mountains and the lake. (*Lilywhite of Sowerby Bridge*)

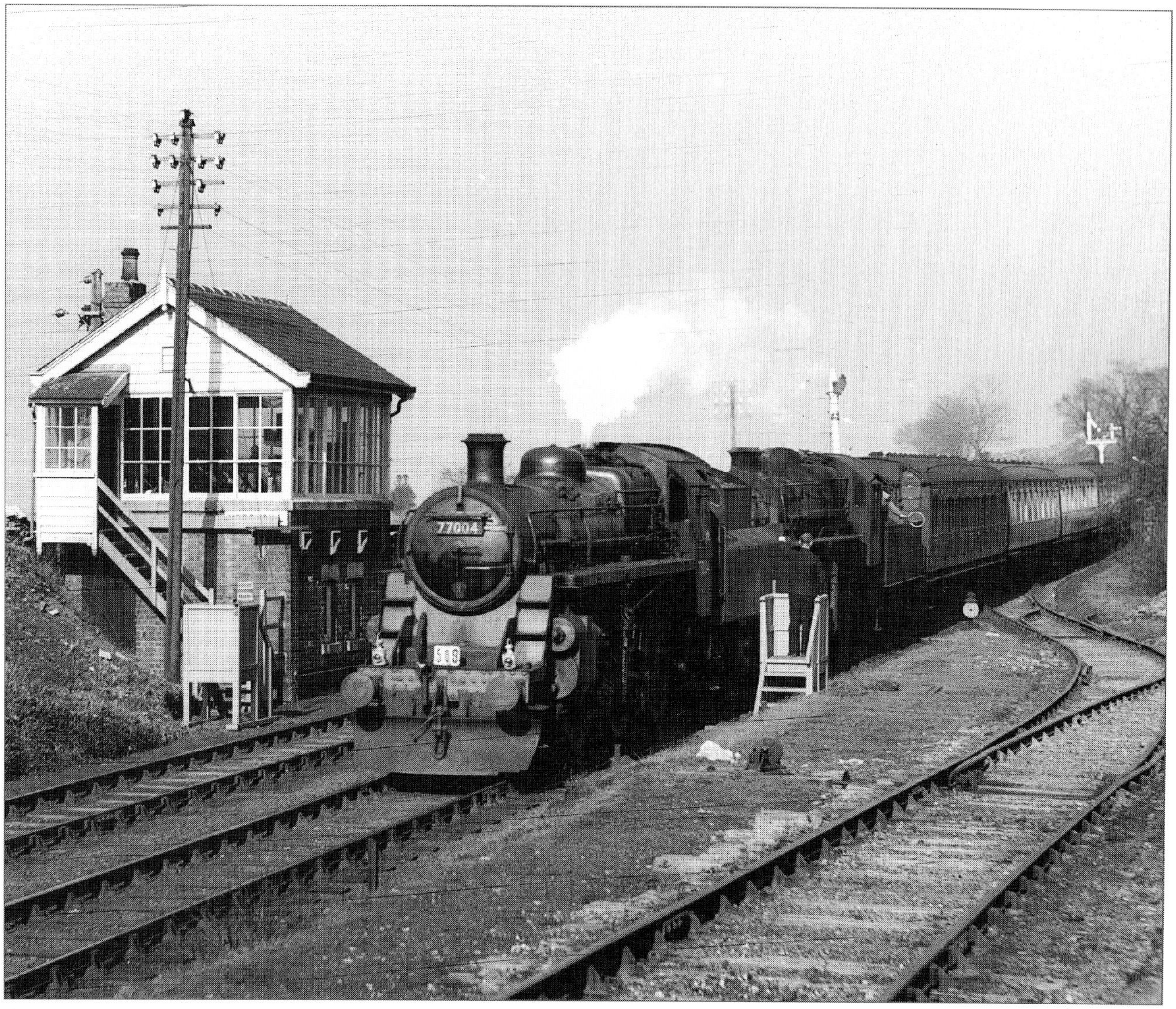

Another railway line that is but a memory is the track that ran over the Pennines at Stainmore into County Durham. The line was opened in 1861 and closed in 1962. It was a mixture of single and double track working all its life and here, in a Neville Stead picture, a double-headed passenger train drops the single line token at the Hartley signal box near Kirkby Stephen. Note the snow plough blade on the leading engine, no. 77004 – a class 3 2–6–0 mixed traffic locomotive. (*Neville Stead*)

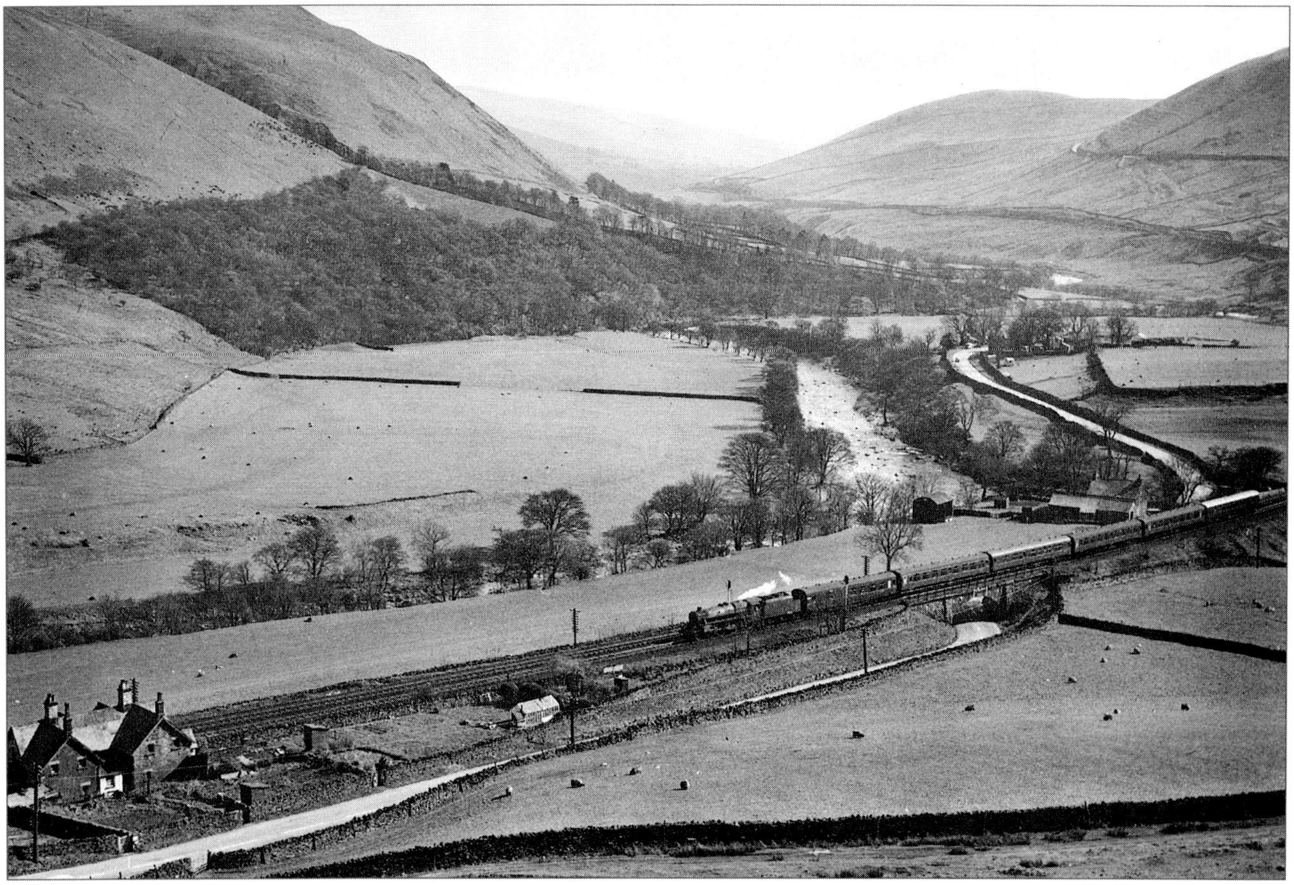

In the Lune valley south of Tebay can be seen the river, the main Carlisle to Preston (and the south) railway and the Tebay to Kendal road. On the right is the site of the Roman fort which nearly 2,000 years ago guarded this valley which allowed easy access north and south through the surrounding high fells. A main line express train travels north. On 15 April 1961 Preston Whiteley photographed this scene which has since changed very much. In 1970 the M6 motorway was opened over the land occupied by the road and houses in the front of the picture, and it now runs parallel to the railway through the valley. Also in the 1970s the line was electrified with overhead cables. This remote valley has many memories. (*Preston Whiteley*)

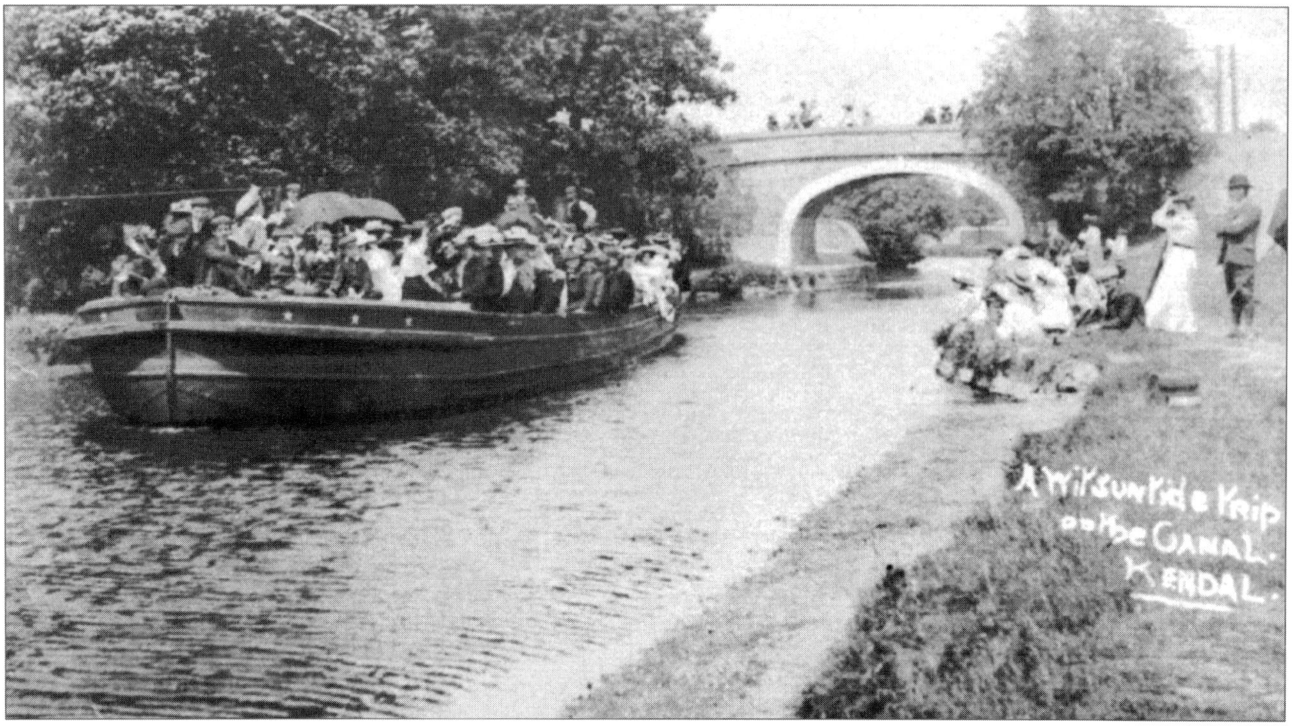

The Kendal to Lancaster canal at Kendal is now but a memory since it was closed and filled in with refuse as far as Stainton. Cumbria's only other canals were at Ulverston, the shortest, deepest and widest and now a factory reservoir, and at Carlisle, which was filled in in the 1850s to carry a railway. The Kendal canal may well be reopened in the twenty-first century but from 1818 to the 1950s its waters provided a welcome source of recreation to the locals. Above, a Whitsuntide trip on a cleaned-up coal barge in about 1910 and below, a row on the Kendal canal near a coal wharf at about the same time. (*John Marsh Collection*)

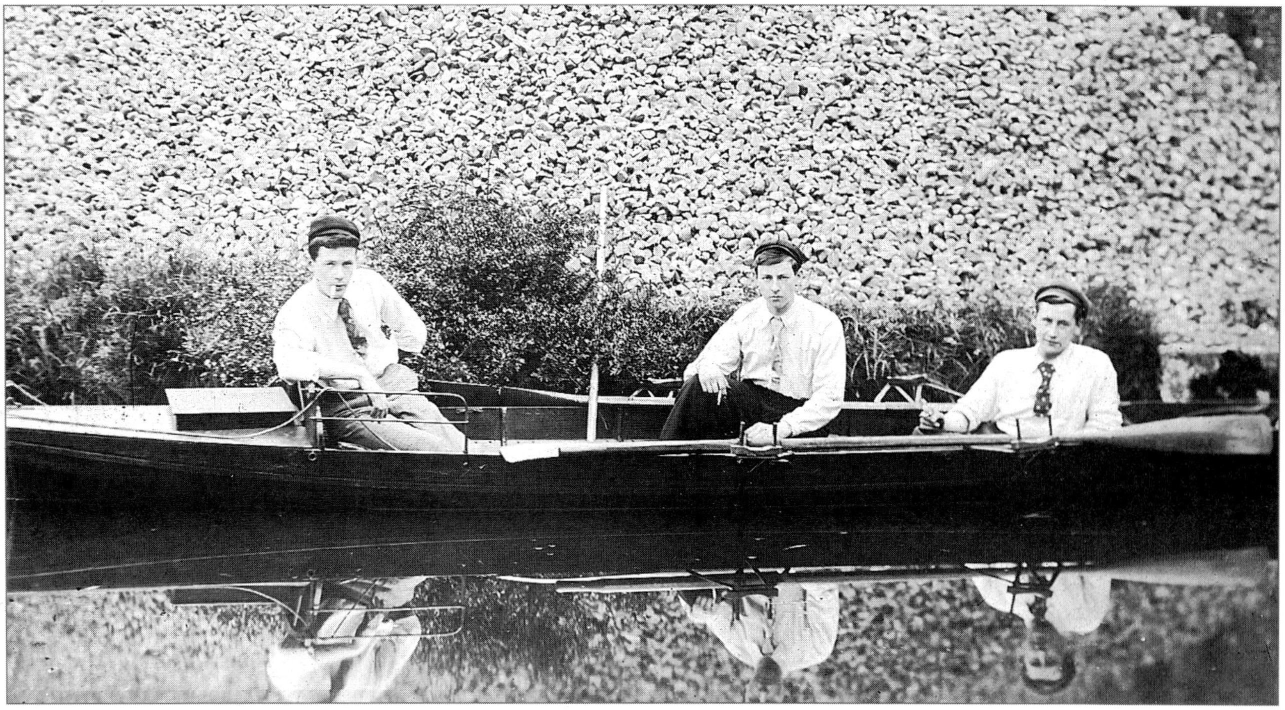

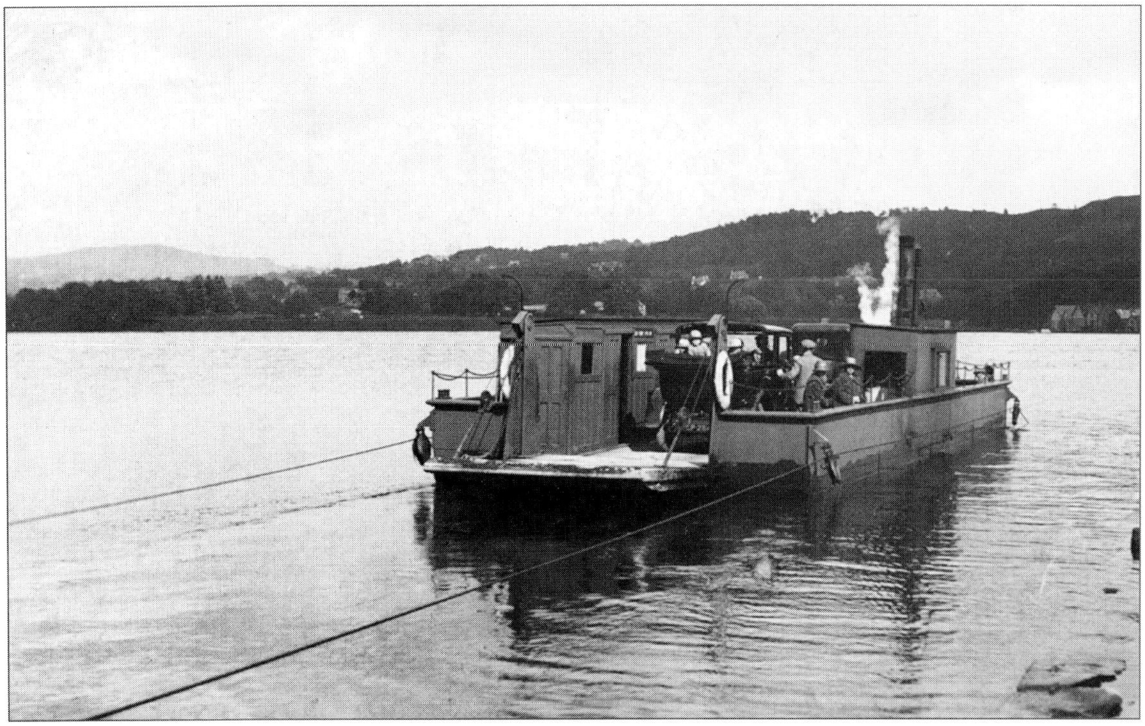

The Windermere ferry in the 1920s. Here the second steam ferry, which ran from 1915 to 1954, was pictured by Atkinson and Pollitt for their postcard series. The 1954 replacement was named after the Lancashire County Council surveyor – the *Drake*. The first steam ferry replaced a large row boat in 1870. The twin guide ropes seen here were introduced when the ferry broke away from a single rope. (*Atkinson & Pollitt*)

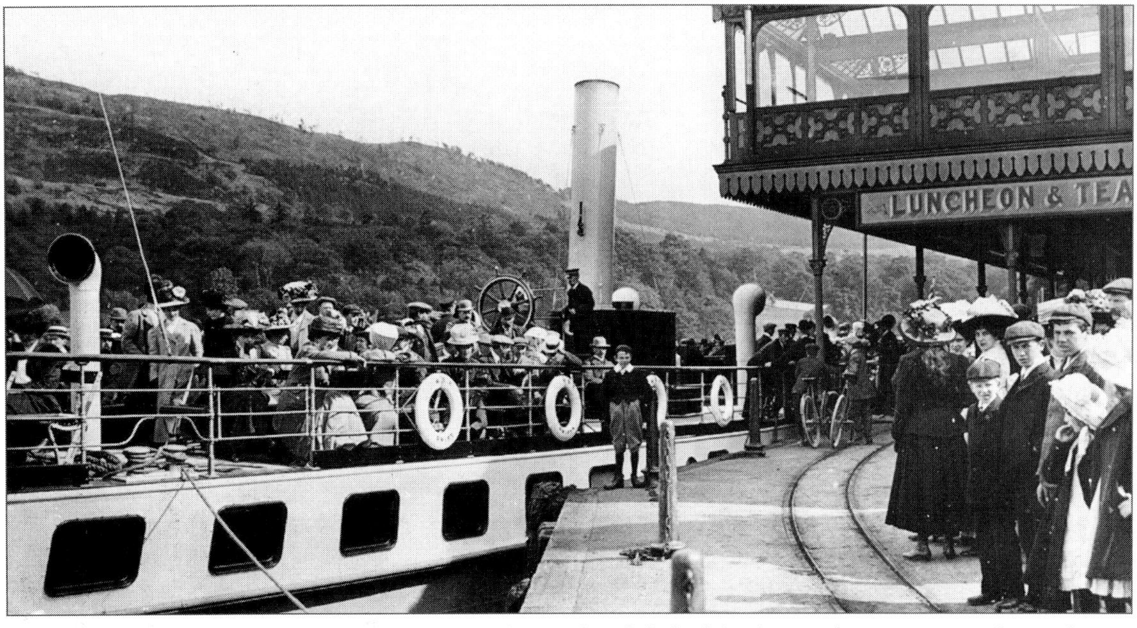

All aboard the *Swift* at Lakeside pier, *c.* 1910. The *Swift* sailed the lake for nearly a century and gives happy memories of holidays to many Cumbrians. One of the authors spent summer holidays working as a crew member in the early 1950s. Put into lake service in 1900 the *Swift* was, for many years, the largest and fastest boat on the lake. The *Swift* was scrapped at Lakeside only a year before the publication of this book. She did not make her century. (*Raphael Tuck*)

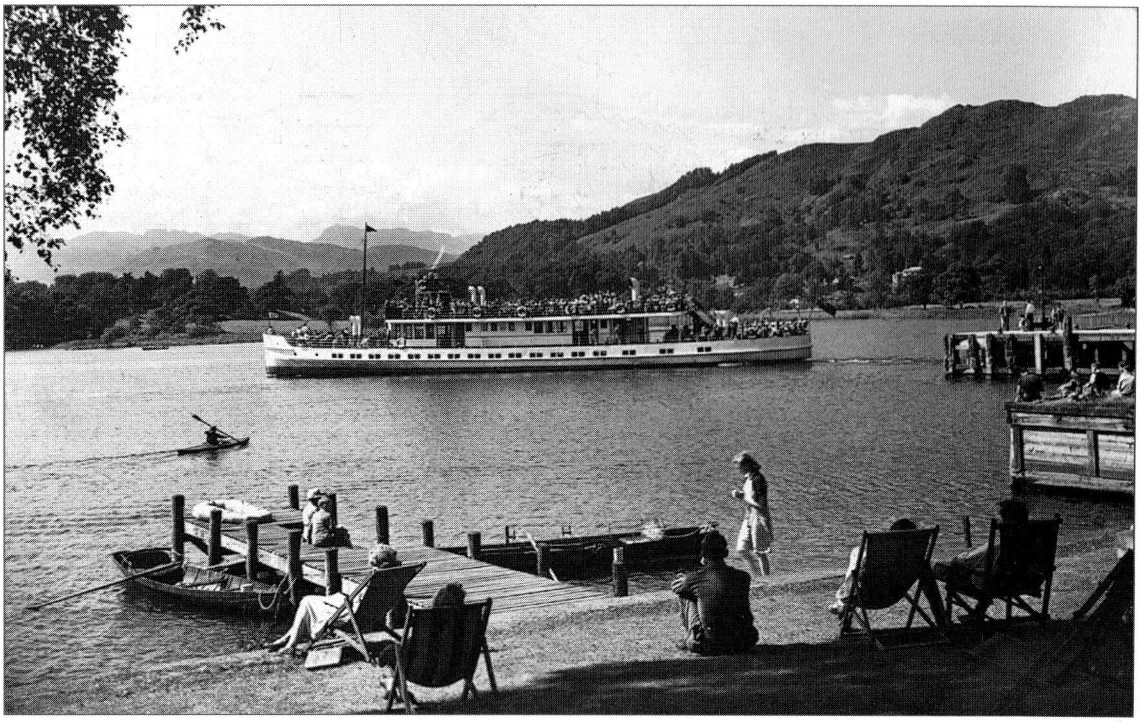

The two new railway steamers of the Windermere service were the *Swan* and the *Teal* which were both built at Barrow-in-Furness in the late 1930s and taken in sections up the railway to Lakeside where they were reassembled, fitted out and put into service. Both were driven by twin diesel engines and were not steamers at all, but they caused much excitement when they were put into service. They have continued in service until the time of writing but now have a much altered appearance having been modernised in recent decades. Above, the *Swan* is seen leaving Ambleside in the late 1940s, and below the stern of the *Teal* leaving Bowness shows the beautiful lines of the original design. (*Atkinson & Pollitt*)

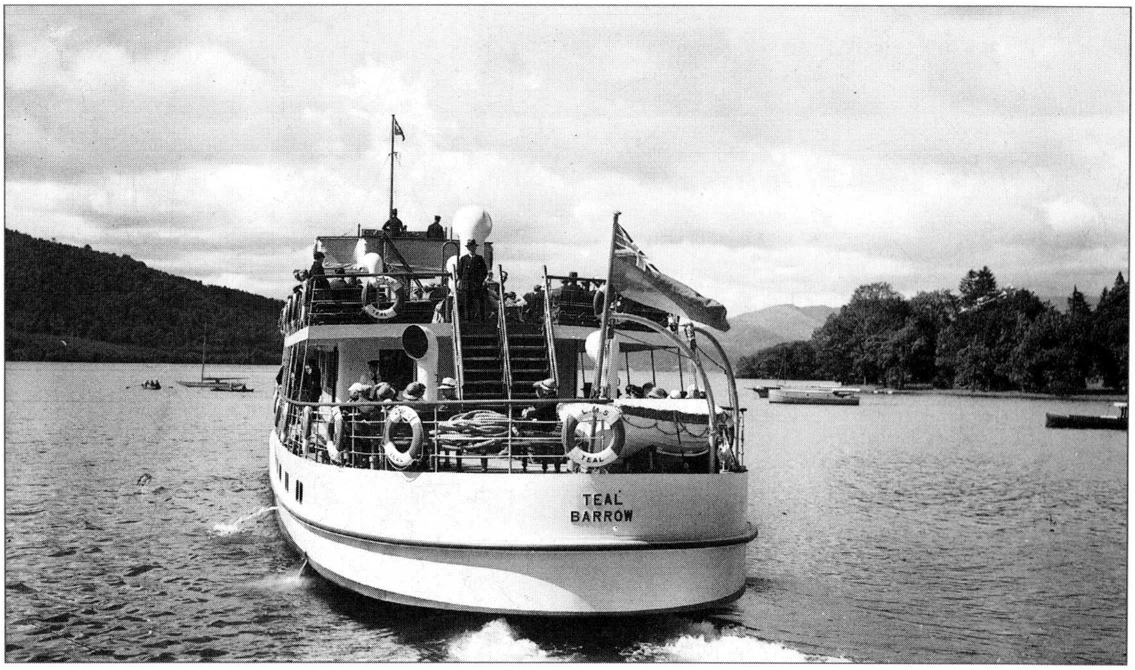

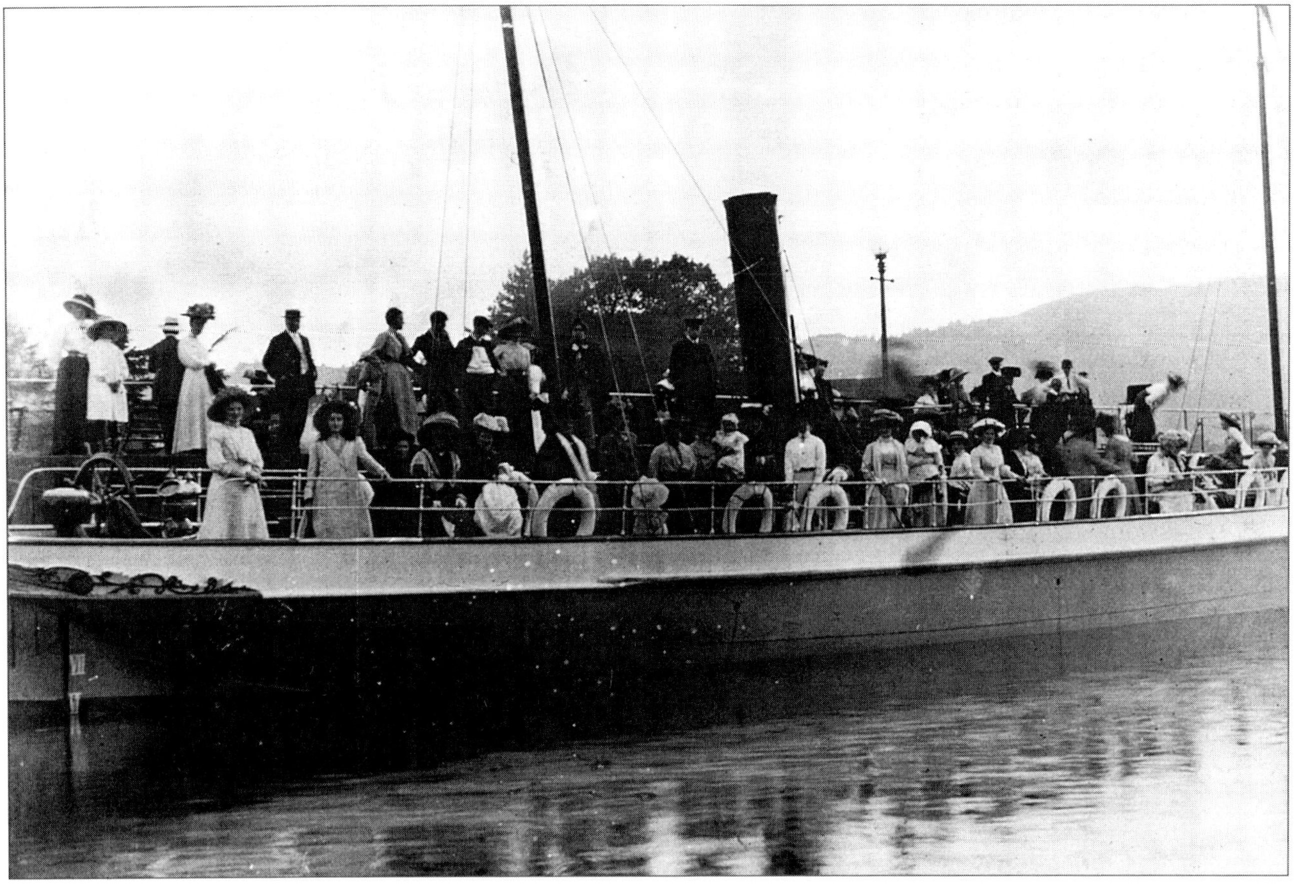

The steam yacht *Britannia* came into Furness Railway service in 1907 after being a private yacht since 1879. She continued working the lake on private hire until 1915 when she was withdrawn, and was scrapped in 1919. Here she is seen against Bowness pier in about 1910 with a party consisting mostly of ladies. (*John Marsh Collection*)

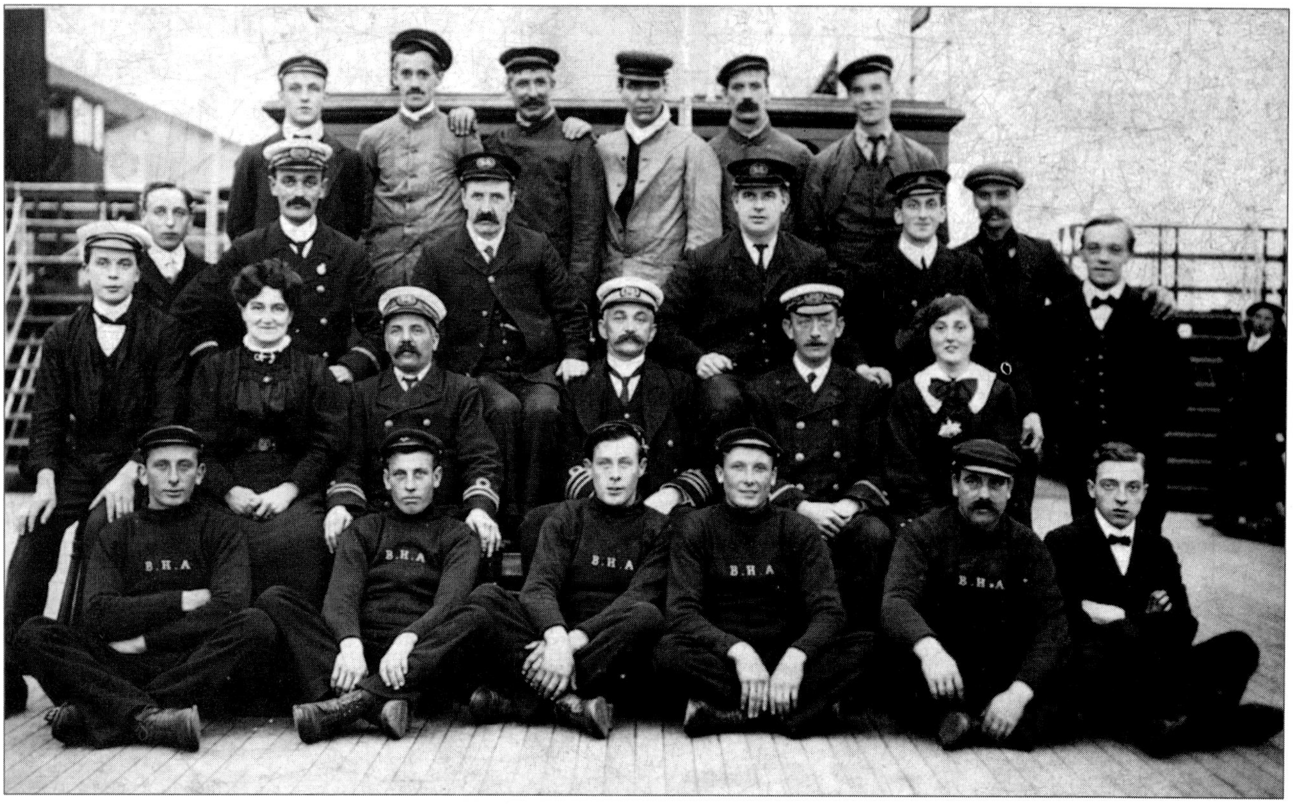

Memories of the Furness Railway paddle steamers which plied between Barrow and Fleetwood in the years leading up to the First World War are evoked by the accompanying three scenes. Above we see the officers and crew of the *Lady Moyra* in 1911, when Captain Ashcroft assumed command with John Helm as first mate and Mr E. Vardon as second mate. The first and second engineers were Mr F. Hewitt and Mr E. Kelsall. The purser was Mr Henry Brown. The top picture opposite shows part of the crowd on 3 June 1911 on board the sister ship, the *Lady Evelyn*. In the lower picture the crowd is crammed aboard the *Lady Moyra* en route to Blackpool on 27 May 1912. She carried 189,936 in the 1911 season without a major incident. Both the *Moyra* and the *Evelyn* survived until they were both sadly lost at Dunkirk in the 1940 evacuation. For illustrations of the boats see *Cumbrian Railways* by the same authors (Sutton Publishing, 1999). (*All three photographs are from the studio of the official photographer on the Furness Railway steamers: Edward Sankey of Barrow-in-Furness, who has left a legacy of photographic memories as important as any in the north-west)*

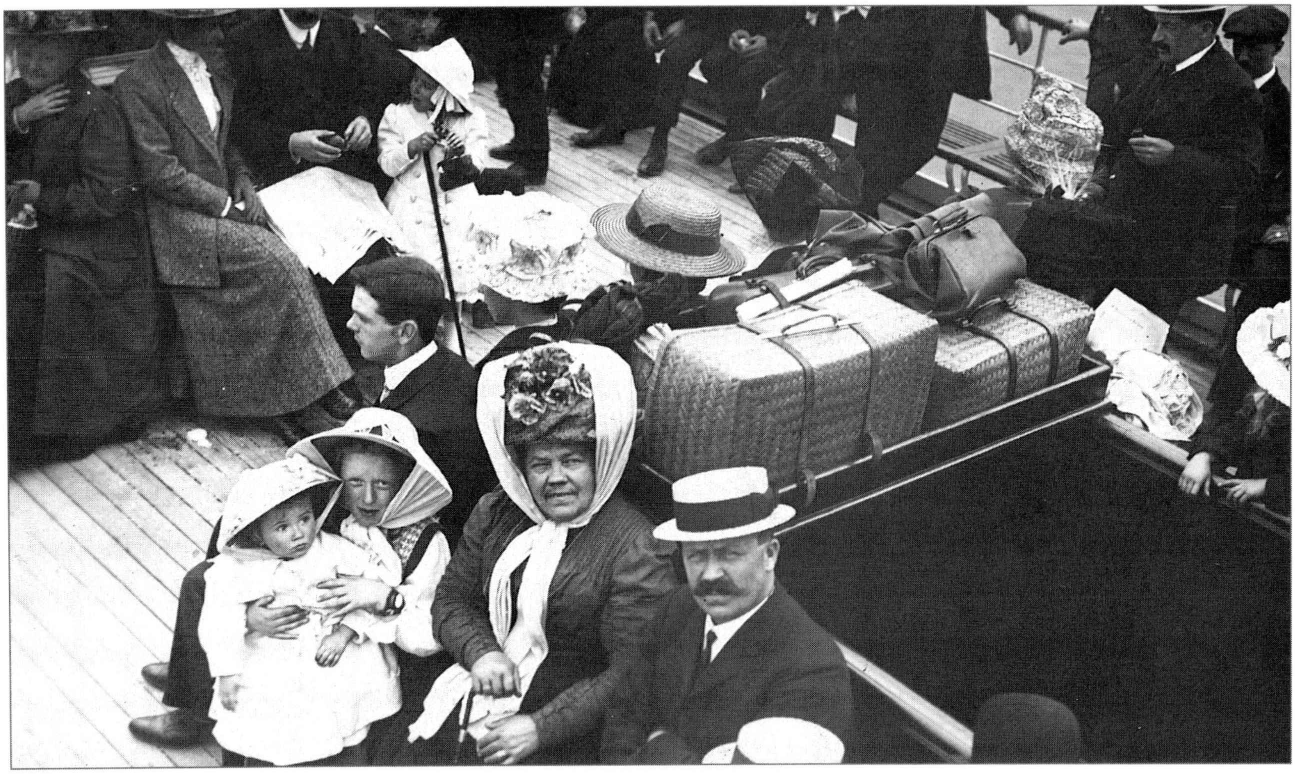

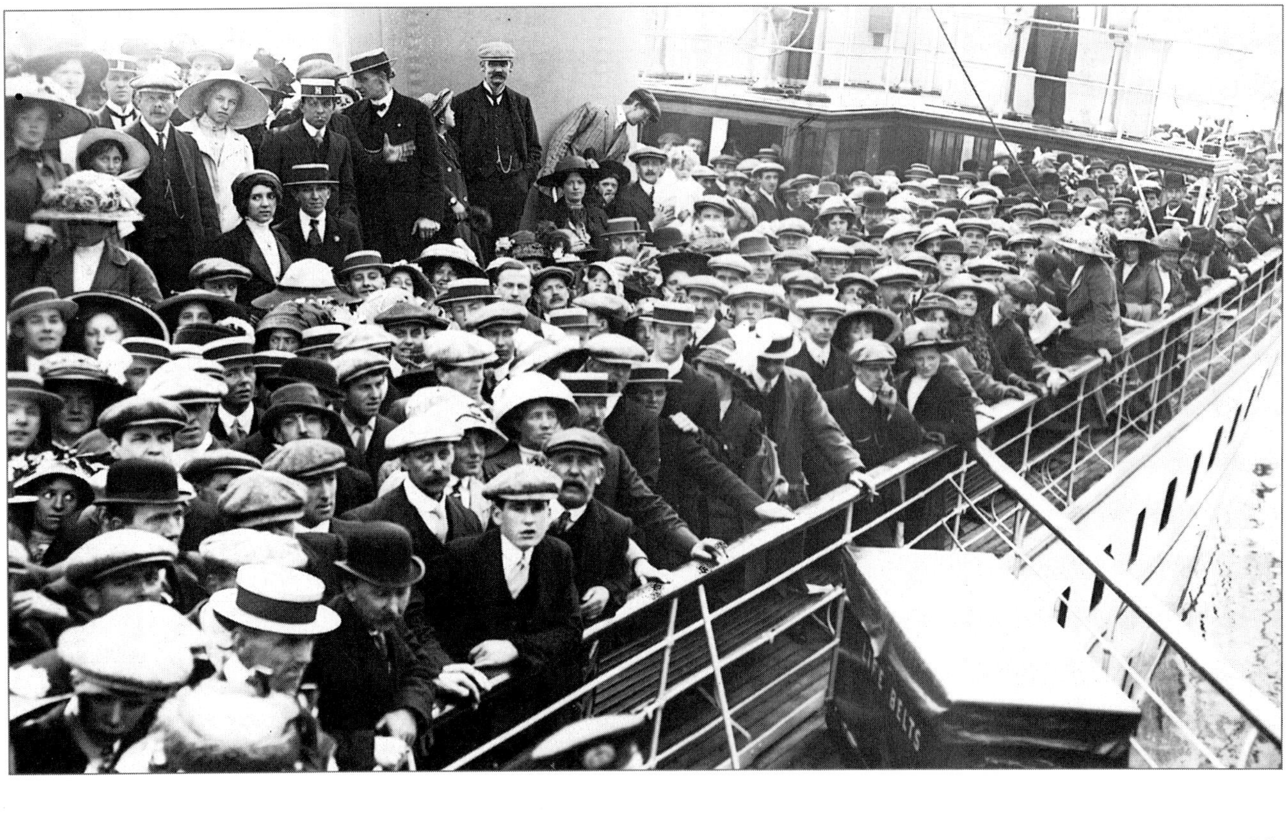
LIFE BELTS

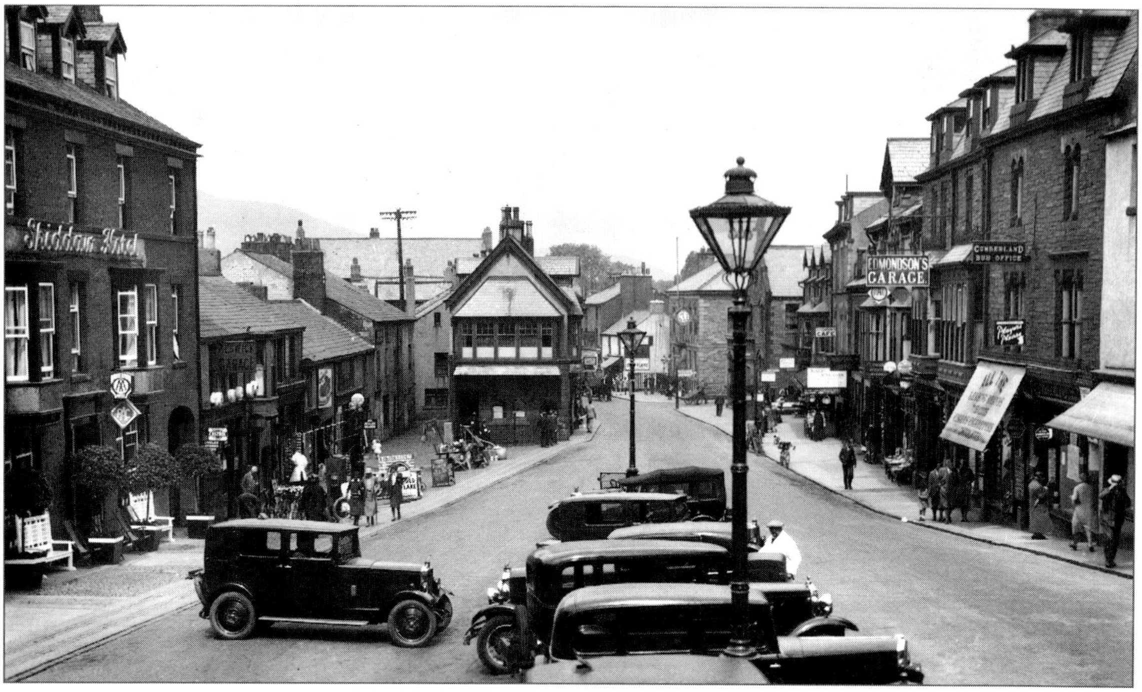

Keswick Market Place was turning into a car park when Maysons, the local photographers, pictured the scene in the early 1930s. A problem which grew and grew over the sixty years since the picture was taken has still not been solved in spite of the huge car park now to be found behind the buildings on the right. There are now just too many motor vehicles of various sizes, and free parking such as this in a town centre is but a happy memory for many. (*Maysons of Keswick*)

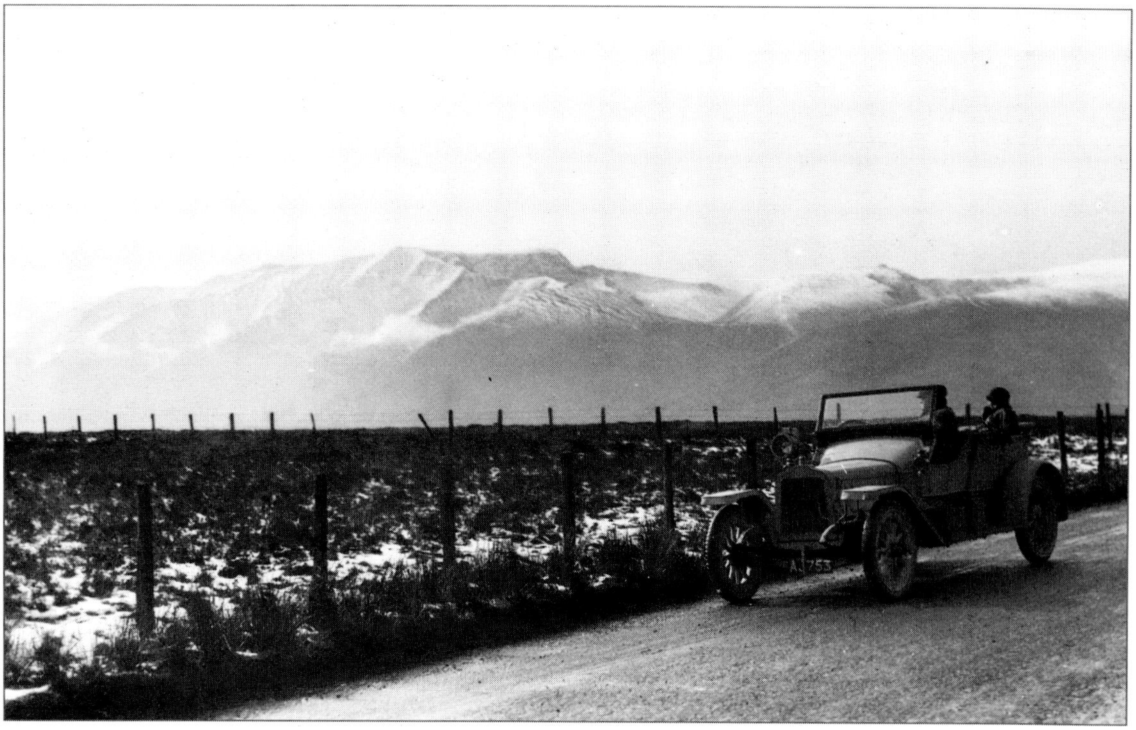

Blencathra from Troutbeck Moor, 30 April 1925. 'It was a wonderful evening with sunshine and snow' said the message on the postcard, which unbelievably was sent from Port Said on 4 July 1925. (*John Marsh Collection*)

Events Large and Small

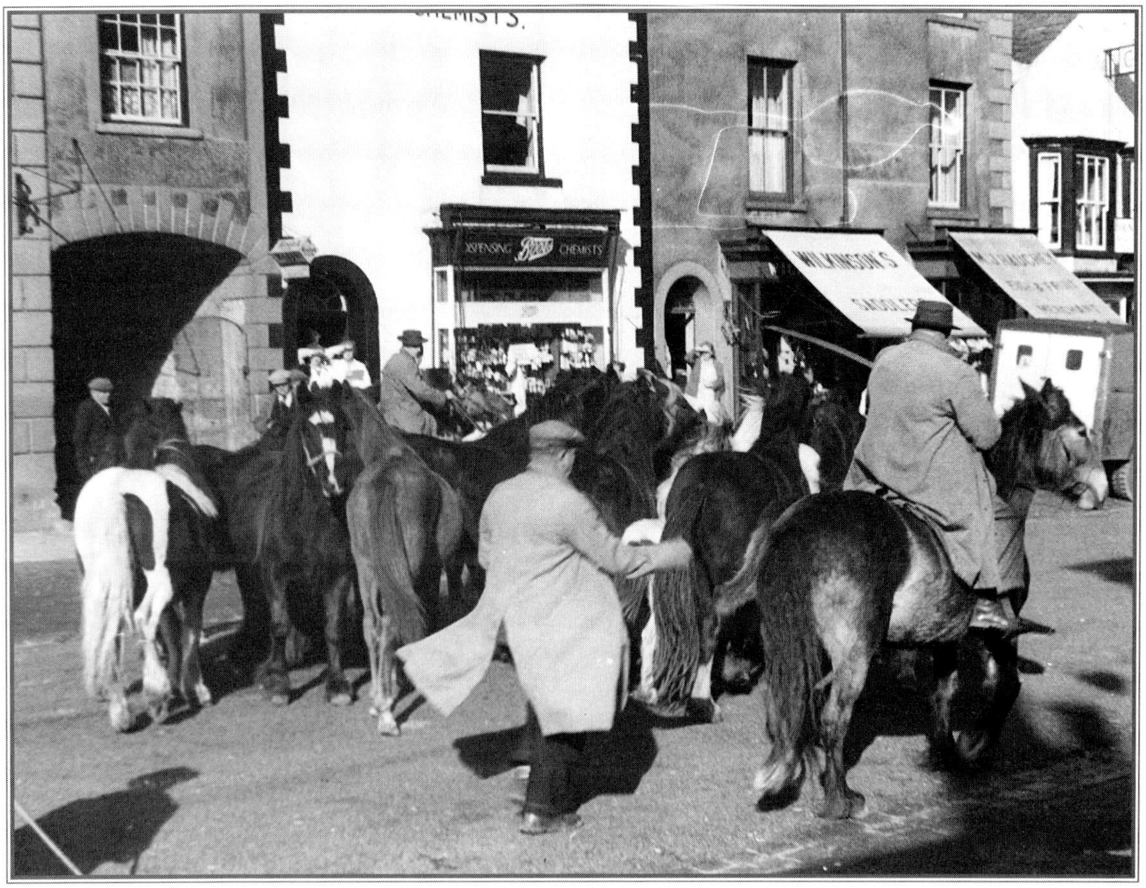

Market Street, Kirkby Stephen, included a Boots the Chemists shop in the 1950s. David M. Williams was the manager for many years and he photographed the annual goings-on in the street such as when Potters from all over the north came together for the Appleby Horse Fair or the by then nearly defunct Kirkby Stephen 'Cowper Day'. The horse dealers had been trading for centuries at horse fairs and Appleby Fair is one of the last to survive as motorised transport replaced the four-legged worker. Many Cumbrian towns had their own horse fair from medieval times. (*D.M. Williams*)

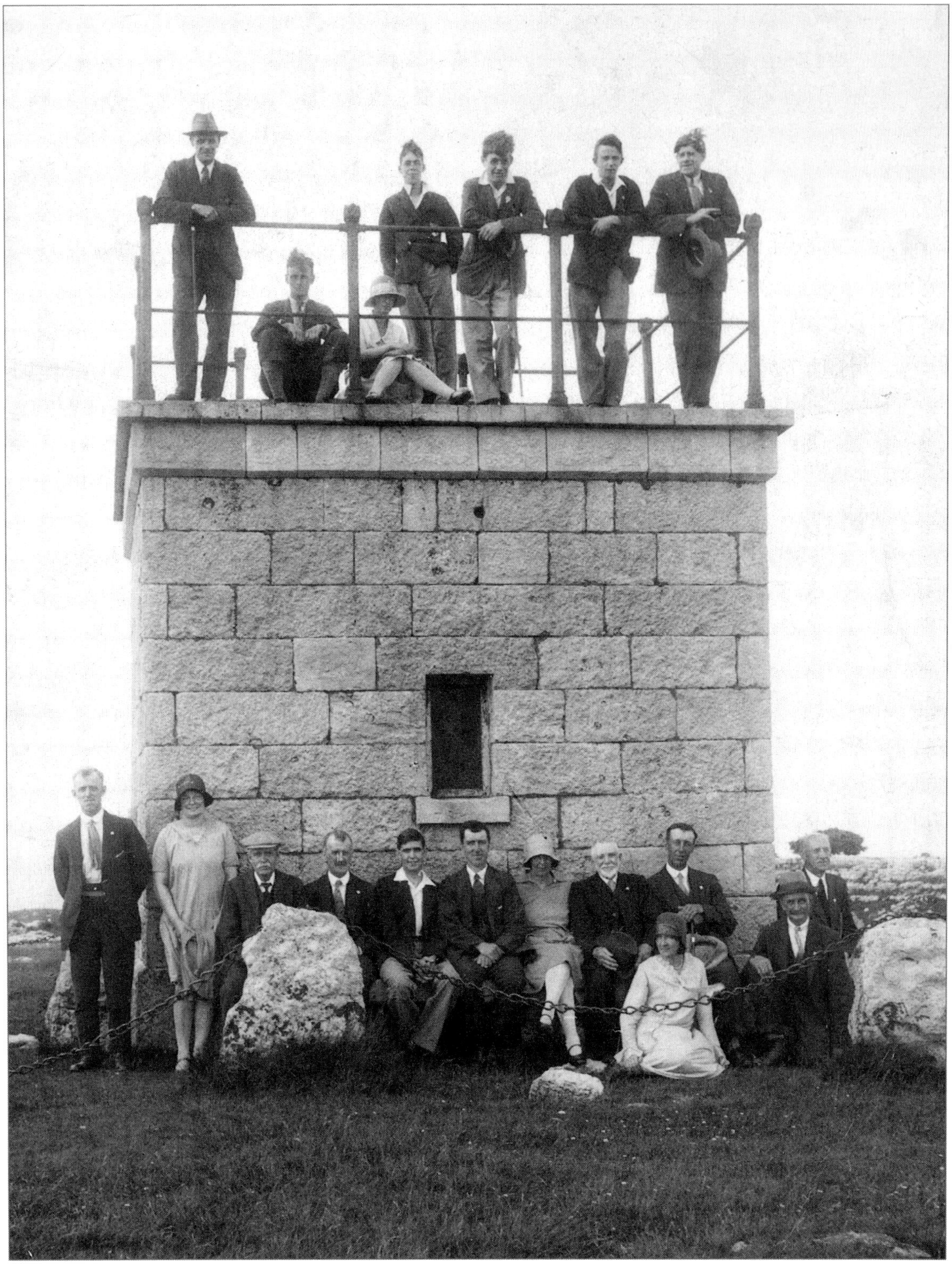

The Hampsfell Hospice above Grange-over-Sands was the objective of the annual Ulverston parish church bell ringers' outing in the mid-1930s. Ulverston church was lucky to have a full peal of bells which the chief bellringer, Joe Kitchin (standing top left), was always eager for his team to use to the full. Competitions, practices, services and outings made for a happy social round. (*John Marsh Collection*)

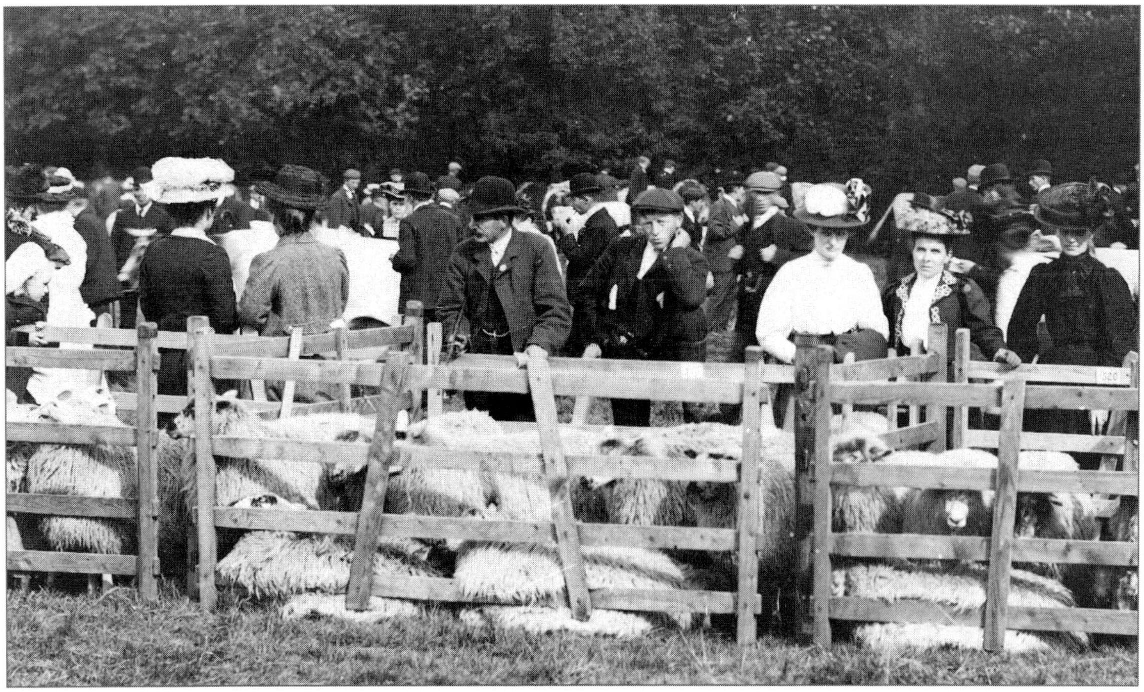

A well-attended agricultural show at Hesket in 1908. This annual event was an opportunity to get away from the daily chores and meet with like-minded neighbours. Prizes at the show would provide the incentive of higher prices at the local market. (*John Marsh Collection*)

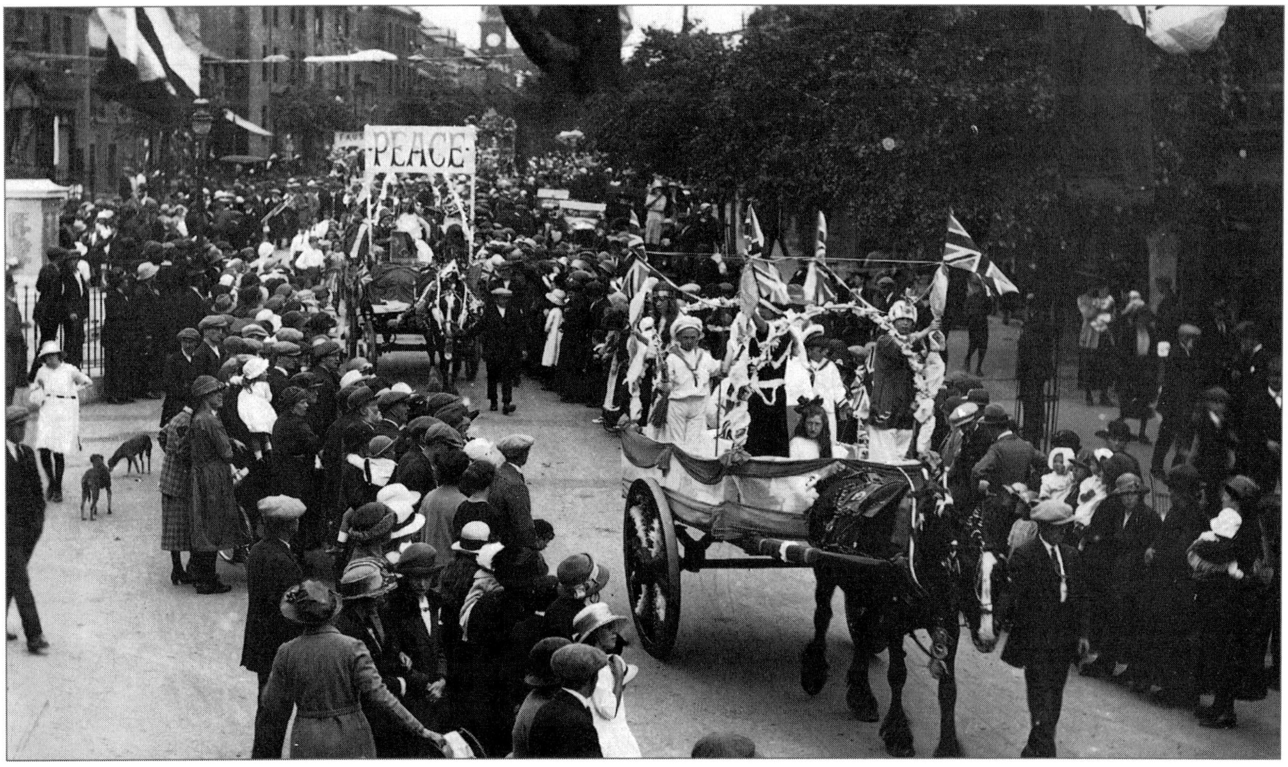

Egremont Children's Gala Day was a popular annual event, seen here in 1923. Smartly turned-out horse-drawn floats are reflected by the Sunday suits of the populace. (*John Marsh Collection*)

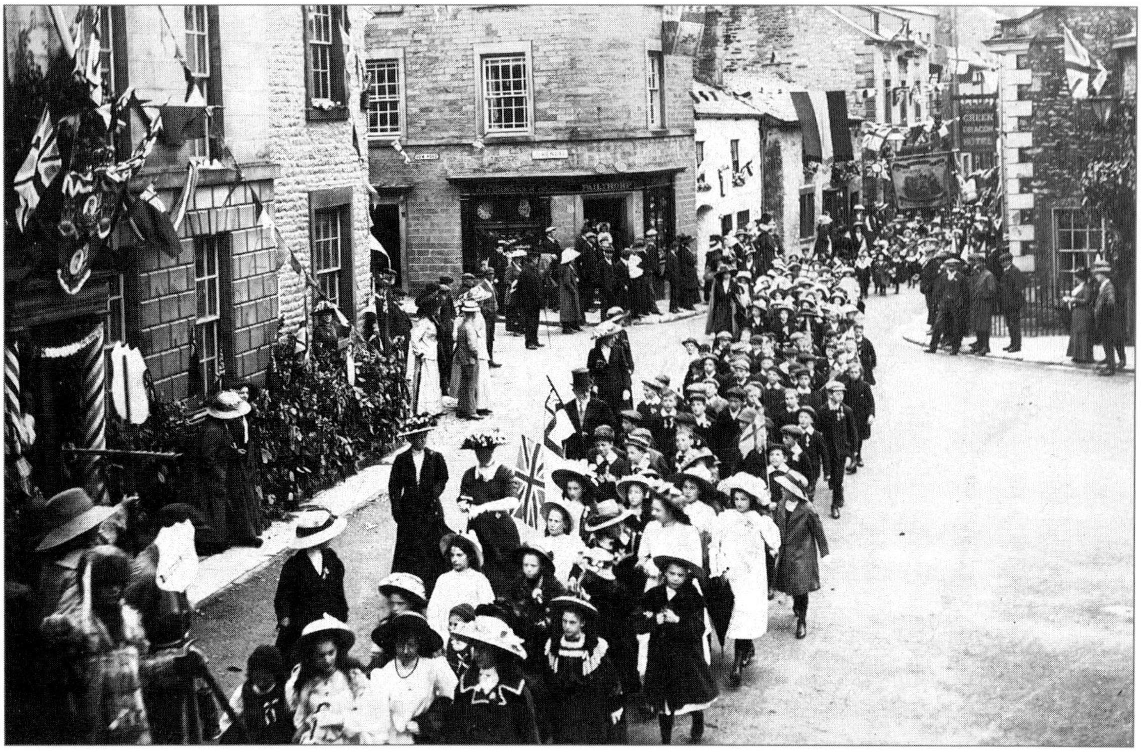

Assembled children at the Kirkby Lonsdale Coronation Day parade in June 1911. Local parades such as this to commemorate a national event have now lost their appeal. (*John Marsh Collection*)

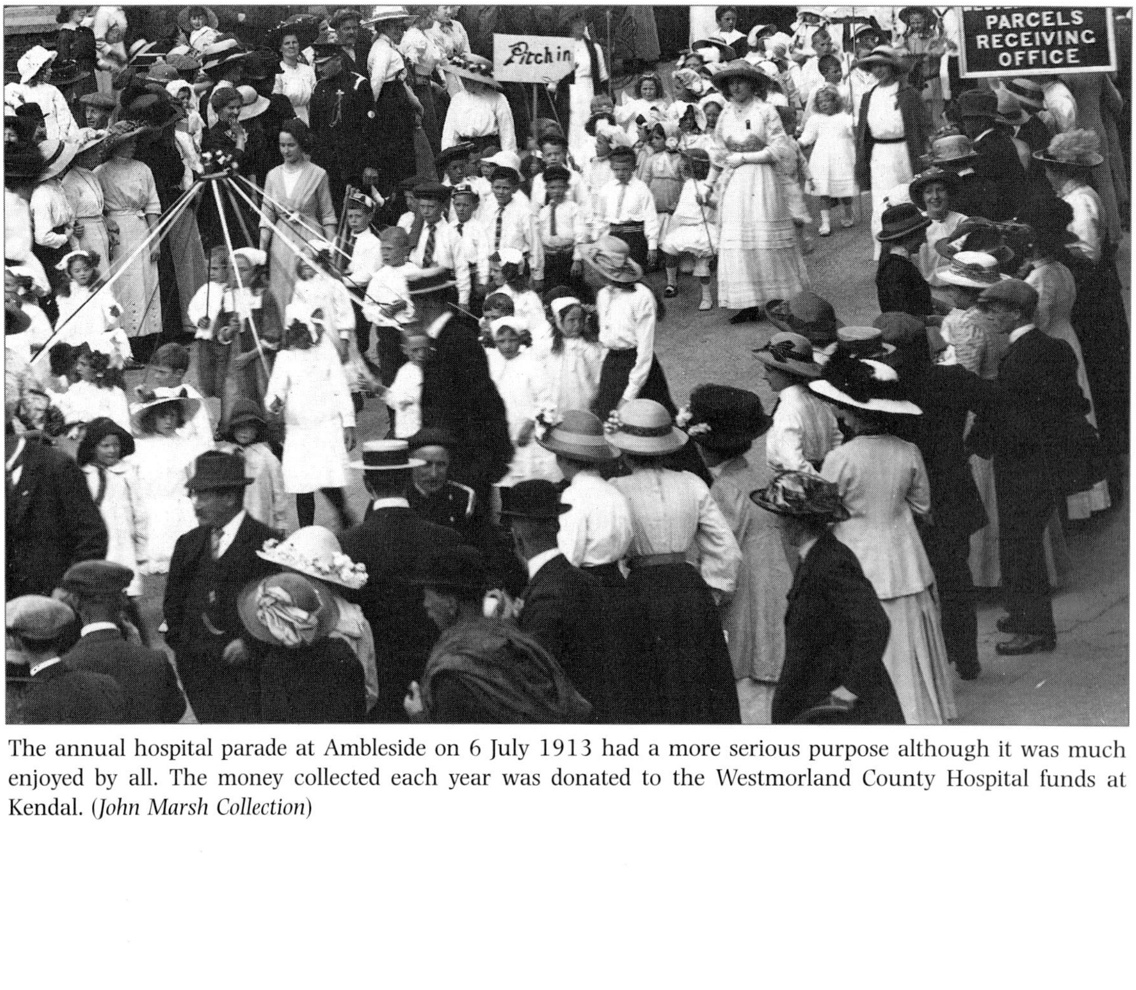

The annual hospital parade at Ambleside on 6 July 1913 had a more serious purpose although it was much enjoyed by all. The money collected each year was donated to the Westmorland County Hospital funds at Kendal. (*John Marsh Collection*)

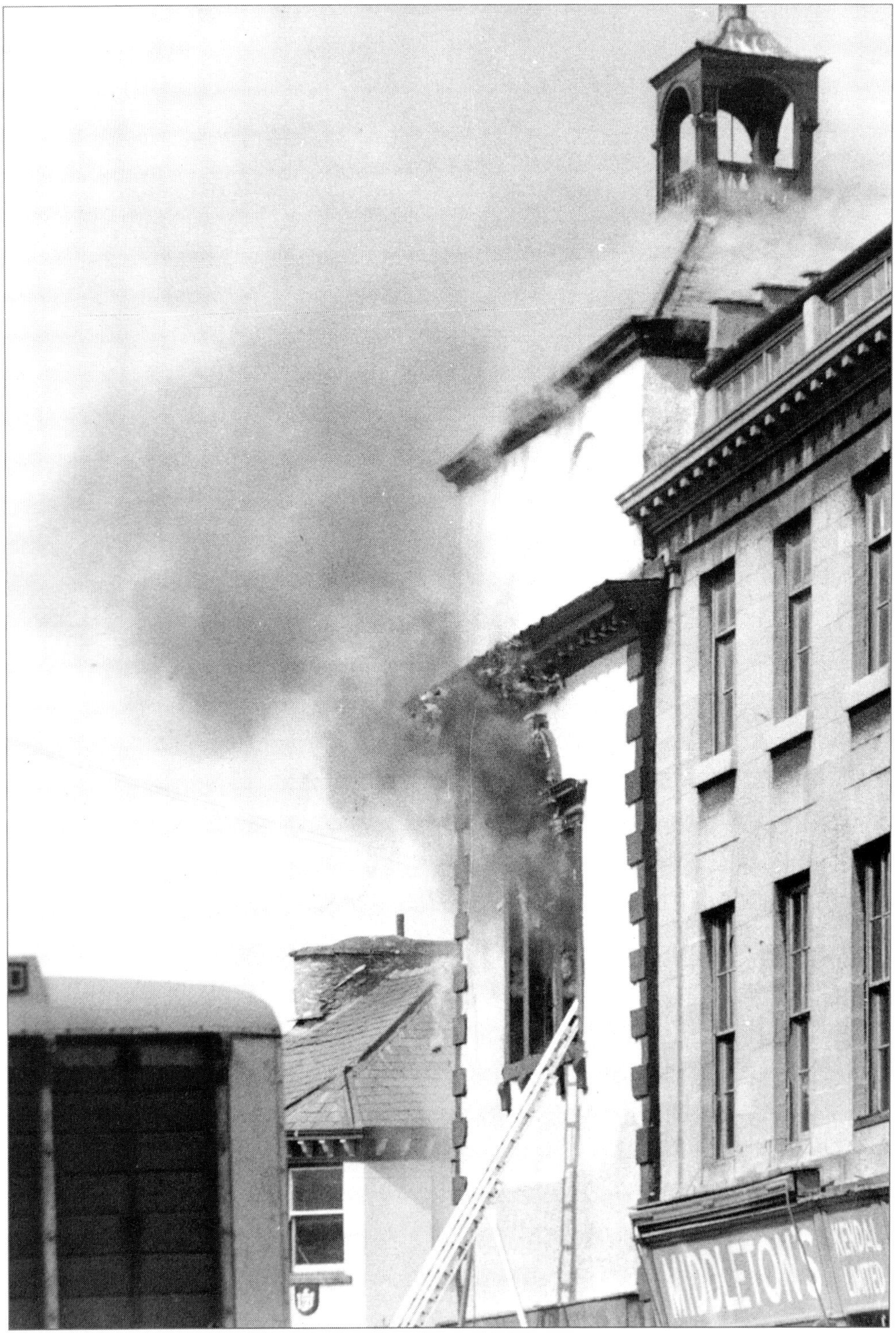

The destruction of the ancient Moot Hall by a criminal act in the 1960s was an important event in the history of Kendal. From the sixteenth century this building had acted as Borough Council meeting place, offices and courtroom. It had other municipal uses until the new Town Hall came into use in the nineteenth century. Unfortunately the building which replaced the old Moot Hall offers few memories of the site's important past, being a building of the 'awful' period of British architecture. (*John Marsh Collection*)

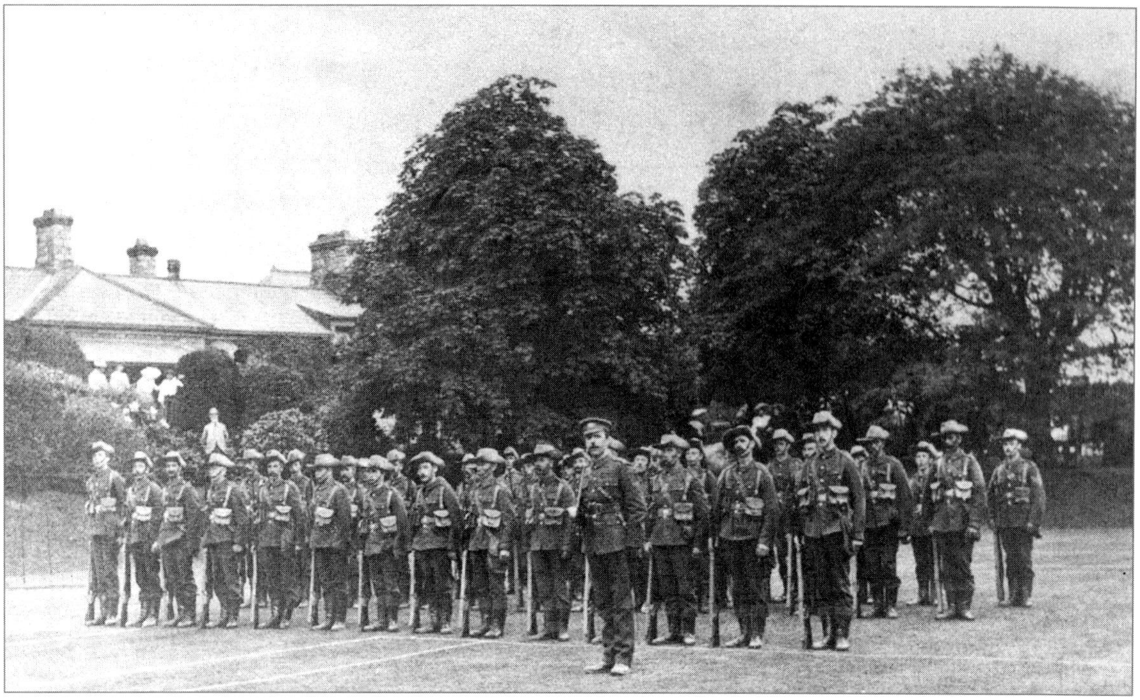

Osborne Paine of Grange-over-Sands photographed the local volunteers on the tennis courts then situated between the railway station and the Grange Hotel. They were about to embark for the South African War complete with wide-awake hats, ammunition pouches and puttees. (*Osborne Paine*)

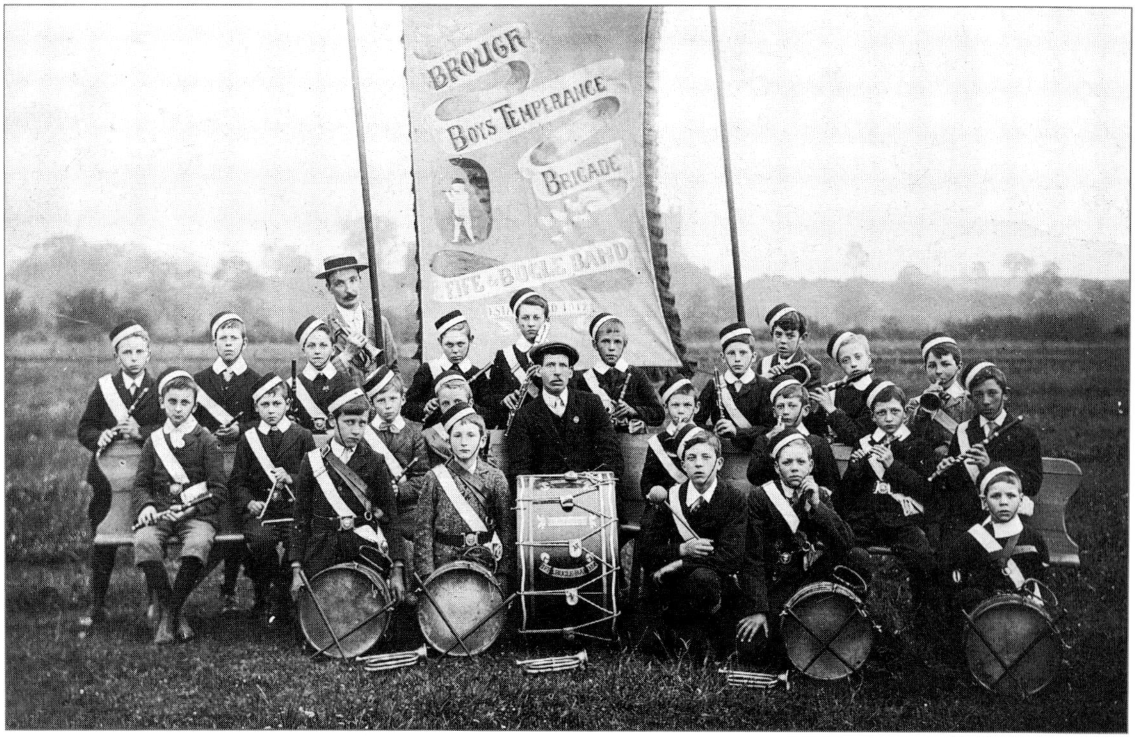

Brough Boys Temperance Brigade pipe and bugle band included five drummers and reflected the ardent interest in the anti-alcohol movement in that area. The band would be used at church parades and Rushbearing ceremonies. (*John Marsh Collection*)

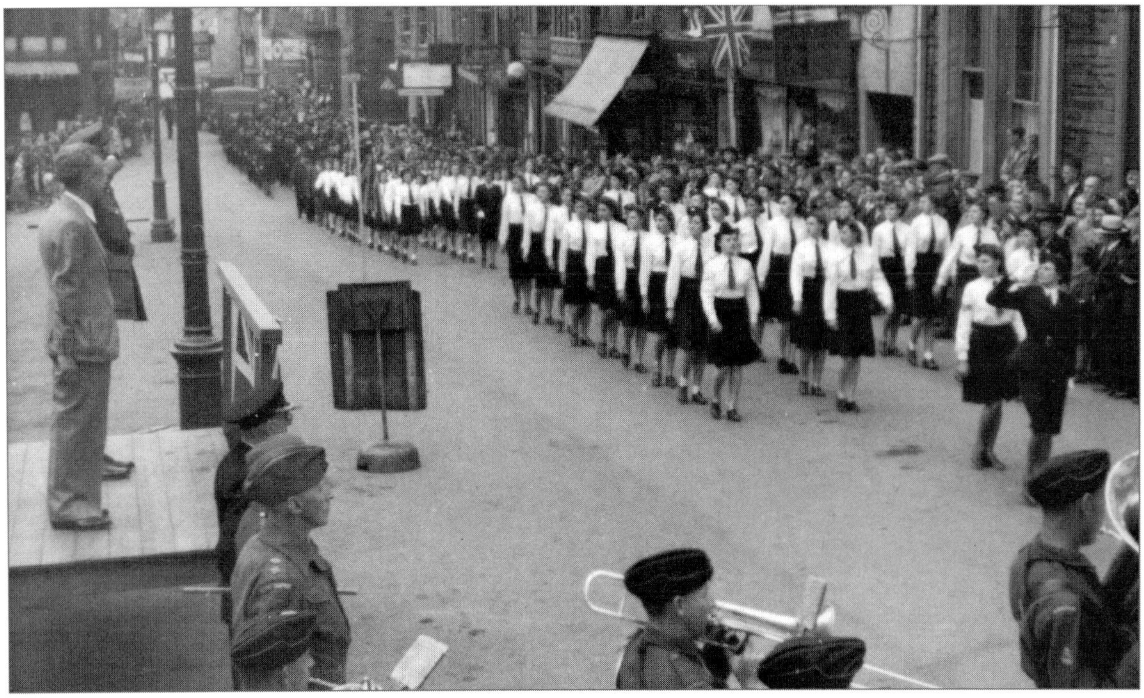

Two very different gatherings at Keswick. Above, in July 1944 we see the No. 228 Company of the Girls Training Corps marching past the saluting base aided by the local Home Guard band. Many were to be recruited into the ATS, the WRENS or the WRAF before the Second World War ended in 1945. (*John Marsh Collection*). Below, the large crowd at a turn-of-the-century interdenominational religious convention. At that time thousands came to Keswick travelling by special trains from near and far. Keswick photographers made certain that everyone attending had a souvenir photograph. (*George Dawson Collection*)

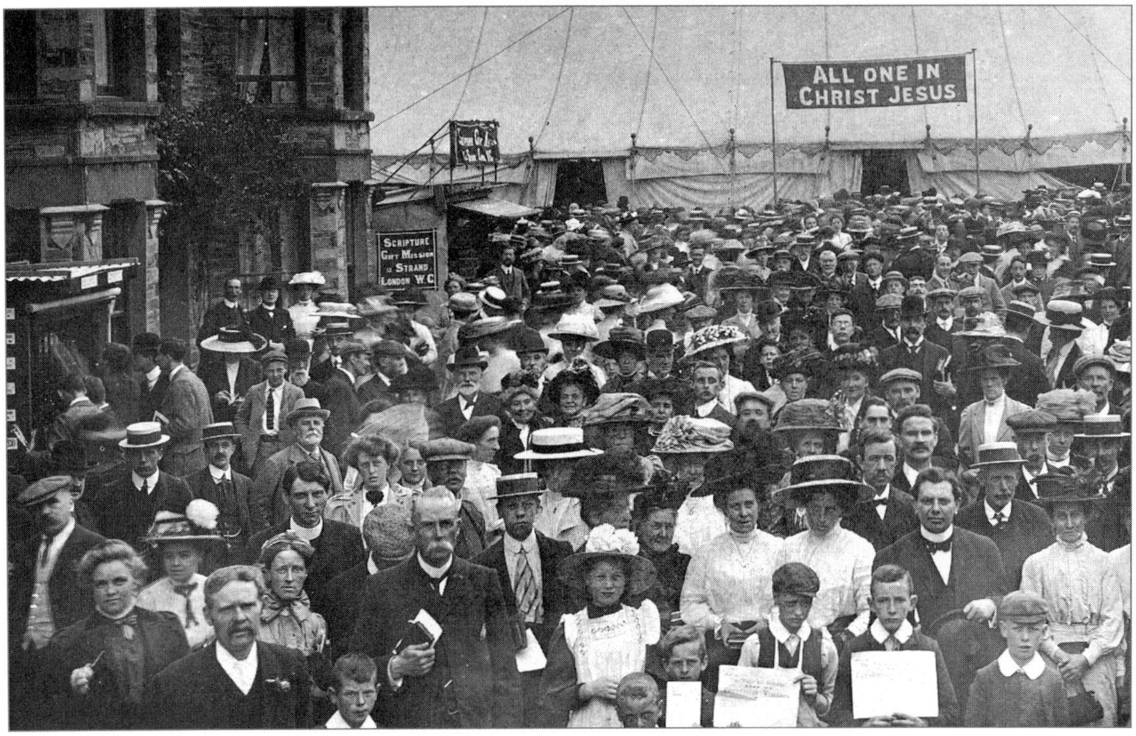

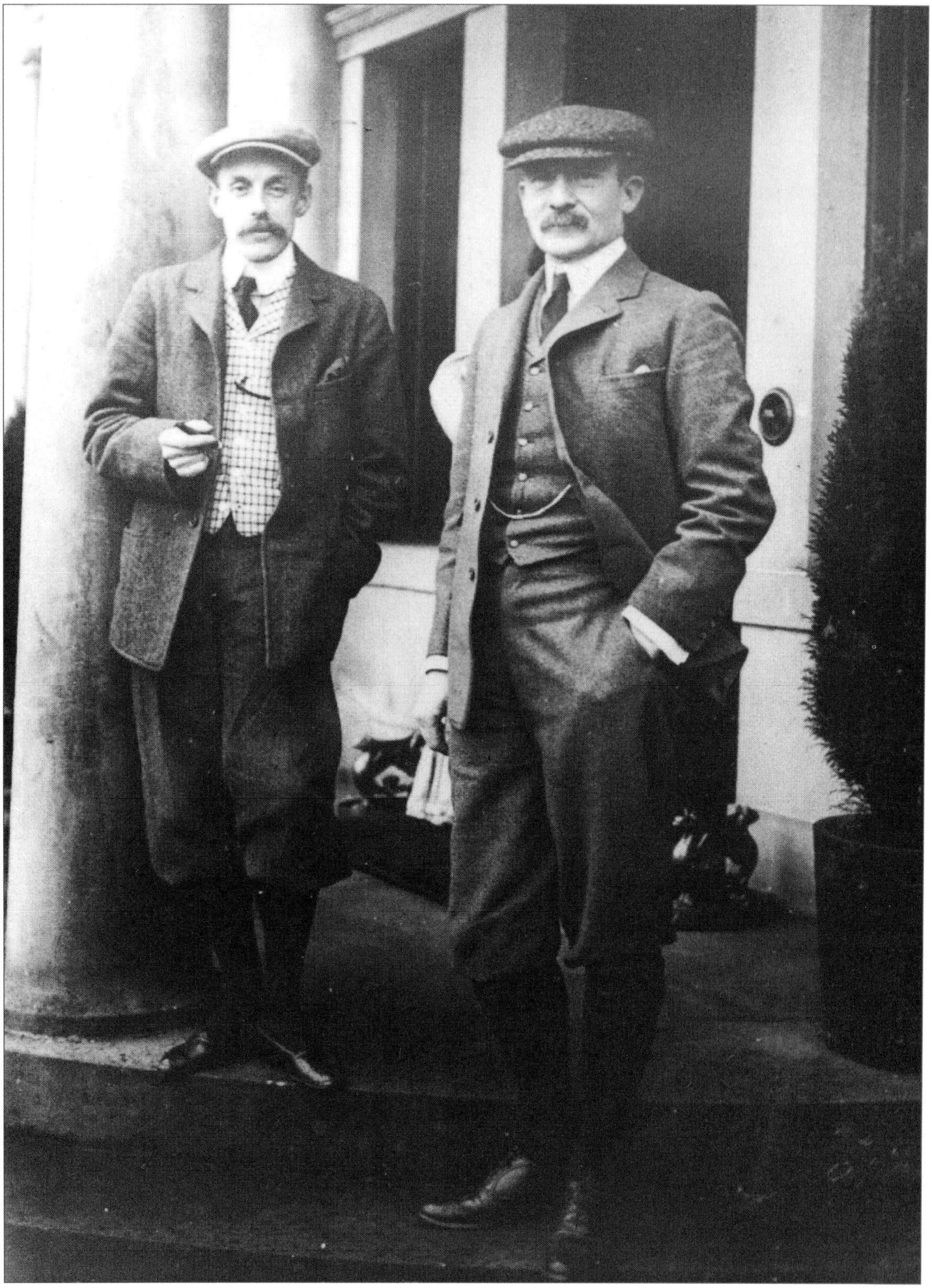

Major Noble of Calgarth Park, Troutbeck, near Windermere, was visited in 1915 by Major General Sir Robert Baden-Powell (right), hero of Mafeking and founder of the Boy Scout movement. (*John Marsh Collection*)

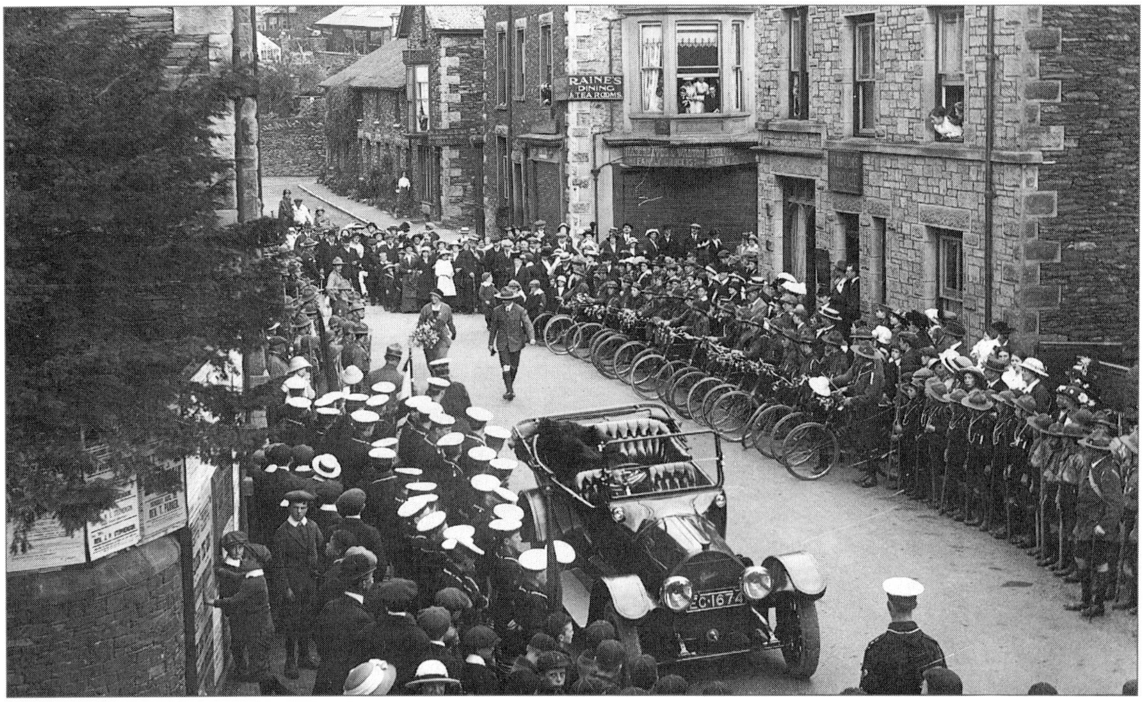

Sir Robert Baden-Powell inspects his Boy Scouts in Crescent Road, Windermere, on 29 August 1915 when Scouts from around the district assembled to meet their illustrious founder. The visit included a trip on Lake Windermere in the *Beaver*, a motor launch owned by his close friend John Mortimer Sladen of Cleeve Howe, Windermere, who had founded the Windermere Sea Scouts in 1912. (*John Marsh Collection*)

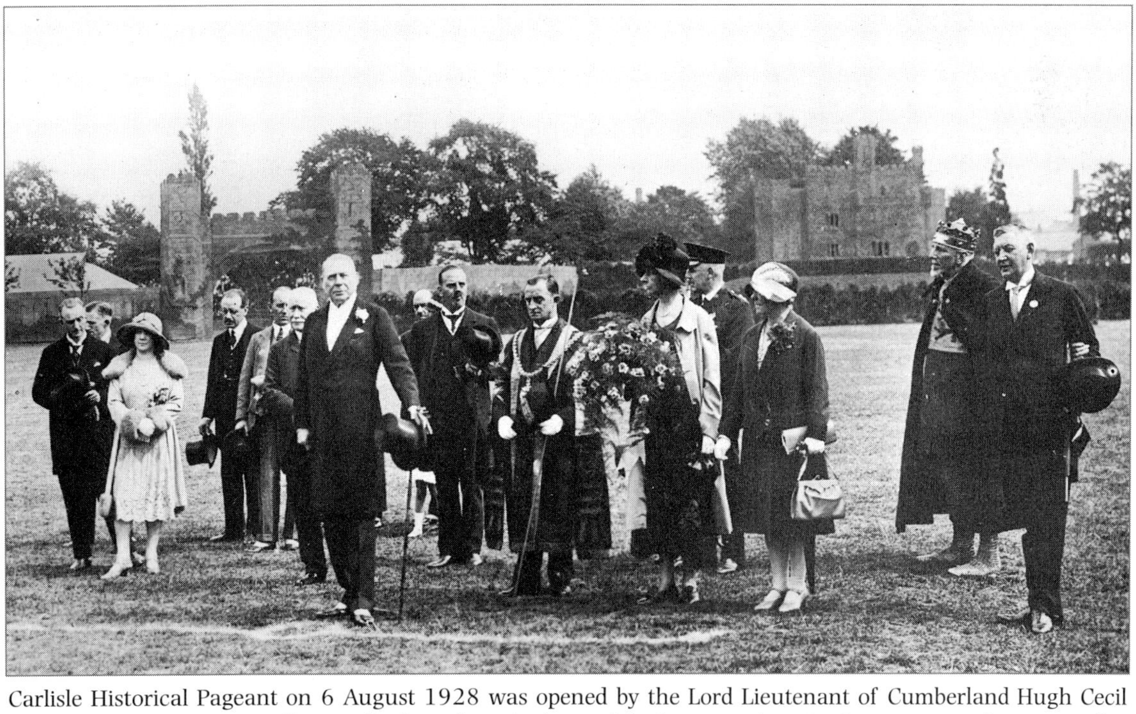

Carlisle Historical Pageant on 6 August 1928 was opened by the Lord Lieutenant of Cumberland Hugh Cecil Lowther, known as the 'Yellow Earl', the 5th Earl of Lonsdale from Lowther Castle, near Penrith. He gave his colour to the Automobile Association when he was its first president, and to his local Tory party (threatening to resign if they did not concur), who use it to this day. (*George Dawson Collection*)

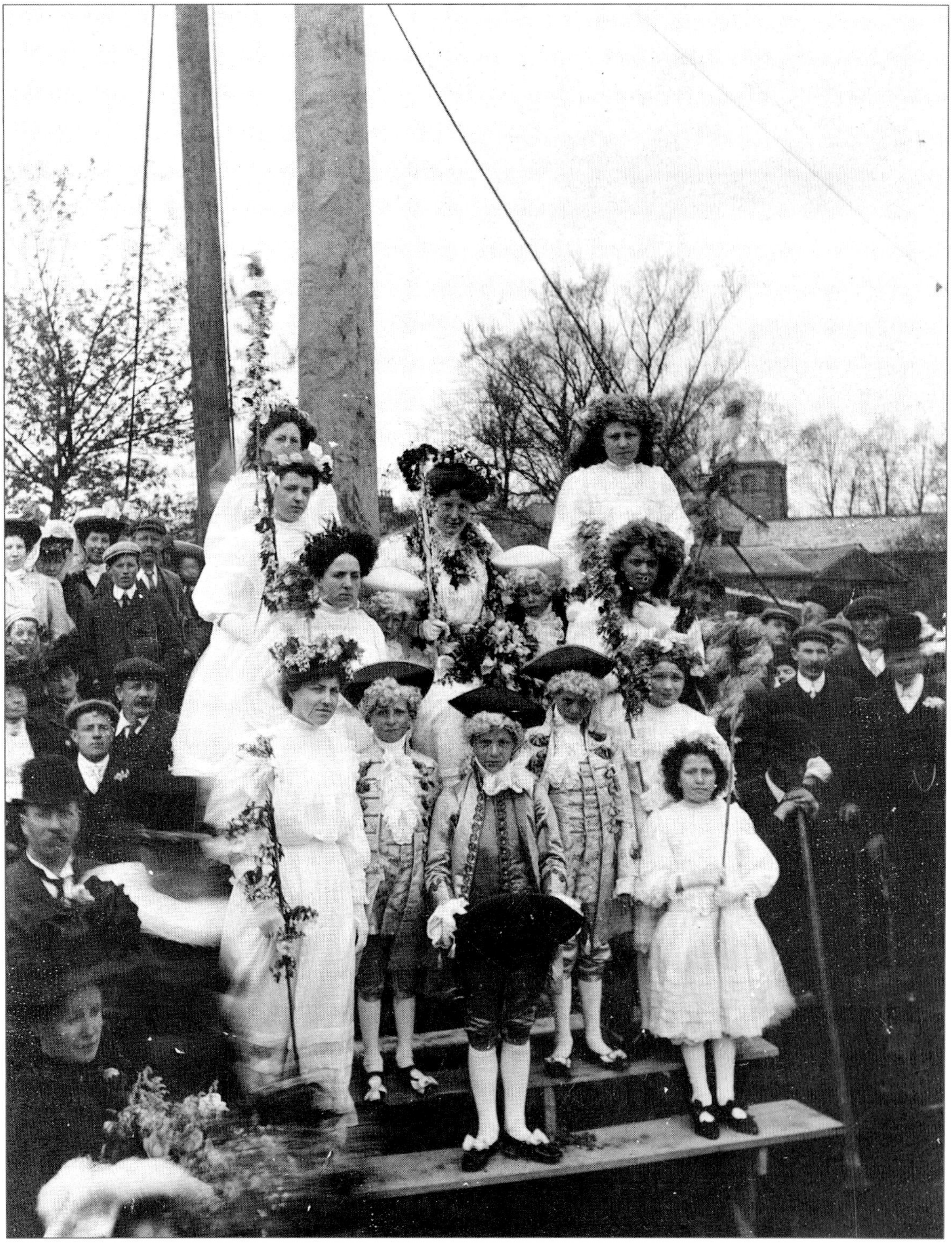

Temple Sowerby May Queen celebration on 14 May 1908 saw the vicar's daughter Ethel Anderson crowned as May Queen. Here she is seen at the giant 75-foot maypole with her retinue of pages and ladies-in-waiting braced against the Eden Valley chilly spring weather. This was the first festivity after a gap of twenty-four years. Lord Hothfield of Appleby Castle had provided the new maypole, which still graces what is now a grass verge on the infamous A66 main trunk road. *(John Marsh Collection)*

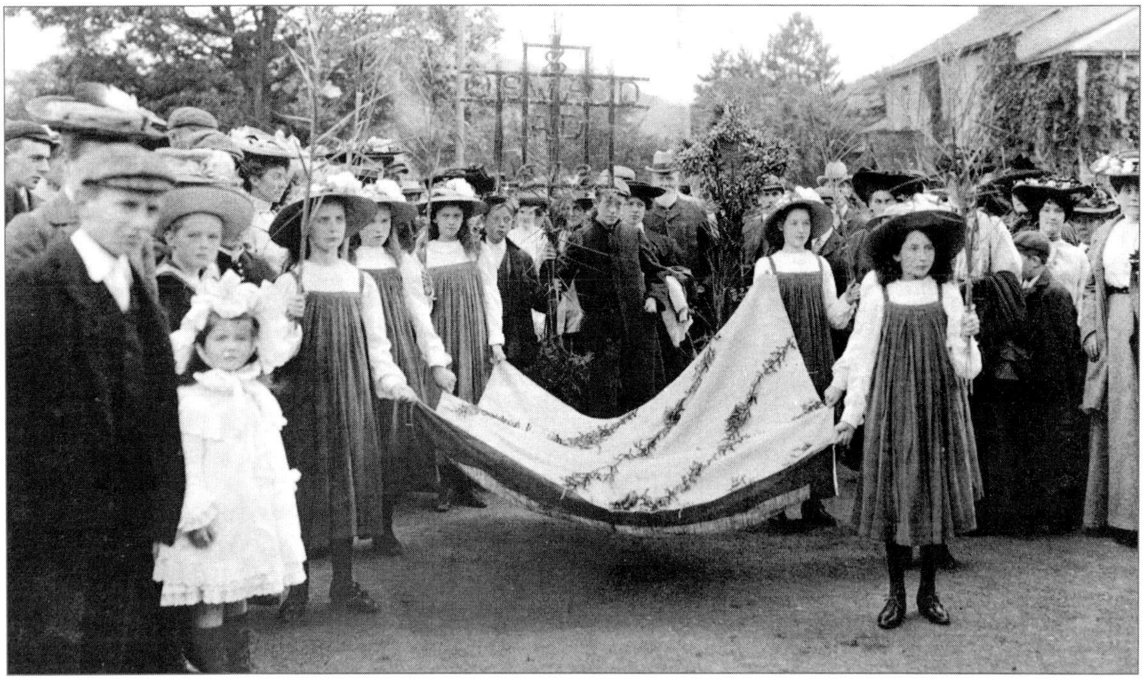

The Grasmere Rushbearing has been held annually for many years. Here, in about 1910, six girls in green and white tunics hold the ceremonial linen sheet, spun locally by the ladies of the John Ruskin Langdale linen industry. The parade to St Oswald's church takes place on the nearest Sunday to the saint's day on 5 August. (*John Marsh Collection*)

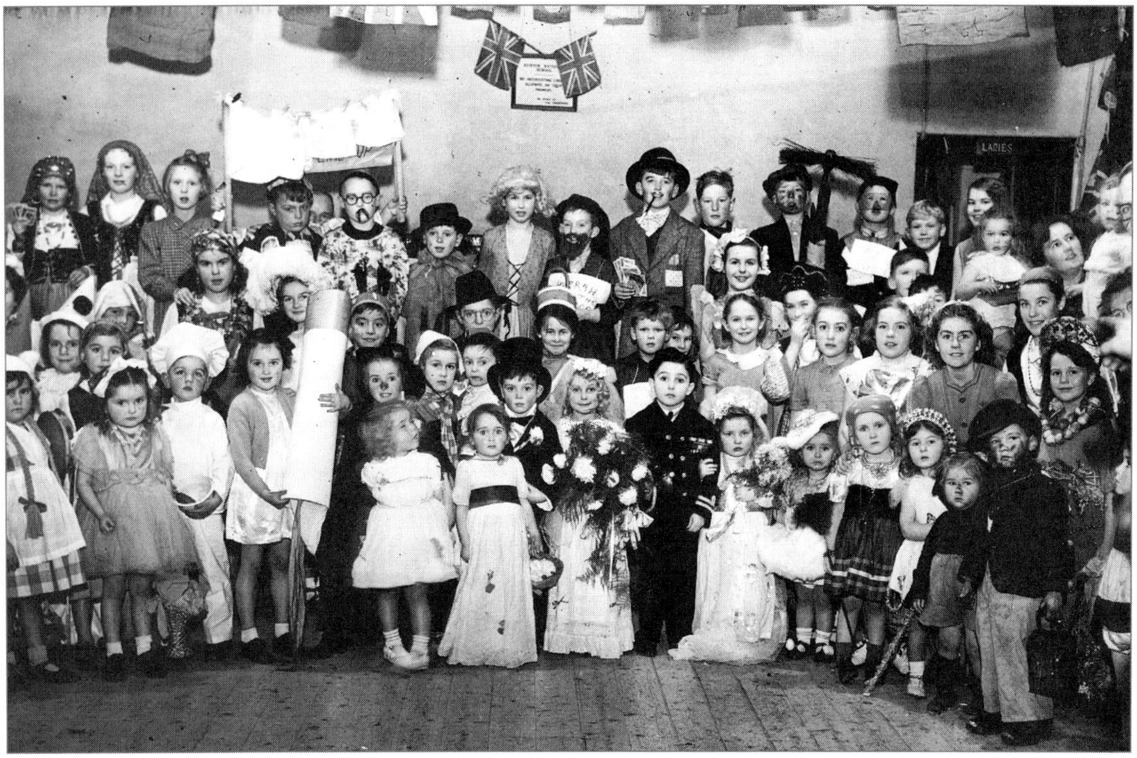

Burton-in-Kendal Morewood School children re-enacted the royal wedding in 1947. The event took place in the old schoolroom, situated opposite the church on Church Bank. (*John Marsh Collection*)

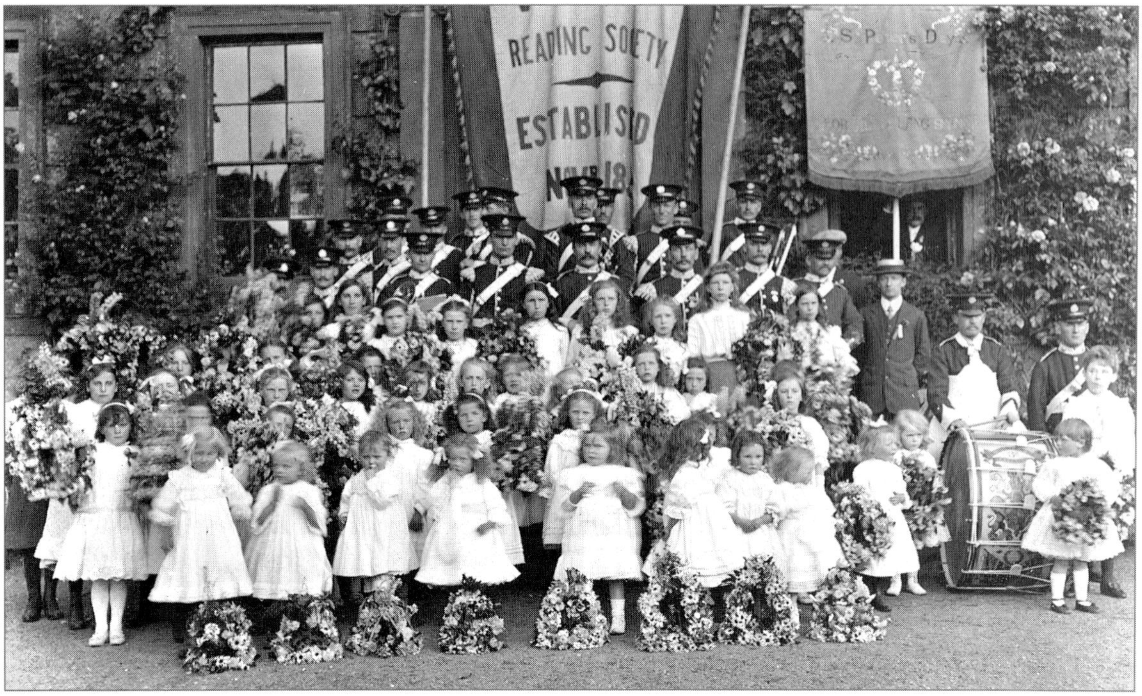

Warcop annual St Peter's Day Rushbearing on 29 June 1909 was a relic of pre-Christian times when pagan rituals were reprogrammed into Christian ritual and, amazingly, survived the schisms of Christian belief over the centuries. The St Peter's Day and Reading Society banners can be seen behind the band and village children with their wreaths and posies at Warcop Hall, which was the centre of events after a church service. (*John Marsh Collection*)

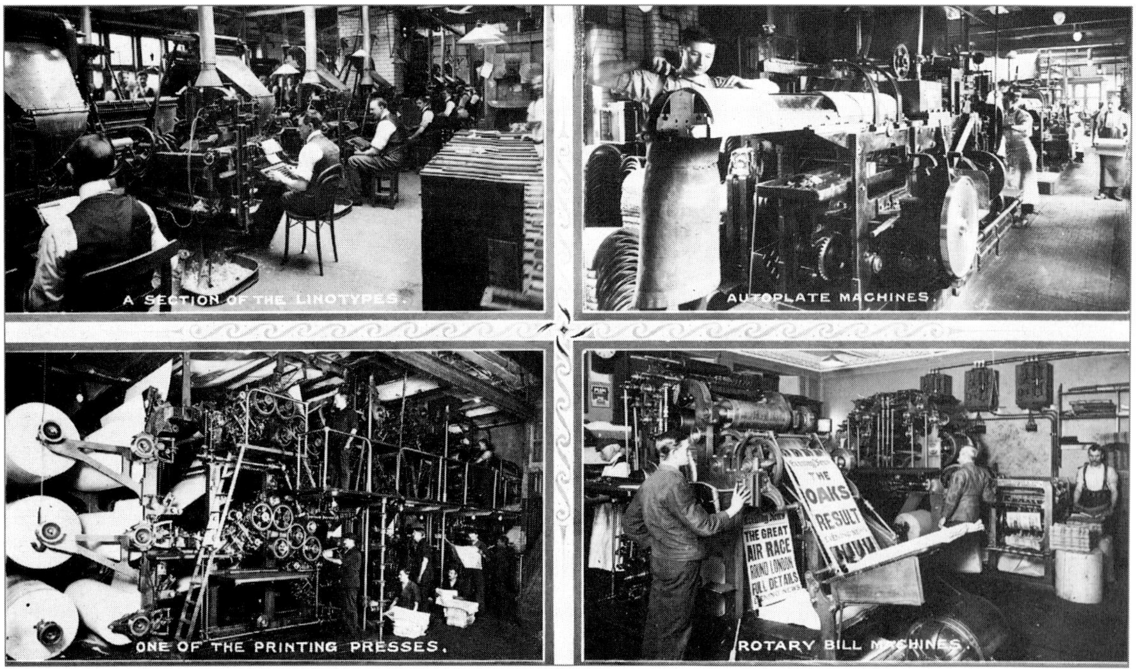

Barrow-in-Furness *Evening News* printing works is illustrated on this special postcard issued by the paper to celebrate its 10,000th issue on 21 November 1913. The paper has changed owners since then but continues to serve the Furness area. Much of the printing process is now but a memory. (*John Garbutt Collection*)

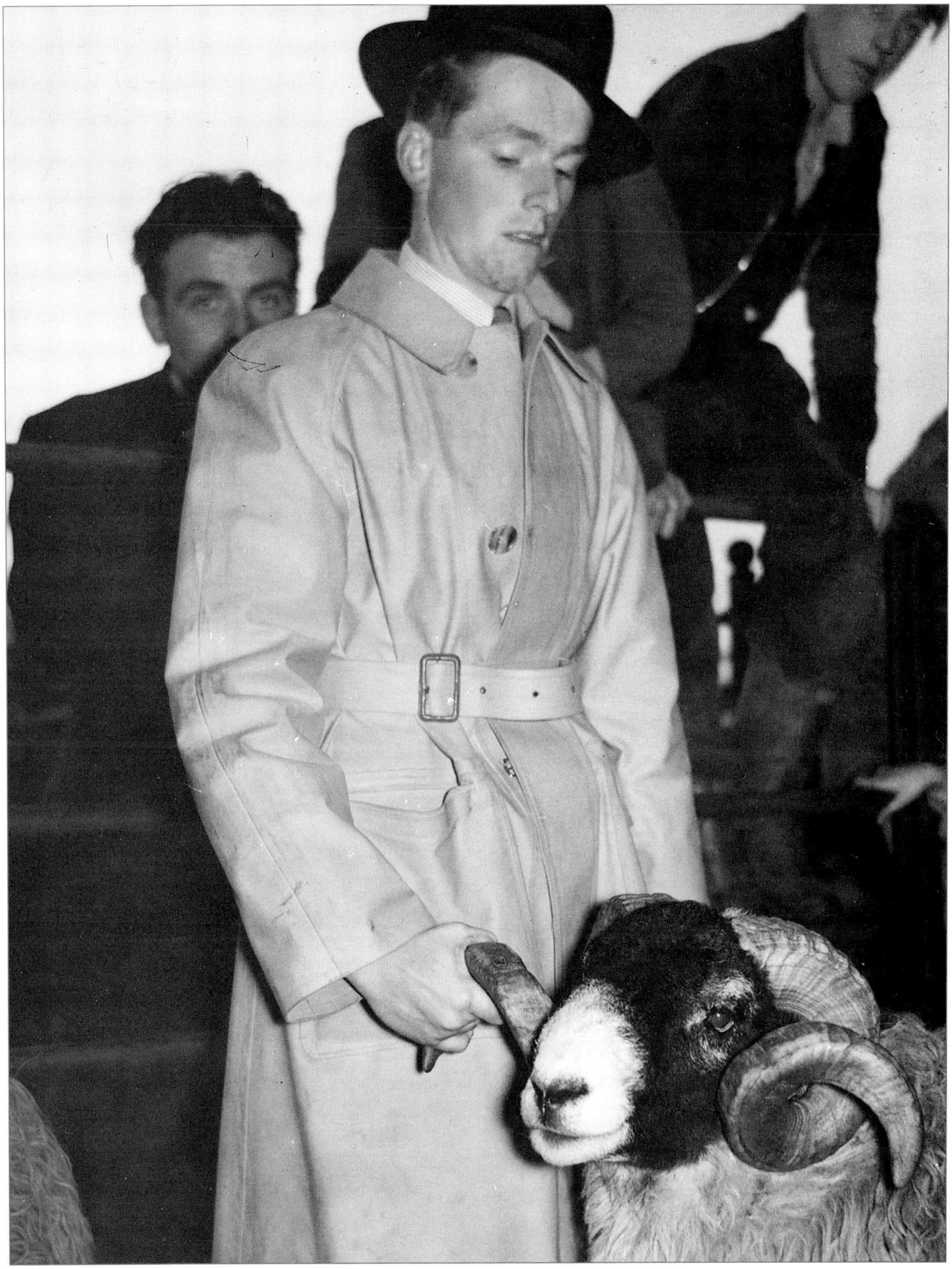

Kirkby Stephen Ram Sale in October 1954 produced a record high price for a ram when this Swaledale shearling ram was sold by J.E. Harker and Sons of Murton Hall for £1800. The fell farmers of the Eden valley could not have expected the harshness of the free market that many of them supported to produce the unhappy situation we see forty years later. (*John Marsh*)

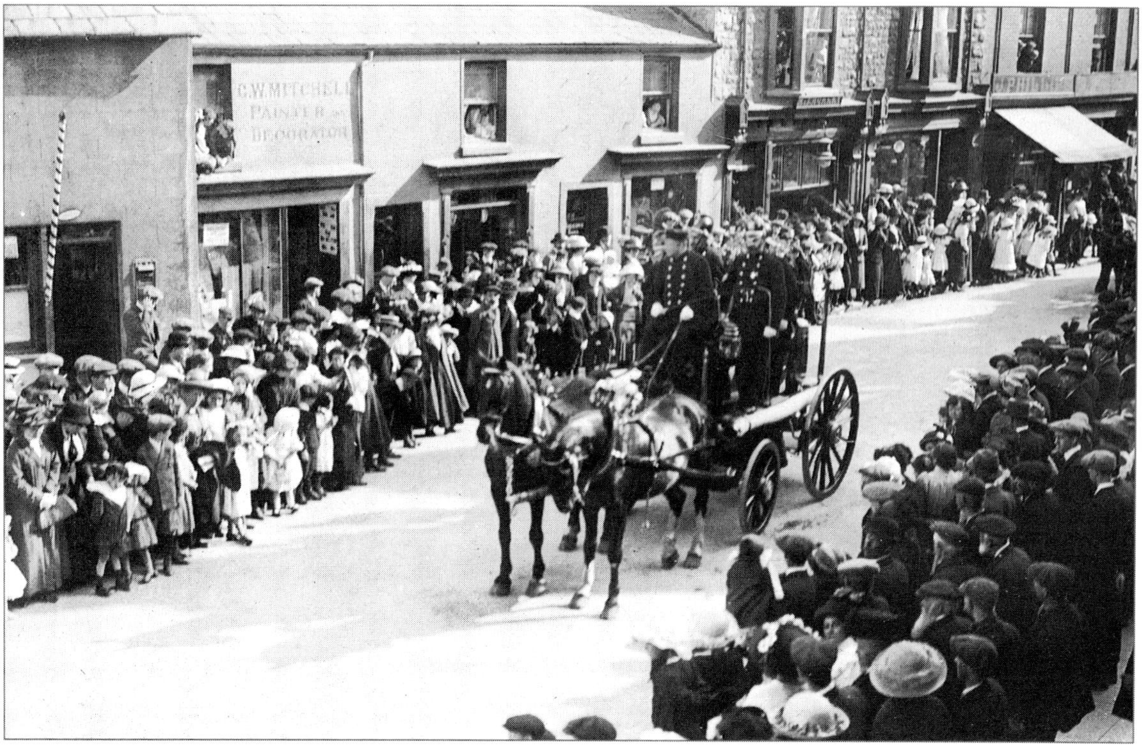

Two hospital parades. Above, the Dalton-in-Furness fire brigade are on their horse-drawn steamer fire engine in Market Street, Dalton, in the 1910 parade. (*G.W. Mitchell of Dalton*) Below, at about the same time, Ambleside children walk down Kelsick Road where today we have a car park on the left and the Public Library on the right of the picture. (*John Garbutt Collection*)

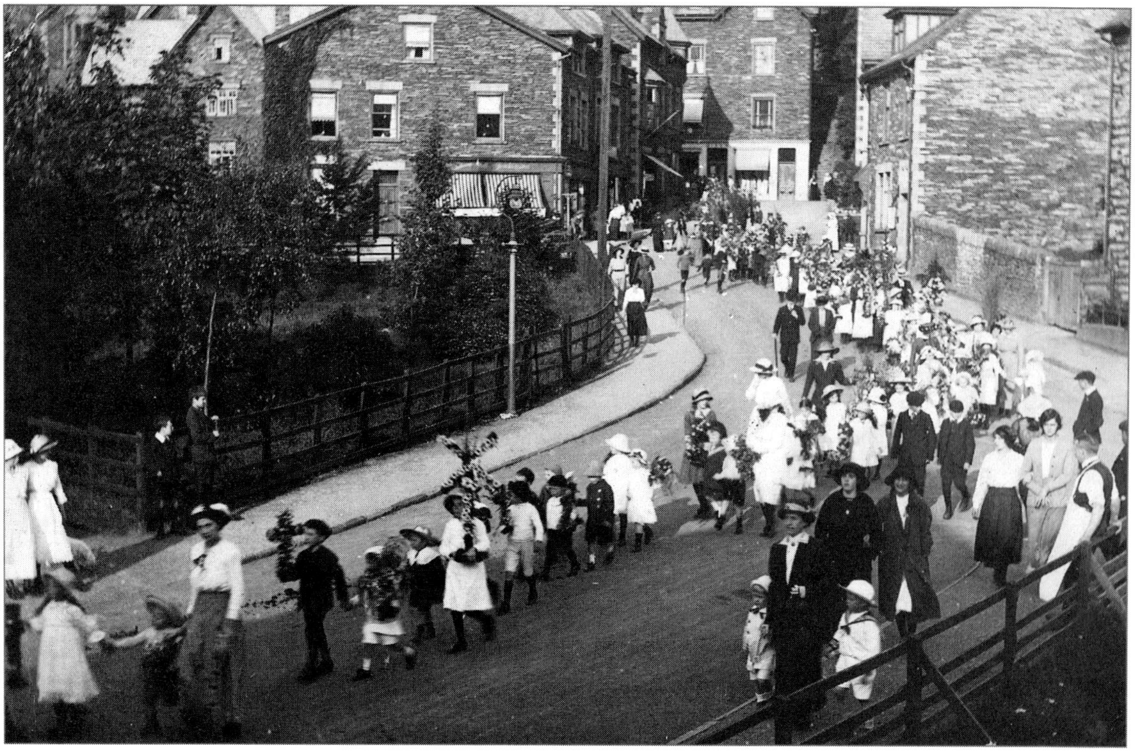

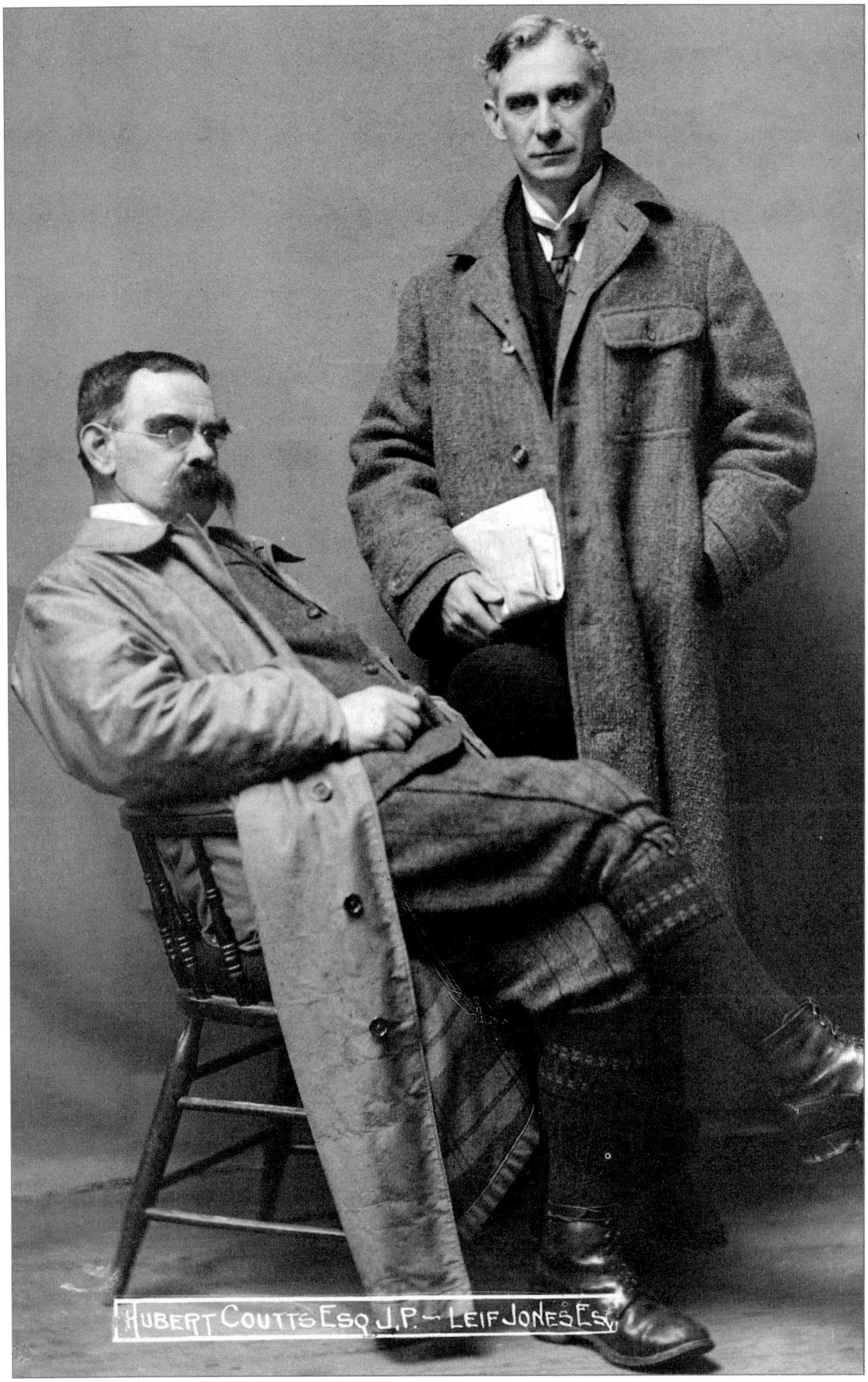

Hubert Coutts (seated and attempting to ignore the camera) was a JP and Liberal agent for Westmorland when Leif Jones (standing) was parliamentary candidate for North Westmorland in the 1905 and 1906 elections. He was elected finally by only three votes. (*John Marsh Collection*)

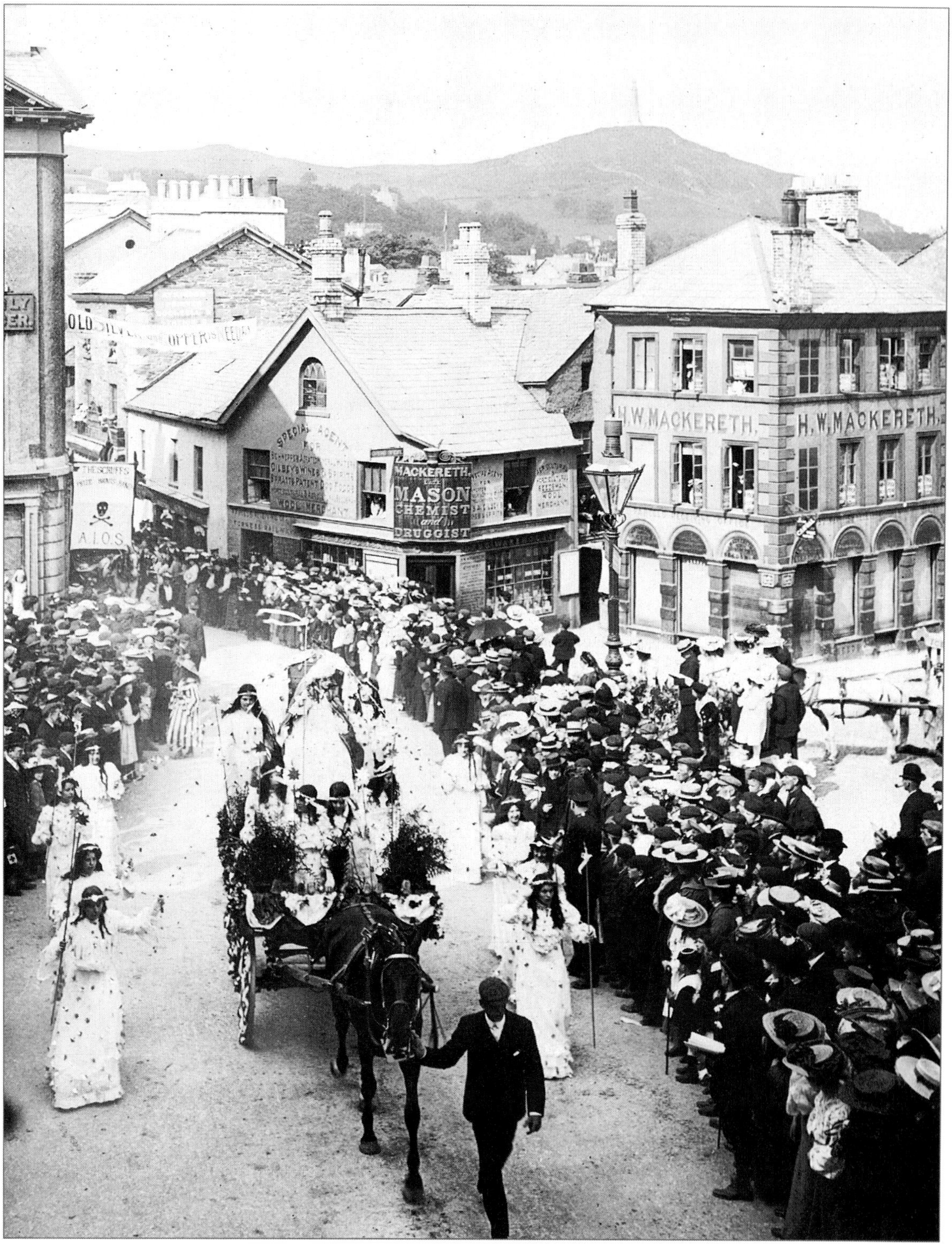

On 10 June 1905, Ulverston Hospital Parade raised £348 *2s 8d* and provided additional funds for enlarging the kitchen at the hospital. The Fairy Queen with her attendants with wands passes through the Market Place, while in the background the banner of The Scruffs brass band with skull and crossbones is just appearing. The town war memorial now stands where the crowds are assembled beside the lamp on the right. *(John Garbutt Collection)*

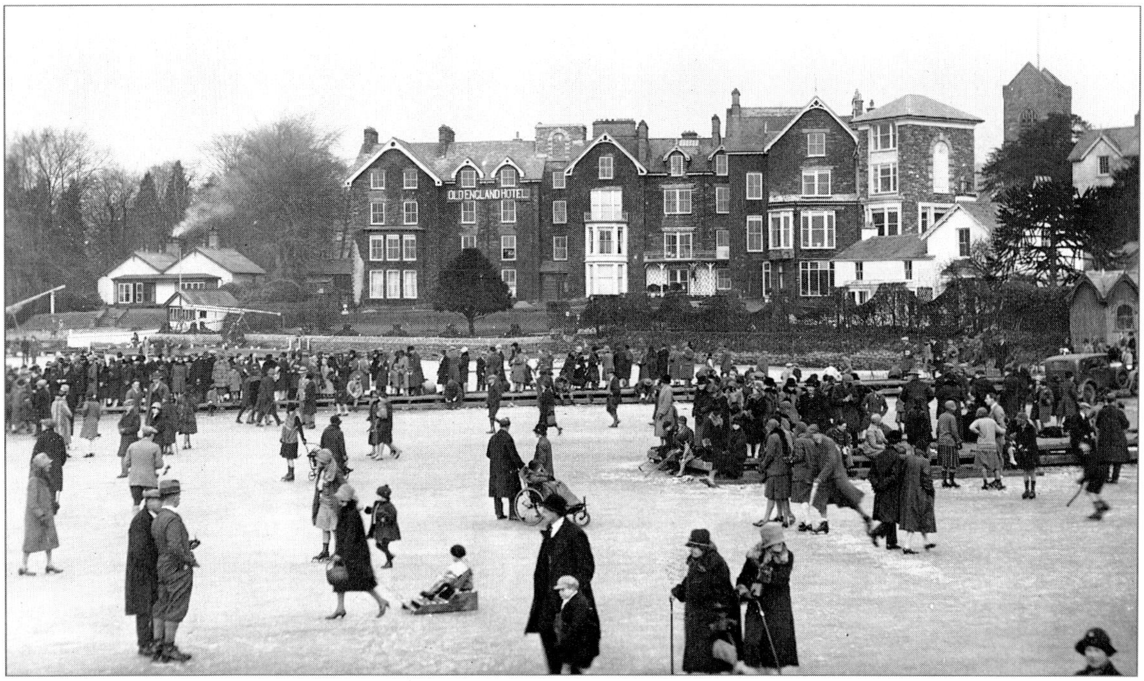

Crowds gather for skating on Windermere at Bowness, 2 March 1929. Atkinson & Pollitt of Kendal illustrated the result of the late frost in a series of postcards. Motor cars were driven on the frozen surface and hotels reopened from their closed season to take advantage of the winter sports. (*Atkinson & Pollitt*)

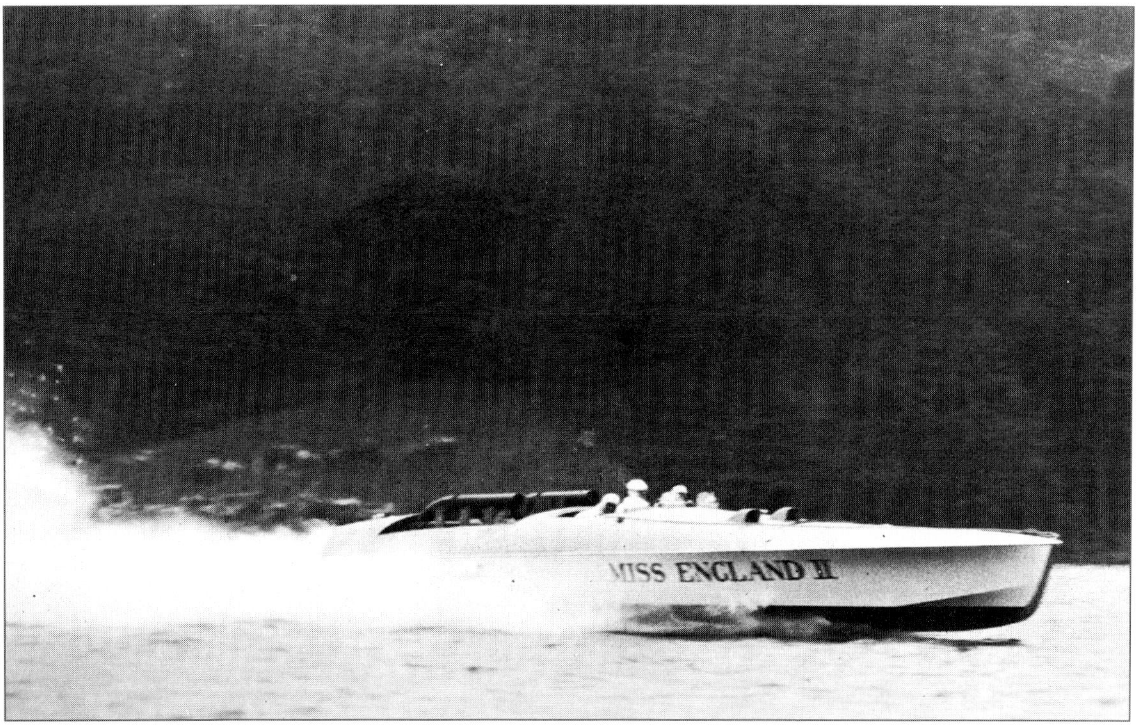

Lake Windermere was often used for speed trials before the Second World War. Atkinson & Pollitt's photographer saw *Miss England II* on Friday 13 June 1930, ten seconds before the speedboat flipped over during a trial run, killing Sir Henry Segrave and mechanic Vic Halliwell. Mechanic Michael Wilcocks survived the 119 mph disaster. (*Atkinson & Pollitt*)

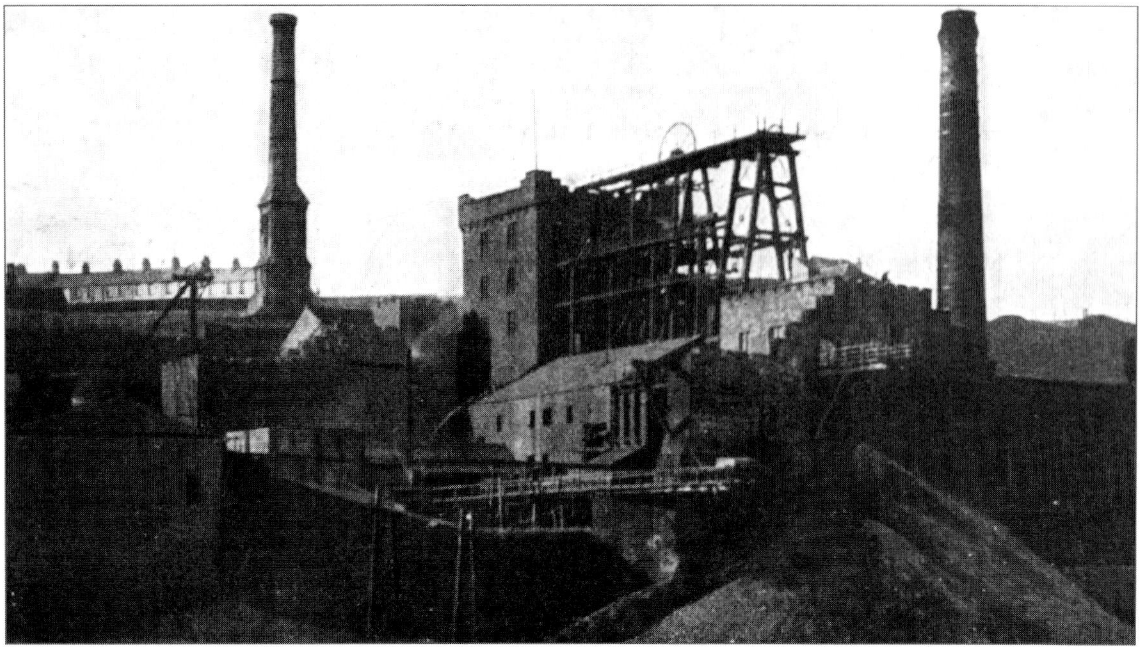

The Whitehaven Wellington Pit disaster on 11 May 1910 was the worst in Cumberland and brings nothing but sad memories of the 136 men and boys killed. Special postcards, of which this is one, were printed and sold in aid of charity funds for the families who lost their menfolk. The Cumberland coalfield was rich but difficult to exploit as much was under the sea. It was always a very dangerous deposit to work as it was a source of highly explosive gas in which any mistake produced high casualties. It has been said that Whitehaven alone had lost over a thousand miners before the final closure of the pits. (*Walter Benton of Newcastle on Tyne*)

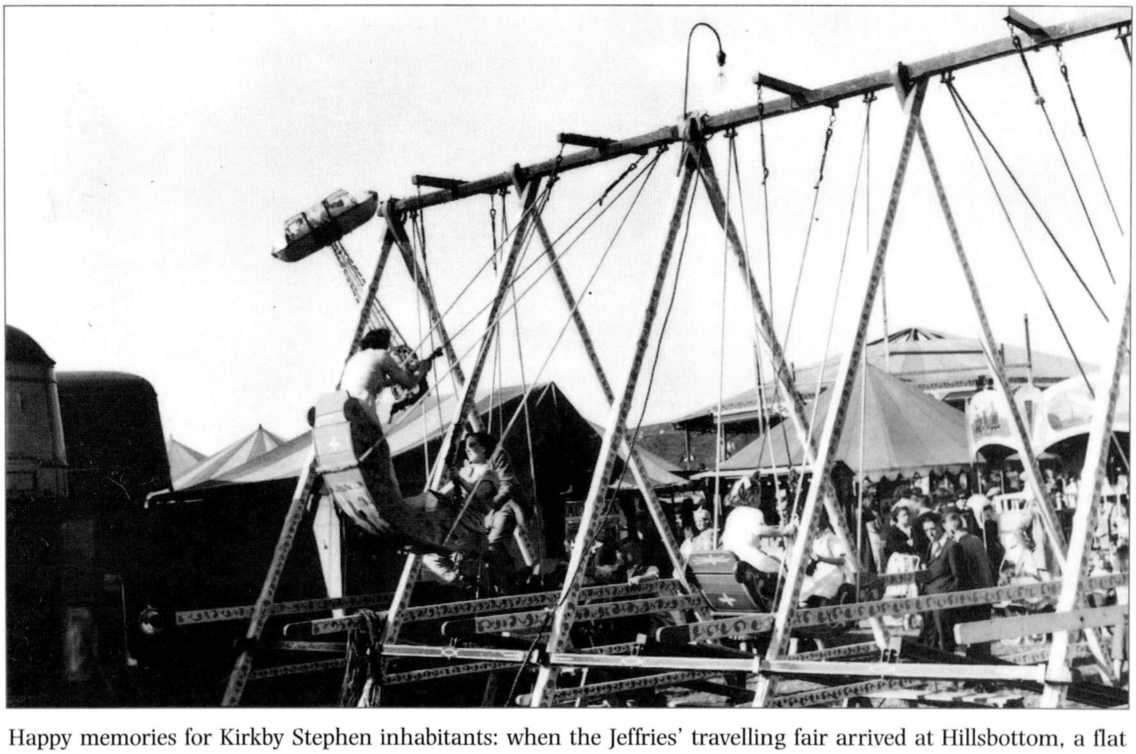

Happy memories for Kirkby Stephen inhabitants: when the Jeffries' travelling fair arrived at Hillsbottom, a flat field by the River Eden was transformed into a showground. The 1954 fair was photographed by one of the authors. (*John Marsh*)

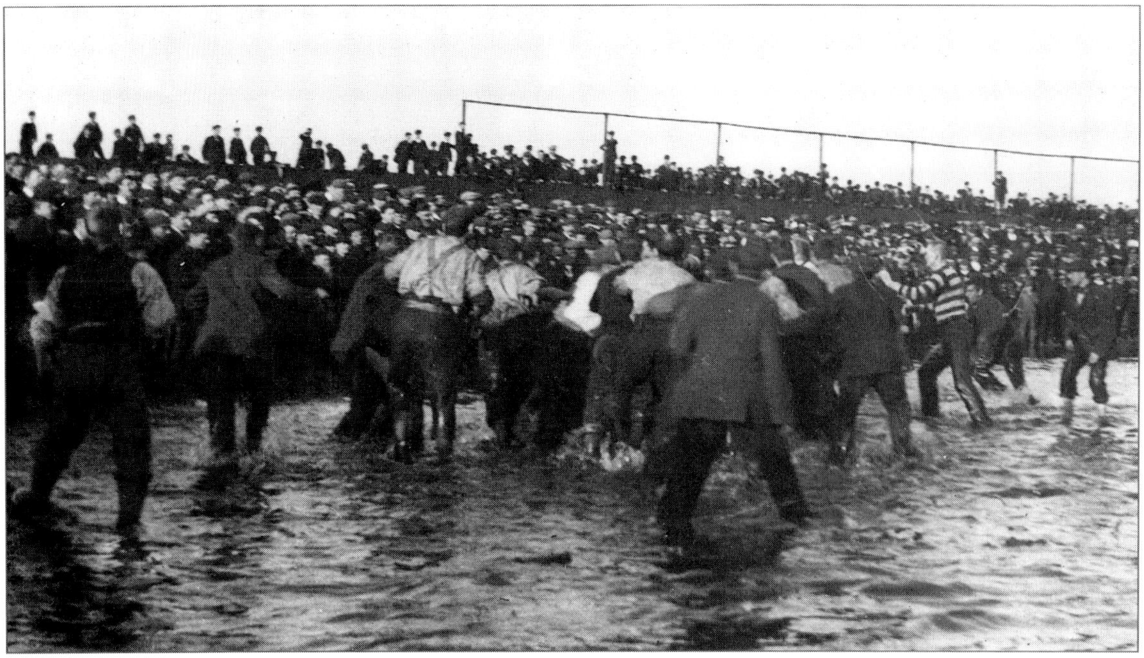

'The "Uppies and Downies" football match at Workington apparently replaced the "Easter football" play,' wrote Daniel Scott in 1899 in his *Bygone Cumberland and Westmorland*. 'How long these Easter Tuesday matches . . . have gone on, no man can tell. . . . The goals are about a mile apart, one being a capstan at the harbour and the other the Park wall at Workington Hall. There are no rules except those suggested by cunning and skill, while brute force is of the greatest importance. . . . The players sometimes number hundreds, and thousands of people attend as spectators.' Our picture shows the crowds assembled for the 1908 contest. (*John Marsh Collection*)

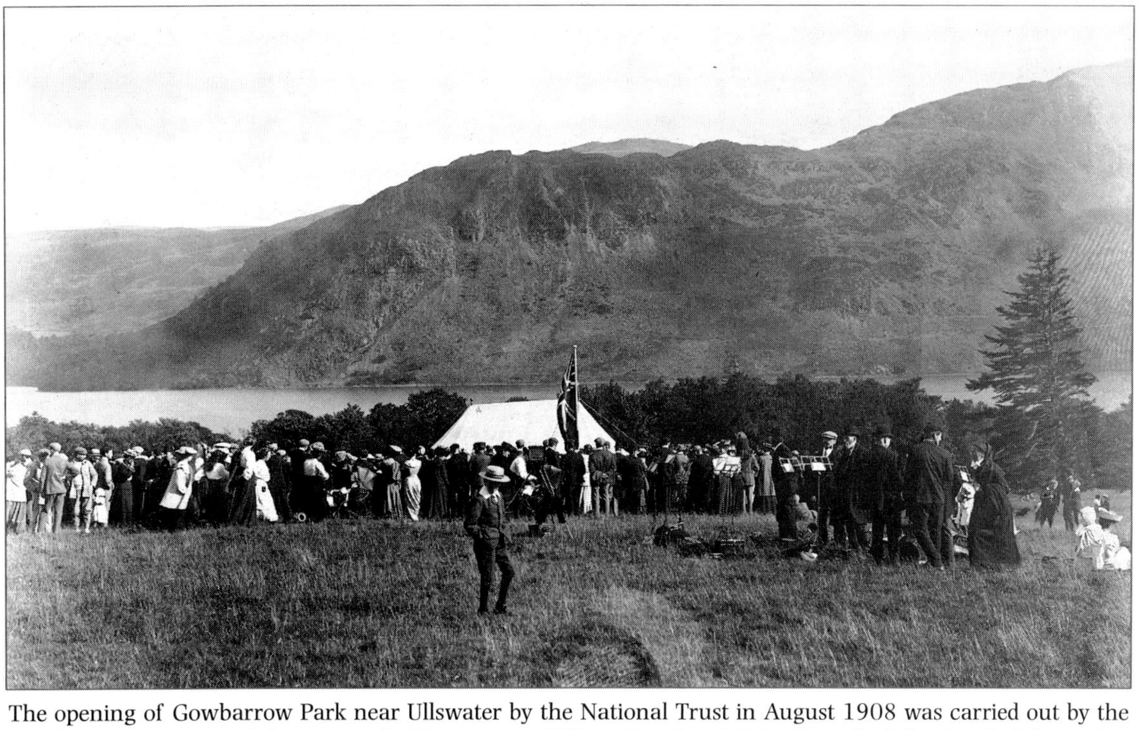

The opening of Gowbarrow Park near Ullswater by the National Trust in August 1908 was carried out by the Speaker of the House of Commons, the Hon. James William Lowther, MP for Penrith. (*John Marsh Collection*)

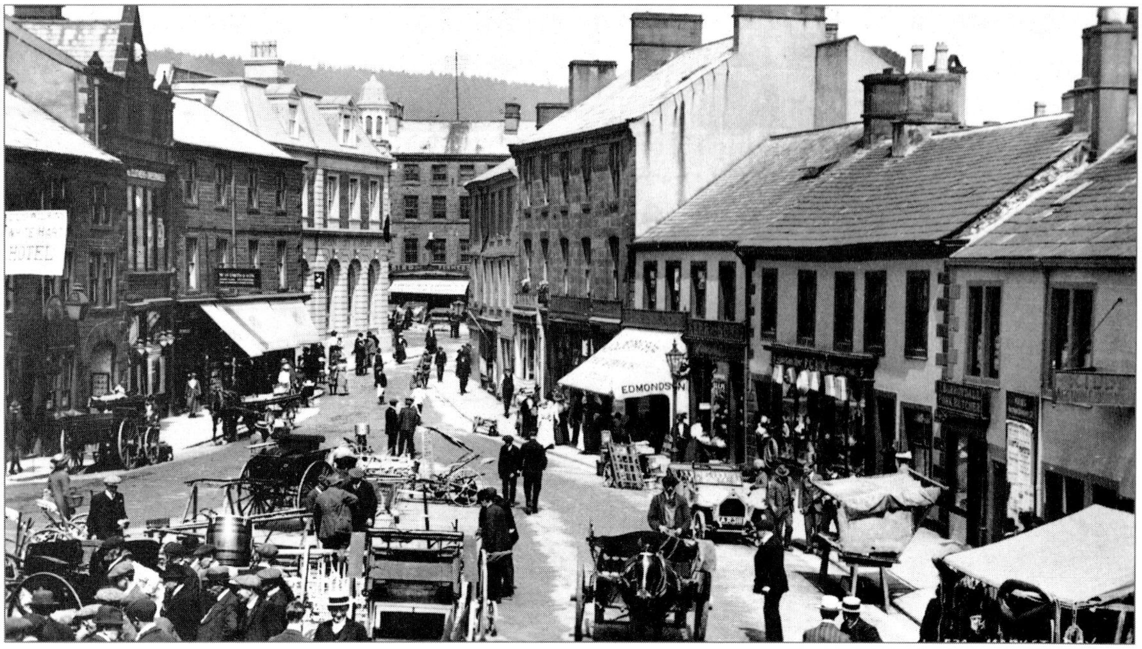

Sandford's eighteenth-century *History of Cumberland* describes Penrith as 'a very fine towne, and great markett and merchants for all kinds of commodities'. Penrith weekly market continues on Tuesdays and here the scene in the corn market at the time of the First World War shows only one motor car and many horse-drawn vehicles. (*John Marsh Collection*)

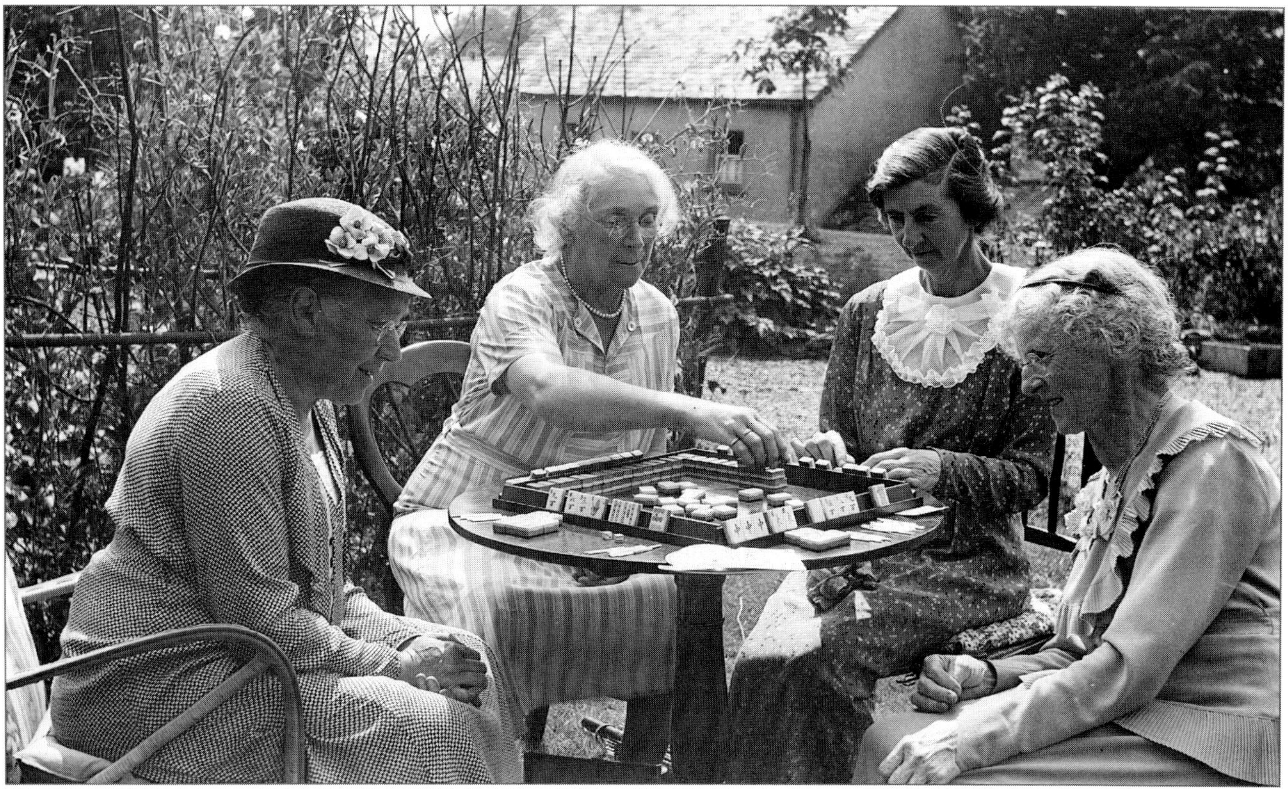

The garden of The Cragg, Satterthwaite, was photographed by B. Coward of Satterthwaite in the 1930s when ladies of the Lightfoot family and friends gathered to play mah-jong. (*B. Coward*)

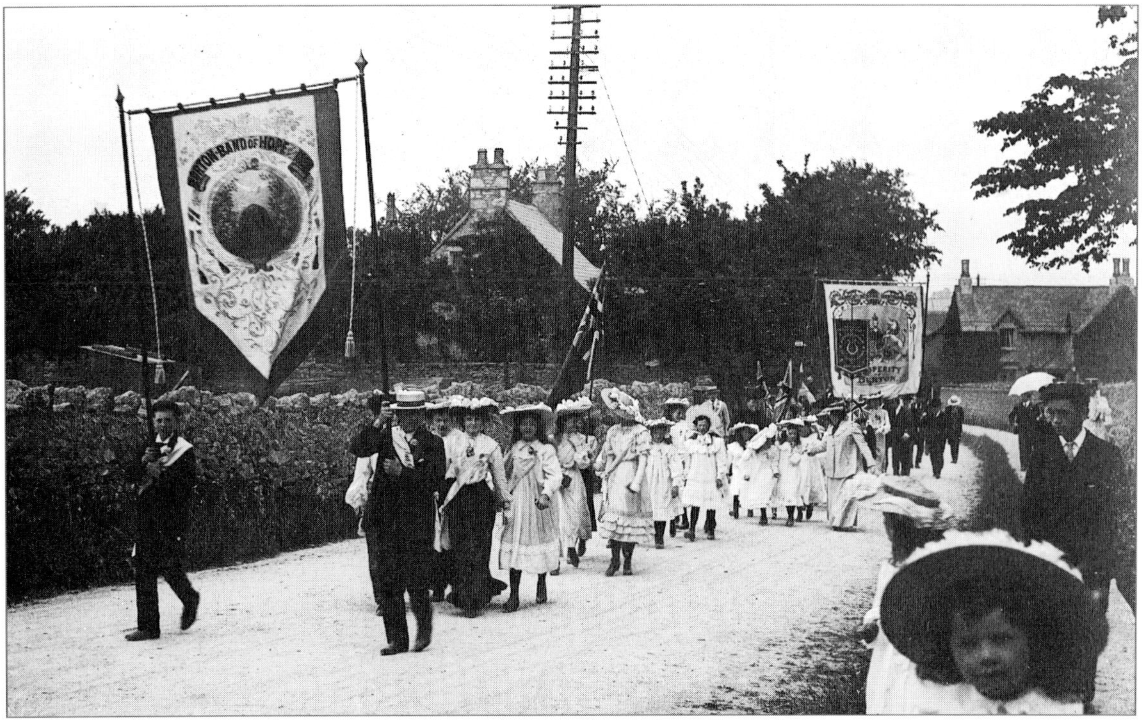

The Burton-in-Kendal Whit Wednesday walk can be seen climbing Church Bank from St James's church on its way to Heronsyke field led by a small contingent of the Burton Band of Hope, 1905. (*Rowbotham of Burton*) In the lower picture, at the corner of The Square at Burton, part of the crowd celebrating the June 1953 Coronation includes children in fancy dress. (*John Marsh Collection*)

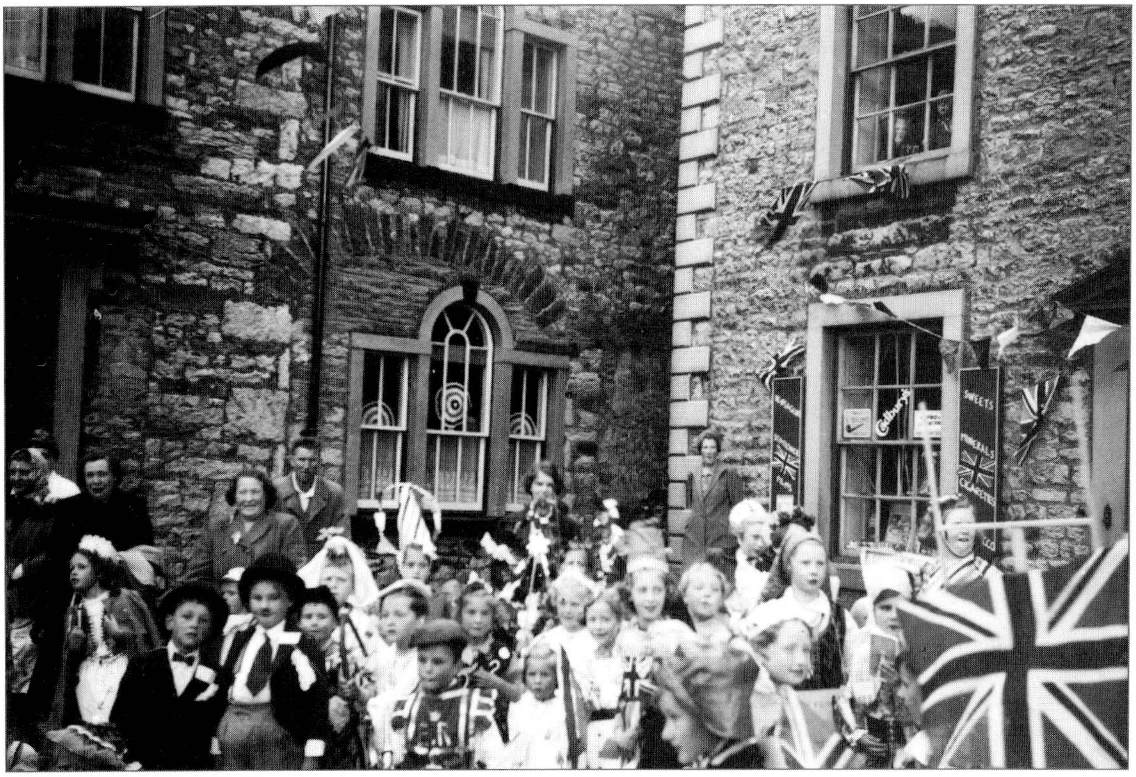

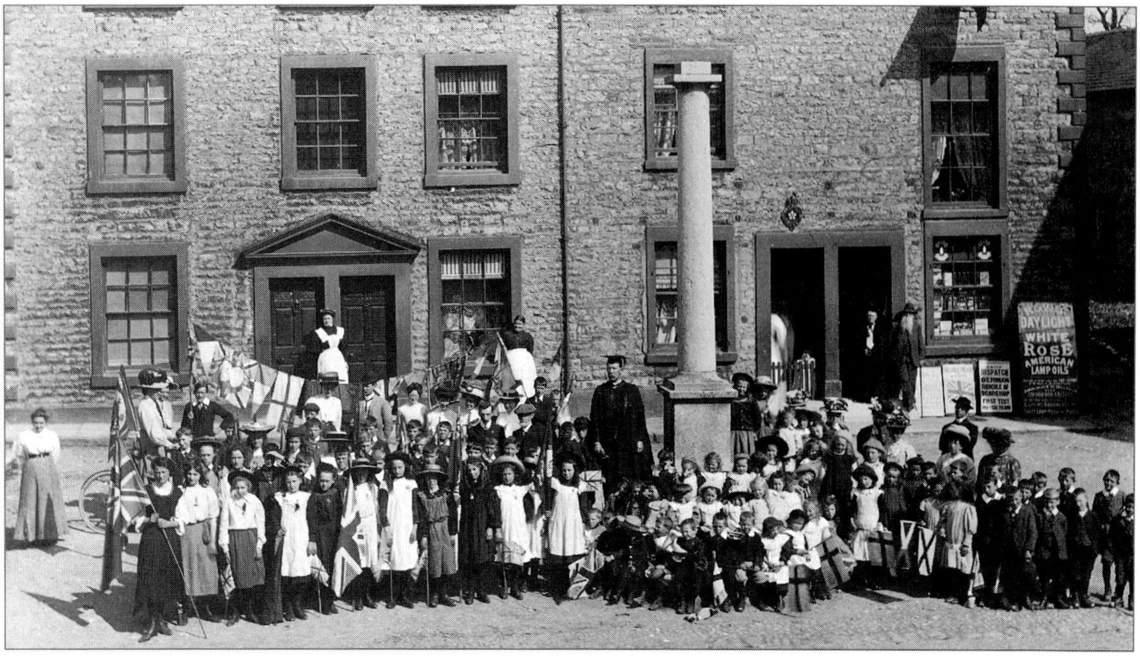

Burton-in-Kendal has a long tradition of celebratory gatherings in The Square. Here we see the Empire Day crowd on 24 May 1909 with the local headmaster in charge, wearing mortar board and gown. In those days he put the fear of the Lord into his pupils, but now the reverse seems to occur. (*Rowbotham of Burton*)

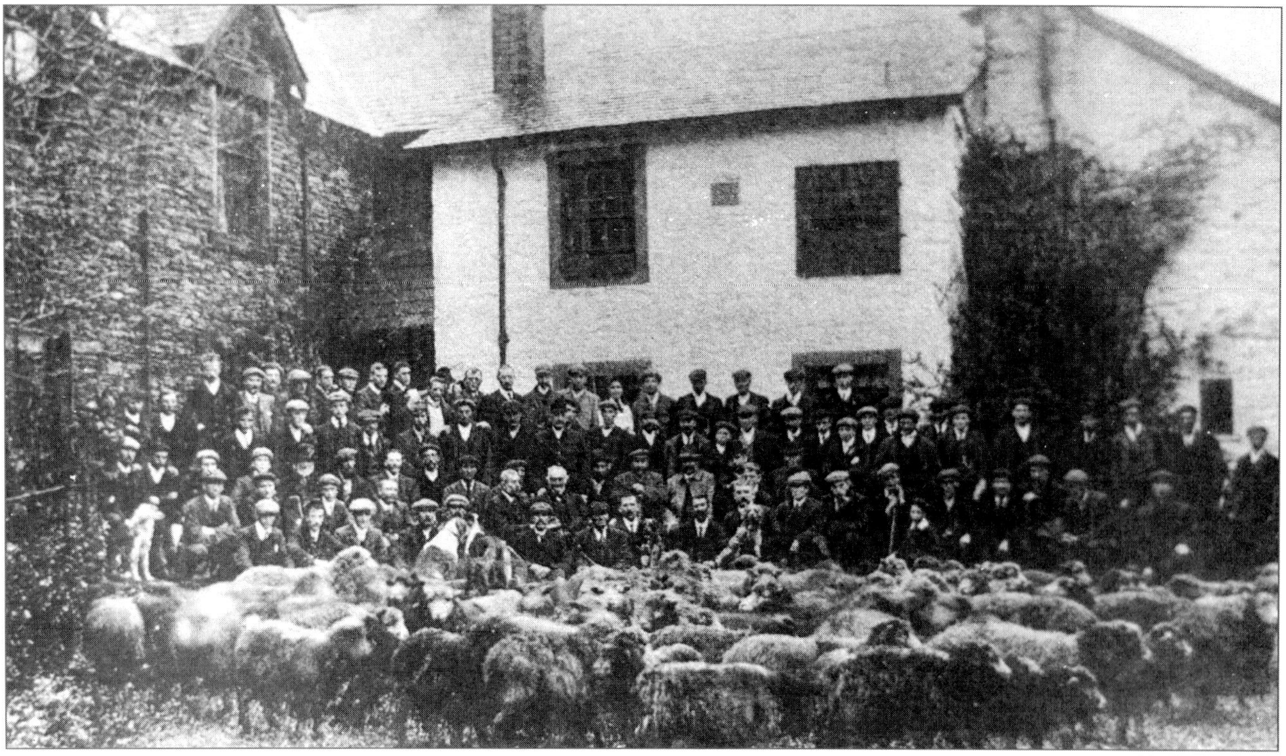

The Dun Bull, Mardale shepherds' meet of 1908, when Harry Usher was the licensee, was but one of an apparently never-ending local farmers' gatherings but the 1930s saw an end to it when Manchester Corporation flooded the valley to make Haweswater reservoir. The Dun Bull, the nearby church and the surrounding farms were all demolished before being submerged. (*John Marsh Collection*)

Along the Coast

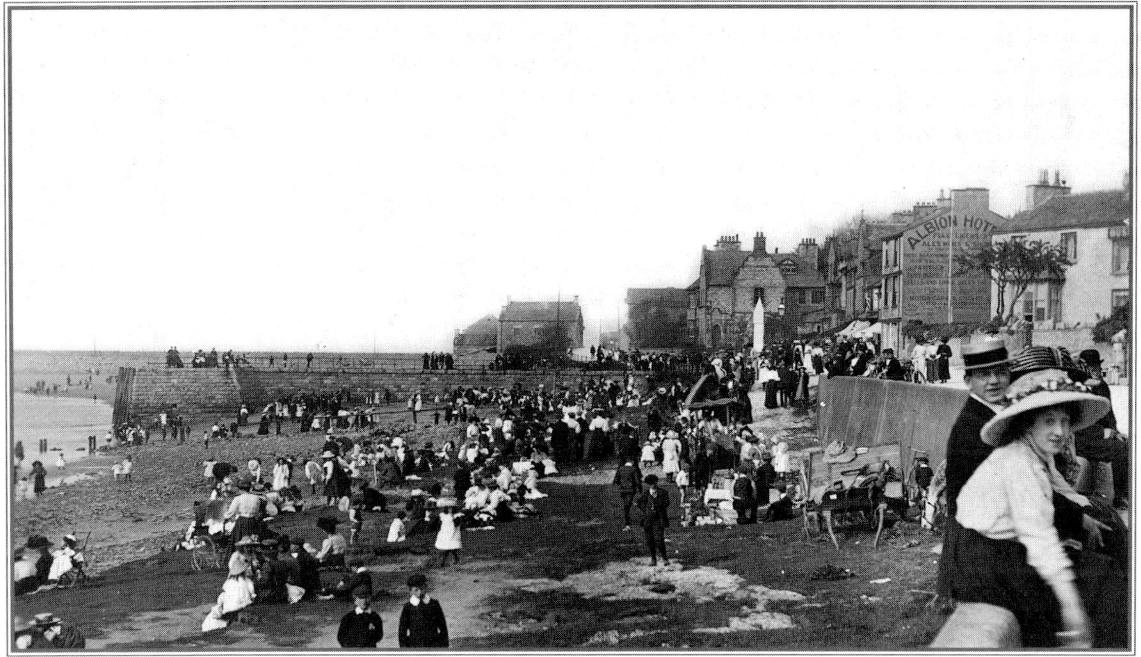

Arnside's holiday crowds in the first decades of the century are remembered in this photograph by J.D. Wilson. The railway brought most but some also came by horse-drawn coach. At one time many came by sea from Morecambe but the silting up of Morecambe Bay following the building of the railway killed the boating business, except for the few trip boats run by enterprising fishermen using their prawner yachts. In the background the Albion Hotel, long run by the Bush family who at one time ran a trade by sea to Liverpool, offered many services – described in their full gable-end advertising. (*J.D. Wilson of Arnside*)

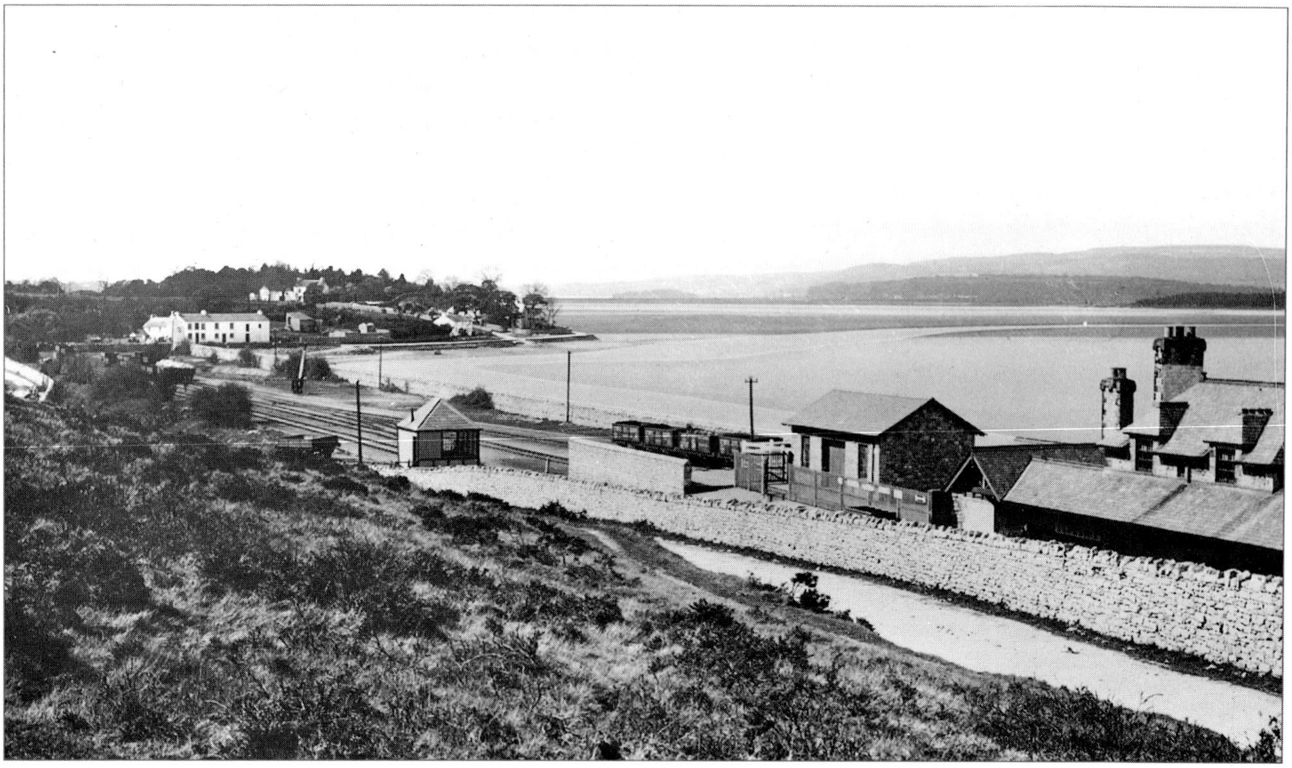

Sandside was a favourite holiday place for many and its station provided easy access. The station also had a large goods yard. It is all now only a memory. The railway is closed, the station swept away and the narrow seaside road carries all the local traffic. Below, a holiday-making family is on the sands at Sandside. Both 1930s pictures are from the camera of Atkinson & Pollitt of Kendal. (*Atkinson & Pollitt*)

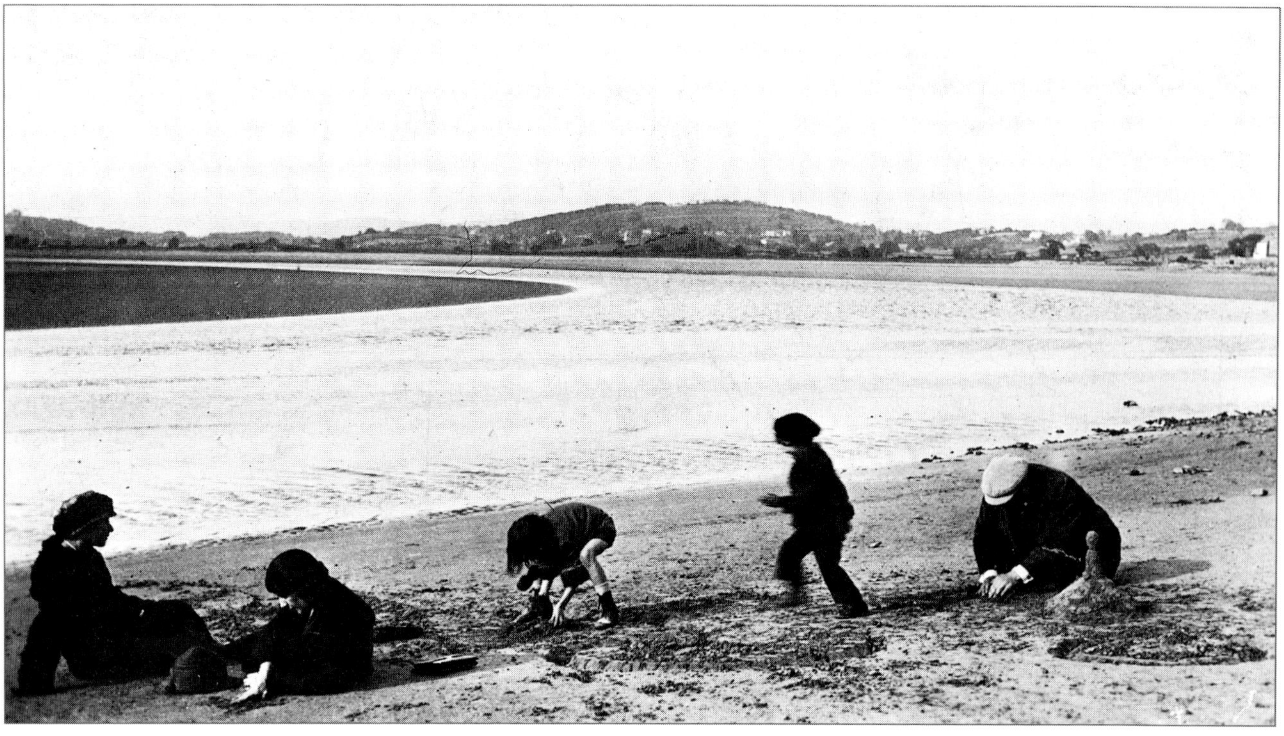

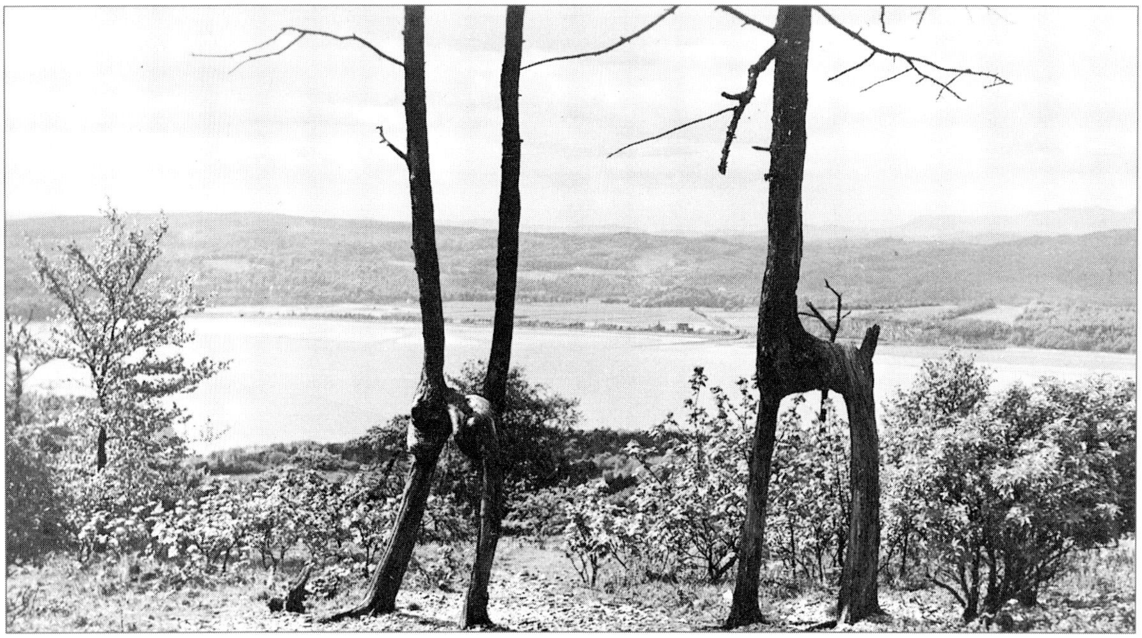

Arnside Knott is the name of the hill on which these four knotted larch trees could be seen until recent decades. J. Anthony Barnes, a local guidebook writer, told his readers that many thought the Knott hill took its name from these trees, but, he points out, the name of the hill goes much farther back in history. Both the limestone hill and its knotted trees were an attraction to visitors for many years. (*Atkinson & Pollitt*)

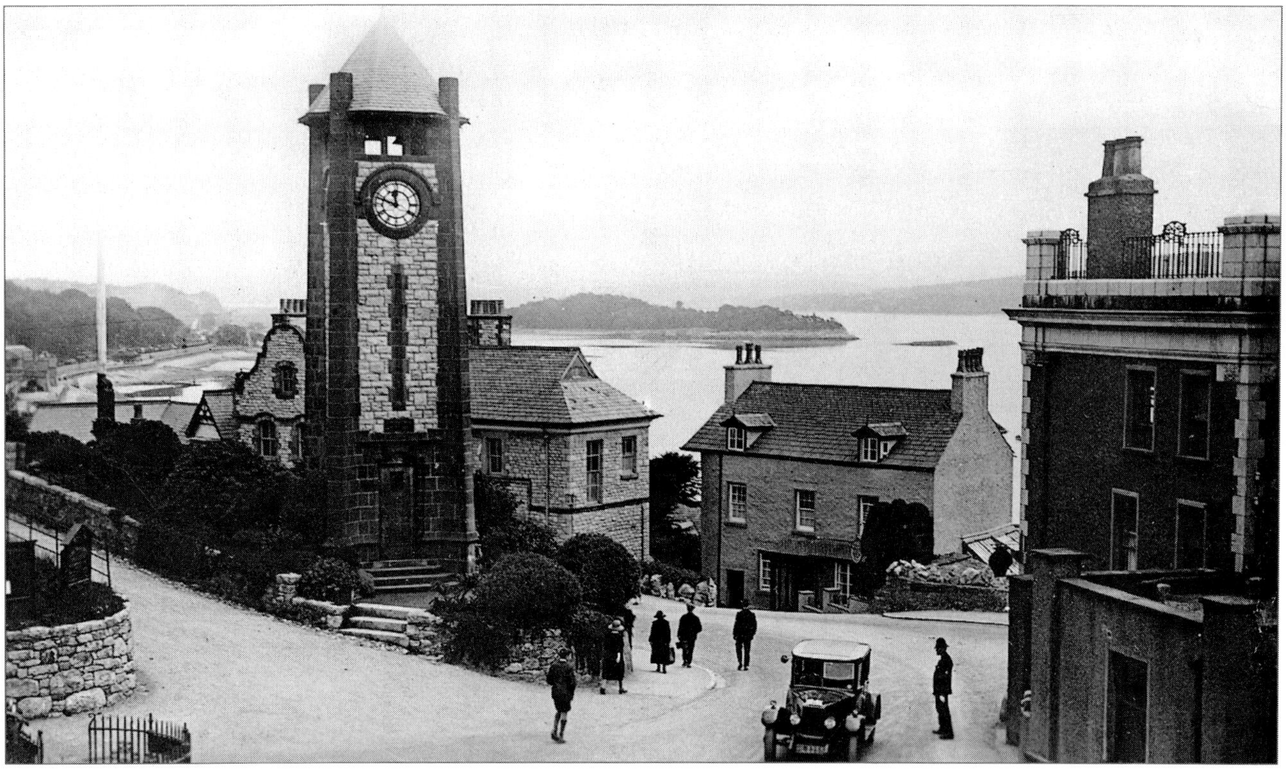

Across the bay from Arnside is Grange-over-Sands. Another Atkinson & Pollitt picture from the 1930s shows a Lancashire policeman observing the little traffic of the day. St Paul's church tower was built in 1912. The corner of the now converted Crown Hotel can be seen on the right. Most of the façade has been retained. (*Atkinson & Pollitt*)

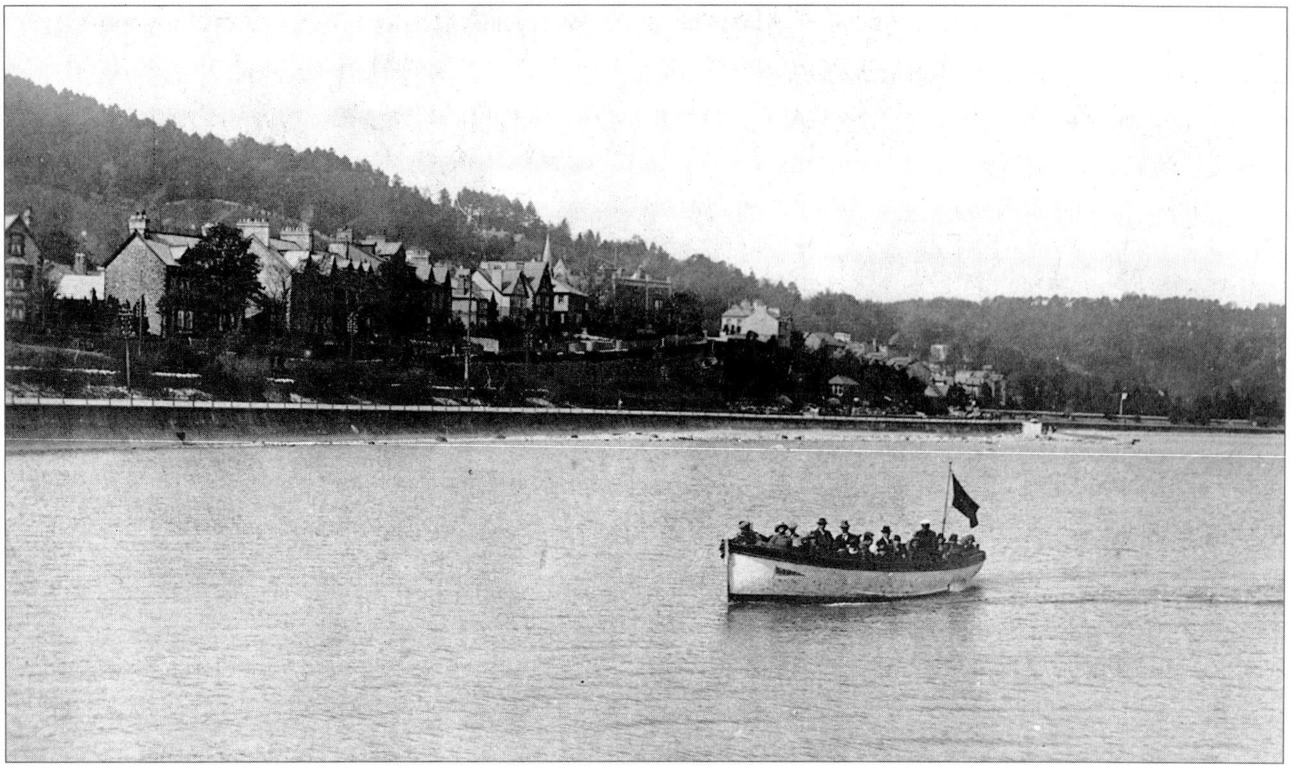

Grange had a busy holiday trade served at one time by two piers. The scenes are so different from today. The Atkinson & Pollitt photographer could hardly have realised that conflicting interests would make these pictures but memories in half a century. Nature conservation and agricultural pollution have spoilt the appearance of the bay at Grange – much changed from that remembered by the authors in the 1930s and '40s. (*Atkinson & Pollitt*)

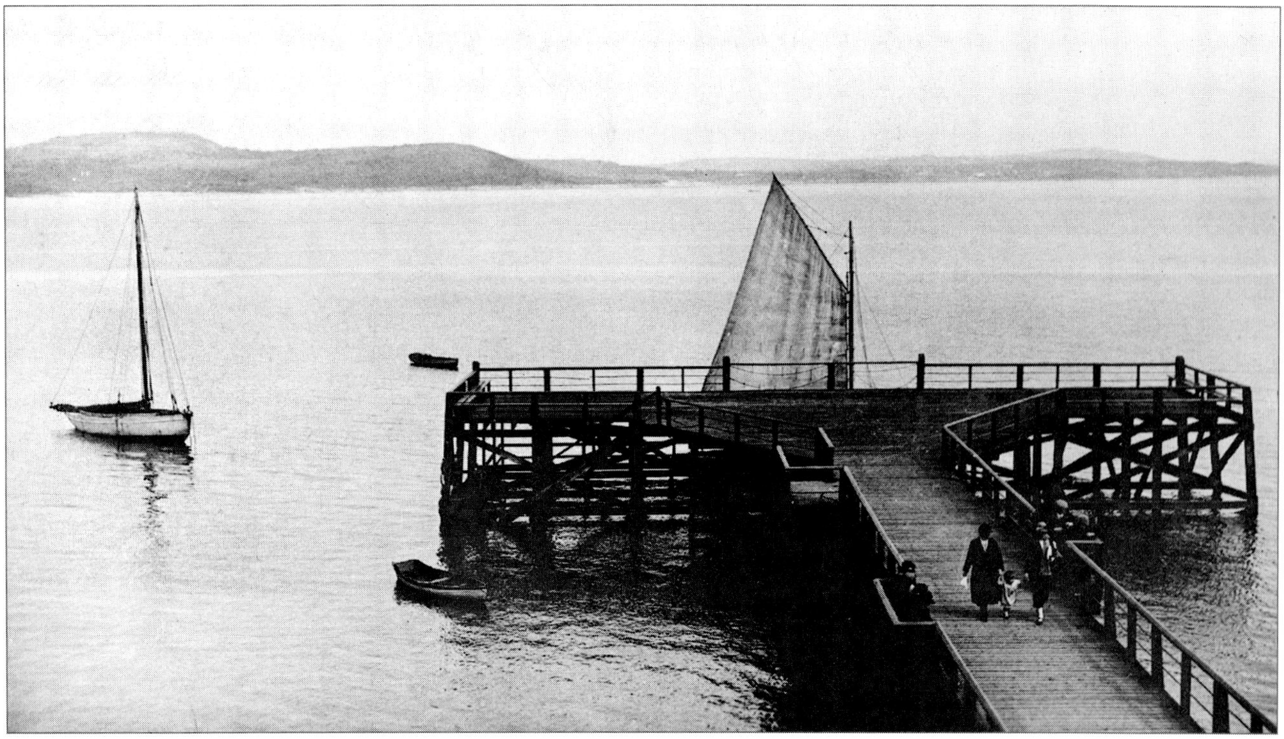

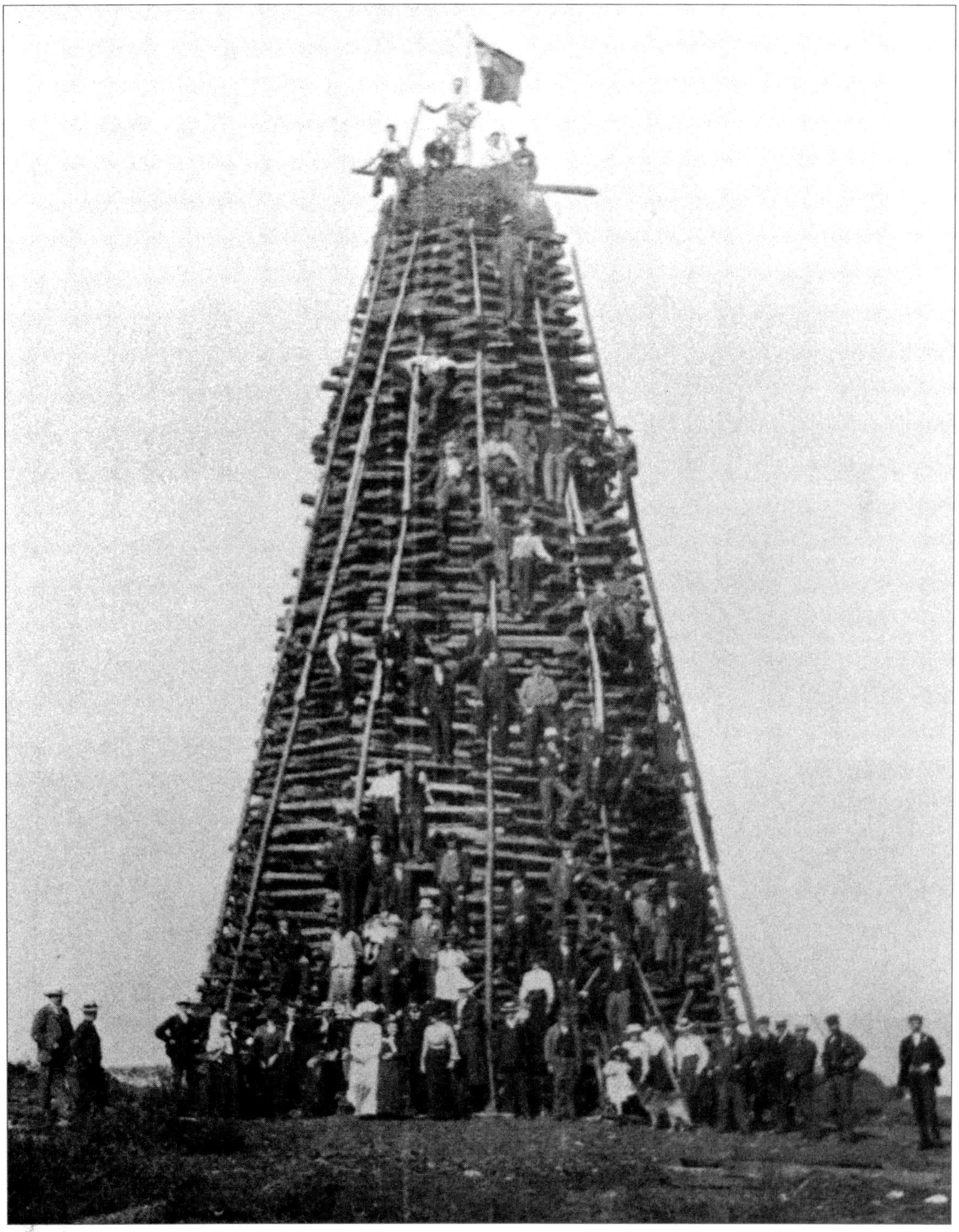

Celebrations for the 1902 Coronation at Ulverston bring memories of many such events up to the Second World War when communities changed after the national devastation. In 1902 a loyal population enjoyed the opportunity to celebrate a royal coronation even though it took place hundreds of miles away in London. This 60-foot high monster bonfire erected on the Flan was, it was claimed, 30 feet round the base and contained 200 tons of material. Lindal Moor mines and the North Lonsdale ironworks provided tons of railway sleepers. *(John Marsh Collection)*

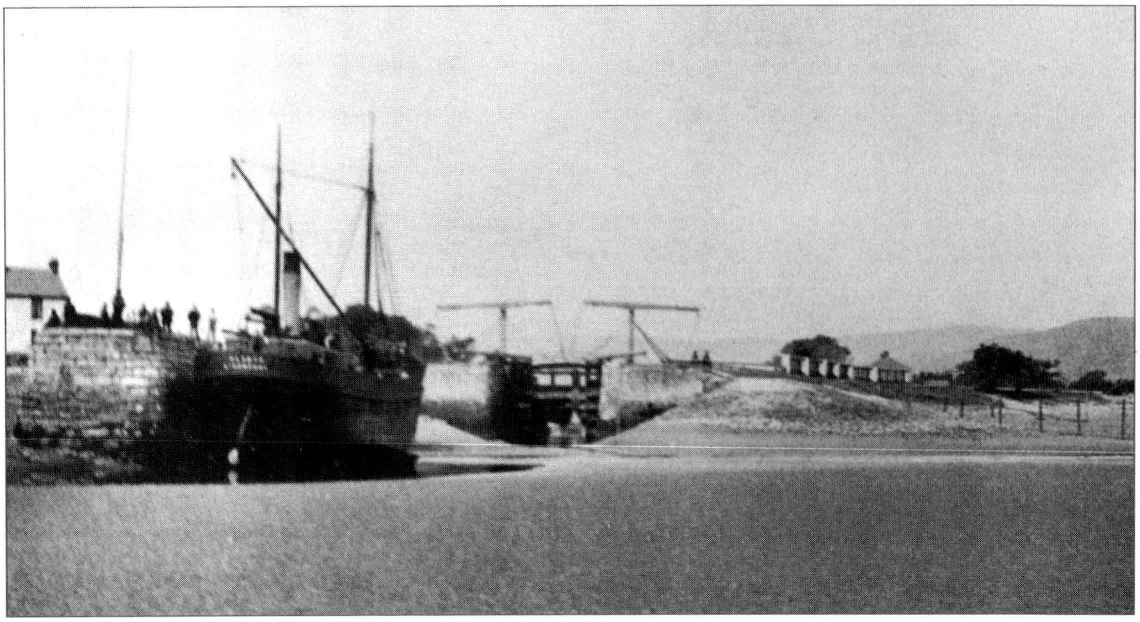

Canal Foot, Ulverston, with the coastal steamer *Gladys* of Liverpool waiting by the pier for a tide allowing access into the canal. Early twentieth-century problems such as this led to the closure of the canal and its transformation into a water supply for the industry on its banks. The picture was taken by James Atkinson of Ulverston in about 1910. (*James Atkinson of Ulverston*)

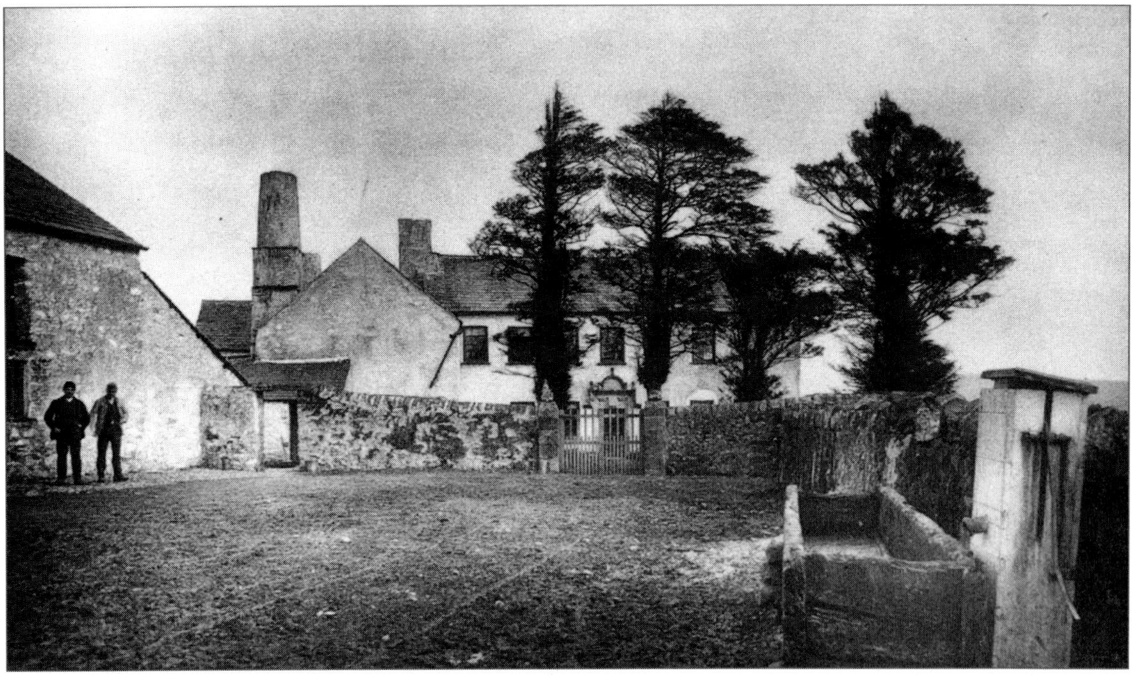

Plumpton Hall, Ulverston, was on the much-trodden walk from Ulverston to the sea and was known to many Ulverstonians who took picnics to the Plumpton beach. Many stories were told of ghosts and hauntings, some so convincing that they persisted into local legend to confuse serious local historians. In truth the land hereabouts was much quarried for limestone and during the Second World War the quarries became ammunition dumps. The traffic for the quarries was by sea or by rail in later years and the wartime traffic was by rail, which provided inquisitive youngsters much to interest themselves in – at the risk of being chased away by armed guards. (*John Howe of Ulverston*)

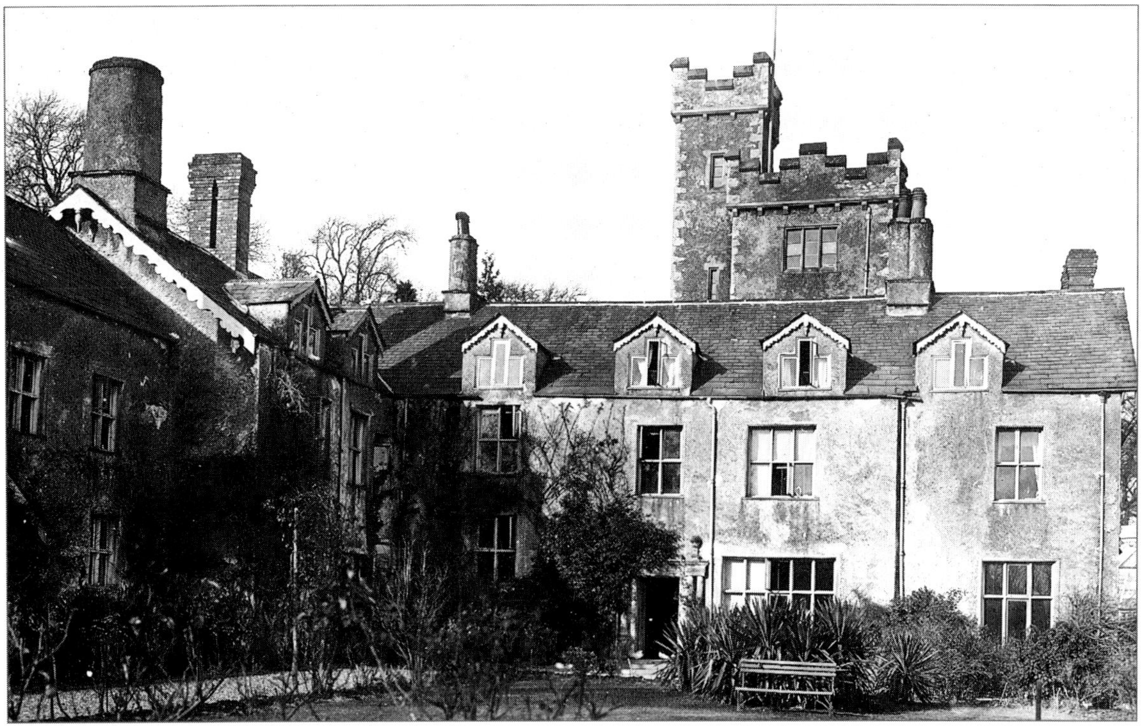

Bardsea village overlooks Morecambe Bay, as does its hall and church. Bardsea Hall was the ancient seat of the local lord of the manor and was demolished in the 1930s. The delightful church at Bardsea, built in 1843–53 by architect George Webster of Kendal, had an unfortunate beginning, being listed among its patron's assets when he went broke. The first vicar had to bid for his church in an auction sale of those assets. (*John Marsh Collection*)

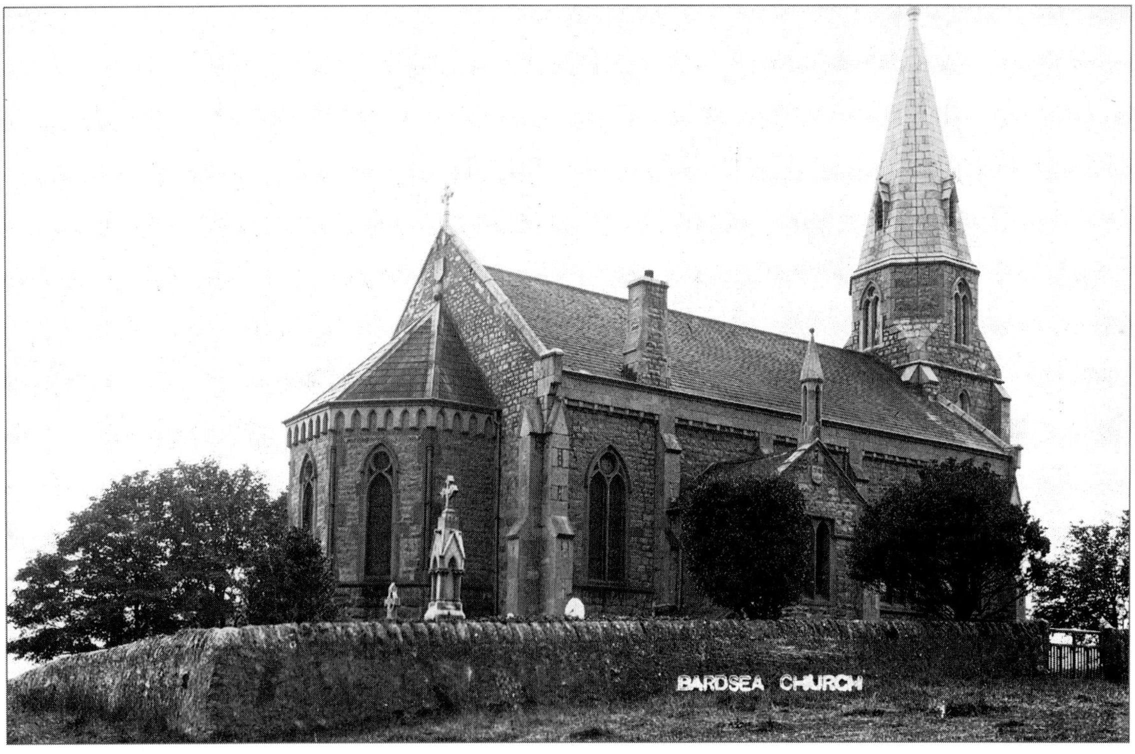

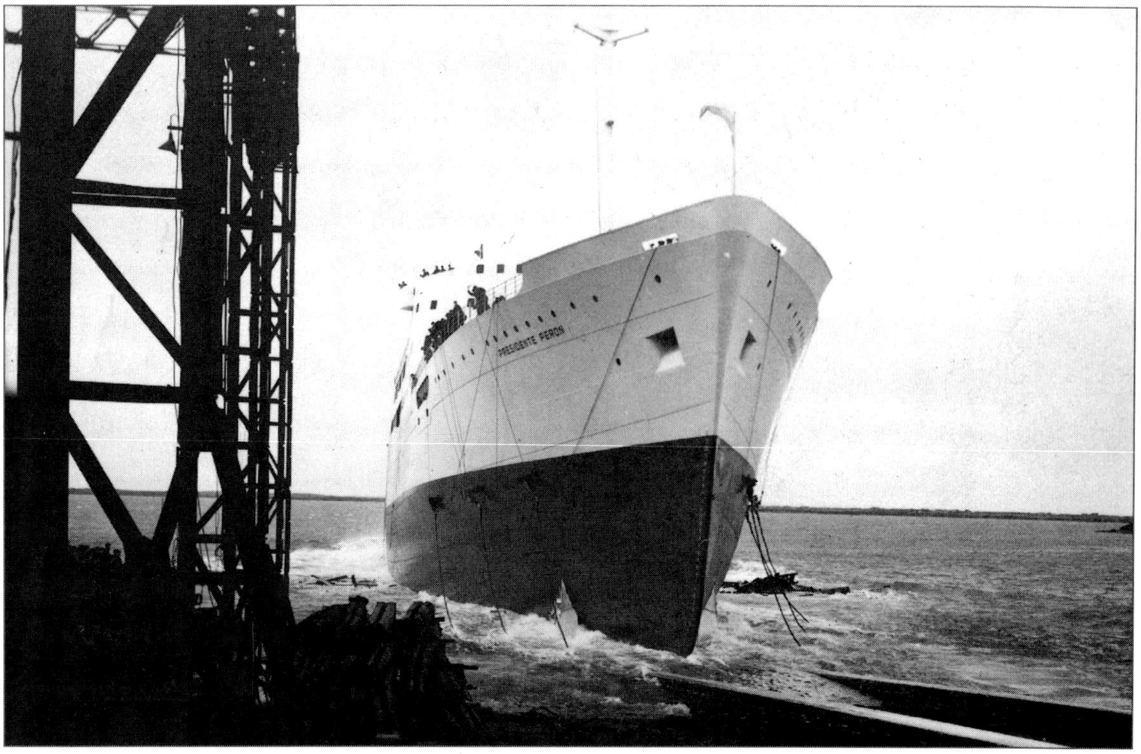

Along the coast at Barrow there was a boom in shipbuilding in the late 1940s when countries from all over the world ordered ships to replace those lost in the war. Here the Argentine government's *Presidente Peron* is launched on 3 November 1948. Such fine ships bring many memories. (*John Marsh Collection*)

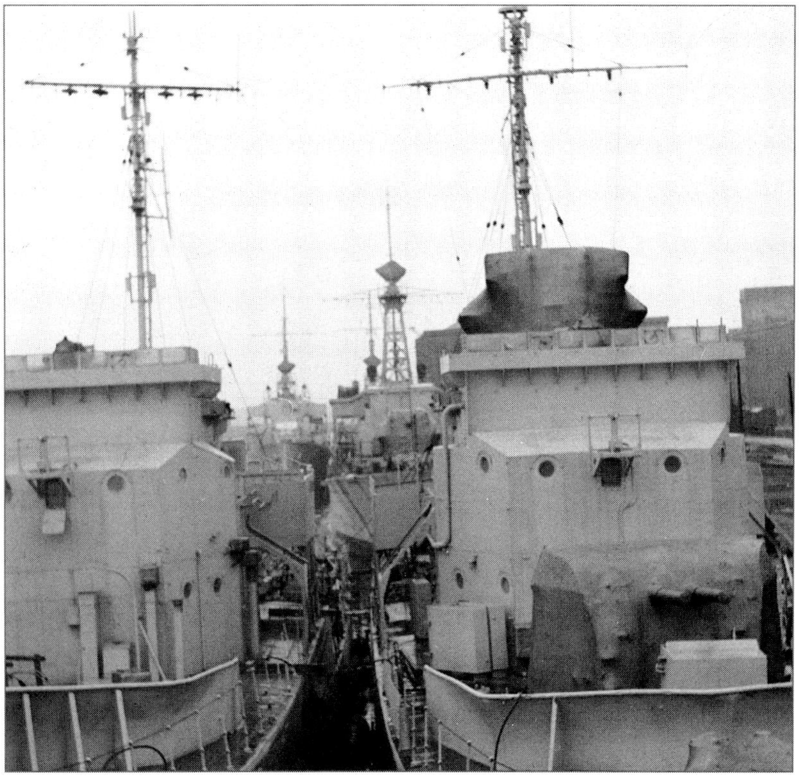

The end of the Second World War left many warships not required. Some of these were not scrapped at once but put into the mothball fleet in docks all round the country. Here a group of destroyers and corvettes is seen in the Devonshire dock at Barrow in the 1950s. (*John Marsh*)

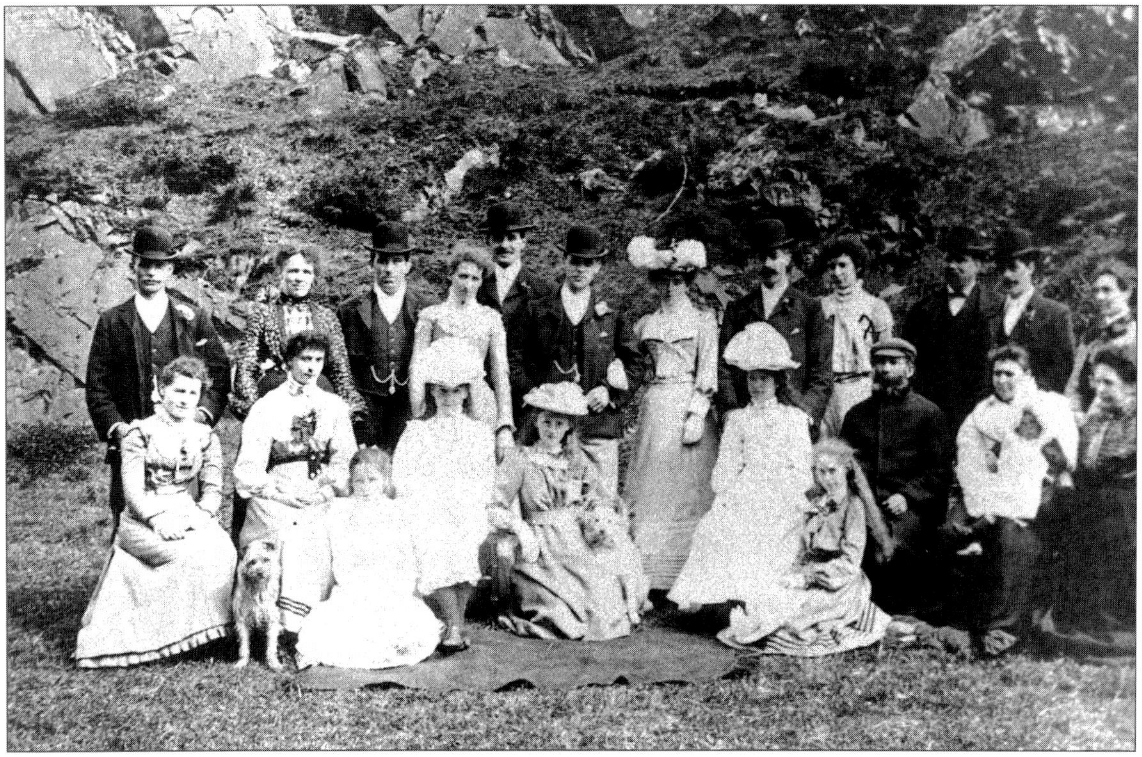

A wedding party at Foxfield on 6 May 1902 when Joseph Kitchin of Ulverston married Agnes Ann Coward. Joe Kitchin was one of the first to go into France in 1914, having been in the Boys' Rifle Brigade which the Church Lads' Brigade became, and one of the last to leave in 1919, but said next to nothing of his experiences to his family on his return. (*John Marsh Collection*)

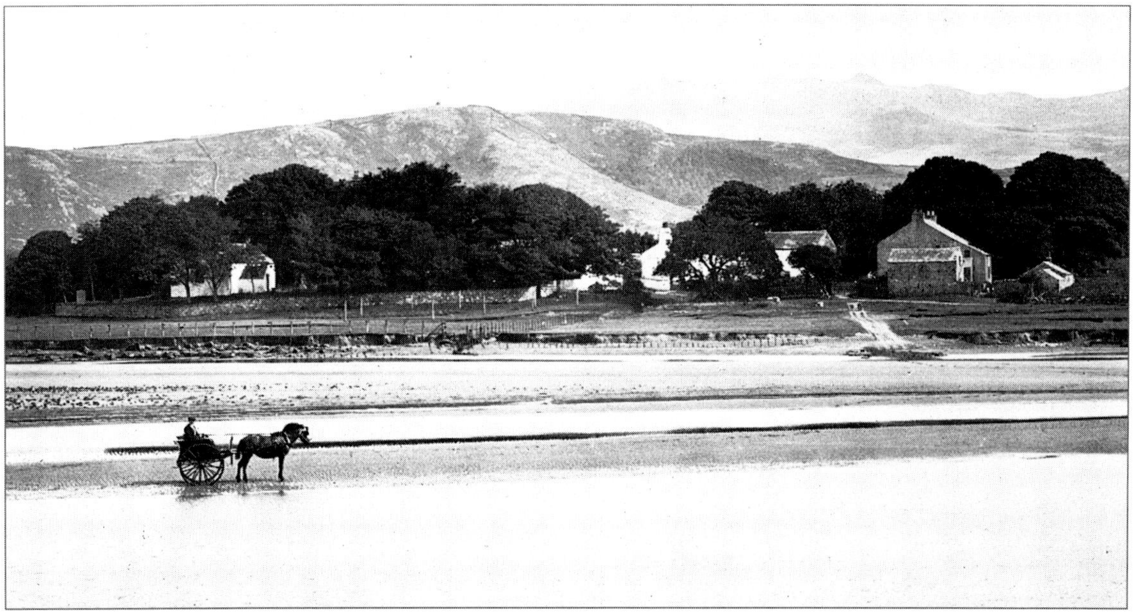

Waberthwaite from Muncaster, photographed by Woodall of Waberthwaite, shows the use of the coast for horse carriage transport at the crossing of the River Esk at the ford probably used by the Romans. This isolated part of Cumbria included a massive gun range at nearby Eskmeals which was serviced by the railway. (*Woodall of Waberthwaite*)

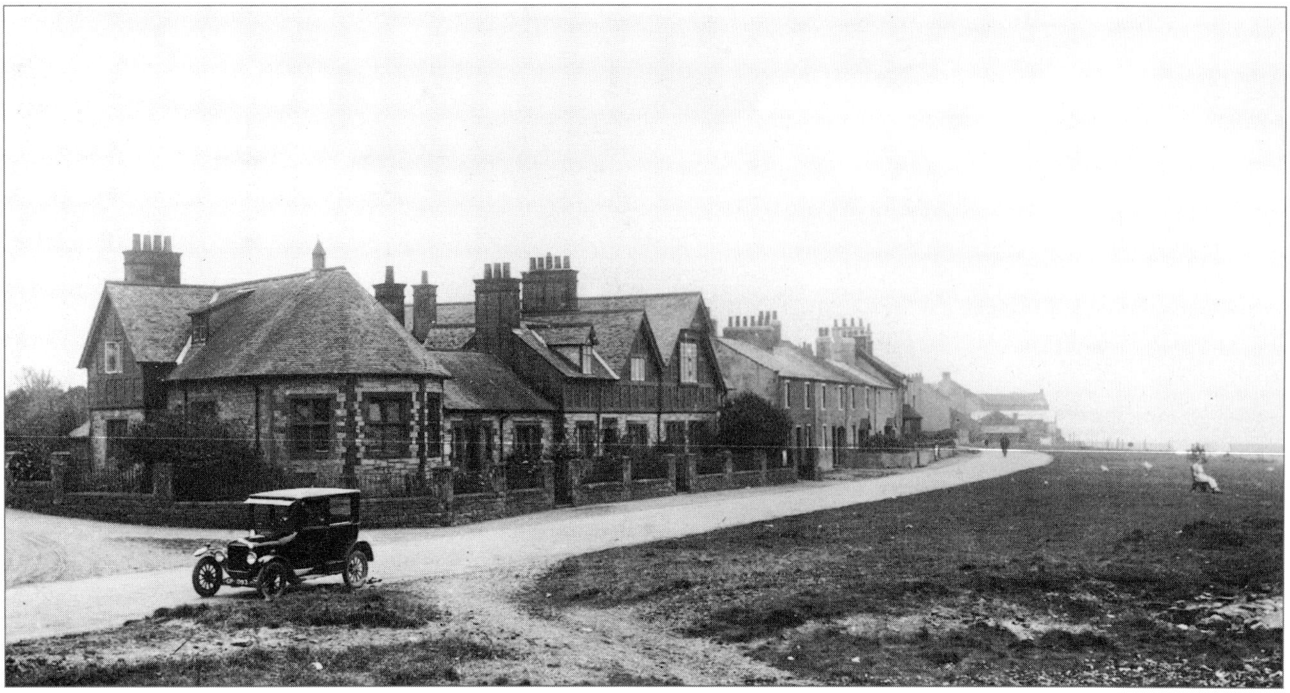

Local firms photographed Ravenglass in about 1930. While Ravenglass has been a port since Roman times, progress has been slow; its main features are now the railway terminus and estuary. Notably, a reading room was established in 1862. The premises were enlarged in 1898 at the expense of Lord Muncaster and a billiard table added, the gift of Miss Ramsden. The area is so peaceful that the nearby sand dunes have been developed as a nature reserve. (*Above, Lilywhite of Sowerby Bridge; below, Atkinson & Pollitt*)

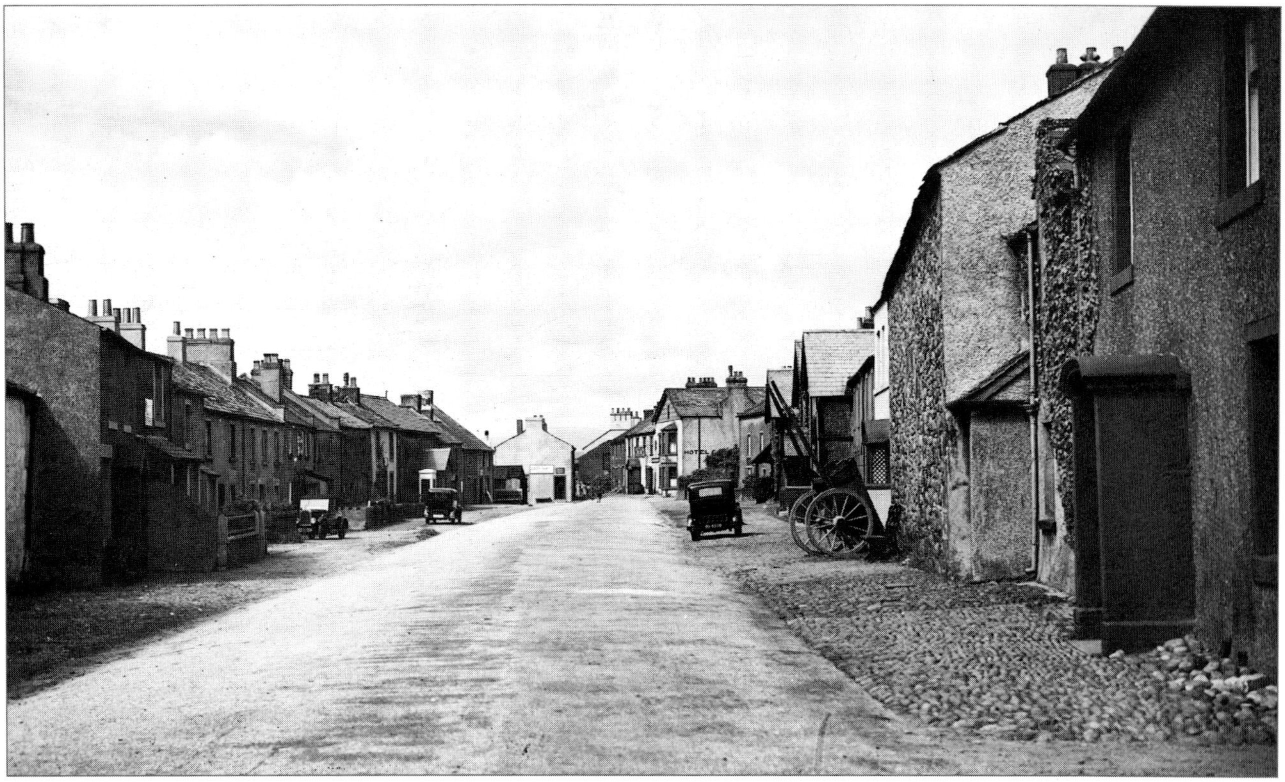

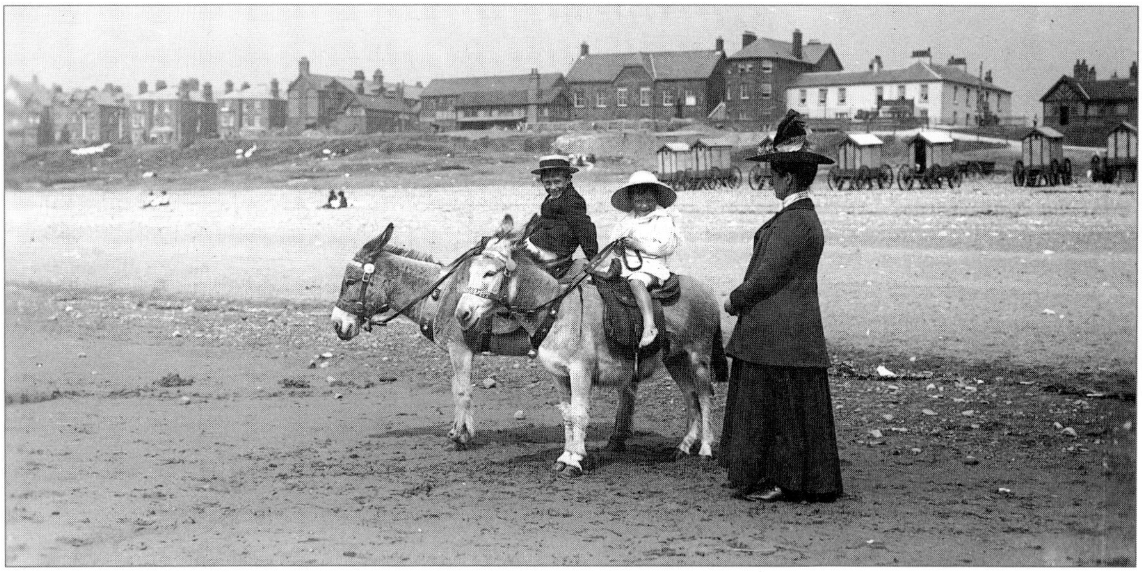

The Furness Railway Co. had grandiose ideas to develop Seascale as a seaside resort in the late nineteenth century but these came to nought, although the bathing huts and donkeys for hire here show some progress in that direction. The eternal problem in the west coast area is the prevailing wind, and at Seascale this was added to in postwar decades by the positioning of a nuclear plant nearby. (*Edward Sankey of Barrow*)

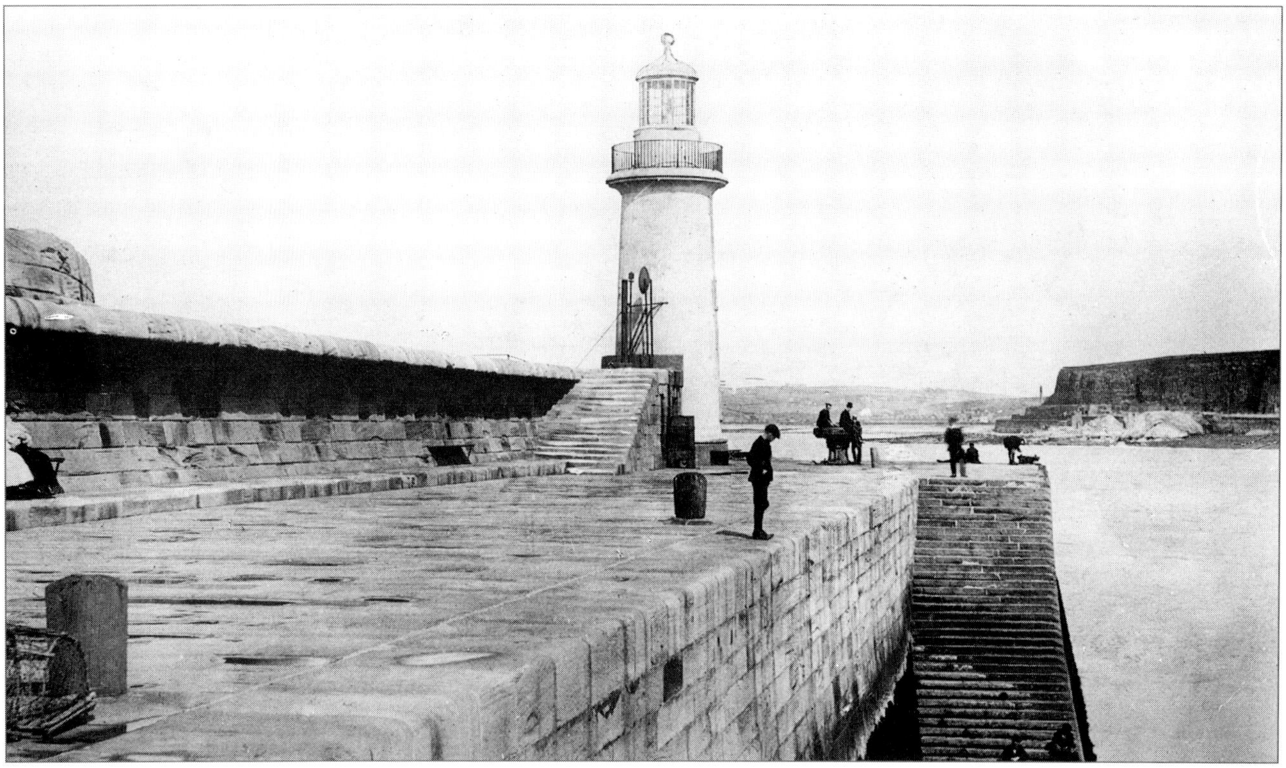

Whitehaven west pier and lighthouse were photographed by Brittain & Wright in 1920. The harbour was mainly financed by the Lowther family who also built the town. Trade developed through exports to Ireland and later the New World, with large imports of Irish peat. At one time in the eighteenth century Whitehaven possessed one of the largest merchant fleets in Britain. Unfortunately the photograph dates from the onset of the economic depression of the 1920s and 1930s, from which West Cumberland never recovered. (*Brittain & Wright*)

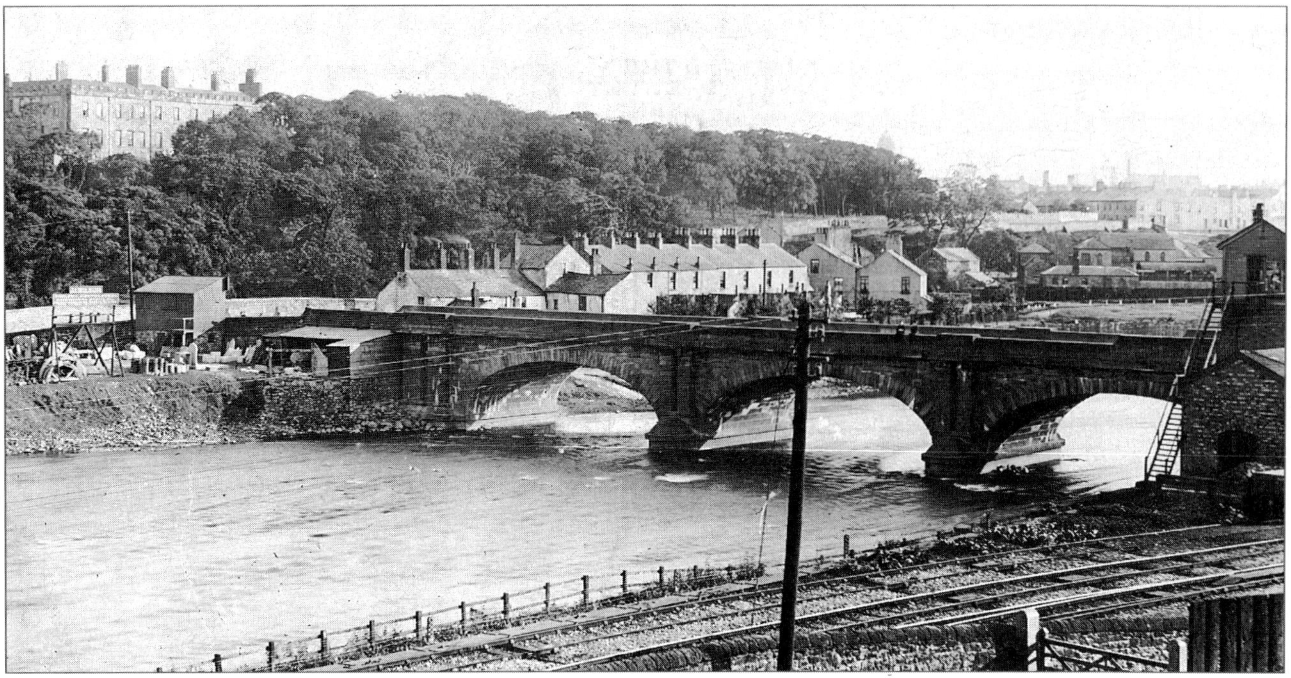

The Curwen family occupied the now derelict Workington Hall for several centuries. Many people will have memories of the hall above the main road north, looking down across the bridge over the Derwent towards the railway station. (*John Garbutt Collection*)

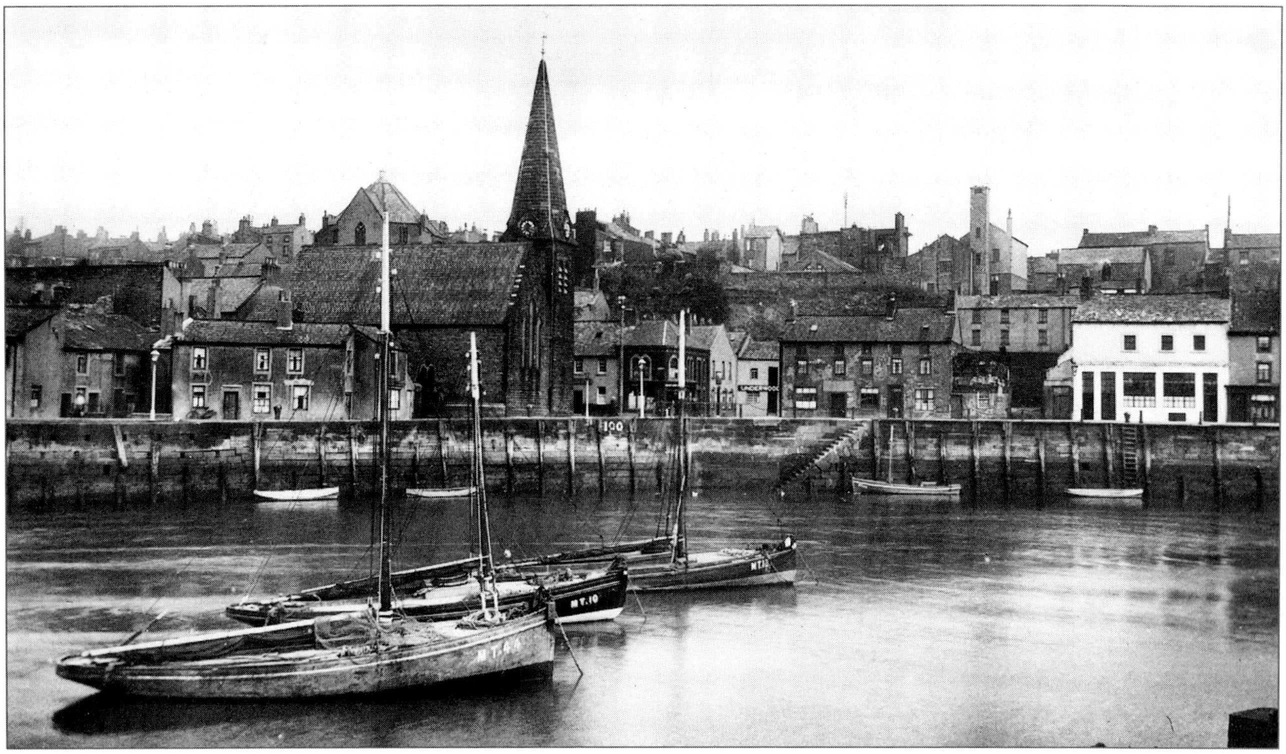

Maryport harbour had seen busier days when photographed here early in the twentieth century. The prawner yacht in the foreground was the last boat to be built on the banks of Ulverston canal. It served as a pilot boat in a number of west coast harbours including Maryport. It is currently being restored by enthusiasts supported by Glaxo Wellcome at Ulverston. (*John Garbutt Collection*)

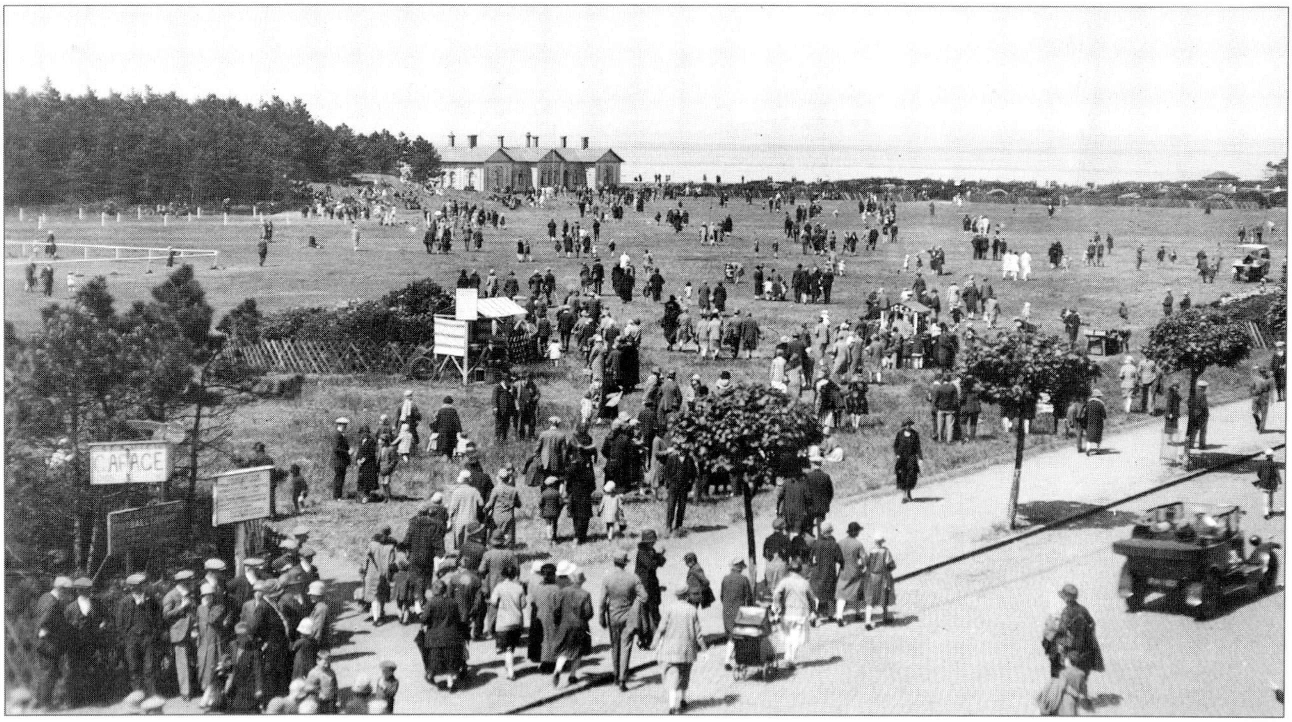

Silloth was a planned west coast resort which was successful for several decades. The crowds on the green above would mostly be from Carlisle having travelled on the Carlisle to Silloth railway. Pedestrians seemed to have the right of way in those days. Users of the putting course, below, seem undeterred by the ever-present sea breezes. (*Above, J.J. Martin of Silloth; below, Valentine's of Dundee*)

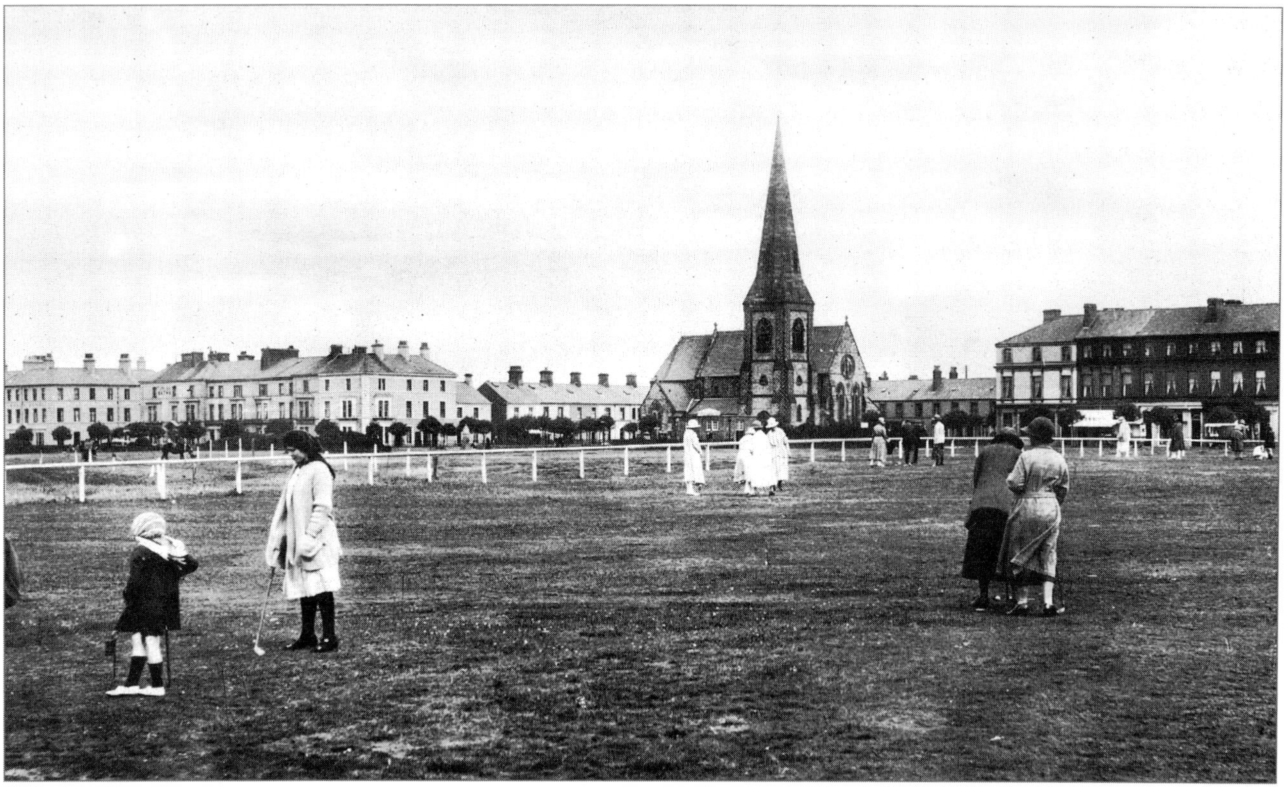

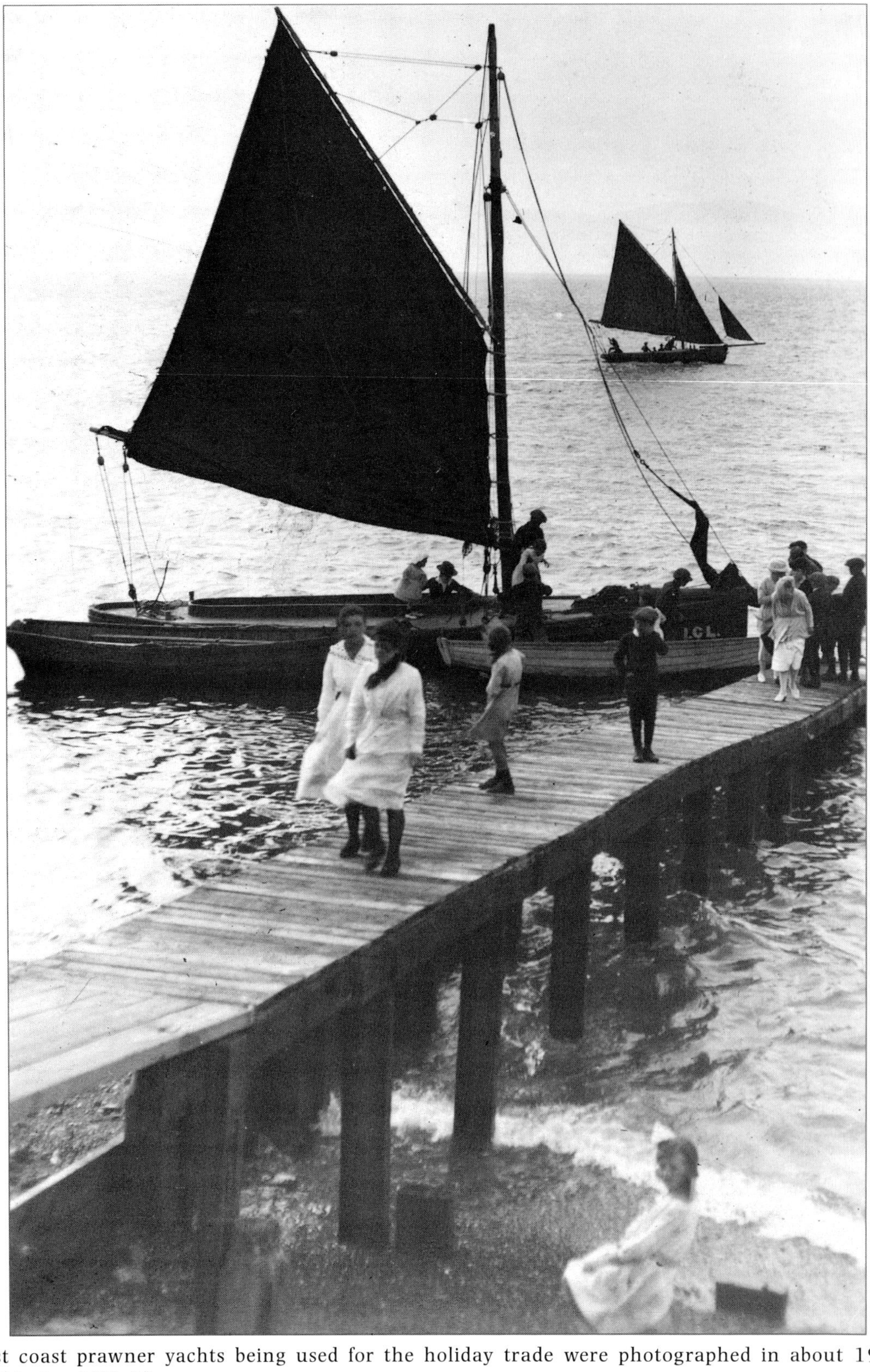

West coast prawner yachts being used for the holiday trade were photographed in about 1920. (*J.J. Martin of Silloth*)

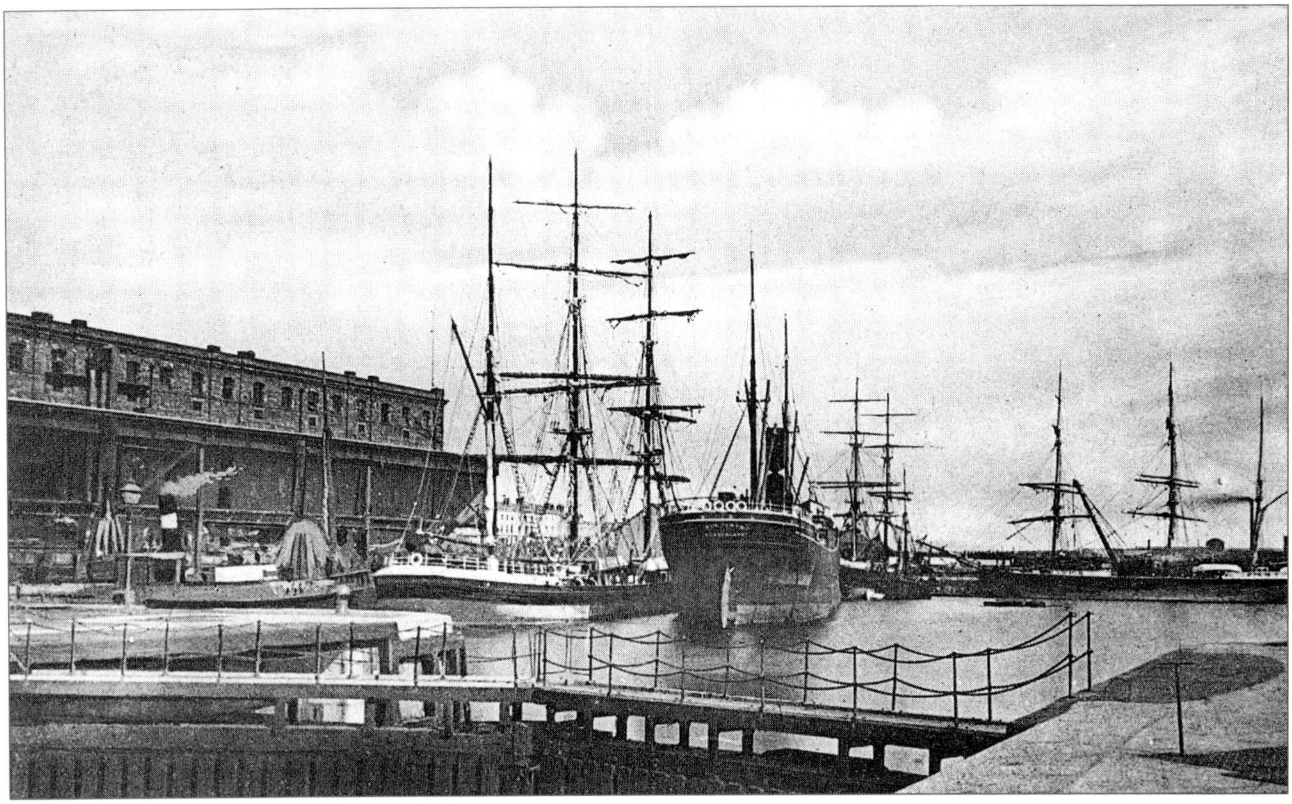

Silloth harbour in the years of transition from sail to steam. Three-masted schooners share the harbour with a Southampton-registered steamer and a steam tug. (*Valentine's of Dundee*)

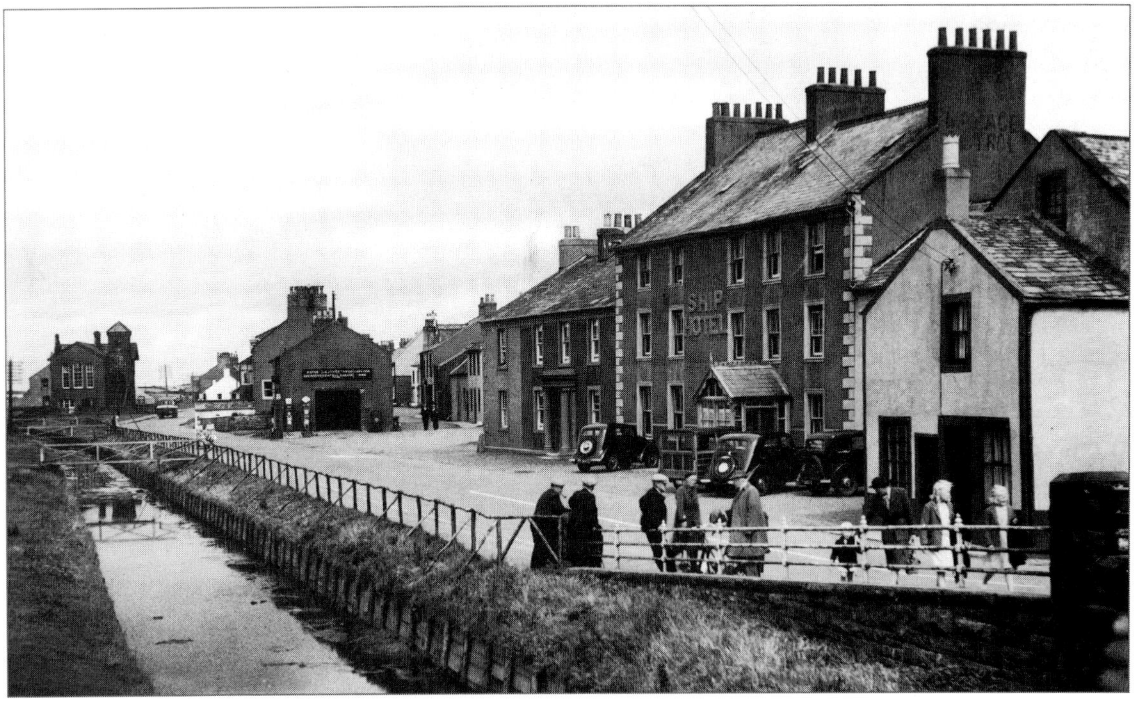

In the 1950s Allonby was still an underdeveloped fishing village surrounding the Ship Hotel. Once visited by Charles Dickens, it was a fashionable seaside resort in the latter half of the nineteenth century. (*John Marsh Collection*)

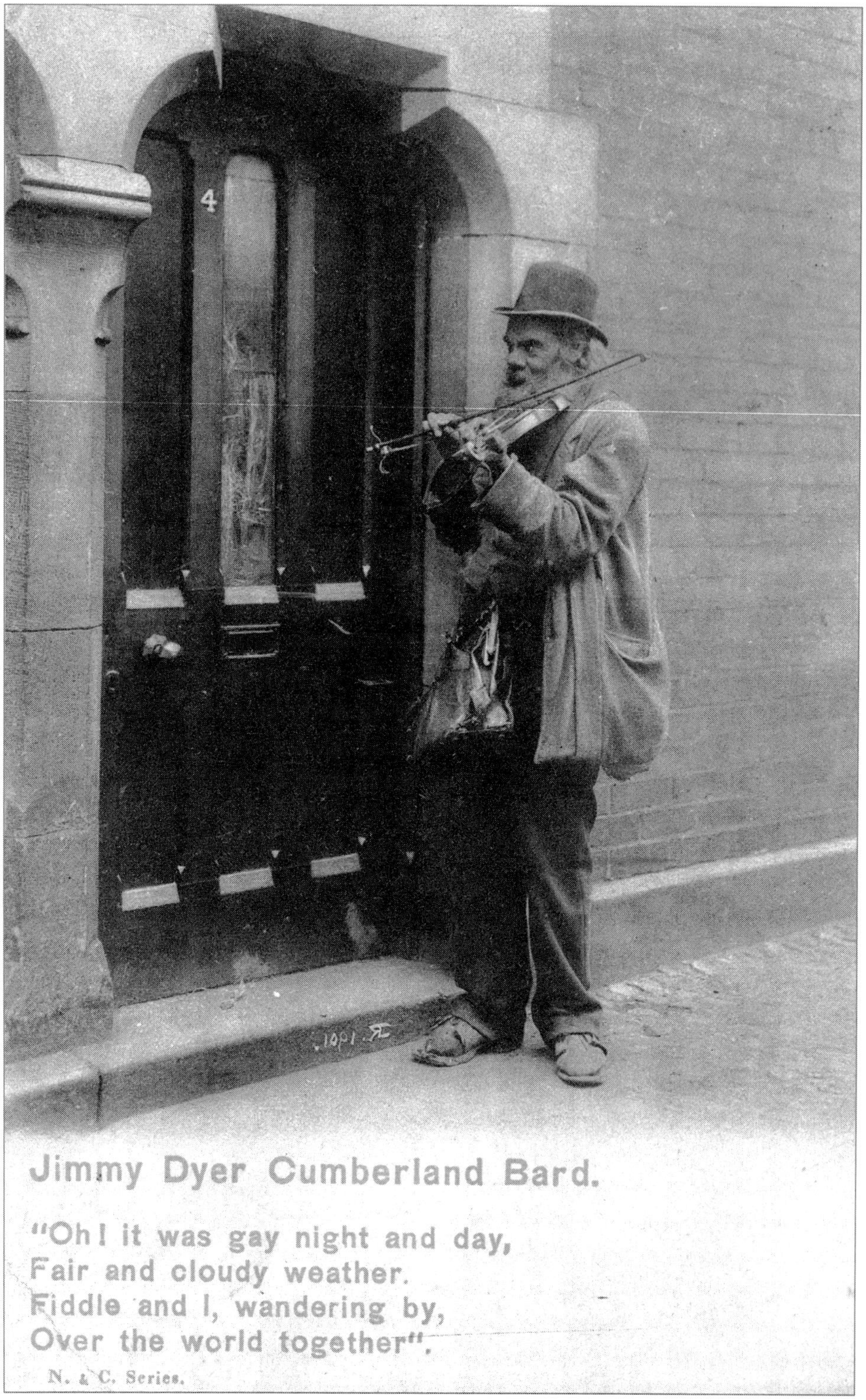

Carlisle area beggar Jimmy Dyer took begging to new levels with his fiddle playing, ballad singing and the sale of postcards of which this is one. Famous even after his death in 1903 at the age of 62, there is now a statue of him in the new Lanes shopping area in Carlisle. It has been argued that such itinerant fiddle-playing beggars are very much part of the Cumbrian tradition, dating back to Norse times. (*John Marsh Collection*)

Cumbrians at Work and in Service

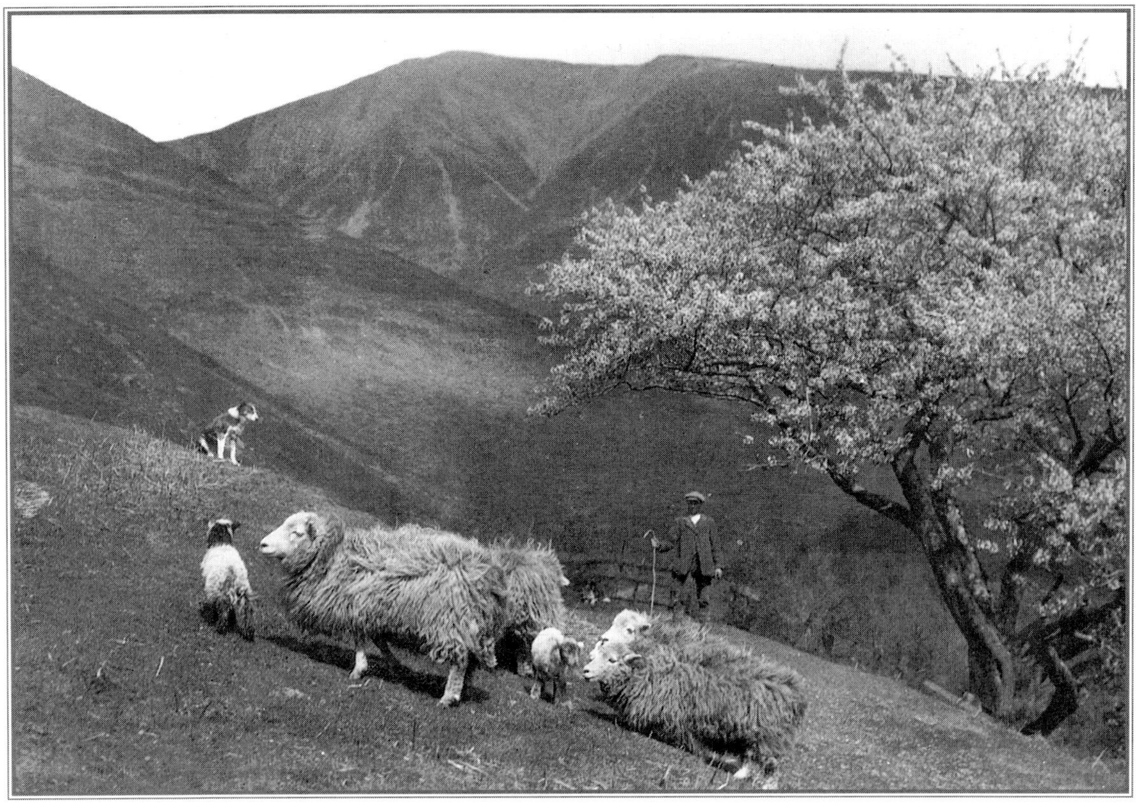

The romance of shepherding on the shoulders of Skiddaw. Keswick produced sales of many such postcards. The actual life of man and dog (and sheep) was, in fact, not romantic at all. The Keswick photographer pictured an idyllic scene with spring blossoms as new lambs are taken to their 'heaf' on the fell. (*Maysons of Keswick*)

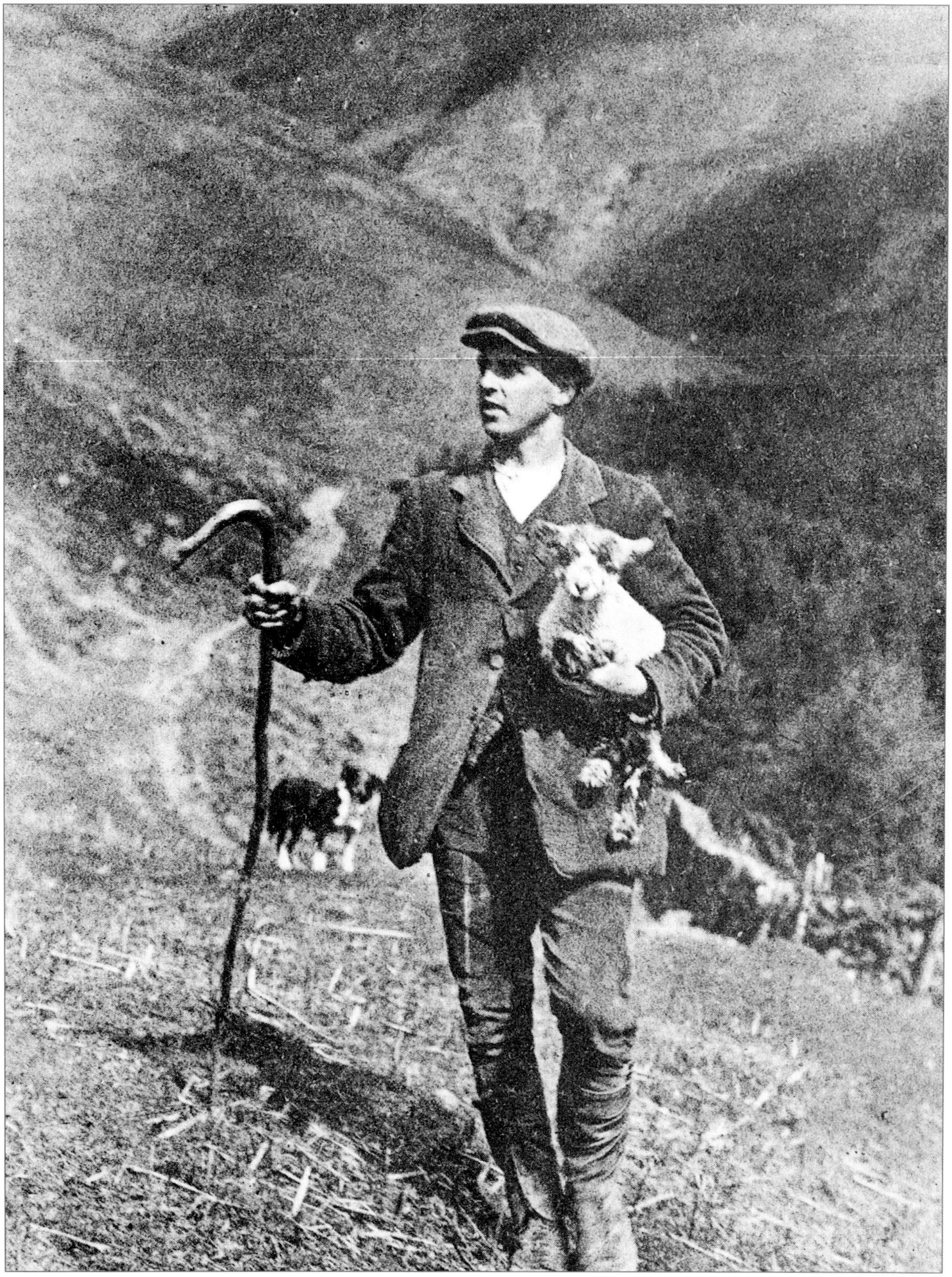

Skiddaw again is in the background for this photograph romanticising the sheep farmer's lot. Heavy boots, leggings, moleskin trousers, tweed jacket, waistcoat and cap were meant to protect in all weathers – maybe also a sack over the shoulders in rain. Visitors to Keswick could not get enough of pictures such as this, although it is doubtful if the farmers shared the profit. (*John Marsh Collection*)

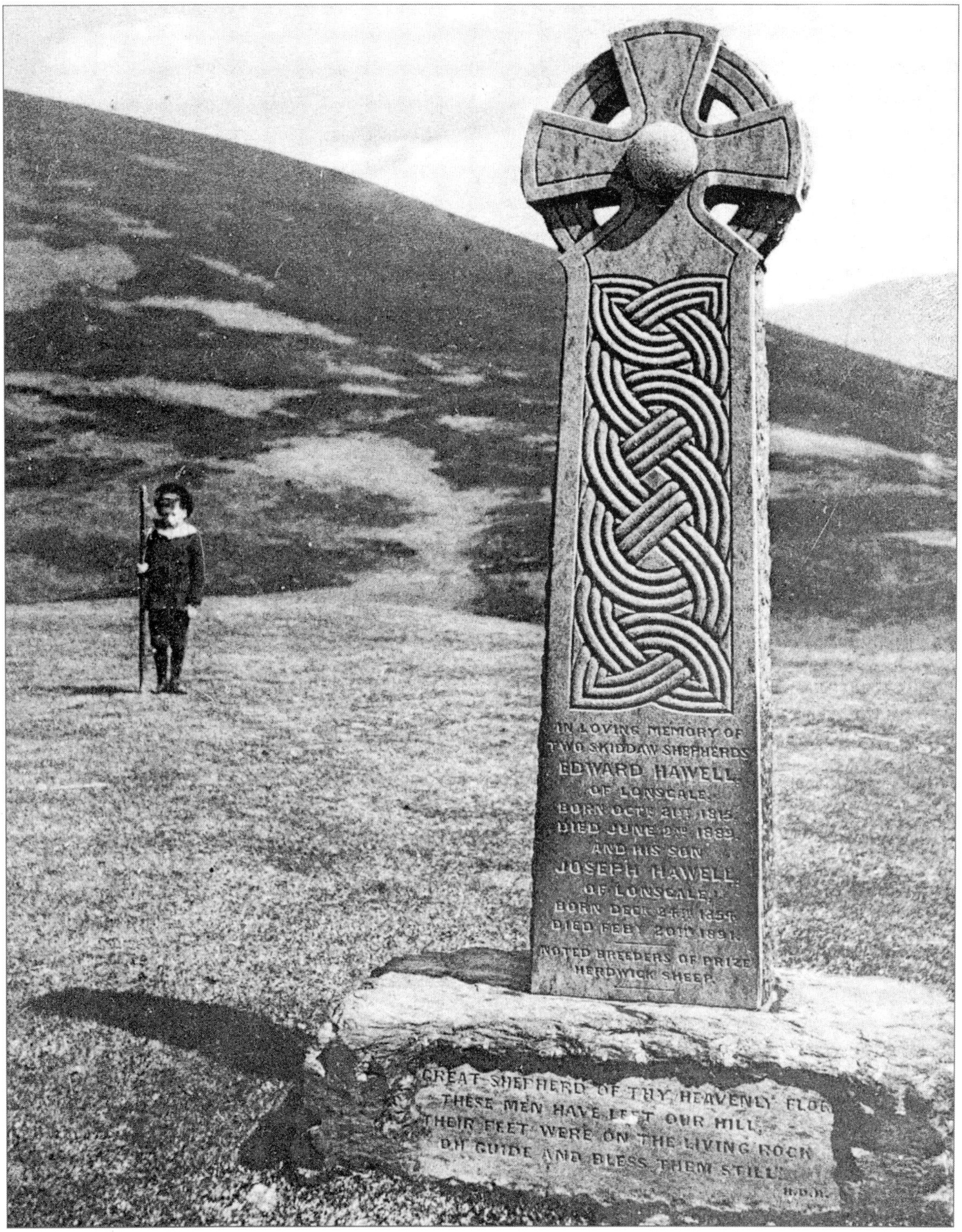

The dirty work of hill-farming reached the heights of the romantic when Canon H.D. Rawnsley of Crosthwaite church, near Keswick, had this monument to the hardworking Hawell family of Lonscale raised on the shoulder of Skiddaw. 'Great shepherd of thy heavenly flock', wrote the Canon, 'These men have left our hill, Their feet were on the living rock, Oh guide and bless them still.' This memory, more of the romantic than of shepherding, comes from the days well before the present crisis in wool and meat sales, dangerous sheep dip and low prices. (*John Marsh Collection*)

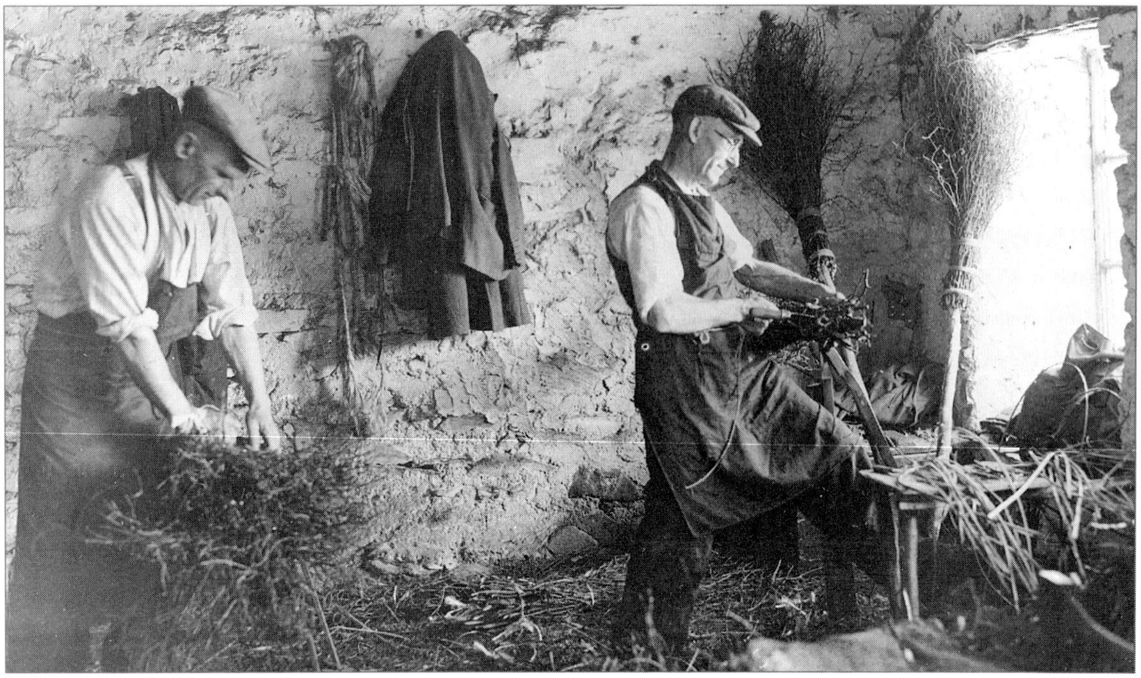

Besom brush making in the woodyards of the Furness fells at Finsthwaite and Backbarrow. The woodland industries of High Furness provided employment for many and transformed the scenery in a way unlikely to be permitted today. Besom and swill basket making, charcoal production, pit prop and bobbin production were the major employers. Elsewhere, the municipal water suppliers and later the government Forestry Commission, both with regimented plantations, changed the woodland scene and its industries. (*John Marsh Collection*)

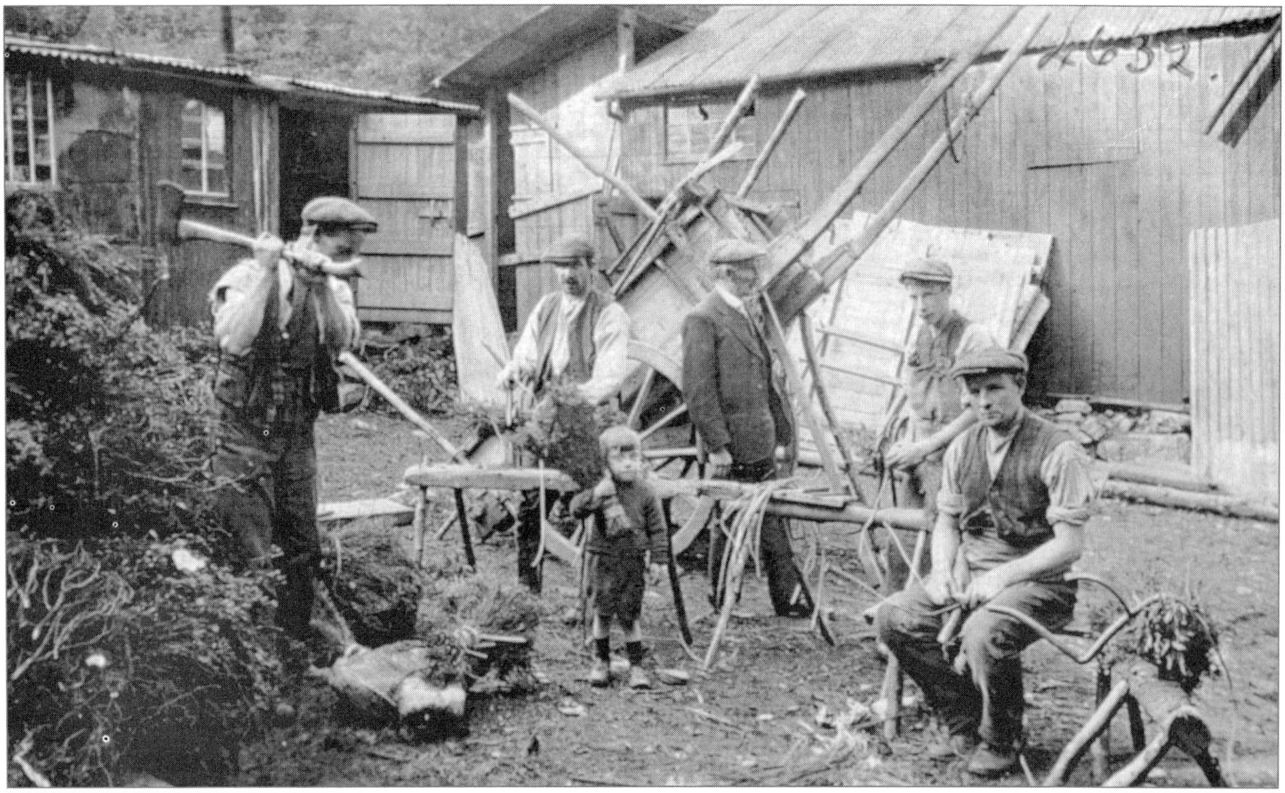

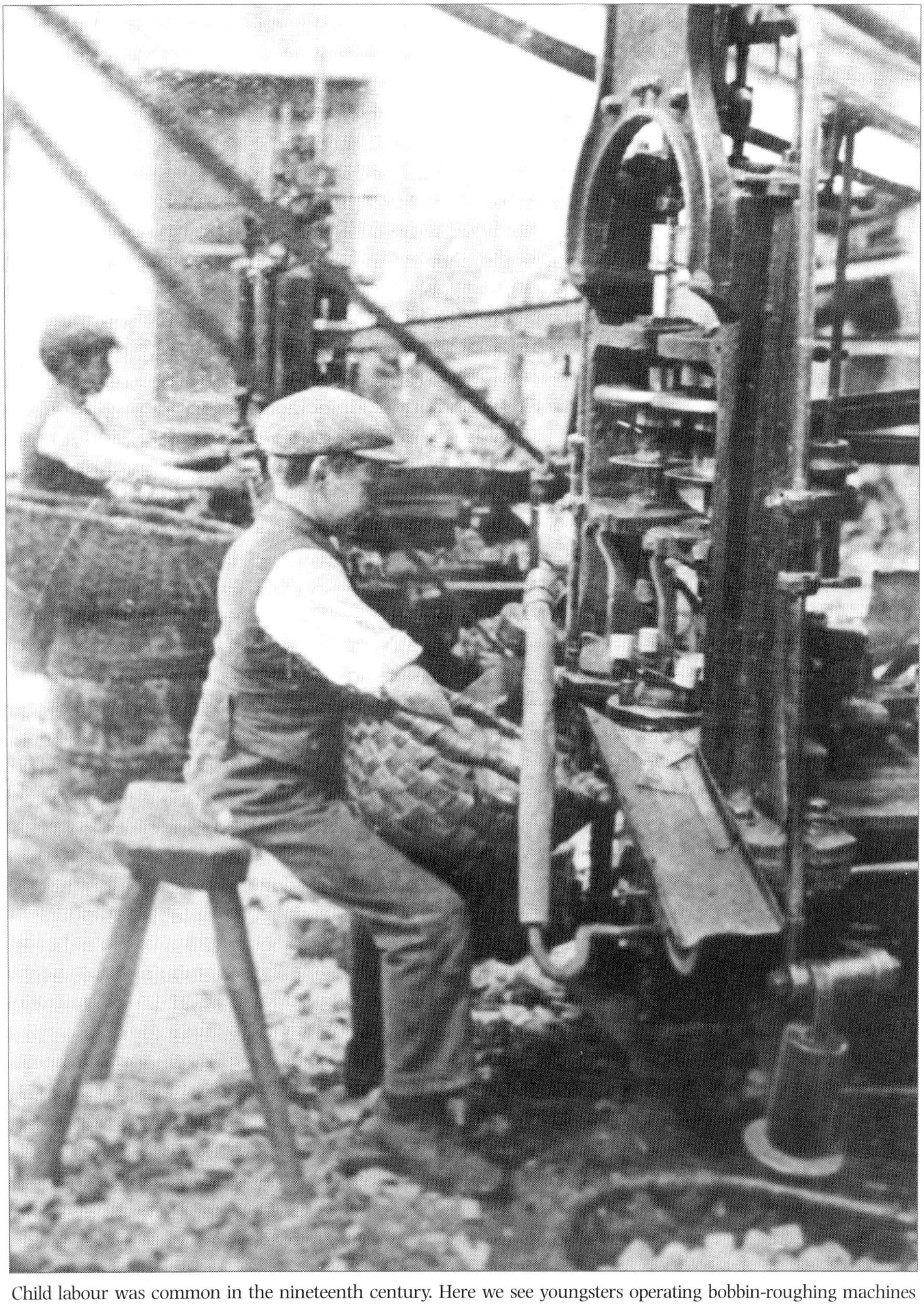

Child labour was common in the nineteenth century. Here we see youngsters operating bobbin-roughing machines at Phillipson's of Spark Bridge in 1899. They continued the practice until the 1930s. (*John Marsh Collection*)

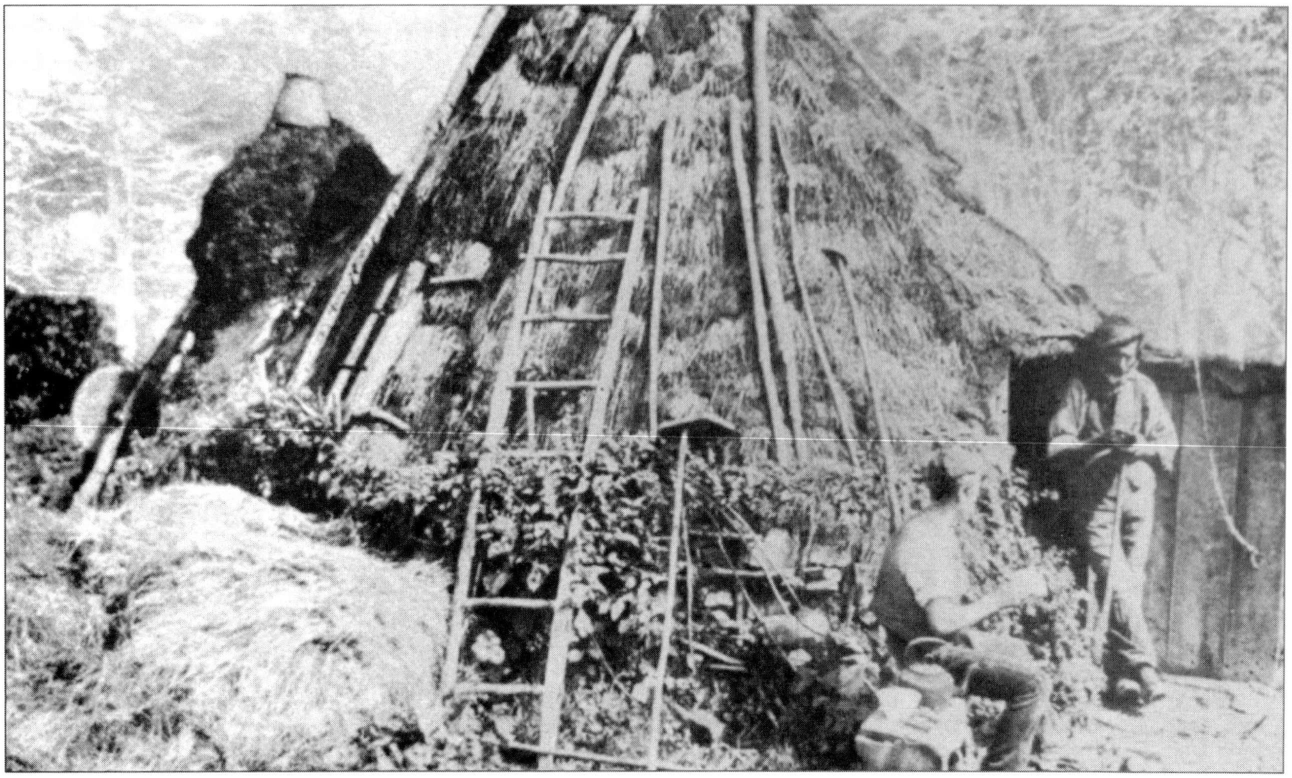

Charcoal burners in the woods of High Furness lived in wigwams near their pitsteads. While the scene appears chaotic the site was kept clean and tidy to avoid the spread of fire. Families with children often lived for long periods on these sites, although most had homes elsewhere. (*John Marsh Collection*)

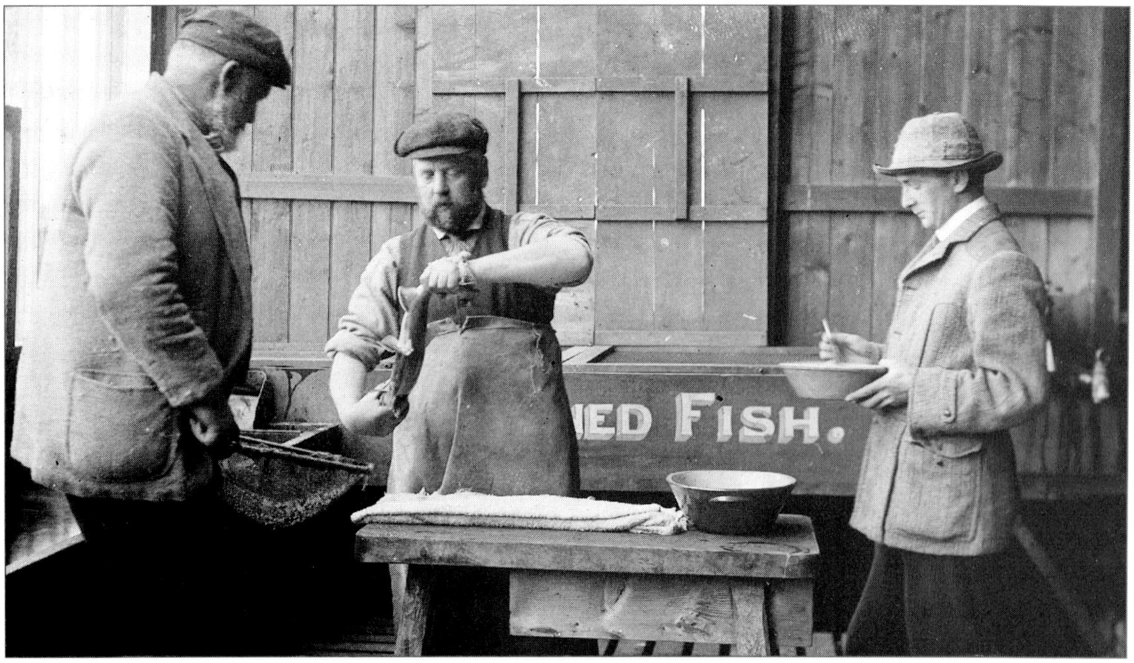

The fishing industry in south Cumbria has been carefully managed for many generations. Photographer Crosland of Arnside photographed Mr Brooks, owner of a local fisheries firm, carefully spawning trout for river stockings to maintain supplies for his customers. (*Crosland of Arnside*)

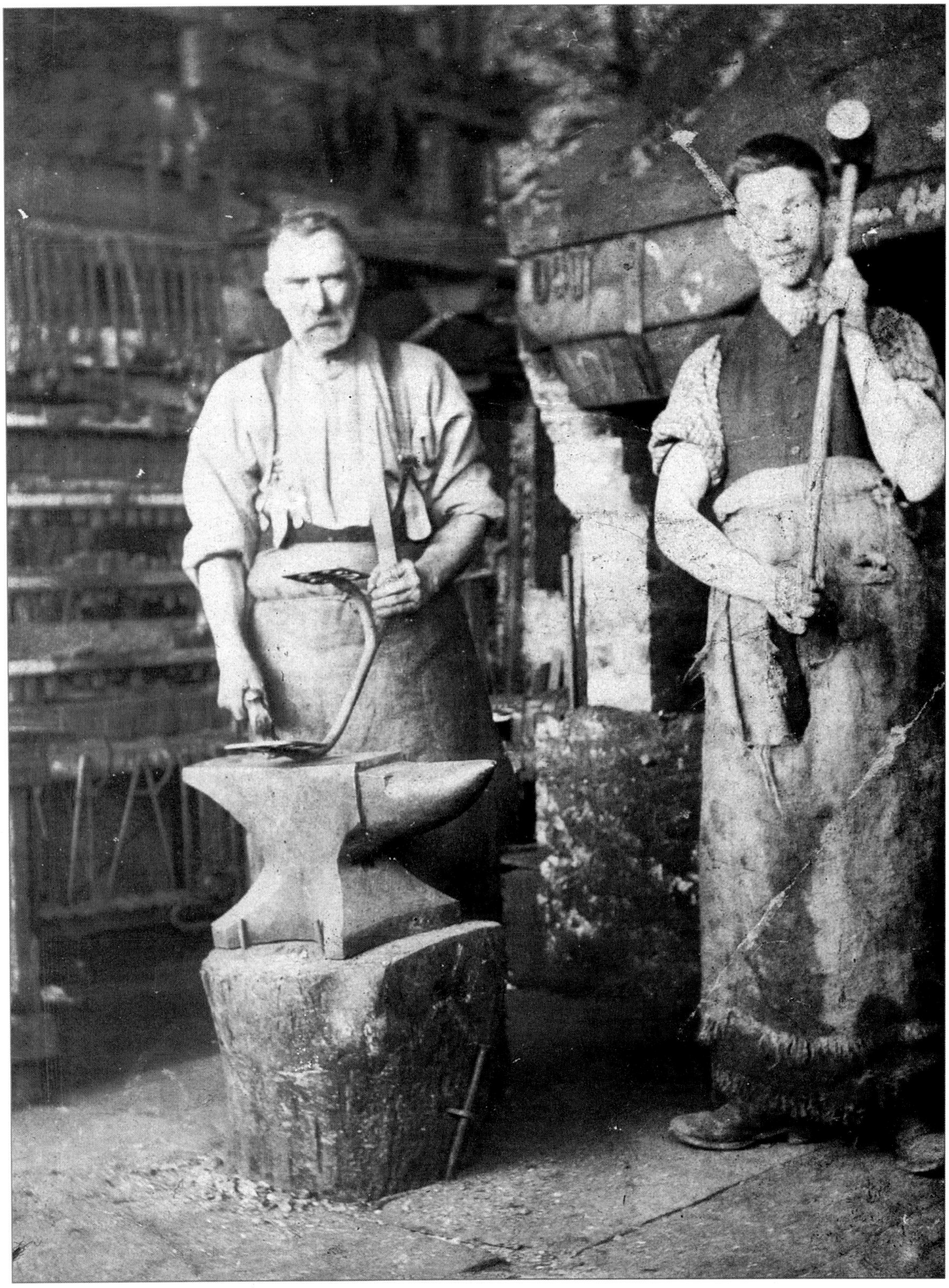

Every village in Cumbria had a resident blacksmith in the days of horse transport. Later, as cars and tractors became popular, many smithies became garage workshops. Here we see the smith and his assistant at Sedbergh before the First World War. (*John Marsh Collection*)

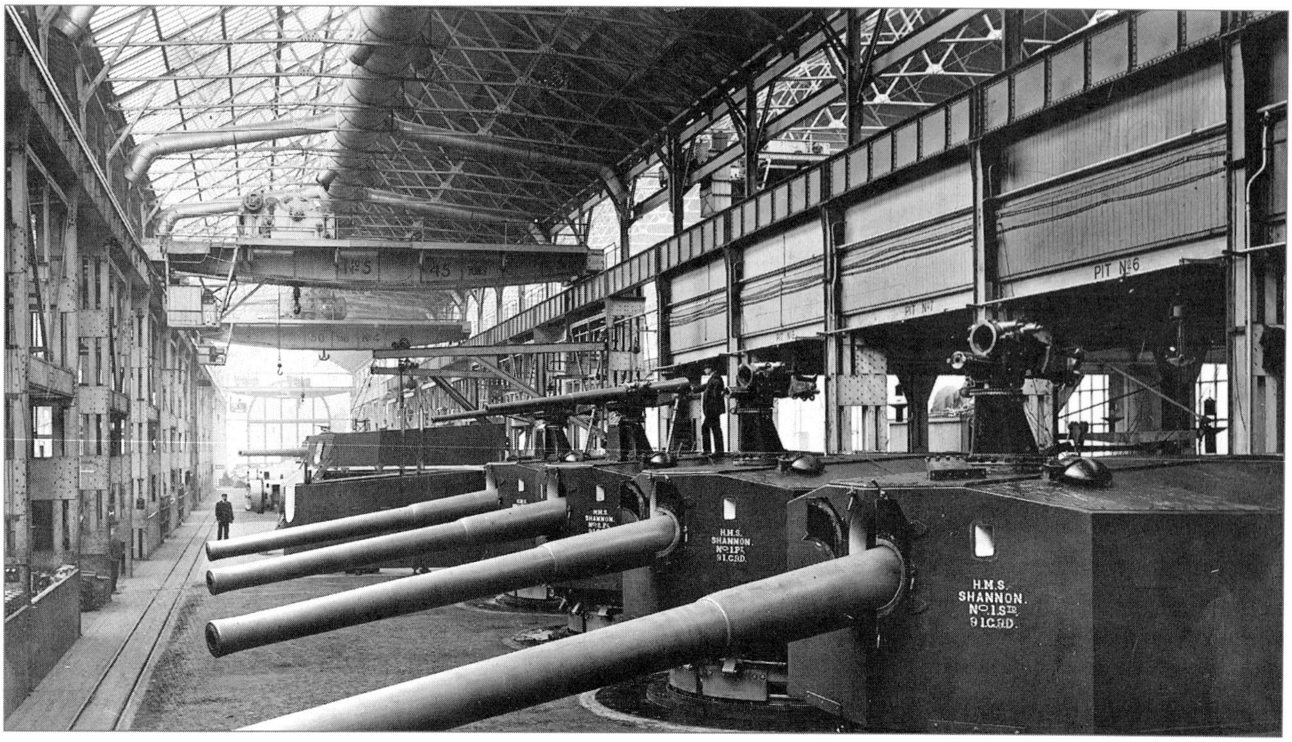

Ironworking and engineering skills merged at Barrow in Furness where Messrs Vickers made ships for both peace and war. Valentine's of Dundee photographed the manufacture of four large guns for HMS *Shannon* (above), and the scene in the boiler shop (below). (*Valentine's of Dundee*)

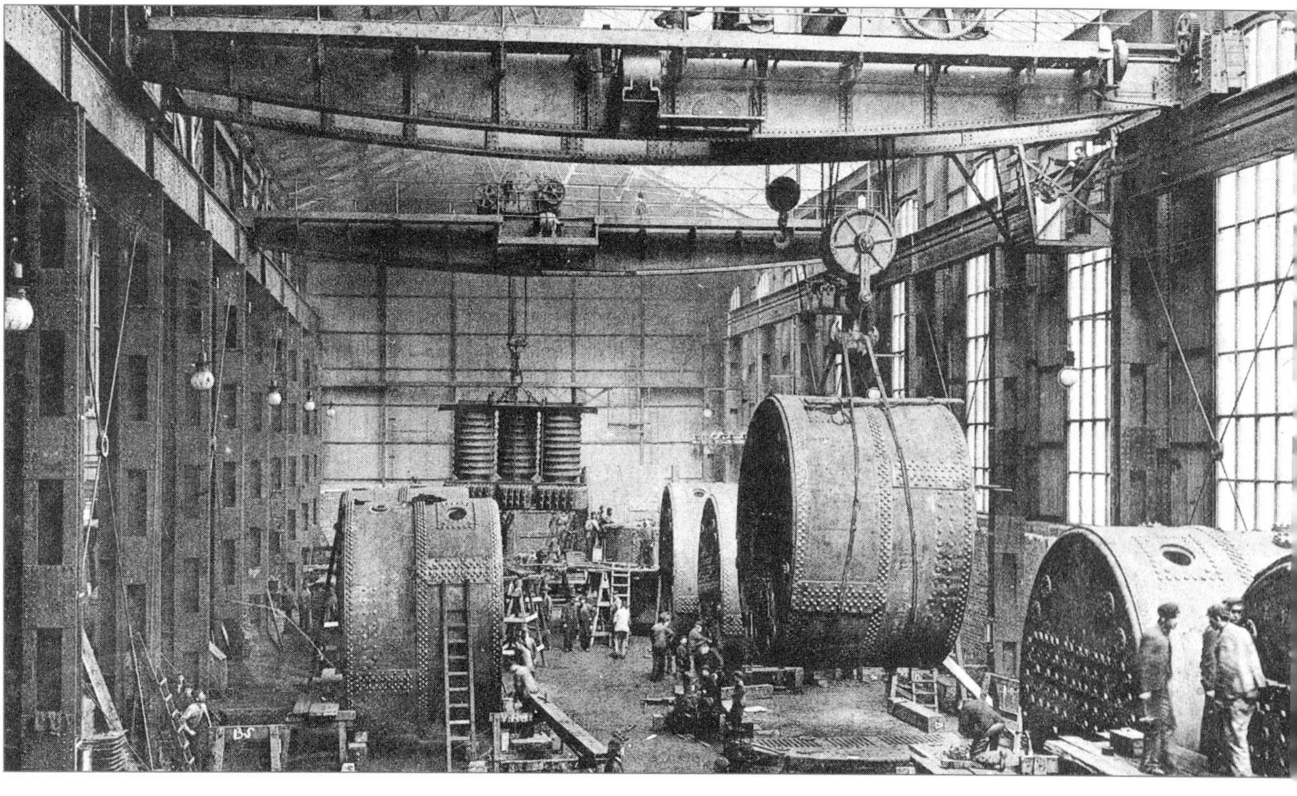

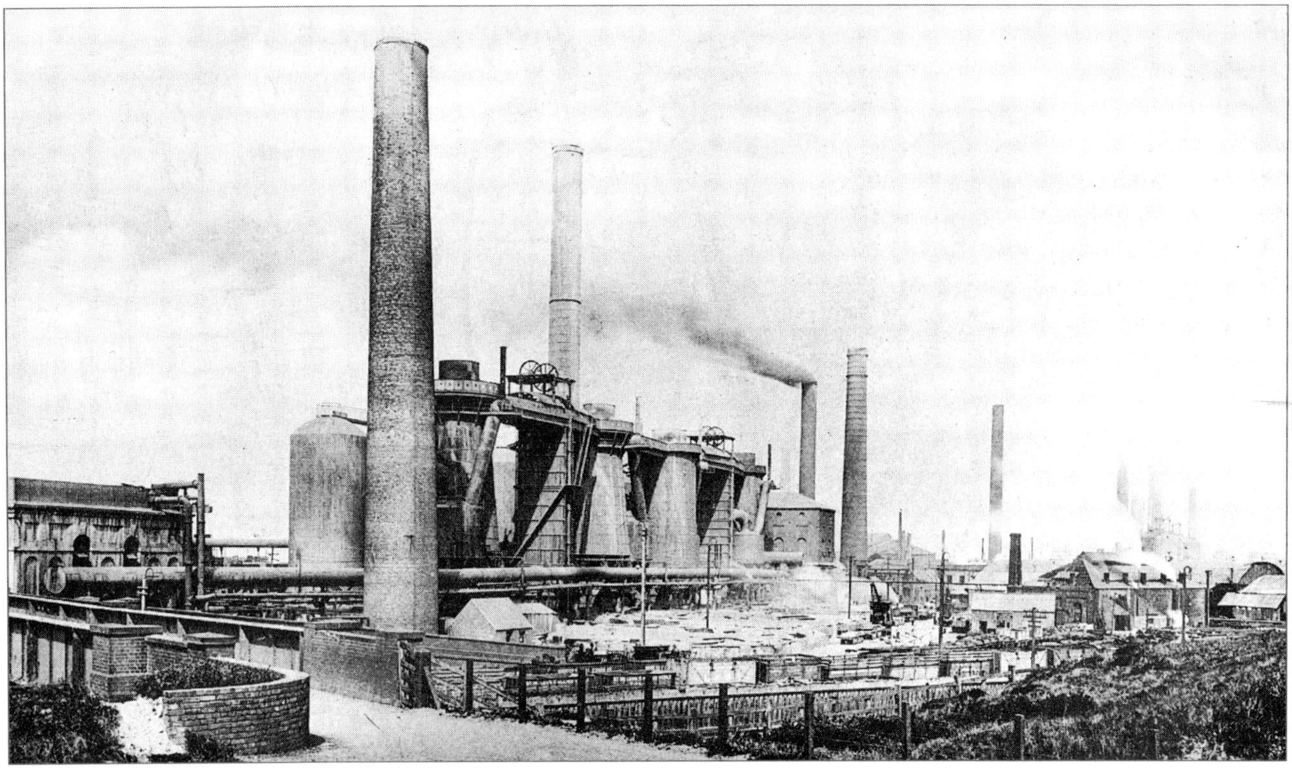

Moss Bay, Workington, with the ironworks was photographed by Valentine's of Dundee. The scene is now only a memory since the works was demolished and the site cleared. (*Valentine's of Dundee*)

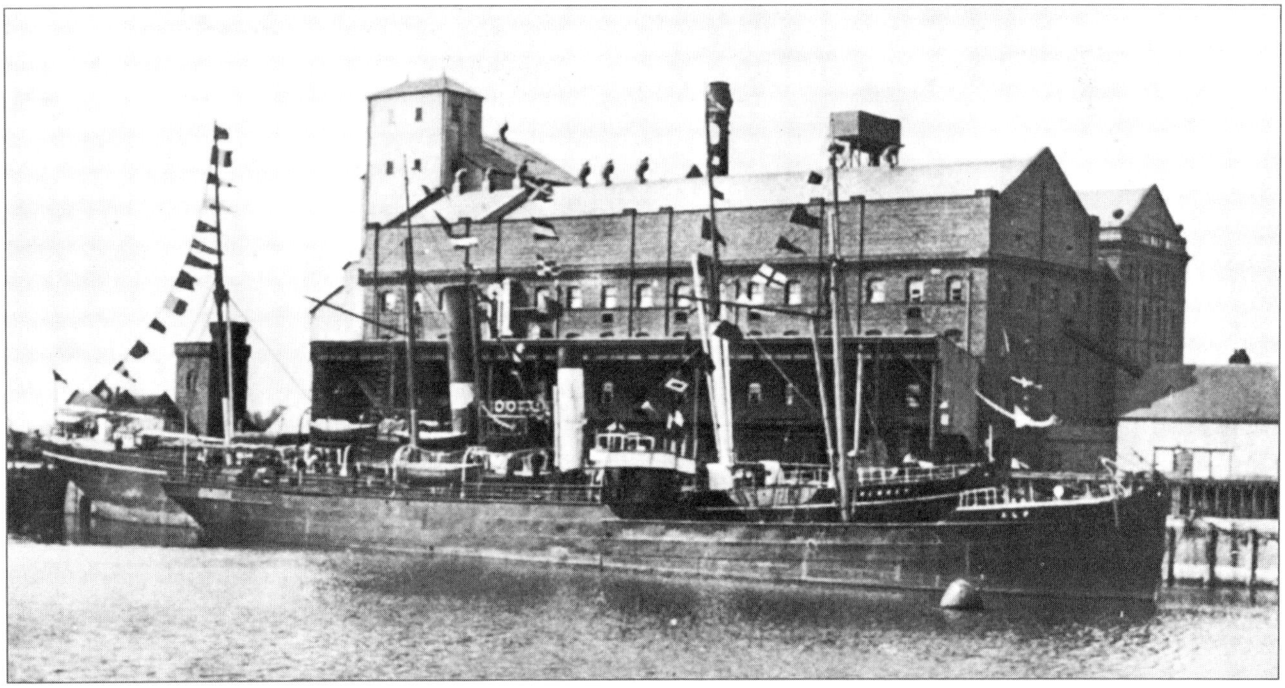

Silloth docks and Carr's mill were photographed at the turn of the nineteenth century by J.J. Martin. Two steam cargo boats are decked with flags and witnessed the constant demand for imported cereals used in preparing animal feed, biscuits and so on. (*J.J. Martin of Silloth*)

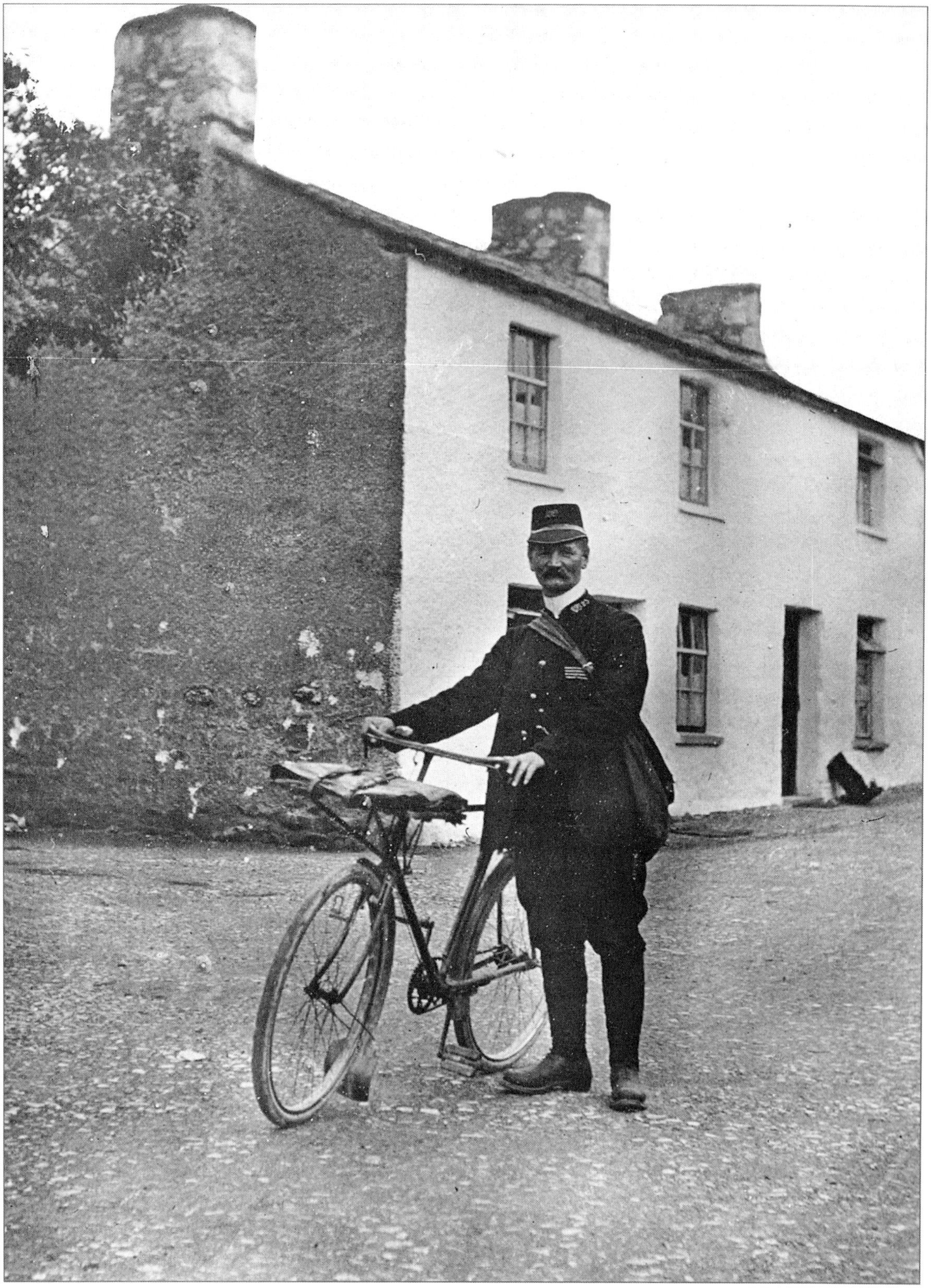

The country postman at Storth, near Arnside, seems unperturbed, having just passed the guard dog seen in the background. His uniform, nowadays, would appear almost continental in style. (*J.D. Wilson of Arnside*)

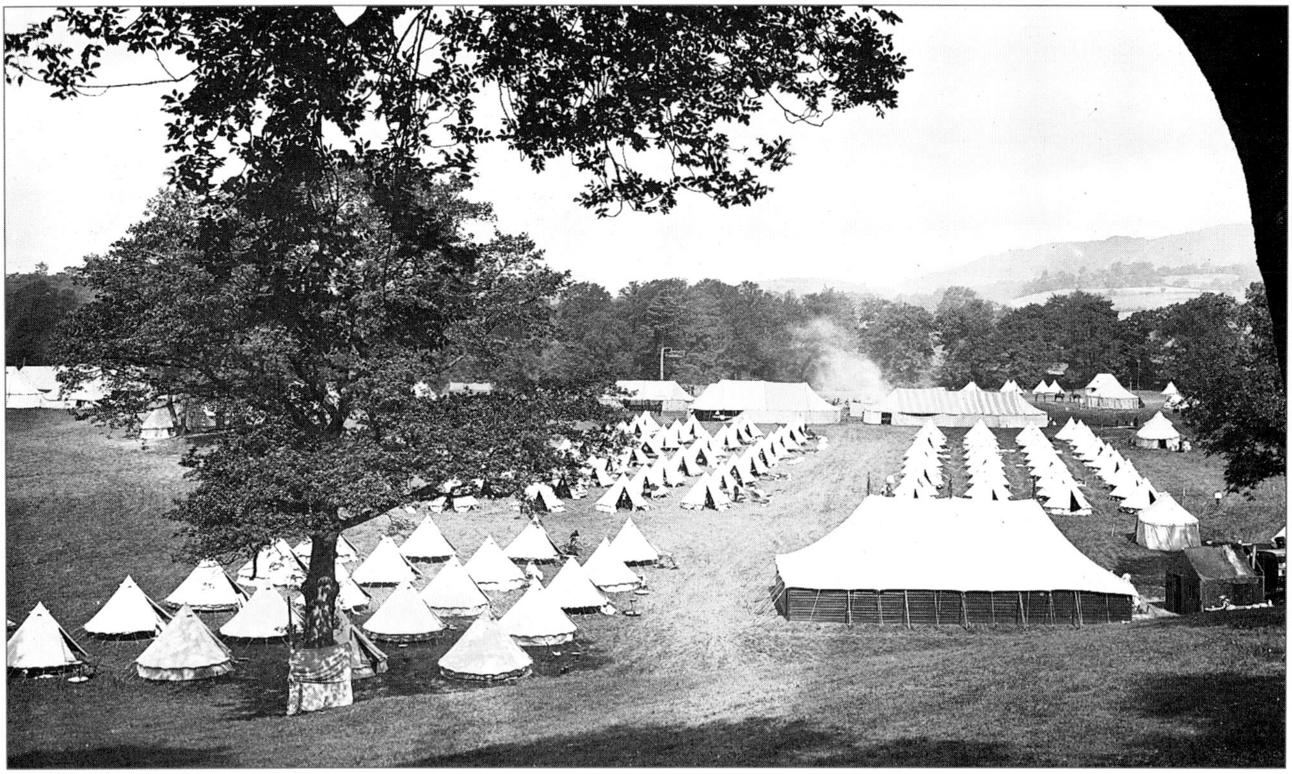

Calgarth Park near Windermere was one of the sites chosen for the pre-First World War annual volunteer camps, of which there were many throughout the county. Many of the volunteers were the first into the trenches in 1914. (*John Marsh Collection*)

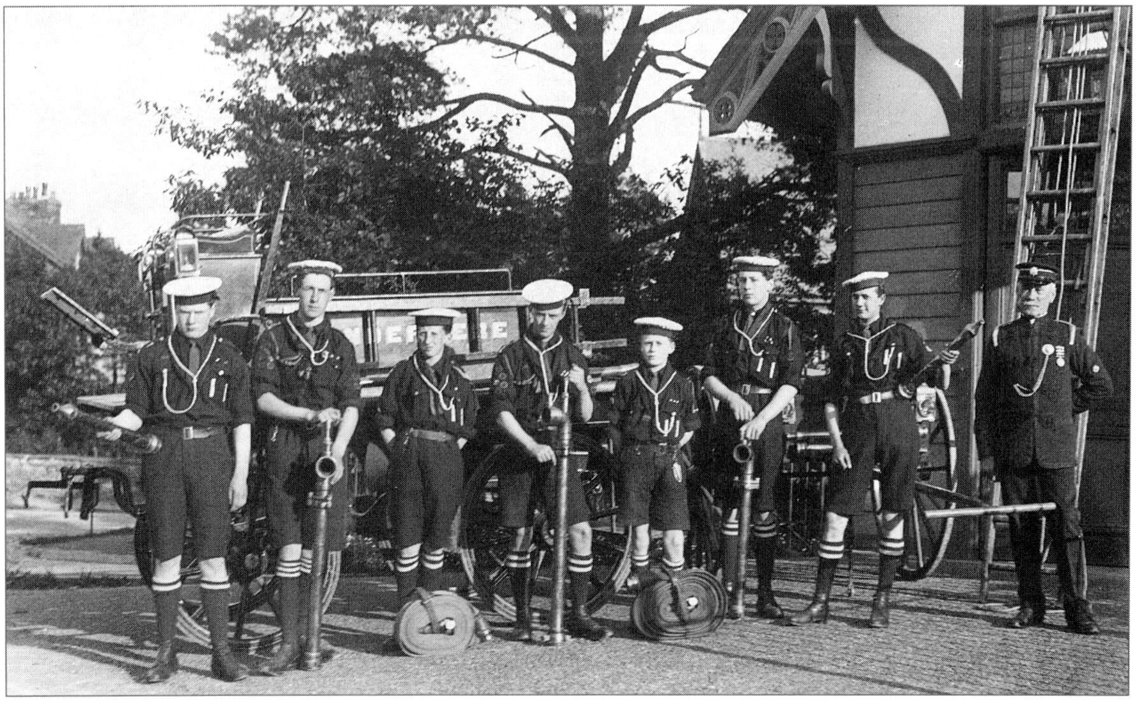

The First World War left many services at home undermanned. Here the Windermere Sea Scouts are pictured at their training with the hand-powered, horse-drawn fire pump at the Fire Engine house at Brook Road, Windermere. 'Be prepared' in action. (*John Marsh Collection*)

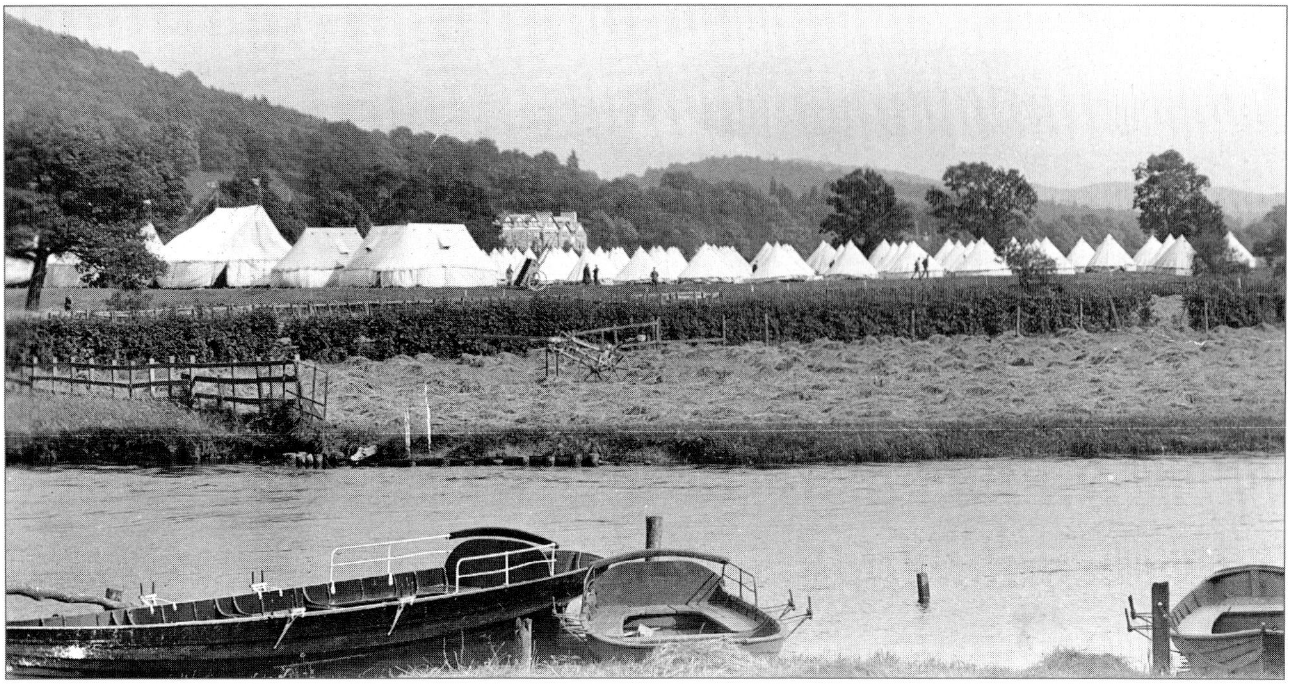

Waterhead, Ambleside was the site chosen for the Officer Training Corps annual training camp, where young men at universities spent part of their vacation training in the art of war. J.C. Capstaff photographed the 1909 OTC camp. *(J.C. Capstaff of Newcastle upon Tyne)*

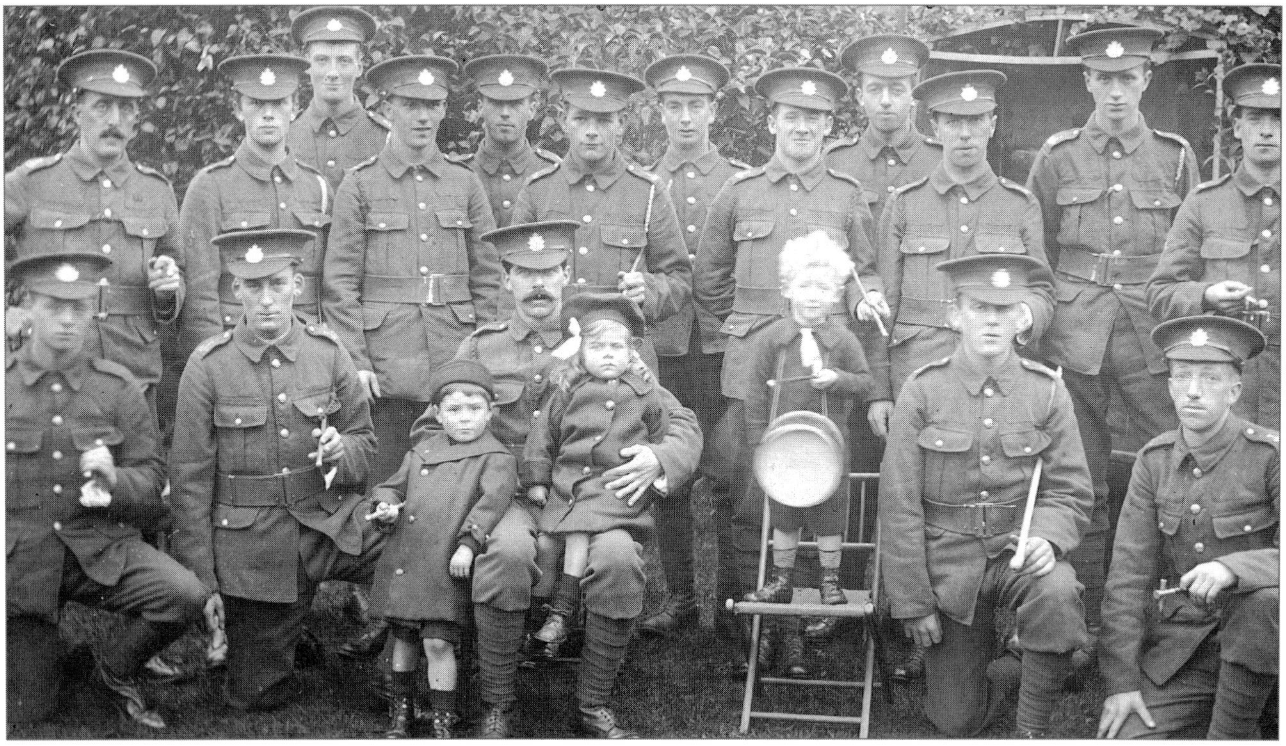

Kirkby Stephen territorials were photographed on the day they left home for India, Monday 19 October 1914. Their role was to replace the regular army units which were withdrawn from the far eastern empire to serve in France. The small boy standing on the chair with a drum was 'Sonny', the only son of Lieutenant Highett. *(John Marsh Collection)*

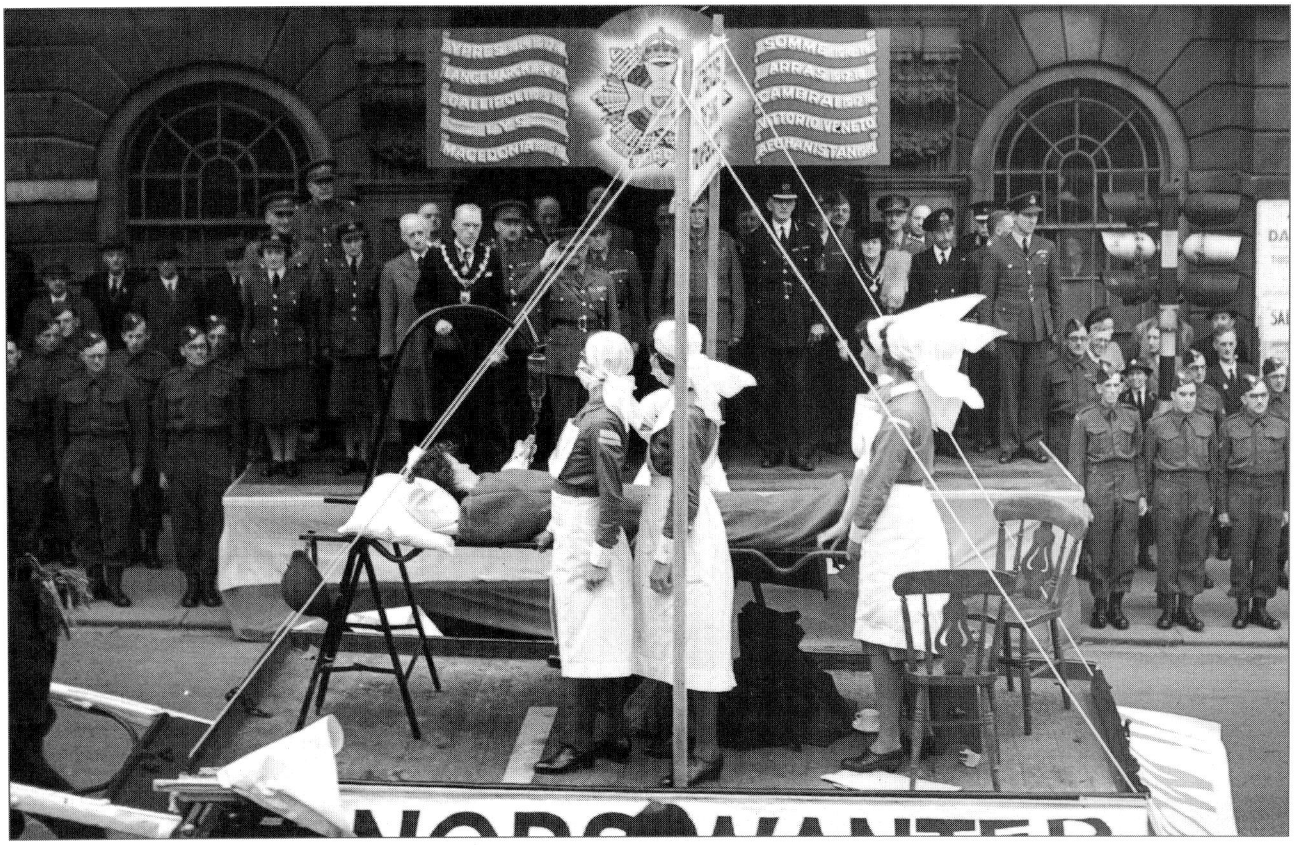

A 'Salute the Soldier' parade passes Kendal town hall in May 1944. The horse-drawn float reflects both the shortage of blood donors and of petrol at that time. Is the patient waving to the officer taking the salute? The nurses hang on to the stretcher while attempting to 'eyes right'. (*Westmorland Gazette*)

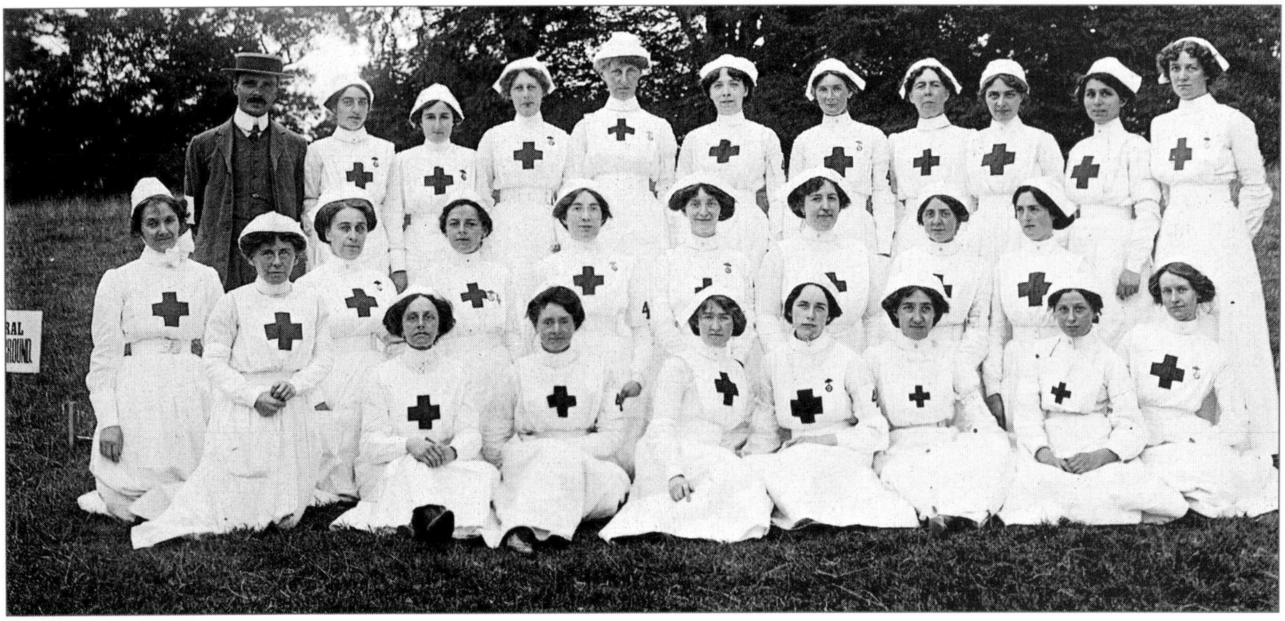

Lowther Park near Penrith saw wartime gatherings in both world wars. Here, in the first, volunteer Red Cross nurses from Workington are seen assembled for the camera. (*Devenham of Workington*)

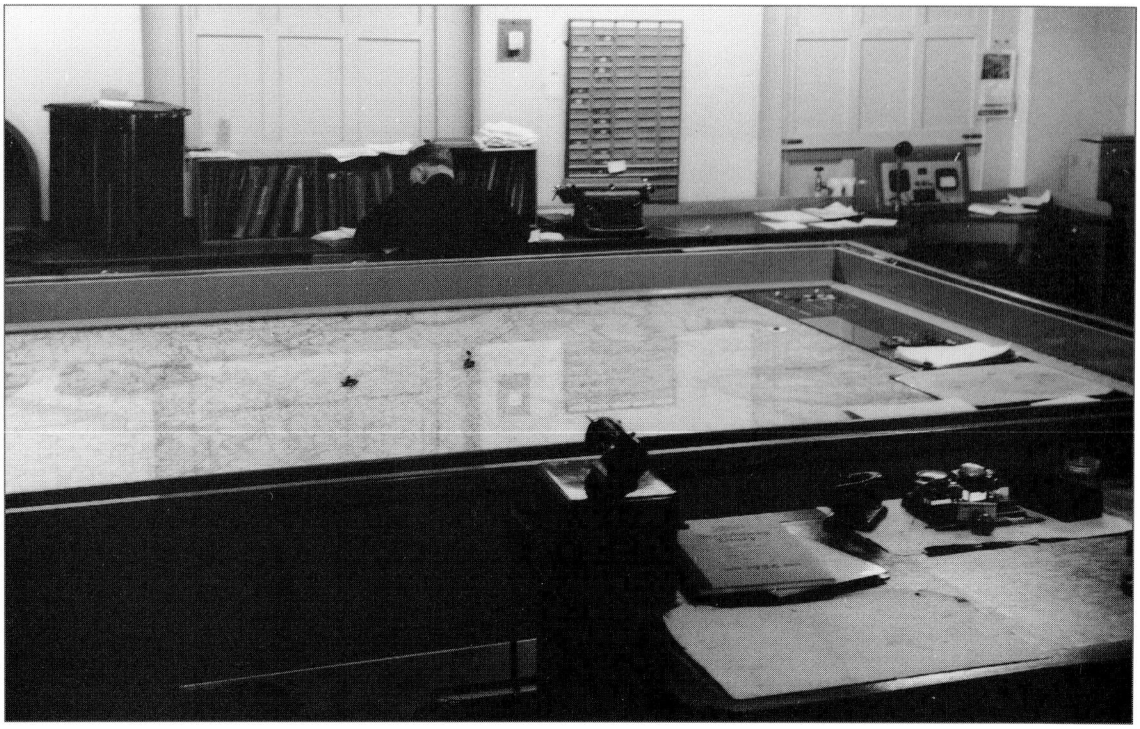

The Cumberland and Westmorland police control room at Carleton Hall near Penrith in the 1950s was planned to resemble a Battle of Britain RAF control room. Numbered model patrol cars were pushed over a glass-surfaced map by staff to the vehicle's last known location. Unfortunately the funds available to the force at that time hardly provided sufficient cars to warrant the elaborate room! (*John Marsh*)

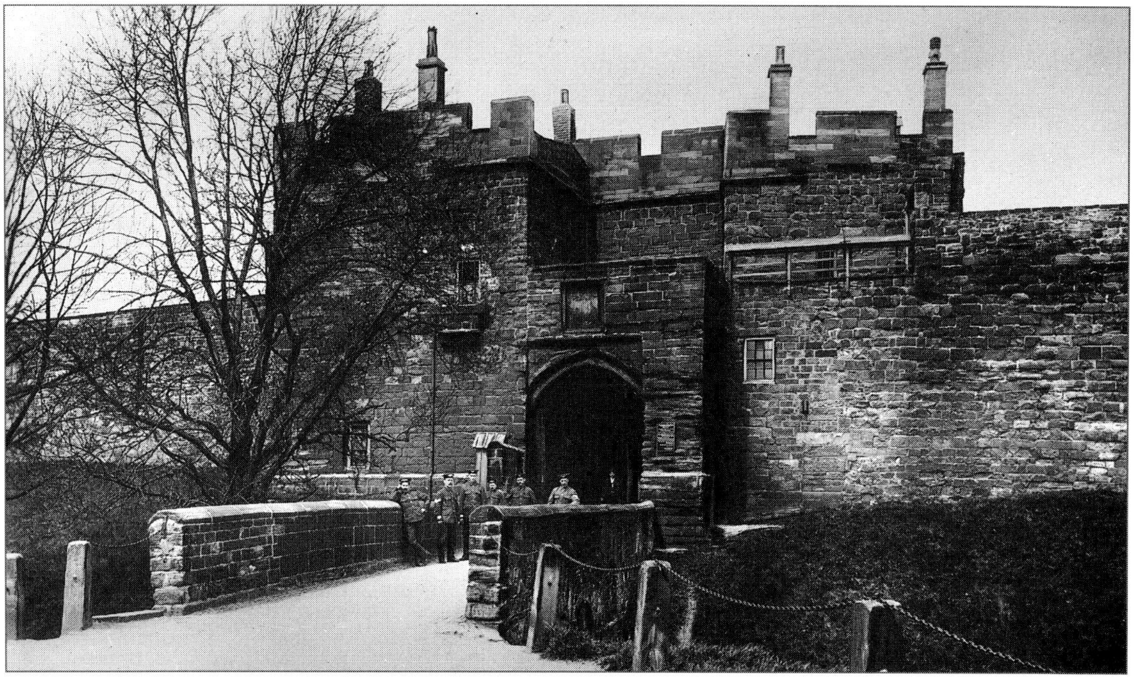

Carlisle Castle was a barracks for the Border Regiment for many years. A small group of soldiers is seen in front of the main gate with its sentry box. The castle was built on the site of a Roman fort by the Normans in about 1092 and served as both barracks and prison until very recent times (see also p. 125). (*John Marsh Collection*)

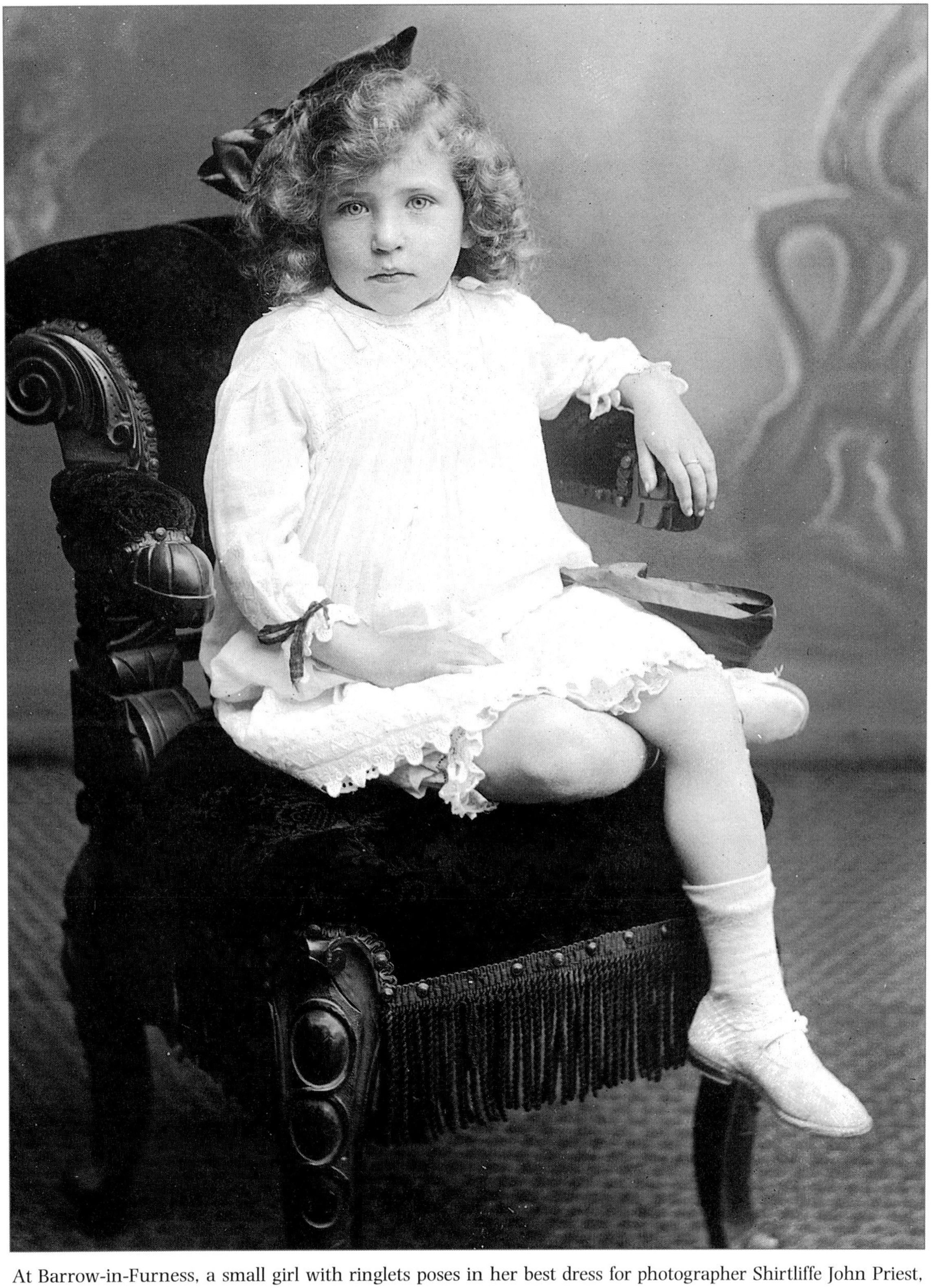

At Barrow-in-Furness, a small girl with ringlets poses in her best dress for photographer Shirtliffe John Priest, 22 Paxton Terrace, Barrow. Family portraits provided a lucrative income for professional photographers in every town in the Lake counties. (*S.J. Priest*)

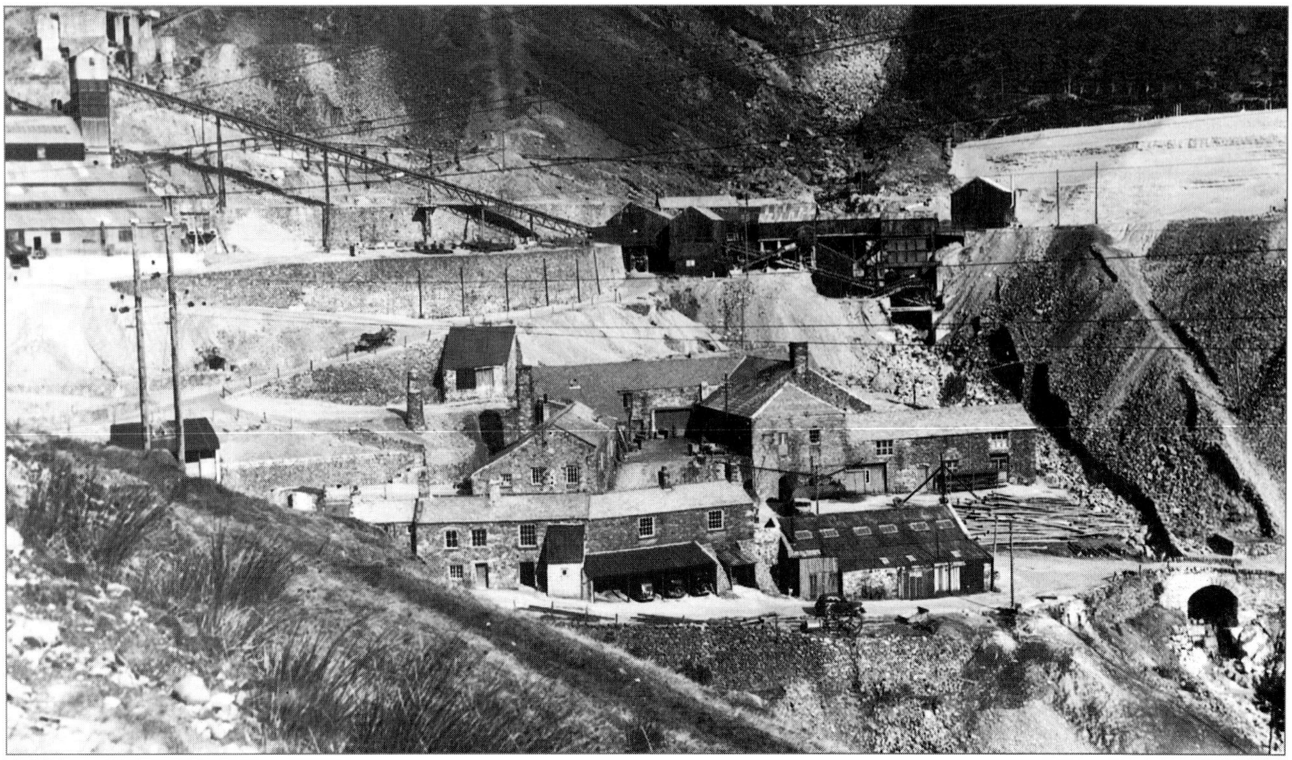

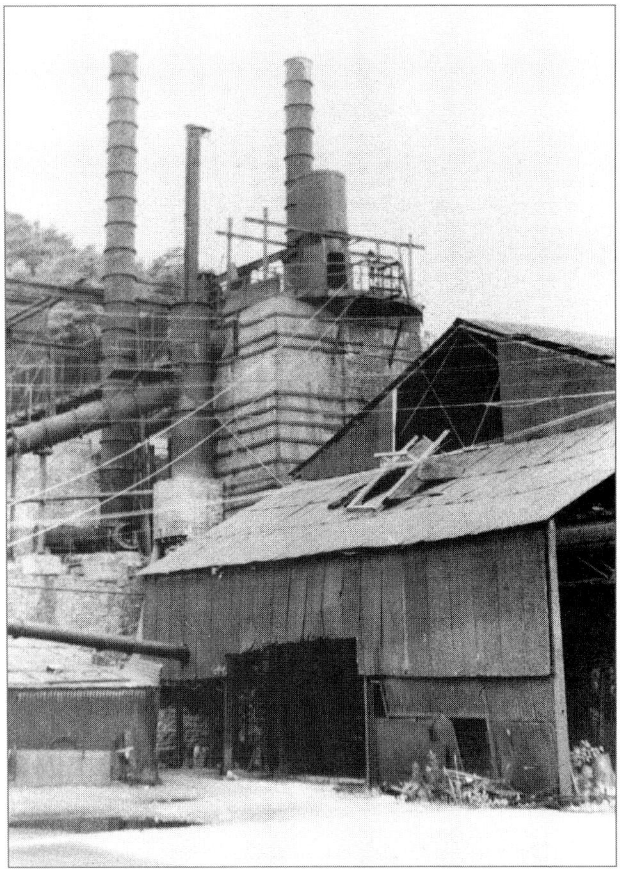

Two industrial sites which no longer exist were Greenside mine in Patterdale, above, and Backbarrow iron works. Lead and silver were mined at Greenside which was notorious for its poor safety record from the middle of the nineteenth century. After closure, seismic testing was carried out in the atomic bomb production programme. Backbarrow iron works started production in 1712 and became the last charcoal-burning furnace in Great Britain. Photographed in its latter working years, we see the furnace with its associated shed and chimney-stacks. The site clearance has been the subject of much controversy in recent years as the surrounding valley became less industrialised. (*John Marsh Collection*)

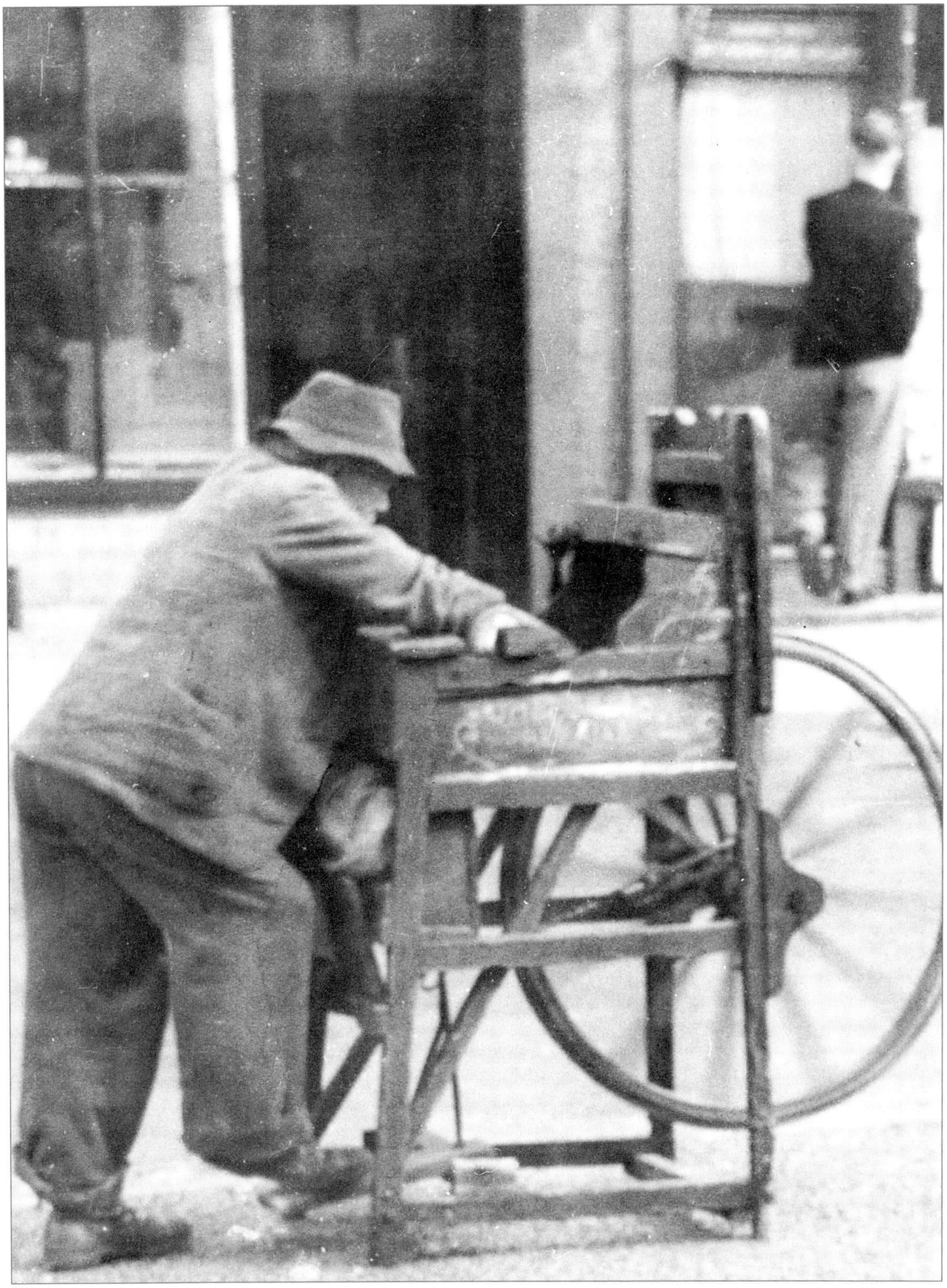

John Marsh photographed this itinerant knife grinder in the main street of Kirkby Stephen in 1954. The fly-wheel also served as a road wheel when the apparatus was moved. The same man toured the northern Yorkshire dales and north Westmorland for many years after the Second World War. (*John Marsh*)

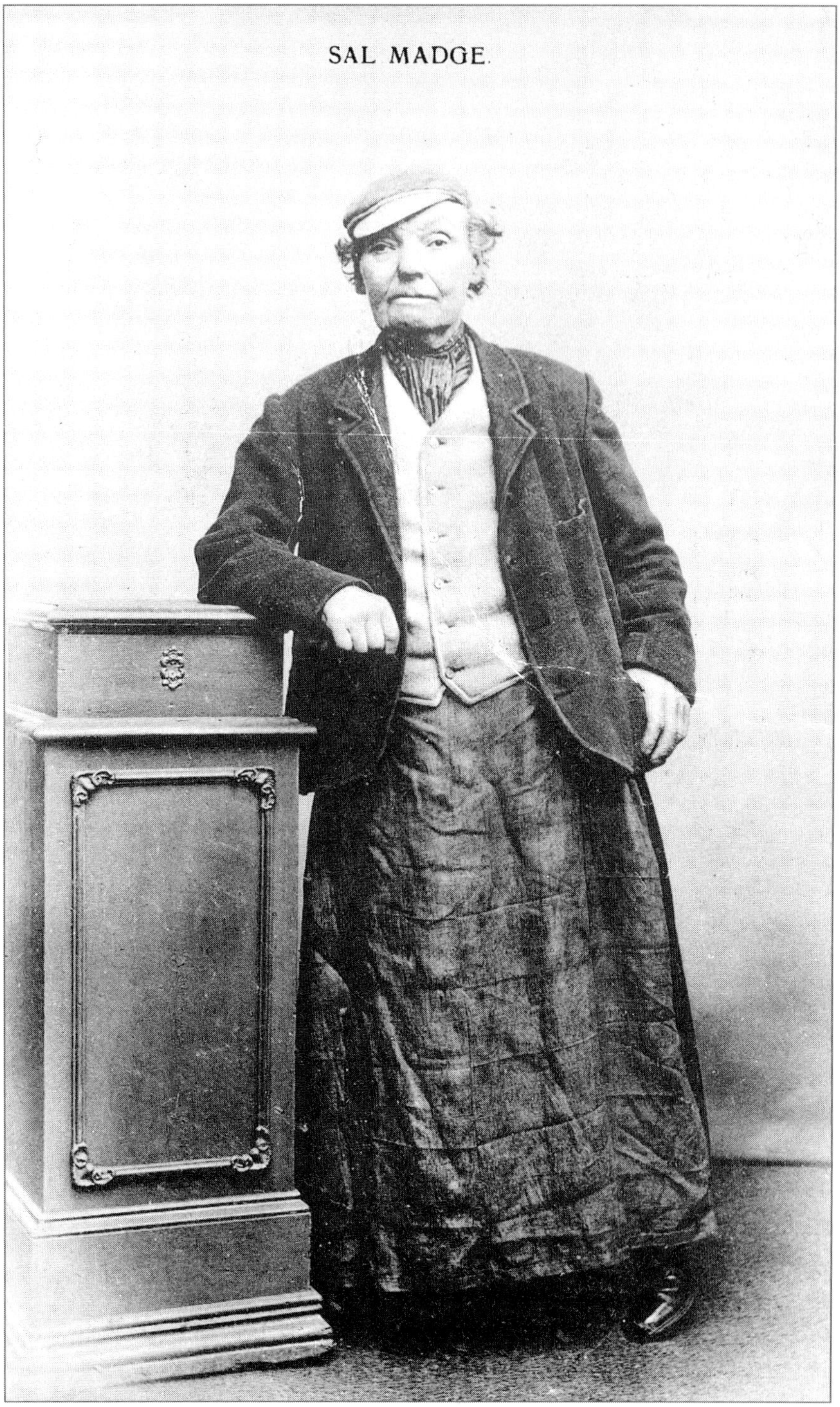

Said to be the last Whitehaven female coalminer, Sal Madge has within the last decade had her story told by Ray Devlin in a booklet obtainable from Whitehaven Museum. Sarah Madgin (1831–99) apparently did not work down the pit, as legend tells, but was a carter in Croft Pit Yard and was also a footballer and wrestler. 'She dearly loved her chew of baccy and drank beer by the pint,' says Devlin, but 'she also possessed a kind heart'. In 1993 the Friends of Whitehaven Museum had a tombstone erected on her previously unmarked pauper's grave. 'Very few women will have had such an arduous life. She is and always will remain part of the history of Whitehaven,' says the dedication. (*John Marsh Collection*)

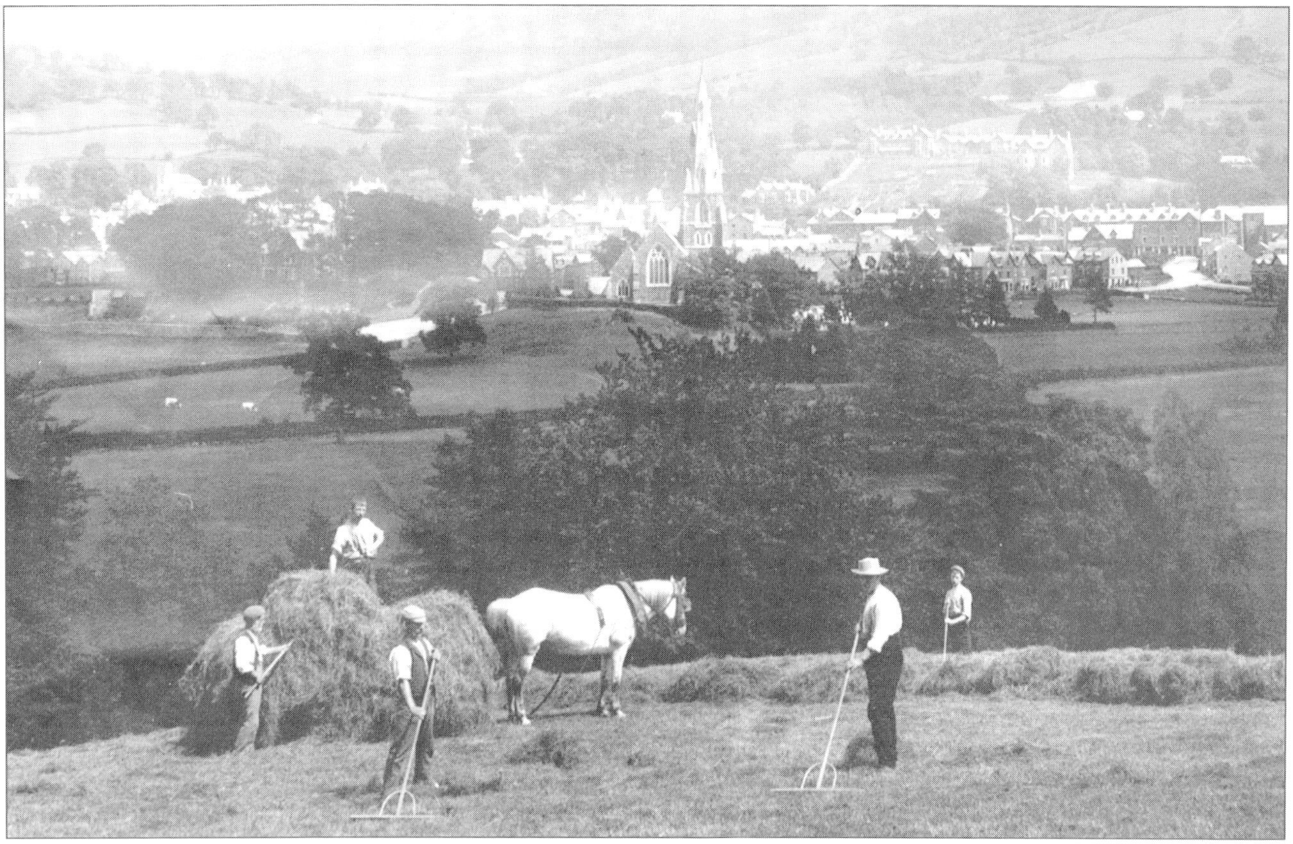

In the fields with the horse at haytime is but a memory in these days of mechanised rolled hay and silaging. In the picture above the hay is being raked together and carted off above Ambleside, and below a youngster poses on the machine when the hay is being turned to dry out above Burton-in-Kendal. (*John Marsh Collection*)

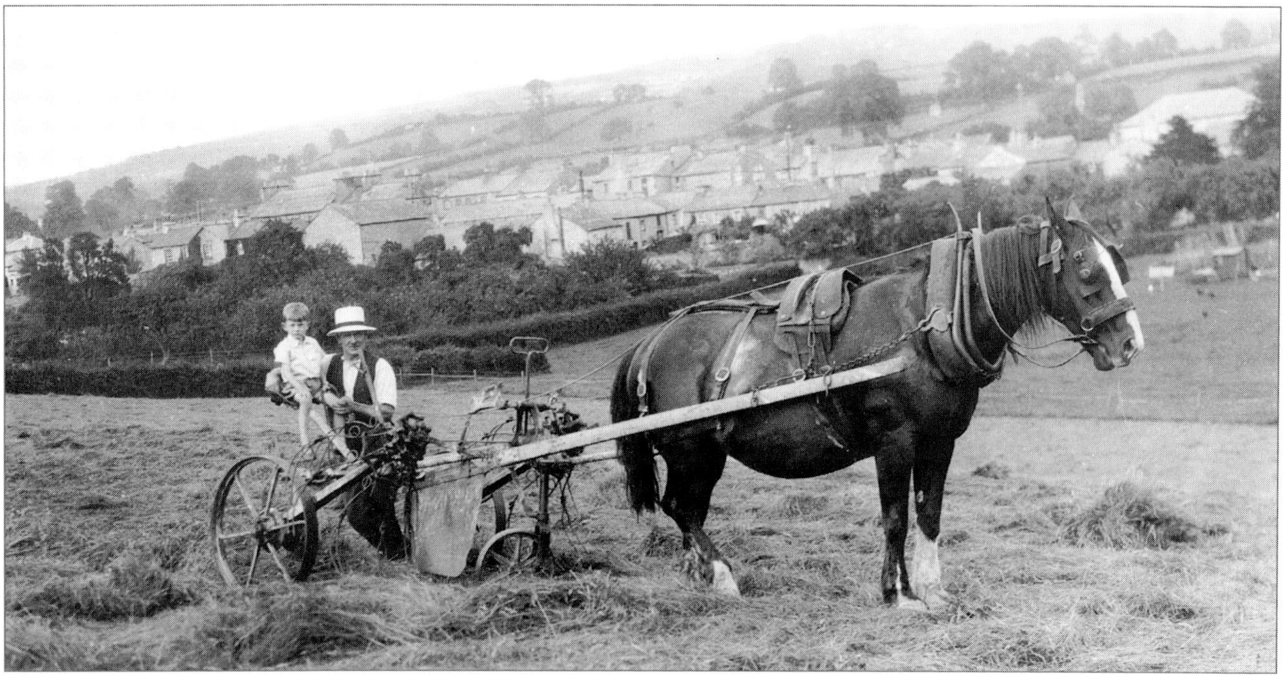

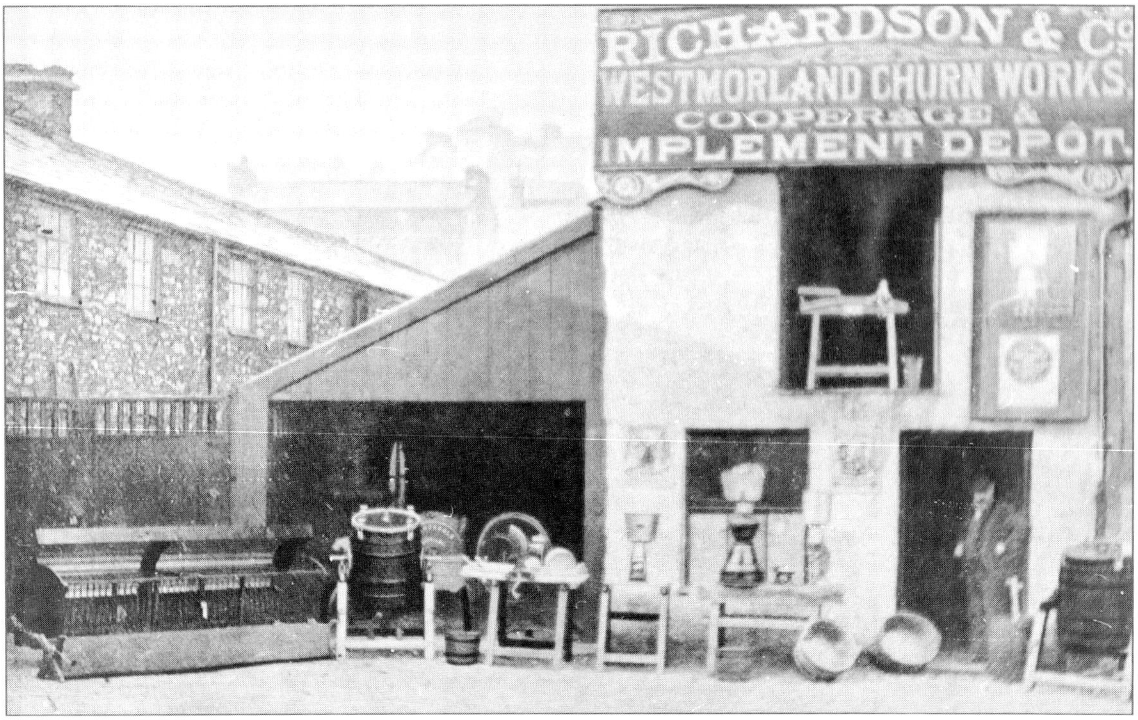

The Westmorland churn works, cooperage and implement depot was run by Richardson & Company in the Old Shambles, Kendal, from the late nineteenth to the early twentieth century. They provided barrels, churns and other implements to local farmers mainly for the dairy industry. (*John Marsh Collection*)

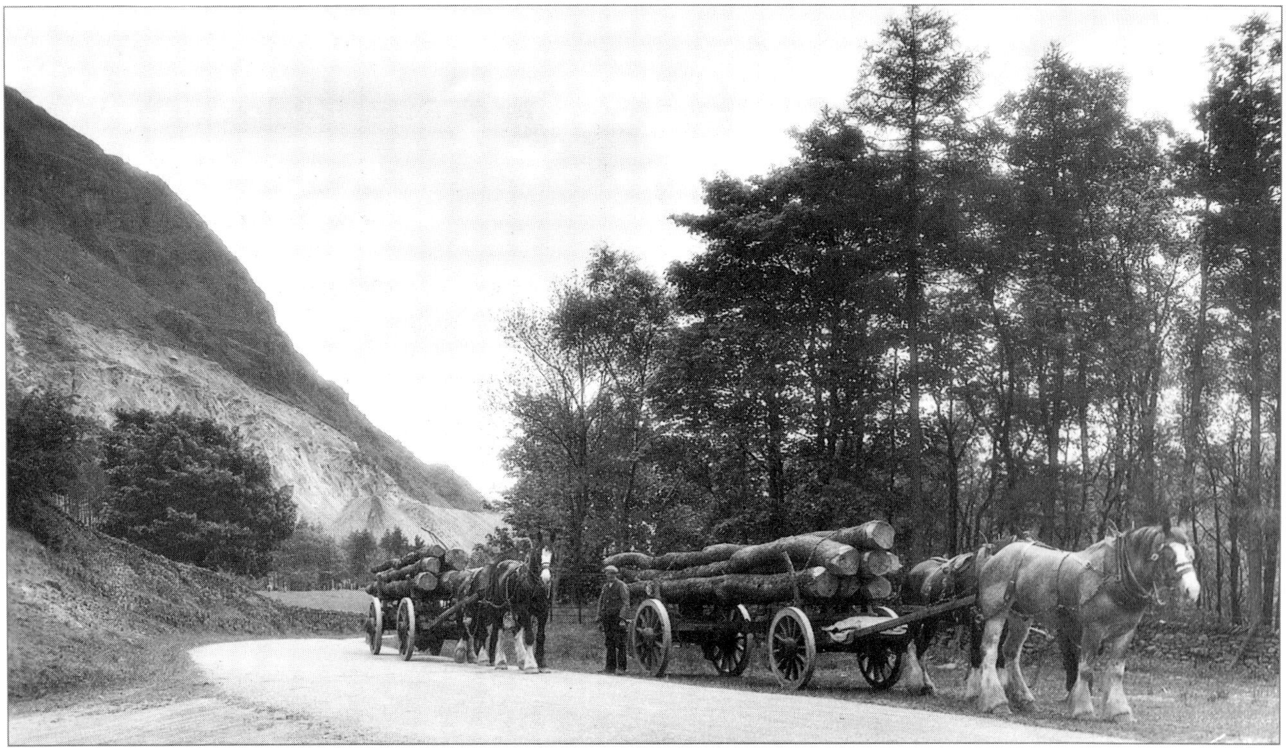

Hauling timber through the vale of St John, 1940s. Horse-drawn wagons were used in the surrounding Manchester Corporation forests, and on the roads, by local timber merchants. (*Walter Scott of Bradford*)

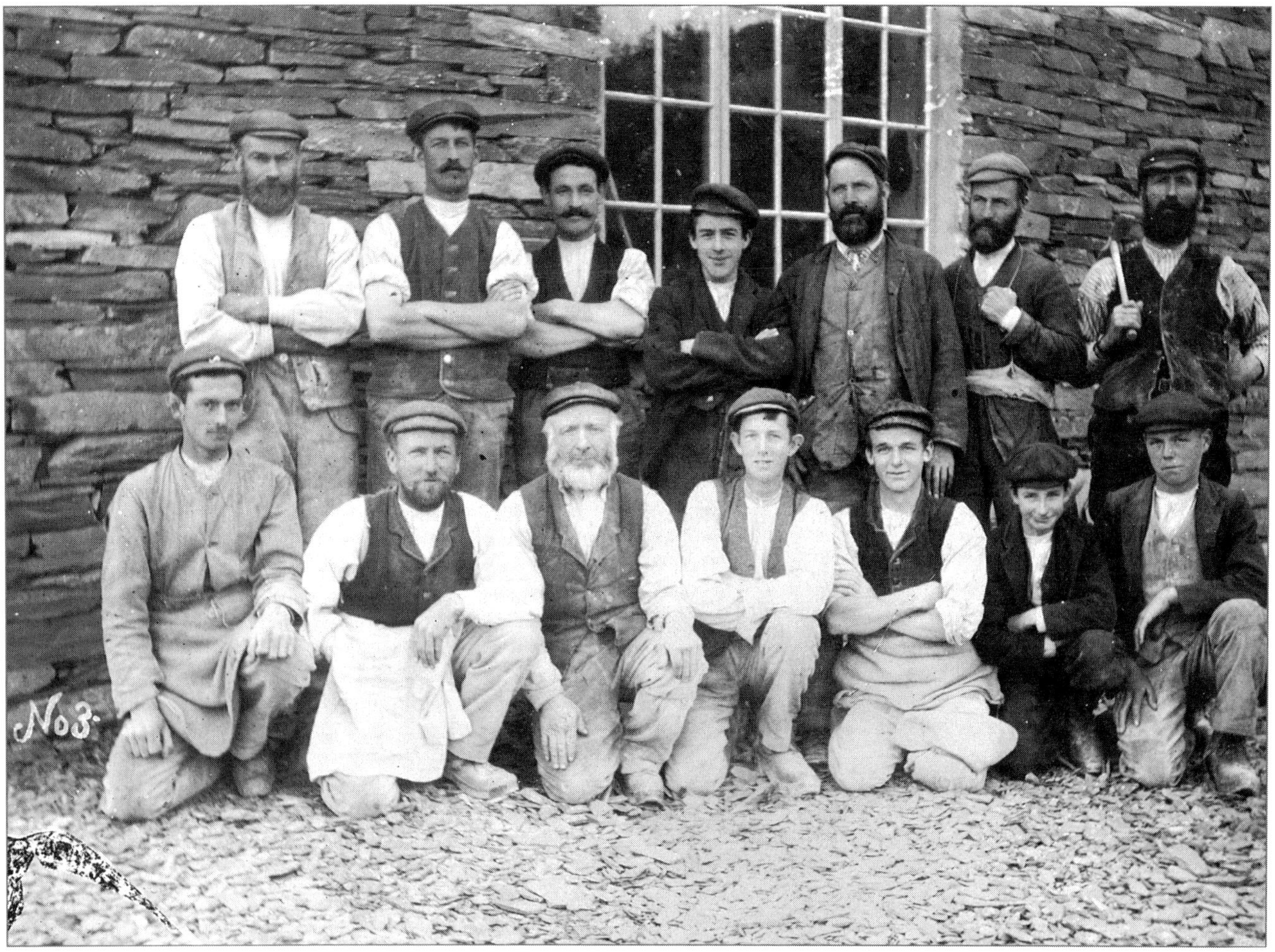

S.G. Lamb of Wellington Street, Millom, photographed this group of Kirkby Moor quarrymen in the early years of the twentieth century. A number of quarry trades can be distinguished by their clothing – stonemasons, slate rivers, labourers and so on. The railway line from Kirkby-in-Furness to Coniston was marked by huge quarries of which the Kirkby Moor quarries of the Duke of Devonshire were the largest. Demand for hardwearing slate for building caused the exploitation of the area, which continues today, with mixed memories for Cumbrians. (*S.G. Lamb of Millom*)

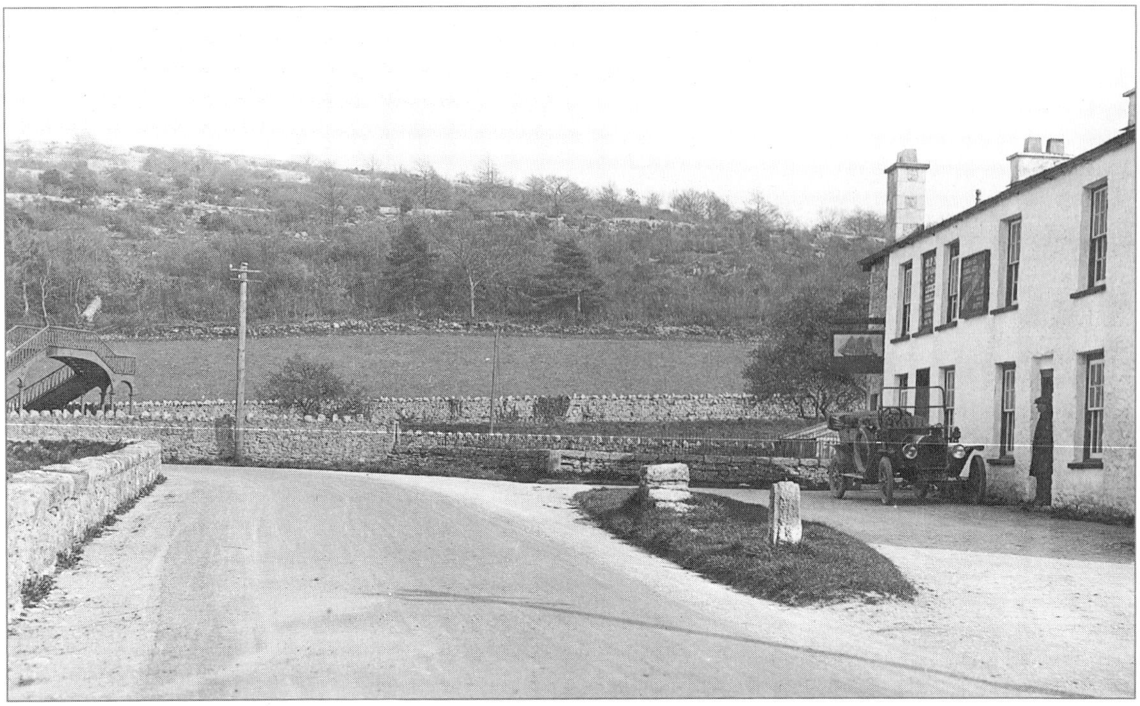

The Ship Inn at Sandside dates from the time when the place was the only port in Westmorland. Atkinson & Pollitt pictured a Model T Ford outside the front door in the 1920s when Sandside was also a minor seaside resort. The footbridge crossed the Hincaster railway branch line which brought most of the visitors to the nearby Sandside station (see also p. 56). (*Atkinson & Pollitt*)

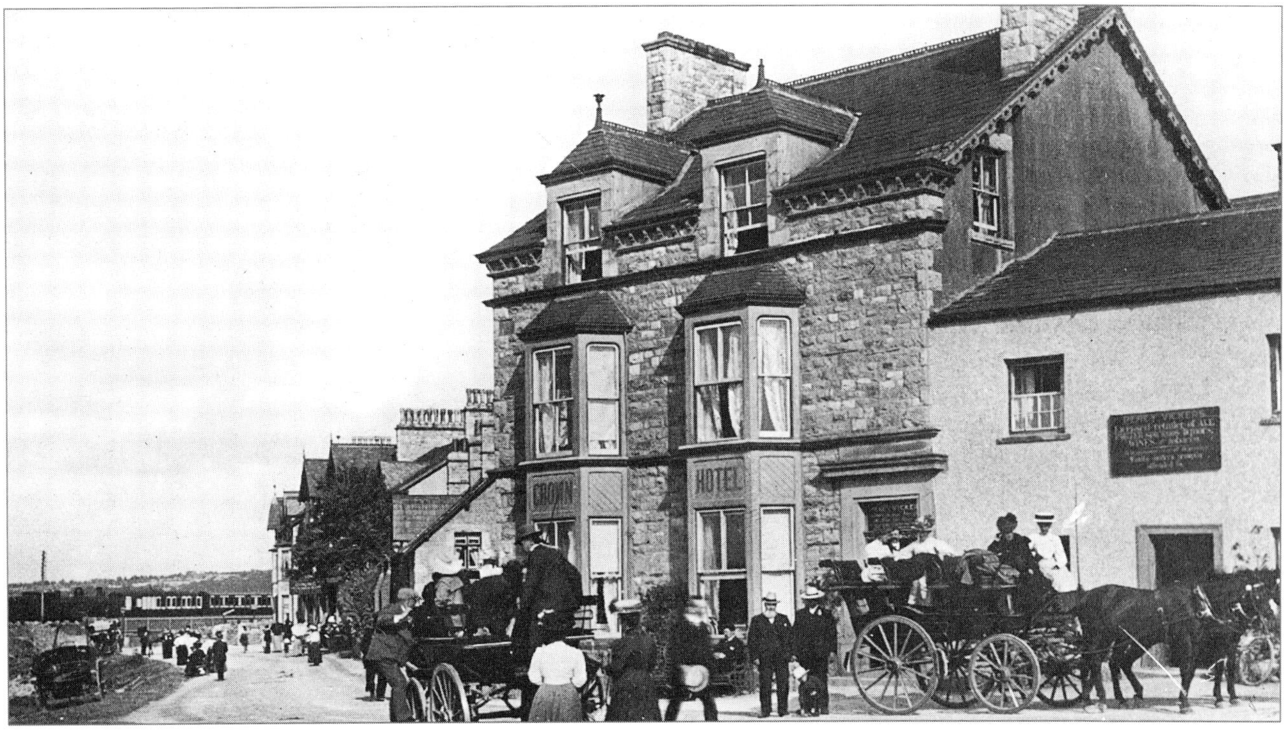

The Crown Hotel at Arnside at the height of an Edwardian summer, with charabanc coaches to convey tourists on trips into the surrounding countryside. In the background a Furness Railway train brings more visitors. (*J.D. Wilson of Arnside*)

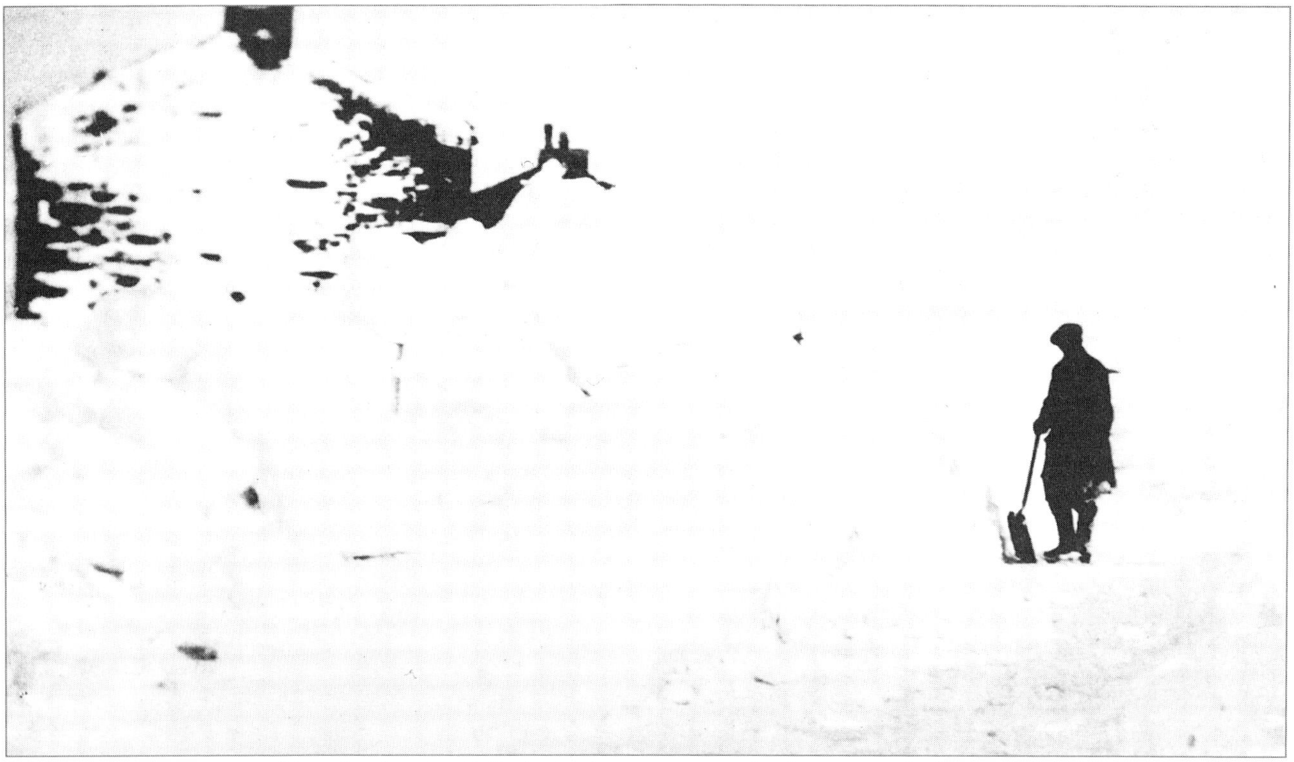

Severe winters were a problem for the Tan Hill, the highest inn in England at 1,732 ft above sea level. Drifts, shown here, almost buried the inn in December 1937. This inn was a place of legend, being surrounded by areas with strong temperance movements. The licensing laws were generally ignored, especially at times of inclement weather, and police supervision was almost impossible until the days of the motor car. (*John Marsh Collection*)

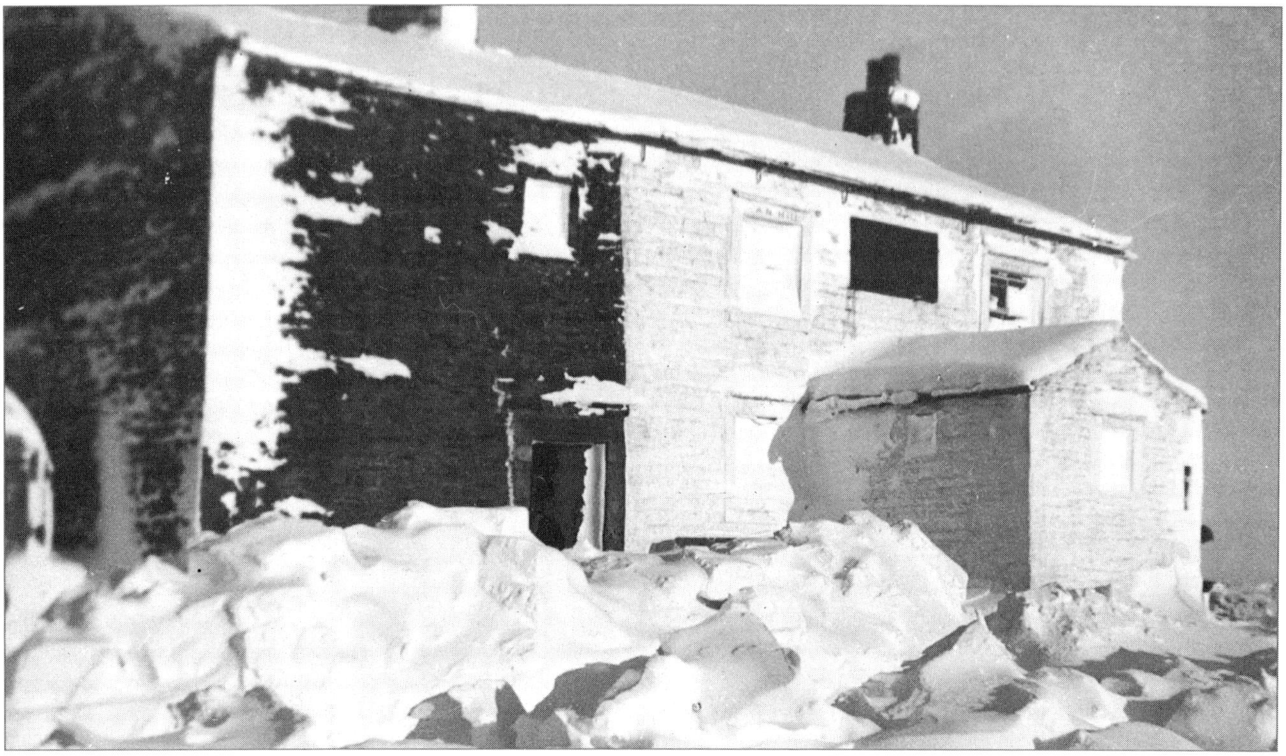

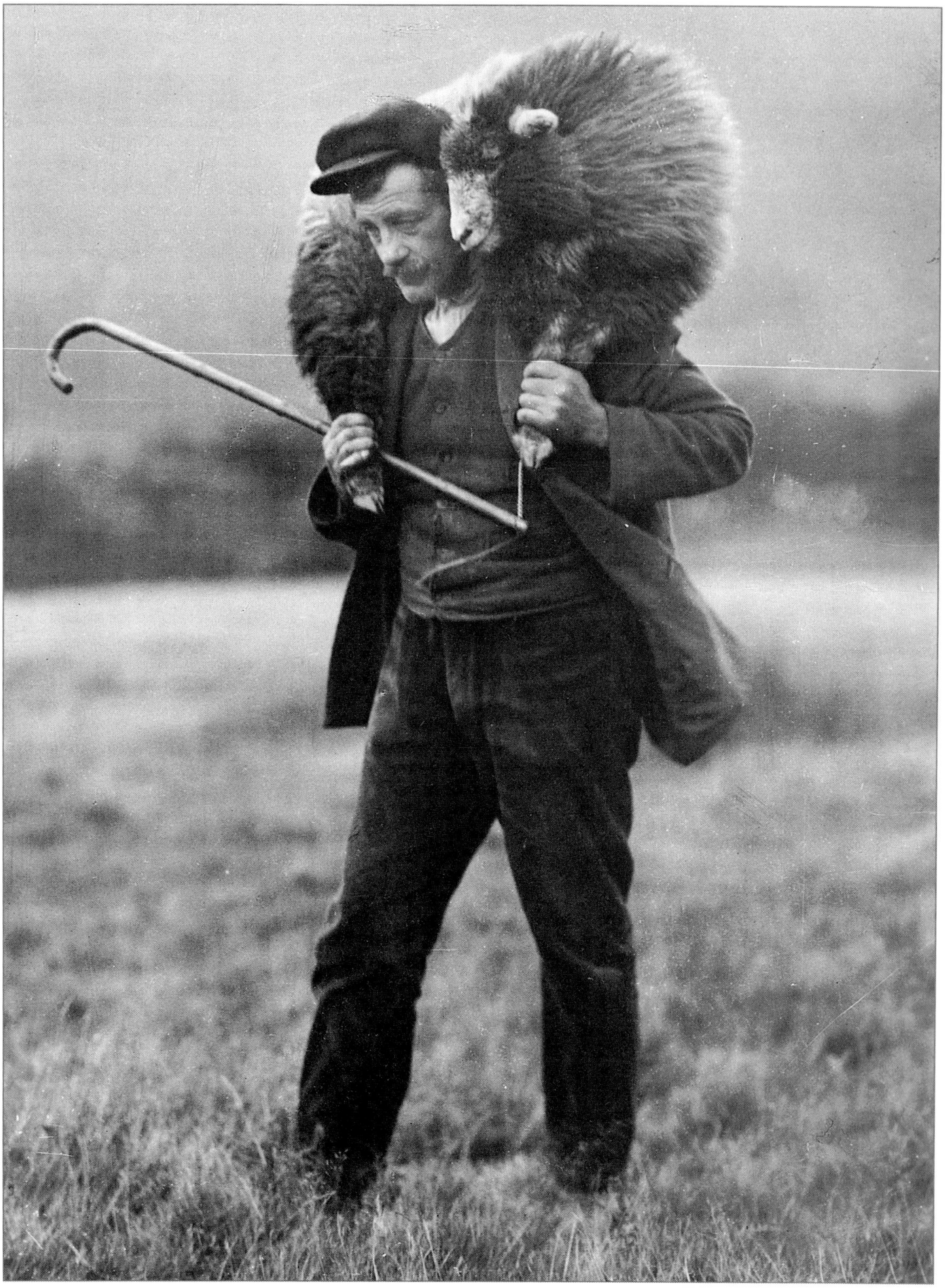

Symbiosis of man and beast warms the shepherd and helps the sheep. Another example of the romanticised version of a shepherd's life was sold by Keswick photographers Abrahams to the thousands of visitors to the Lake District every year. (*Abrahams of Keswick*)

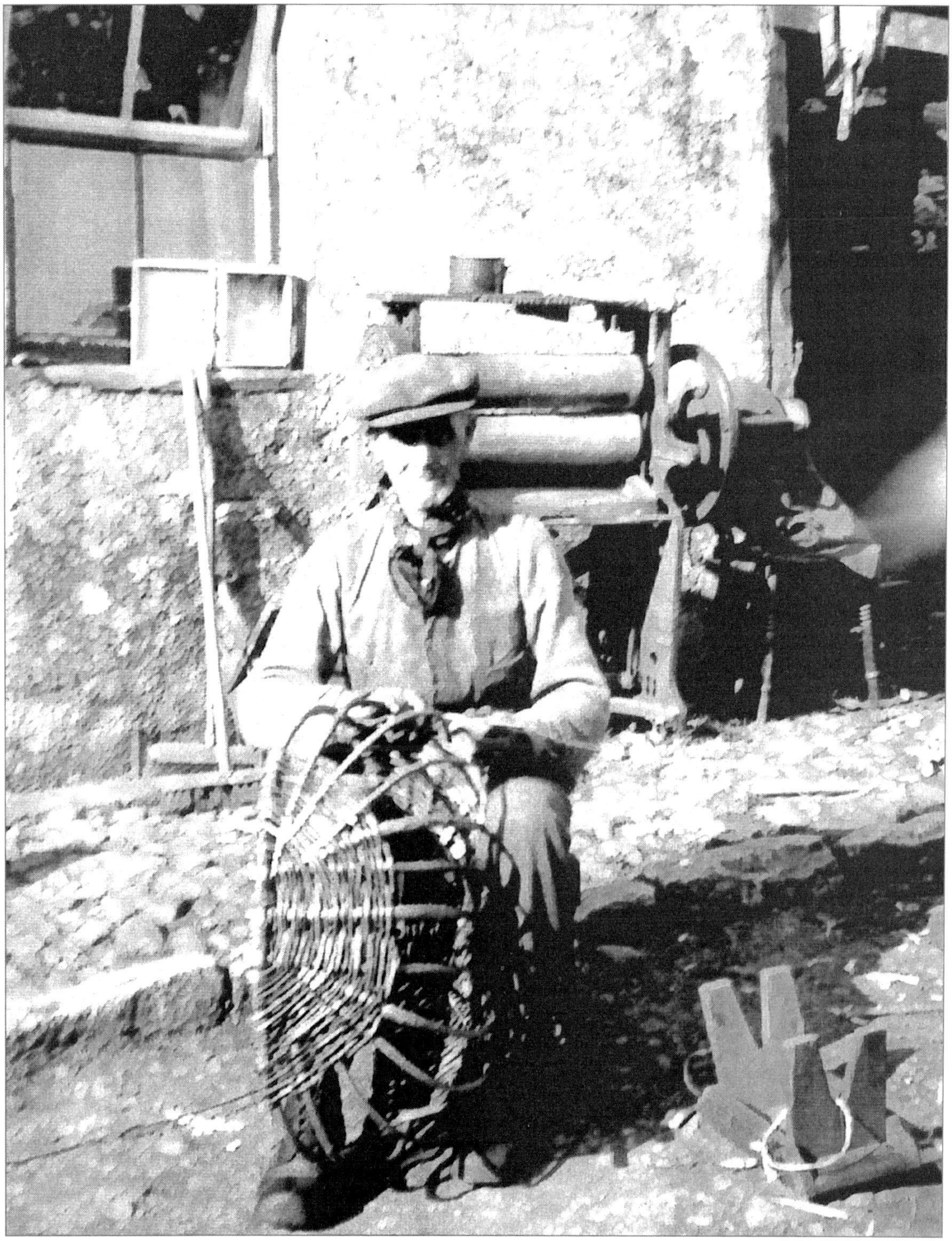

Swill basket making was a traditional home industry when everyone used the useful baskets for both industrial and domestic purposes. Here in a yard in Cockermouth a local expert works to supply the demand in that area. In some areas swill baskets (or skips) were produced in near factory conditions, but production still depended on what is now almost a lost skill. Possession of traditional skills such as this kept the wolf from the door all over Cumbria up to the time of the Second World War. (*T. Allan Collection*)

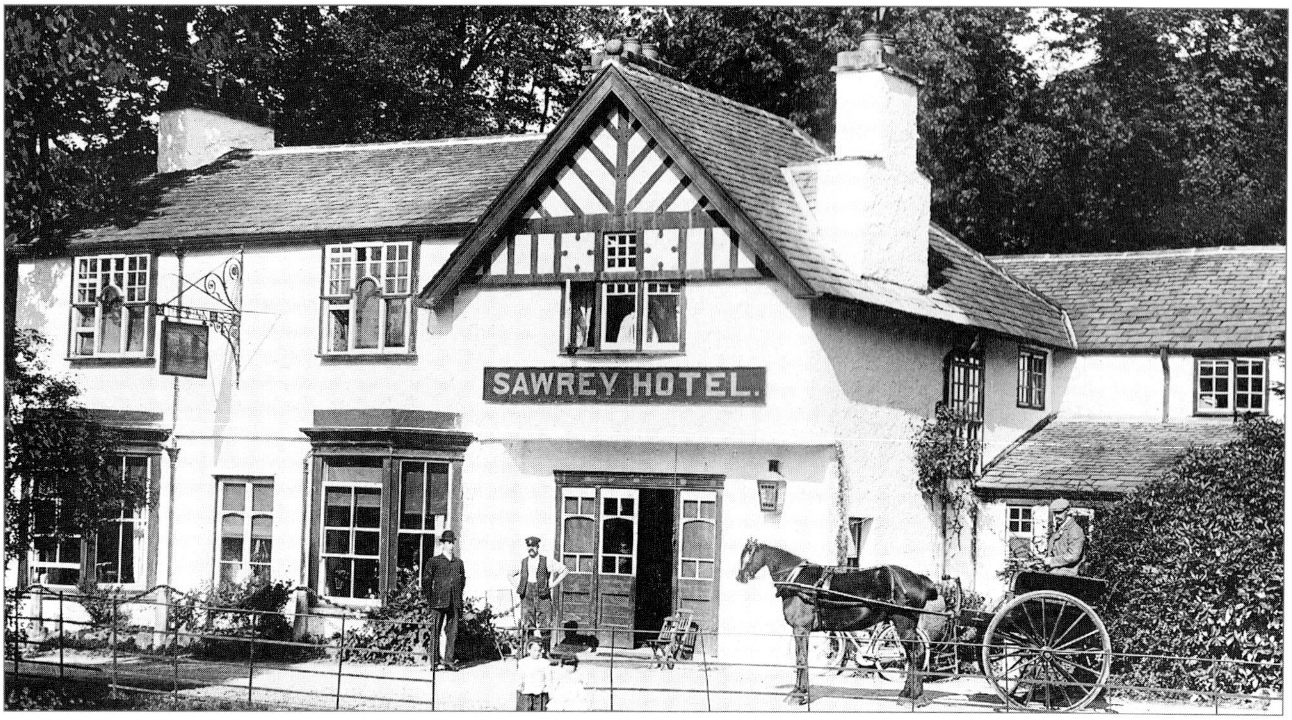

Hotels at Far Sawrey and Ferry Nab housed many Lakes visitors between 1900 and 1950. Above, Nelson Coward of Brinstock is seen in his trap in Far Sawrey. (*Brittain & Wright*) Below, one of the rowing boats for hire at the now closed Ferry Hotel is in the typical Windermere style. The Ferry Hotel became the laboratories and offices of the Freshwater Biological Association, which led the way for environmental studies in the Lakes. (*Maysons of Keswick*)

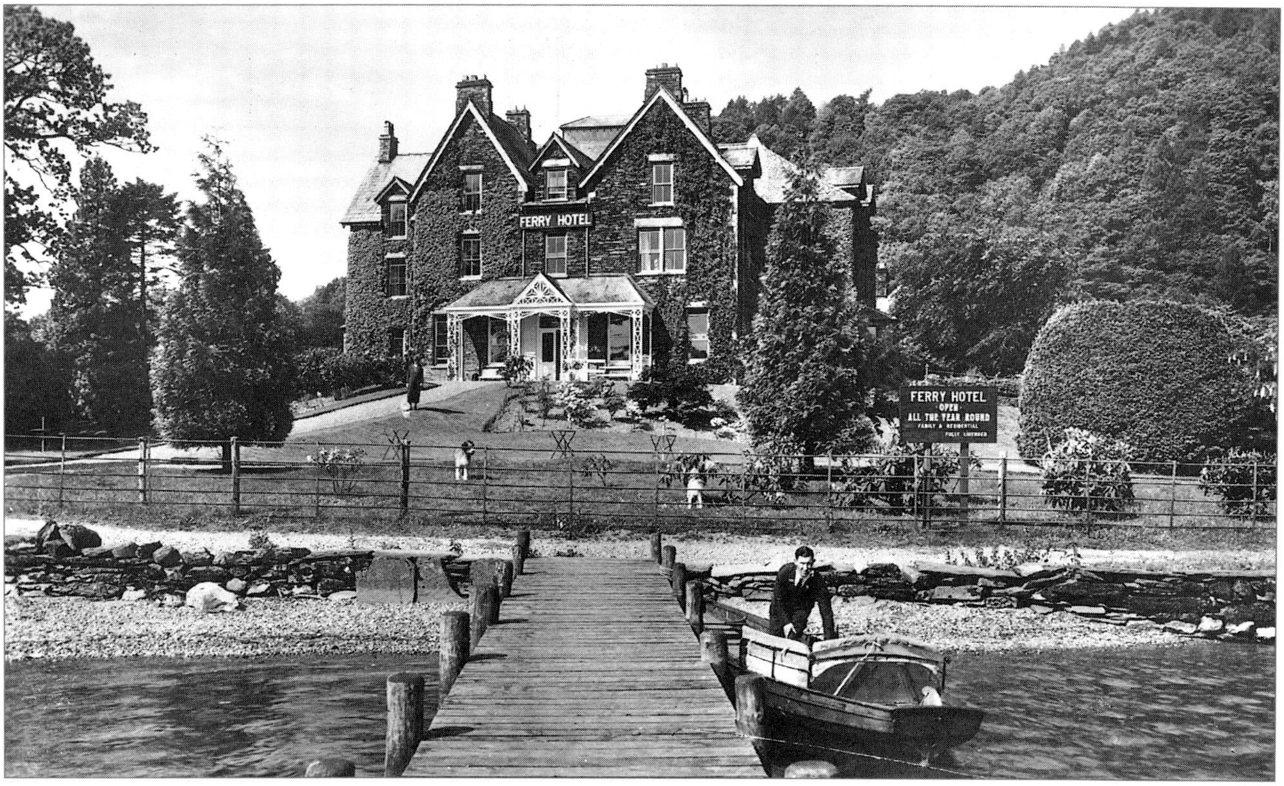

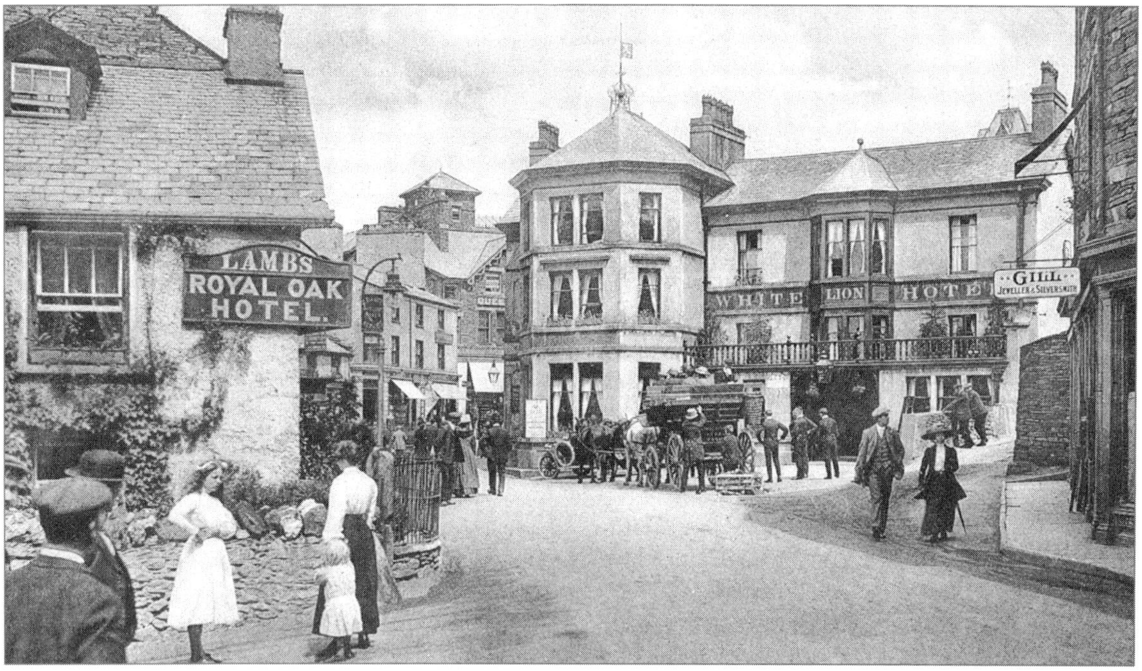

Ambleside main street is seen in differing circumstances: above is a Rigg's horse coach loading outside the White Lion Hotel. (*Frith's of Reigate*) Below and later, in the 1920s, the Rushbearing procession is passing the front of the Queen's Hotel. The motor transport age has ruined this ancient thoroughfare in living memory and Ambleside traffic now remains a problem for which politicians apparently can find no answer. Similar villages in continental beauty spots do not seem to have the same difficulty, using tunnels and bypasses to clear the pollution off their streets. (*Wilmot of Ambleside*)

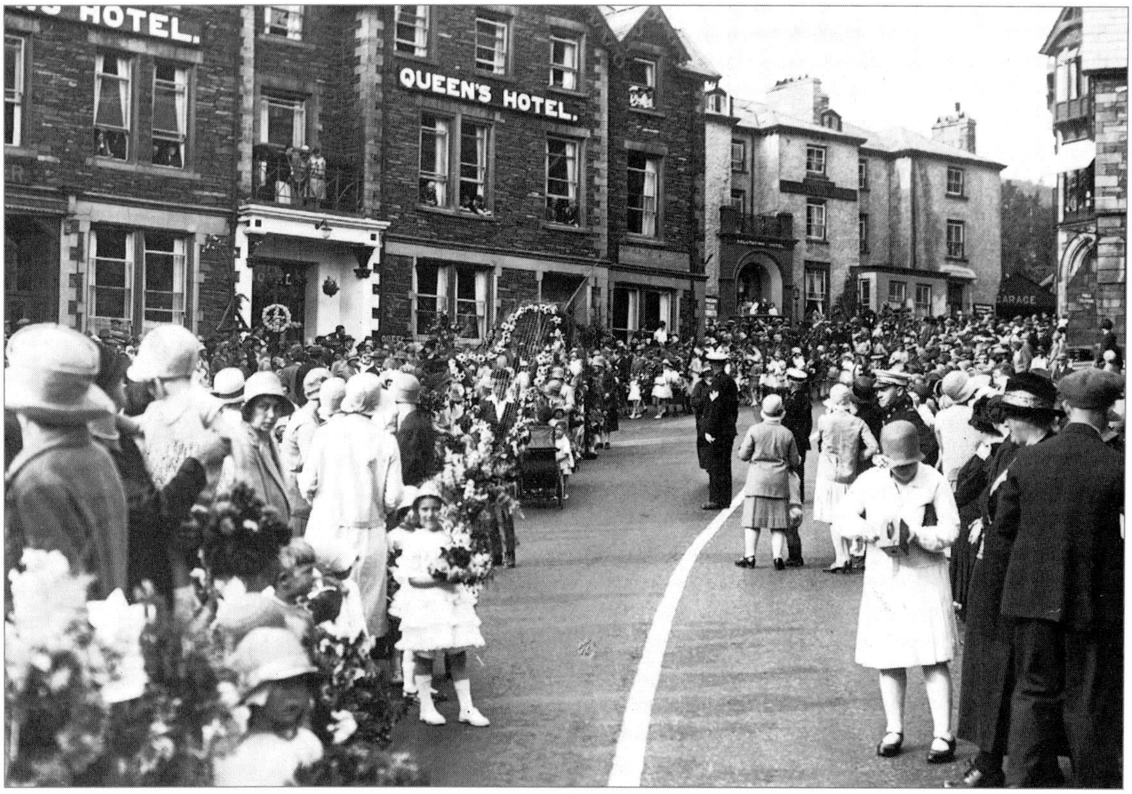

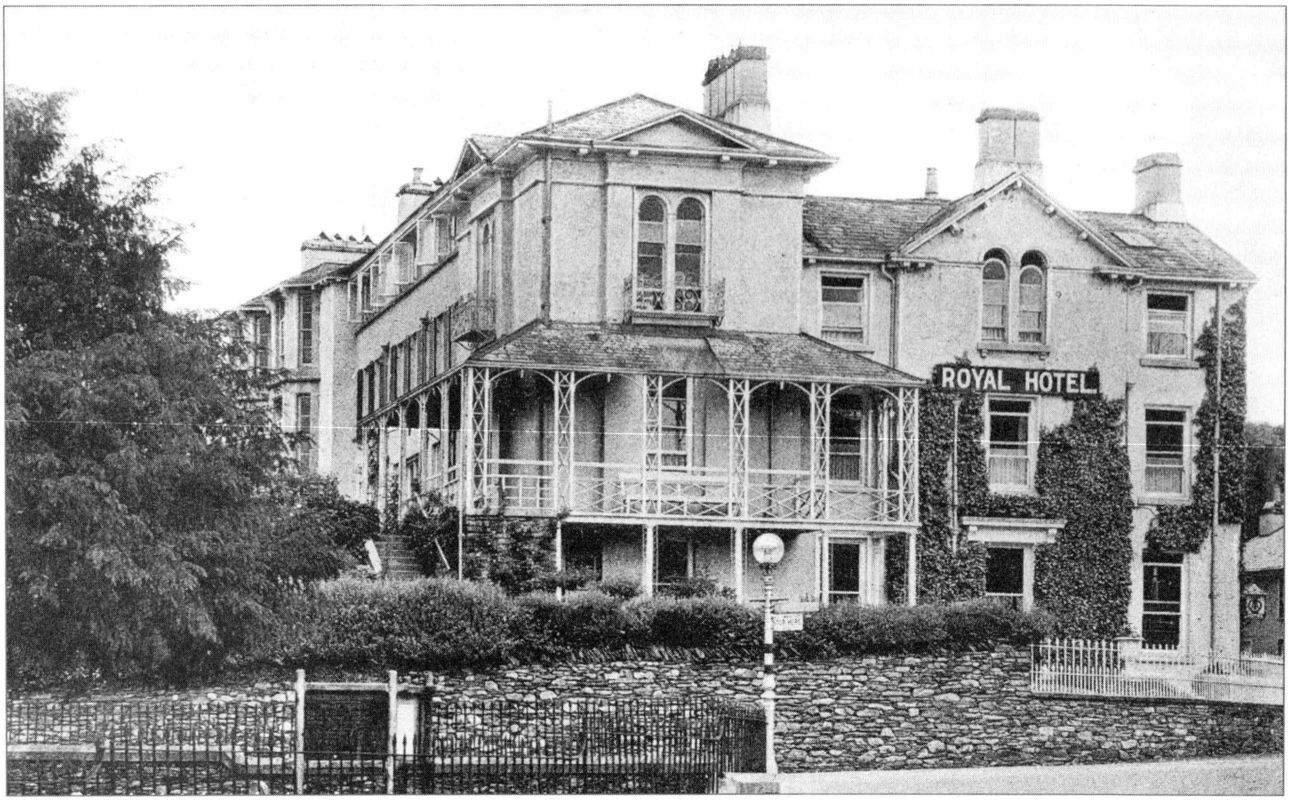

The change in appearance of the Royal Hotel at Bowness-on-Windermere is marked in these two photographs taken some decades apart from St Martin's Square. The balcony and street lamp have disappeared, cars have arrived but the AA sign persists. (*John Marsh Collection*)

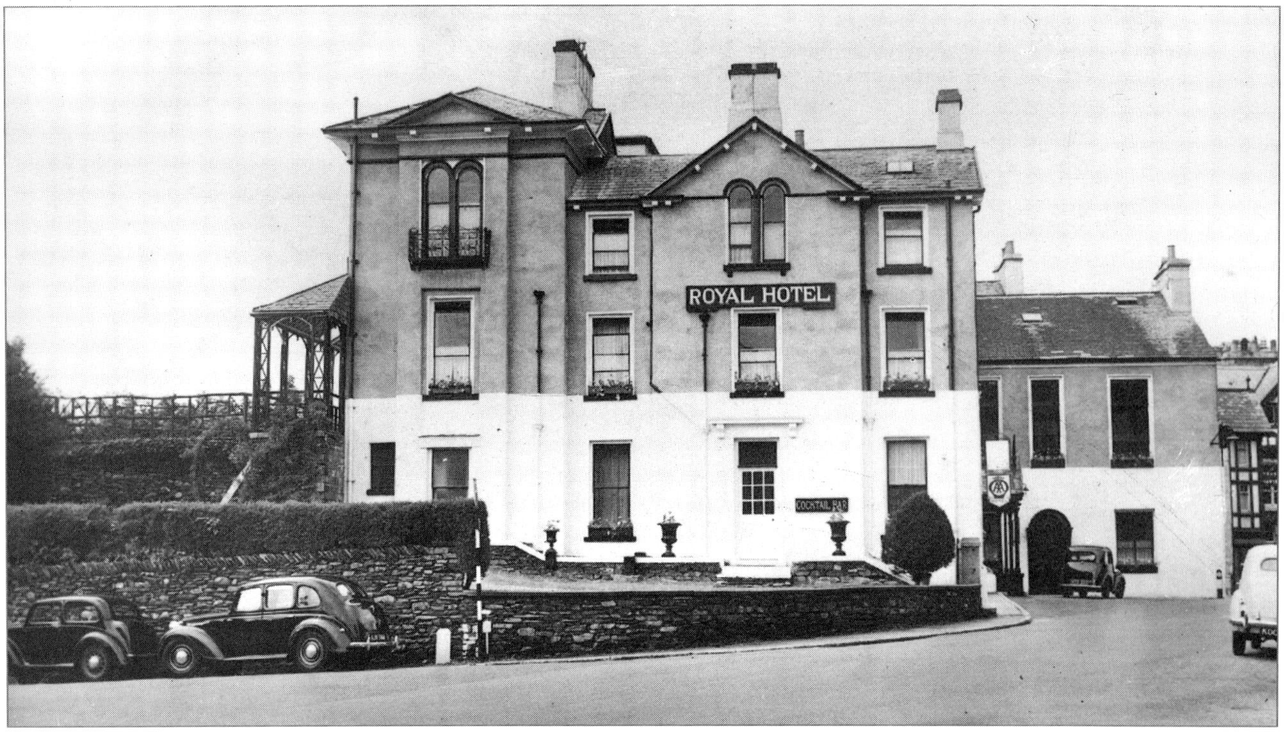

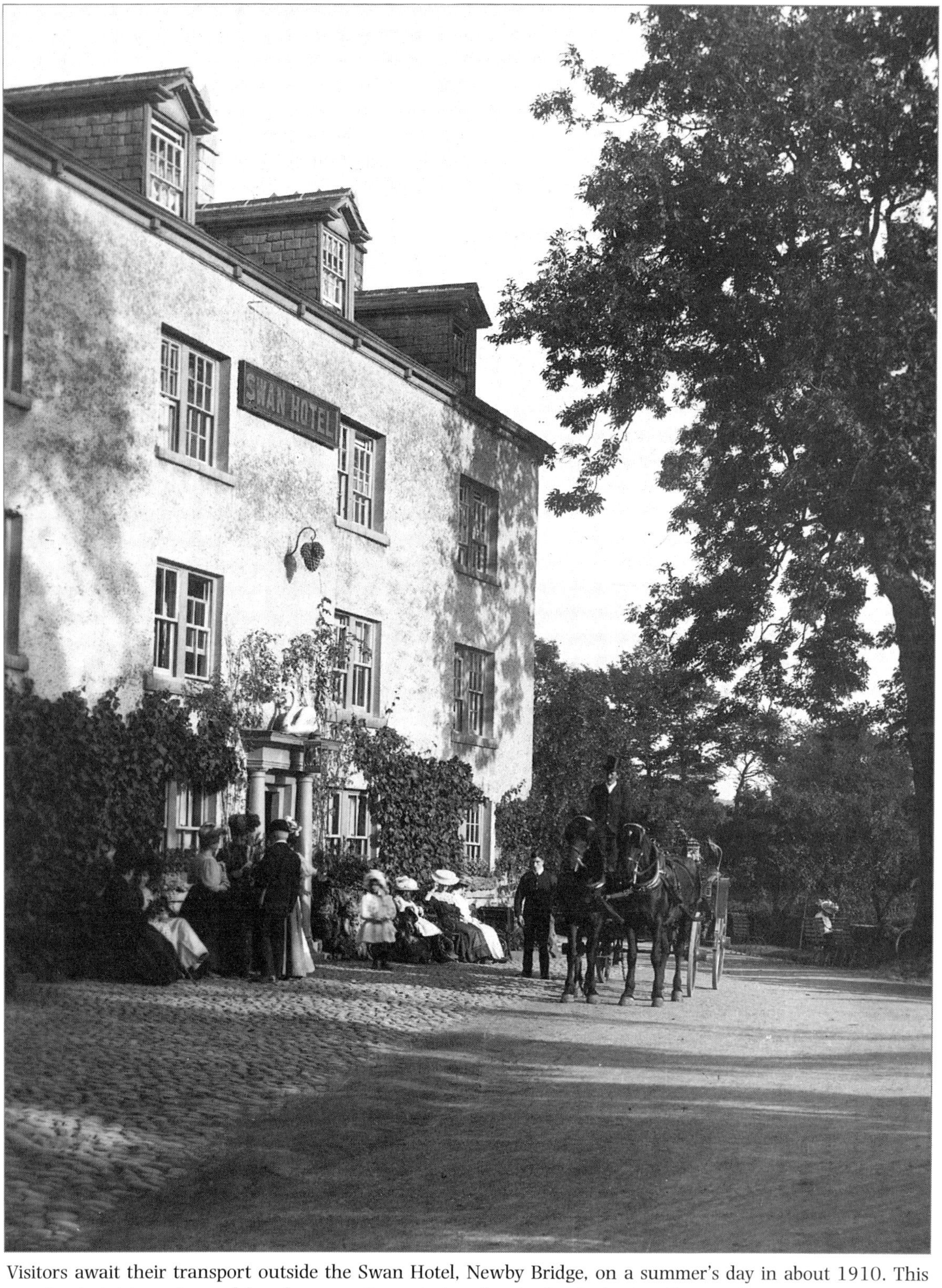

Visitors await their transport outside the Swan Hotel, Newby Bridge, on a summer's day in about 1910. This popular hotel has changed hands many times, but owing to its choice location continues to attract many visitors. Formerly it had almost its own station on the Furness Railway Lakeside branch from Ulverston. (*John Marsh Collection*)

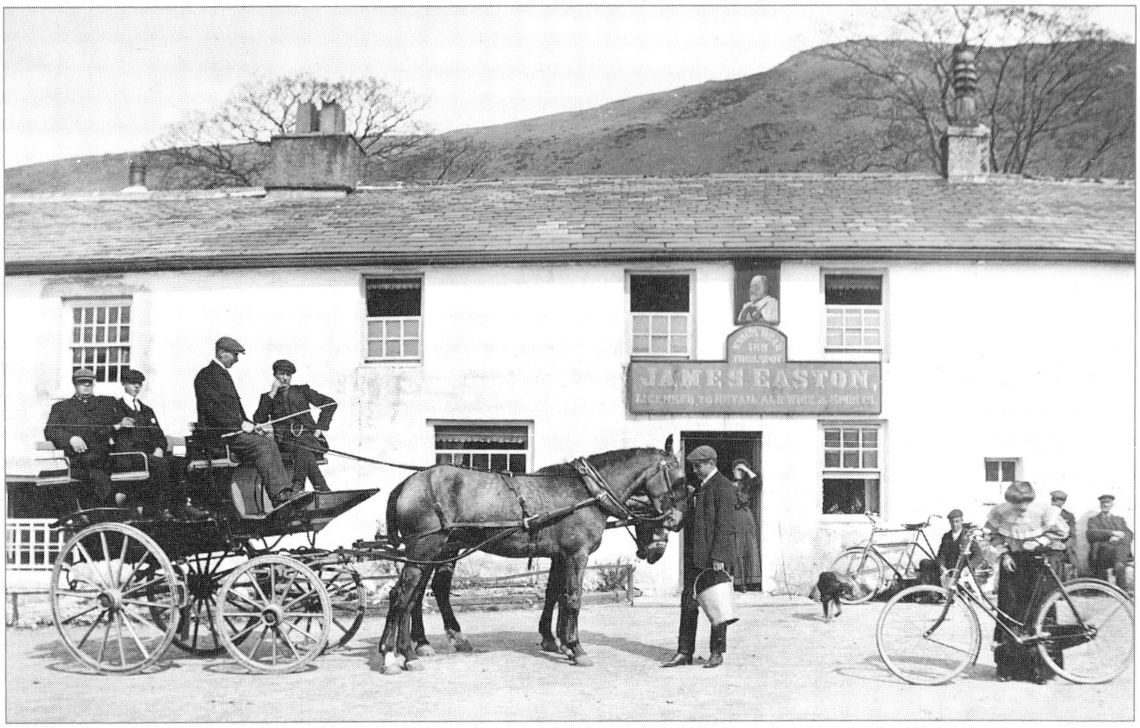

The King's Head, Thirlspot, survived the 1890s flooding of the valley and is now a busy roadside hostelry, seen here before the First World War. The horses are being fed and watered in anticipation of the long climb past Thirlmere and over Dunmail Raise. (*John Marsh Collection*)

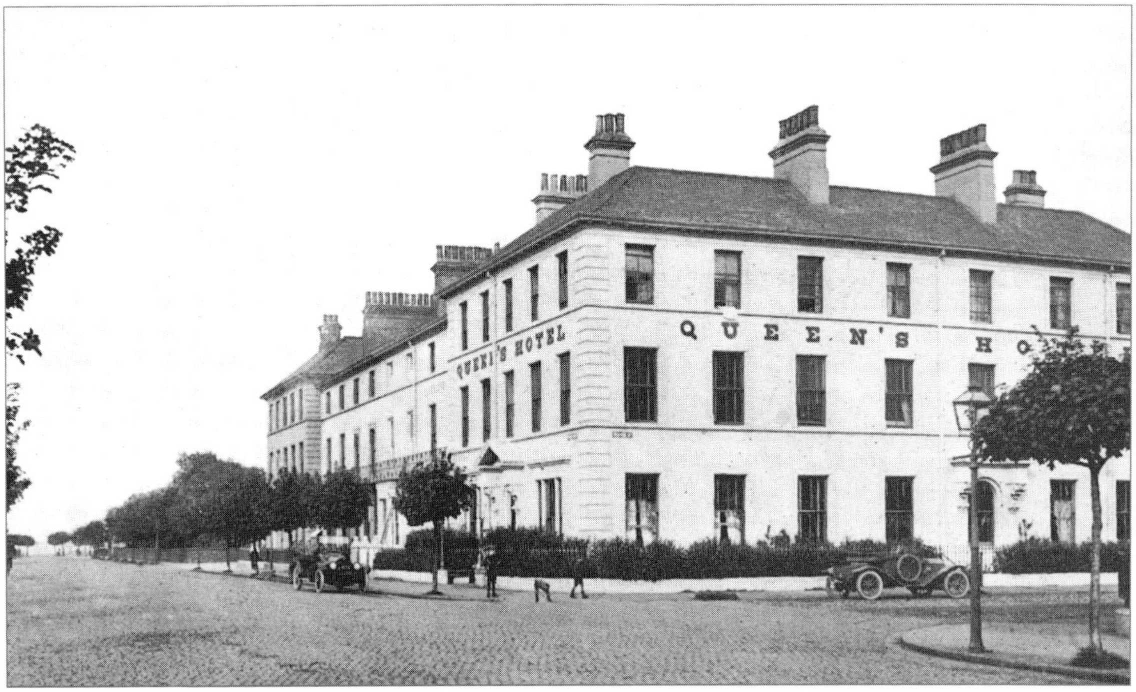

Criffel Street, Silloth, included the Balmoral Hotel, the Criffel Hotel and the Solway Hotel as well as the magnificent Queen's Hotel, seen here around the time of the First World War. Silloth was a purpose-built holiday resort from the middle of the nineteenth century and the profusion of boarding houses and hotels indicates the expected number of visitors. (*Armstrong of Silloth*)

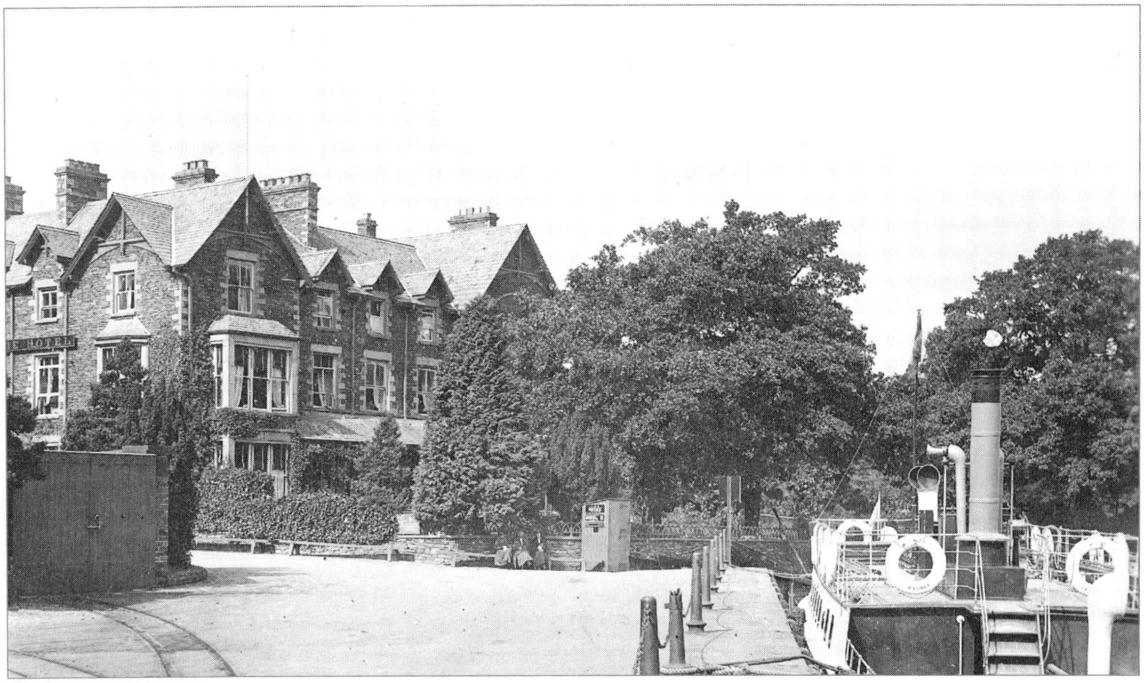

The Furness Railway motor yacht *Cygnet* stands guard over the Lakeside Hotel and empty quayside in the 1920s. The large doors on the left hide the coalyard from which skips of coal were used to refuel the lake steamers before diesel was introduced by the LMS railway. The Lakeside Hotel was known to issue postcards with the adjoining railway station and quay obscured by drawn-in trees. (*Atkinson & Pollitt*)

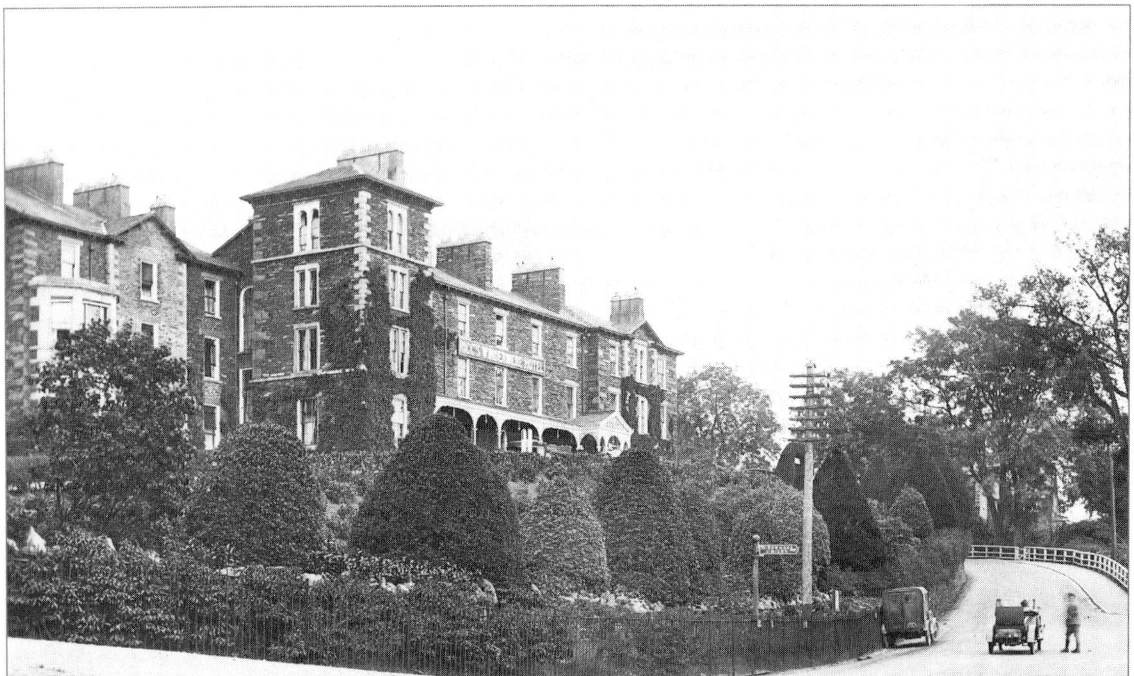

Atkinson & Pollitt visited Windermere on a quiet summer's day in the 1920s and there photographed the imposing Rigg's Hotel. The Rigg family was sufficiently connected to the LNWR to be allowed to erect this large hotel next to Windermere station from where they ran horse coaches to Keswick. (*Atkinson & Pollitt*)

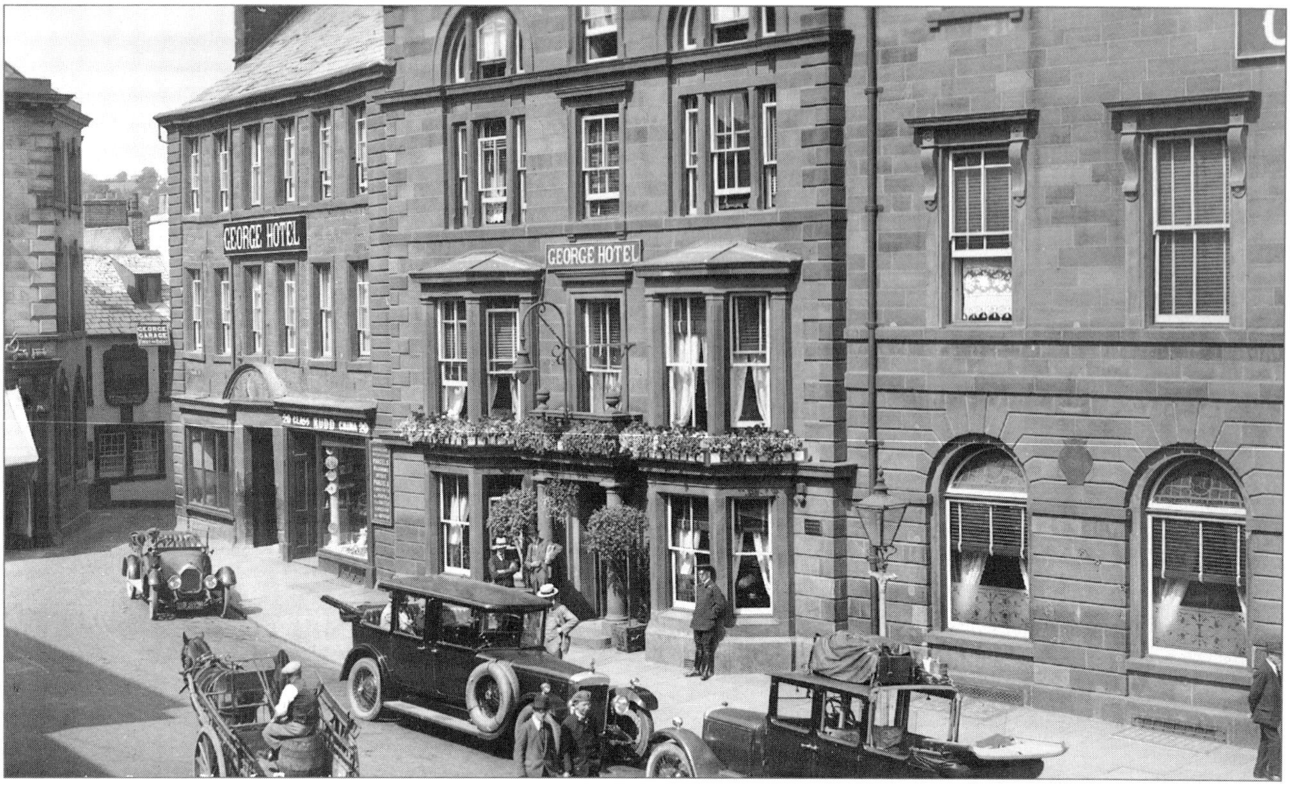

Two views of the George Hotel in the centre of Penrith show, above, the exterior in the 1920s and below, the interior somewhat earlier. Note the staff time-clock on the left among the potted palms. (*John Marsh Collection*)

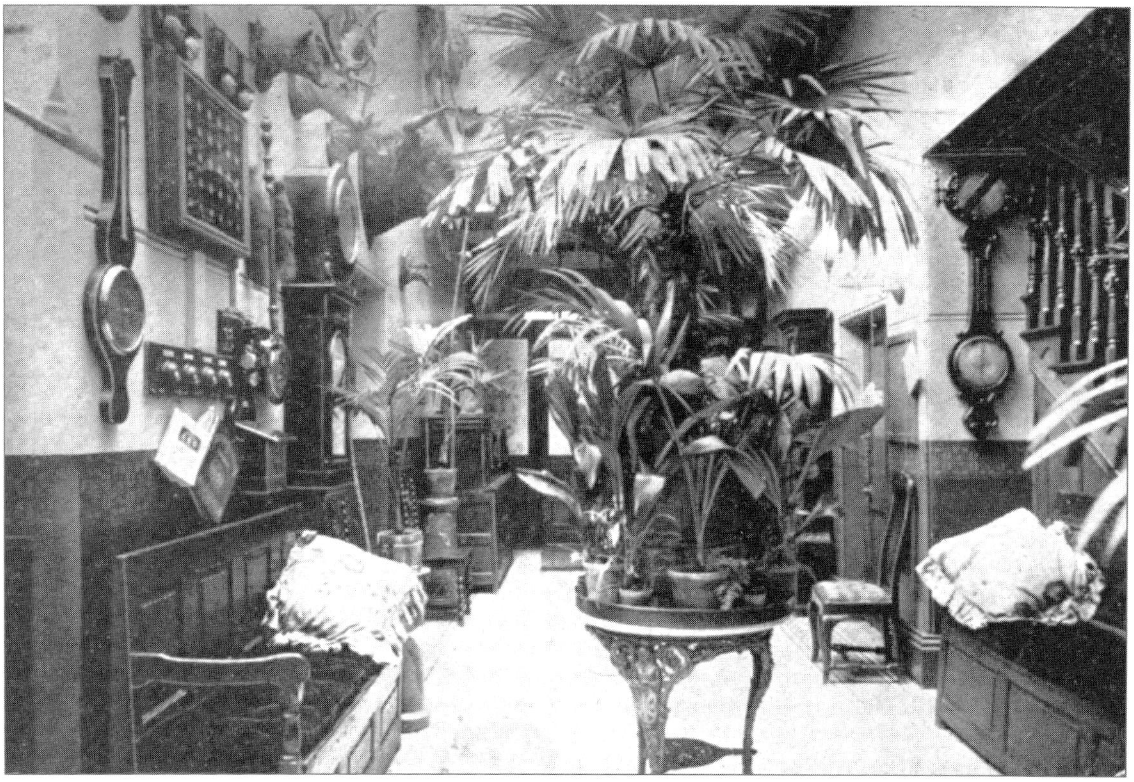

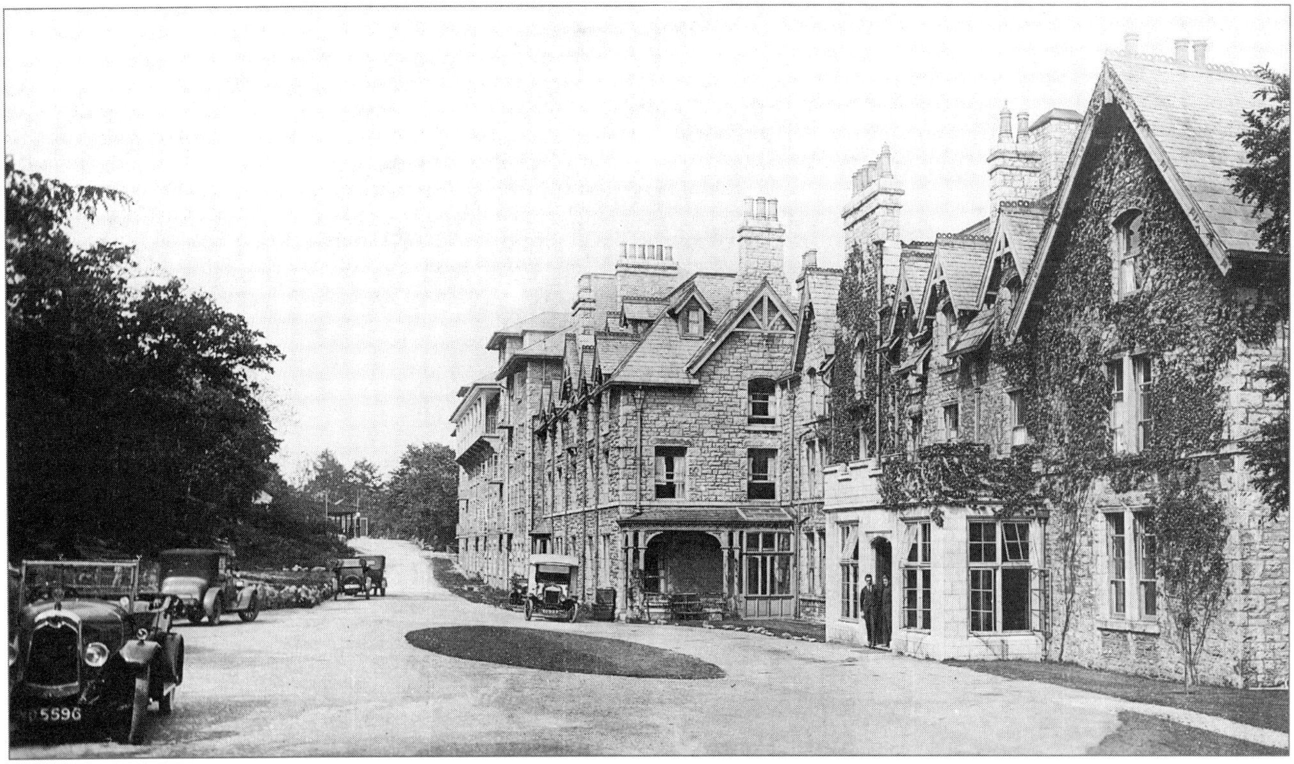

The Golf Hotel at Grange-over-Sands has changed its name frequently since it was photographed by Atkinson & Pollitt in the 1920s. Above, the exterior when a group of motor cars had no problem in finding a place to park and below, the 1920s-style plainly furnished lounge. (*Atkinson & Pollitt*)

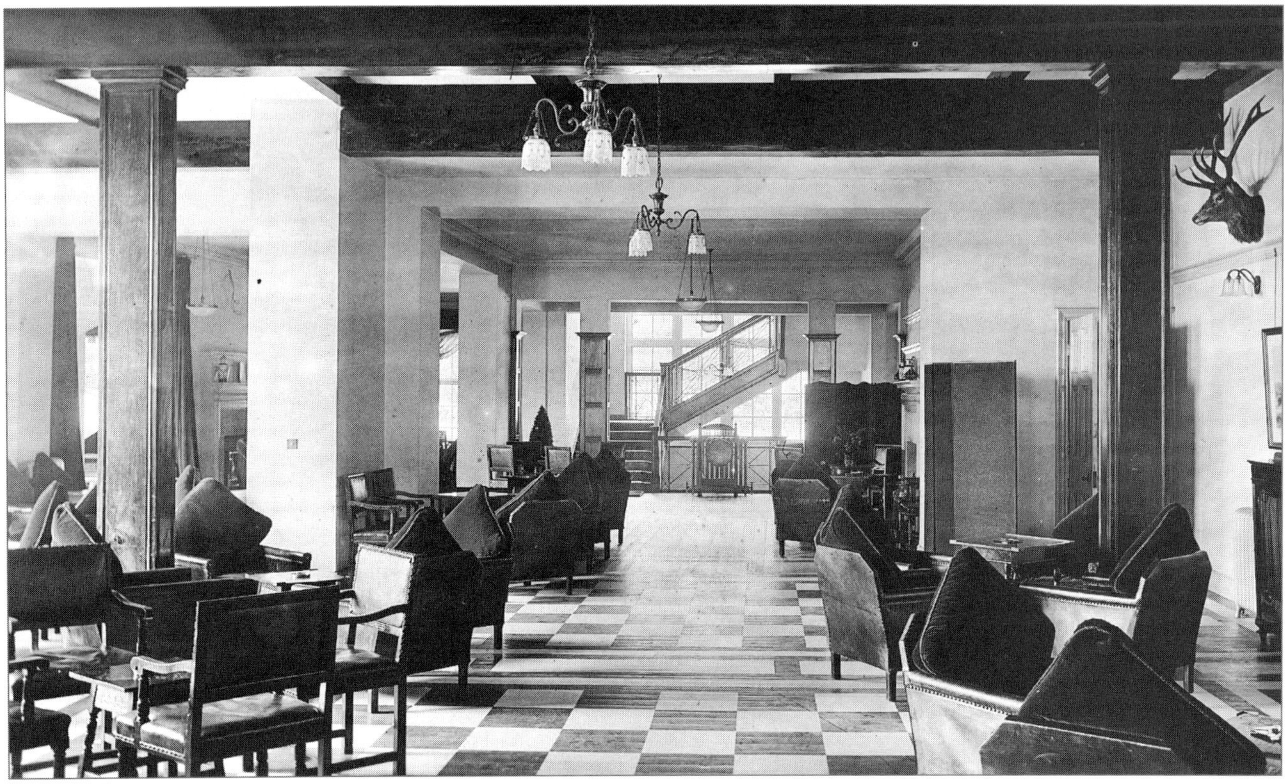

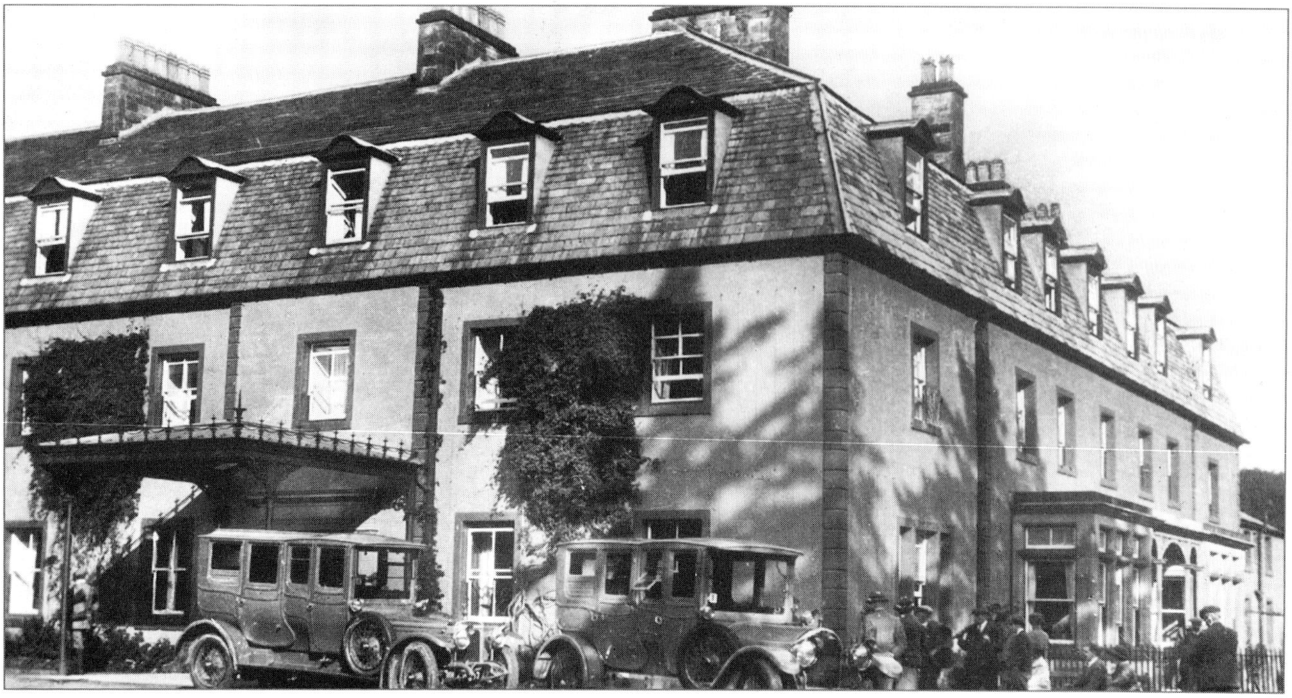

The Shap Wells Hotel on 3 July 1936 when R.J. Clark was the proprietor. This hotel was to be surrounded by barbed wire and transformed into a prisoner-of-war camp for Nazi officers only a few years later. Some of the prisoners found the experience so pleasant that they returned frequently after the war was over. The guards who lived in huts in an adjoining field showed no similar inclination, it is reported. (*John Marsh Collection*)

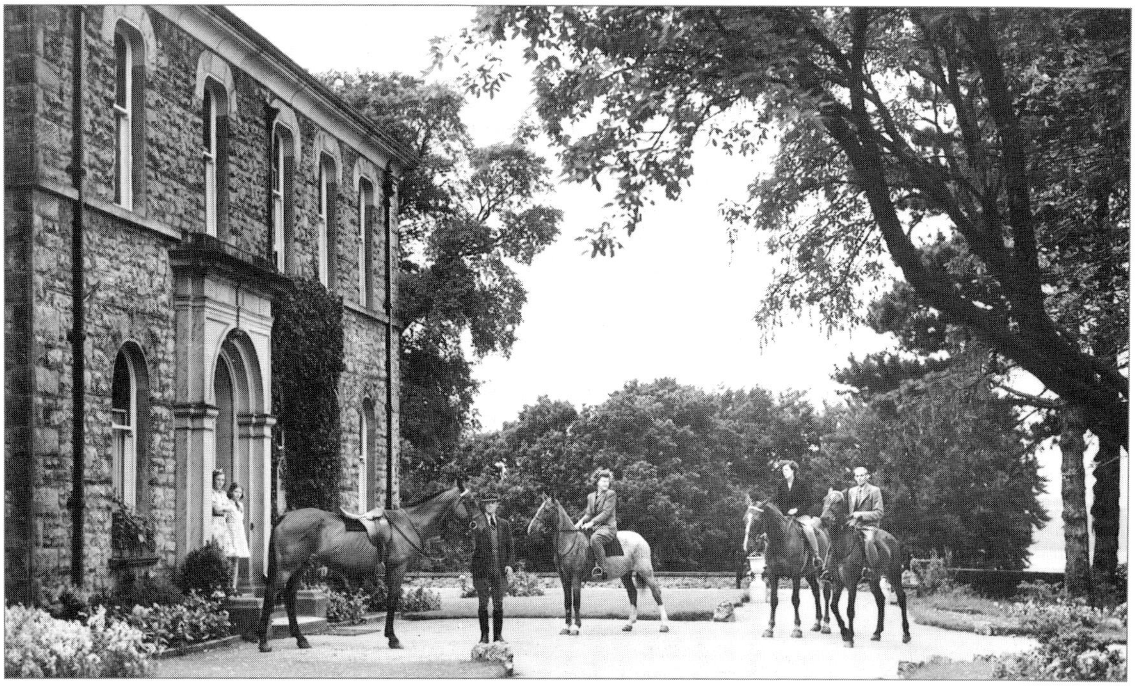

The Inglemere Hotel at Arnside was in a building designed as a house by a Kendal solicitor. It later became a private school for girls. Between the wars the headmistress decided that it would make a better hotel. It must be a loss to the village of Arnside that after the Second World War it was demolished to make way for houses and bungalows. (*John Marsh Collection*)

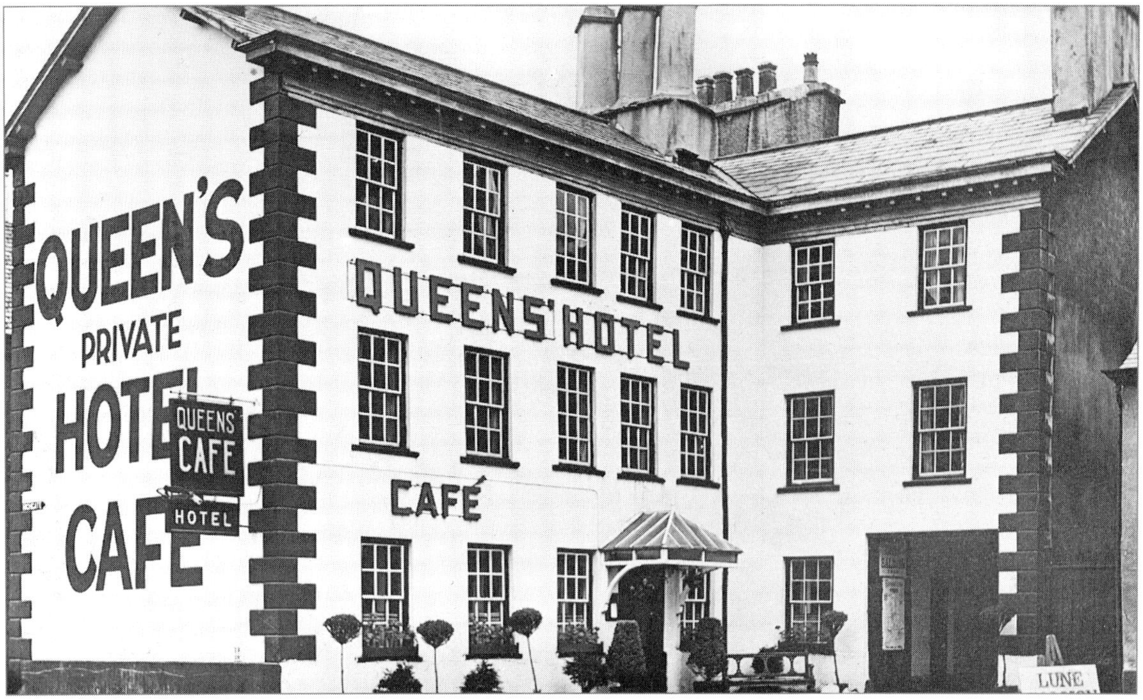

Atkinson & Pollitt of Kendal sent their photographer to record these two A6 roadside hotels in the 1930s. Above, the Queen's Hotel in Kirkland in Kendal. This building started life as a town house of the Wilson family in the late eighteenth century and has been variously used as a nunnery, a nightclub and flats. Below, the Heversham Hotel was the result of converting a vicarage beside the 1930s Heversham bypass. Much extended, this is now named the Bluebell. (*Atkinson & Pollitt*)

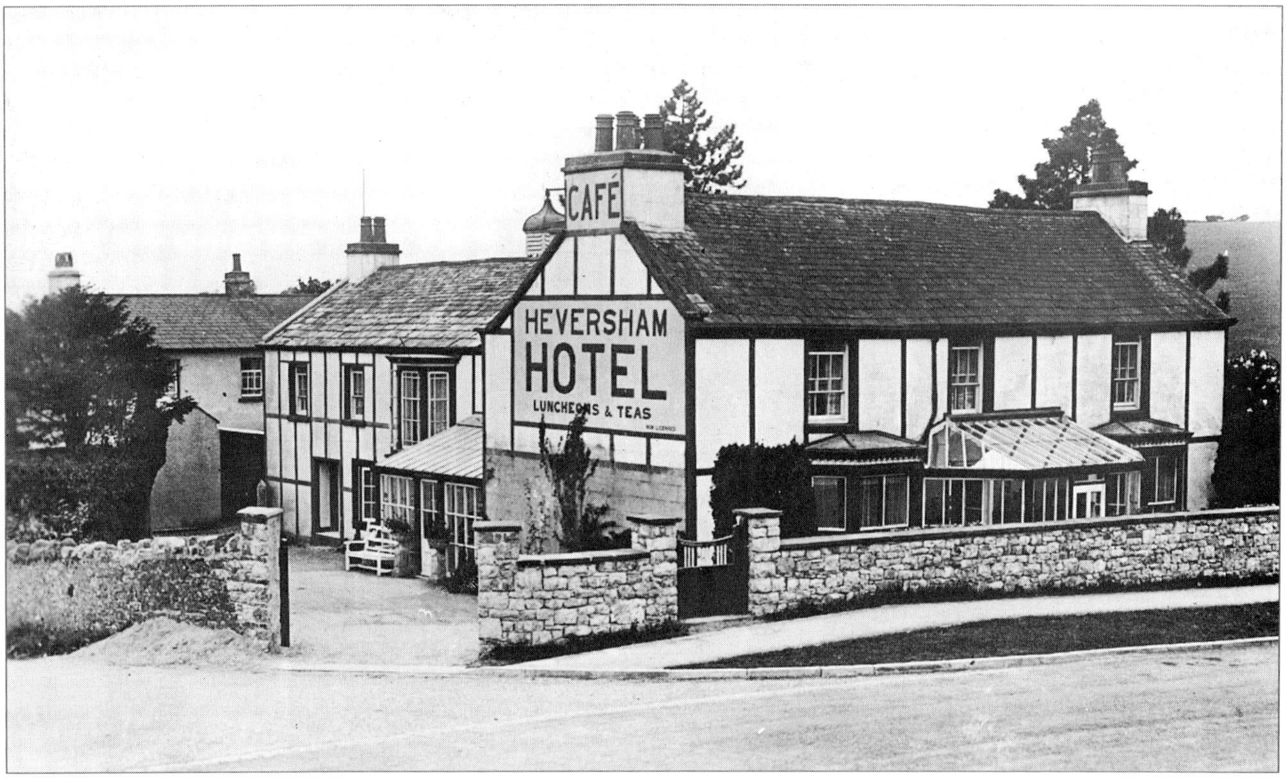

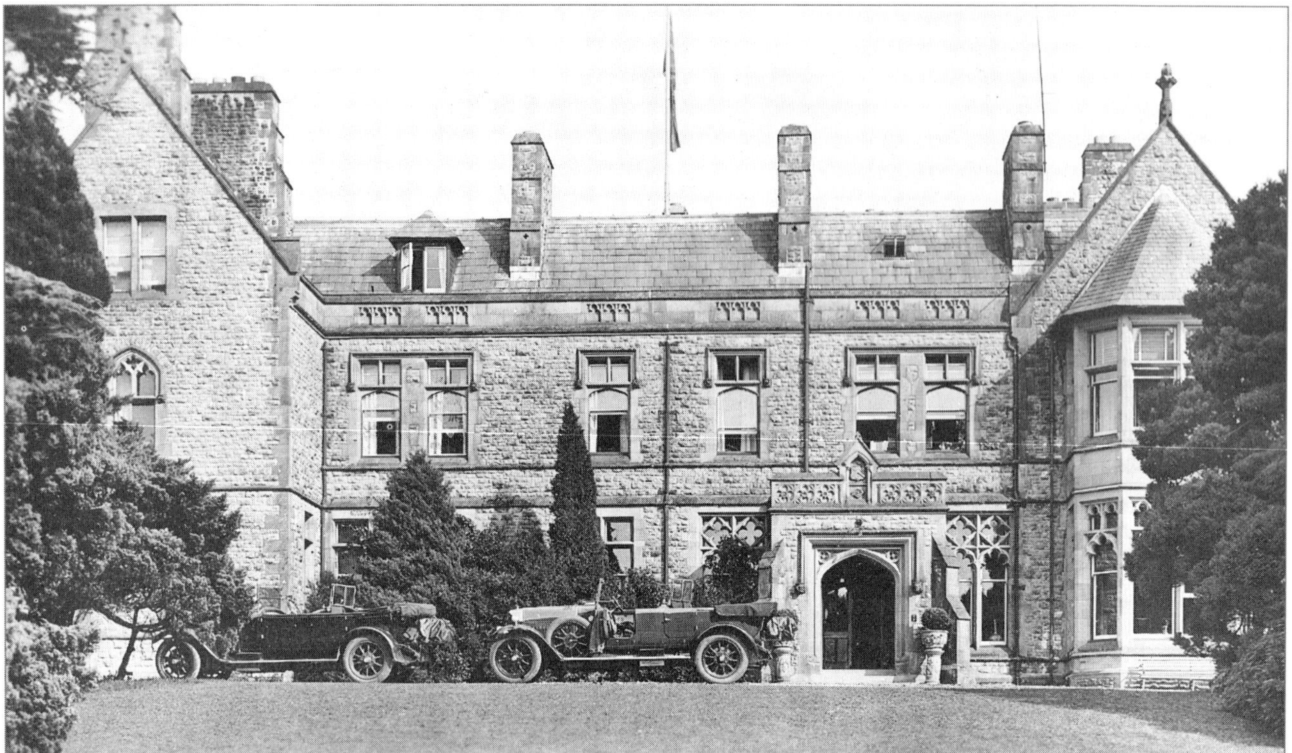

Another A6 roadside hotel was the Levens Hotel at Sedgwick, south of Kendal. Starting life as a private house, the building known as Brettagh Halt is now a nunnery occupied by the Salesian Sisters. Above is the exterior in hotel days and below, the gloomy entrance hall with potted palms and stuffed animal. (*Atkinson & Pollitt*)

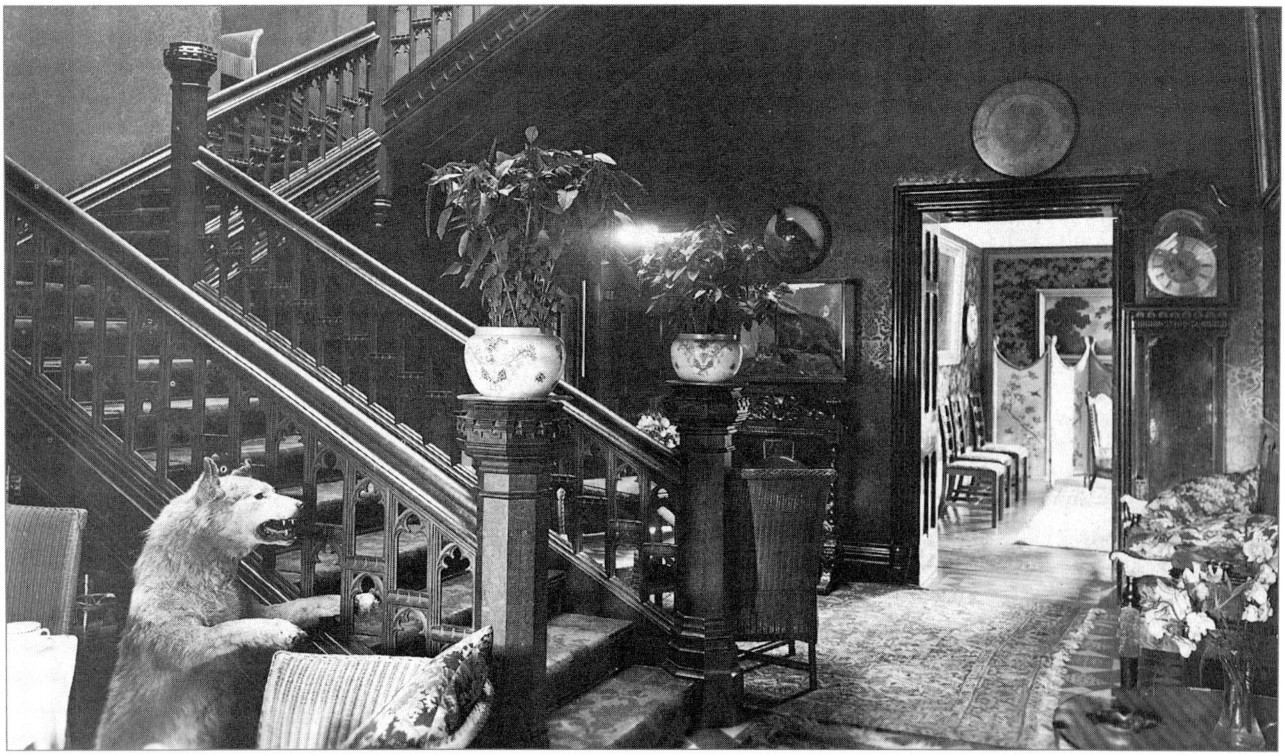

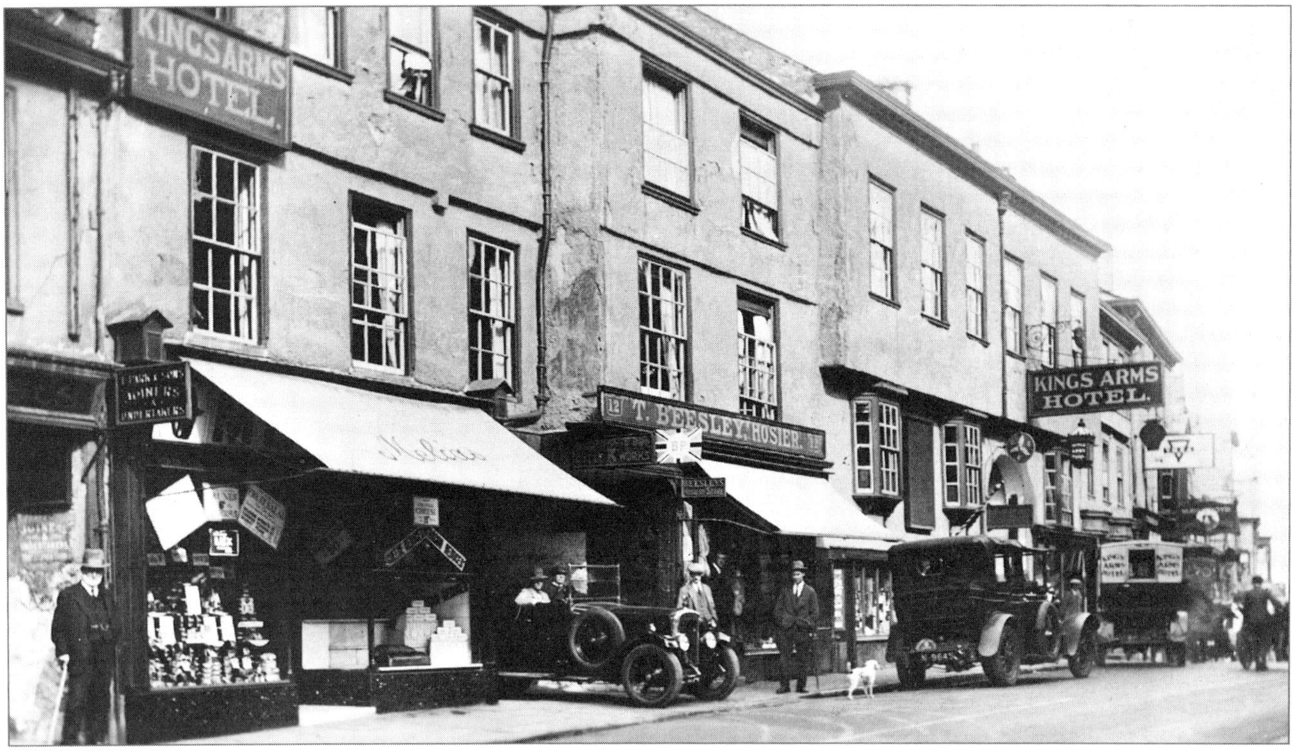

Two more hotels in the 1930s. Above is the magnificent timber-framed ex-coaching hotel, the King's Arms in Stricklandgate in Kendal. This fine building was demolished only a few years after the photograph was taken to make way for the 1930s Marks & Spencer's store. Below, the Royal Hotel at Kirkby Lonsdale has hardly changed. The horse-drawn hotel bus is seen bringing customers from the railway station as it had done for over fifty years. (*Atkinson & Pollitt*)

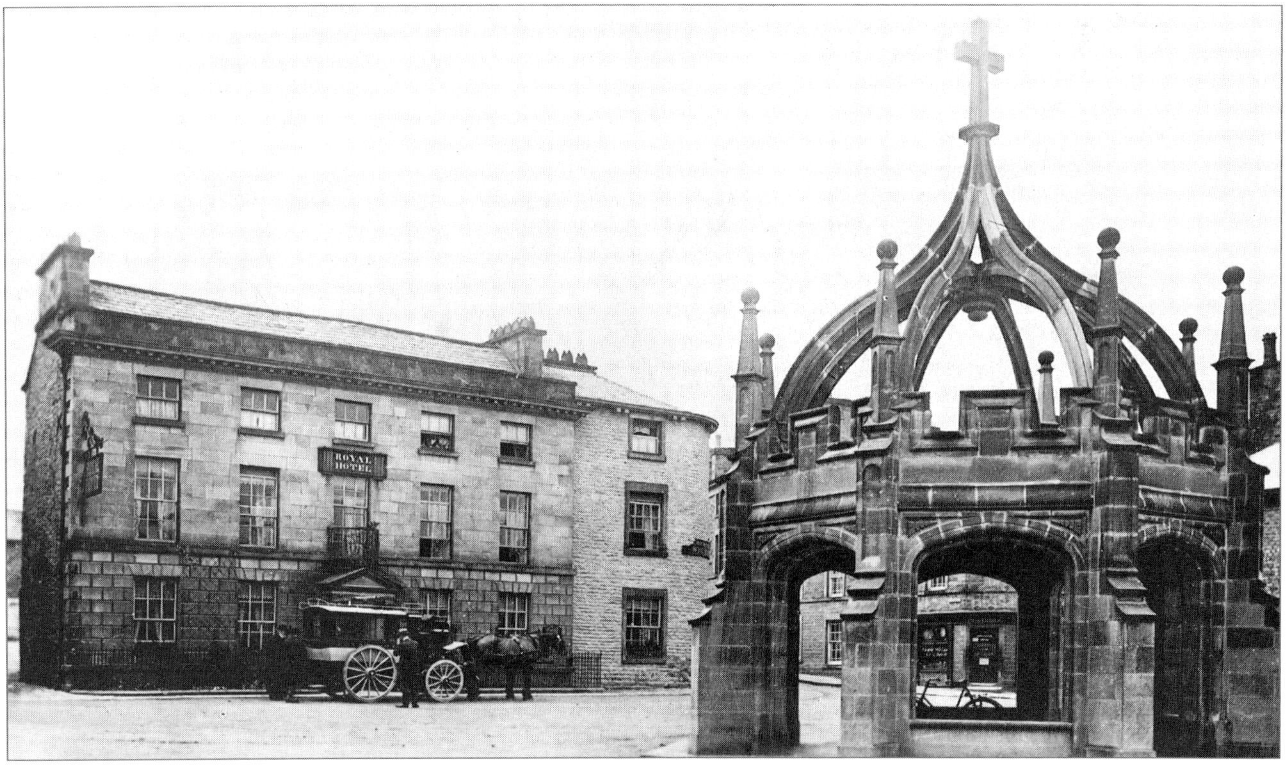

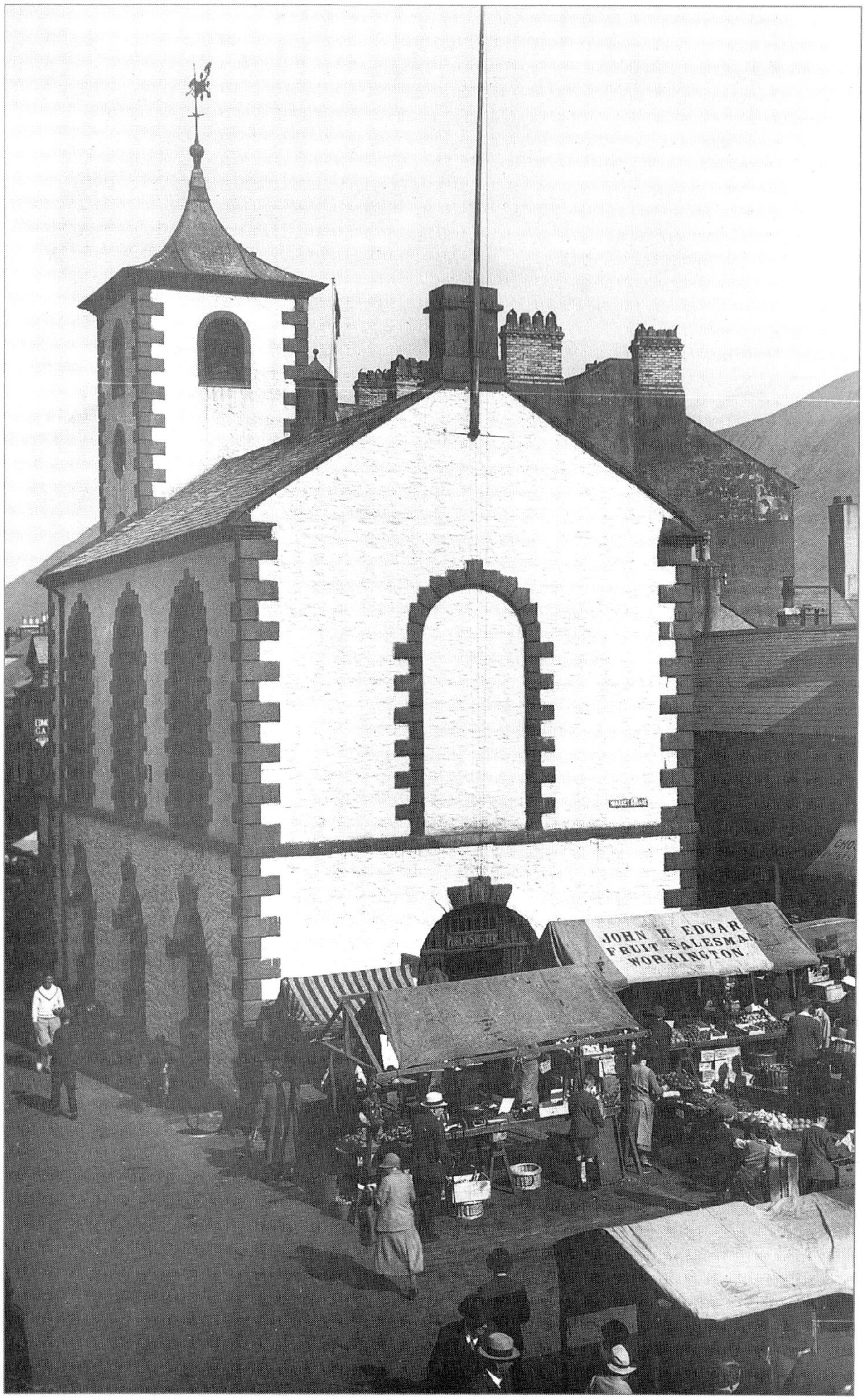

Keswick market was founded in the reign of Edward I. The Moot Hall was built in 1813 where the ancient court-house formerly stood. Pevsner described the building as 'an extremely pretty sight'. This 1930s picture by Maysons of Keswick shows busy market stalls on both sides of the building. (*Maysons of Keswick*)

Sport and Recreation

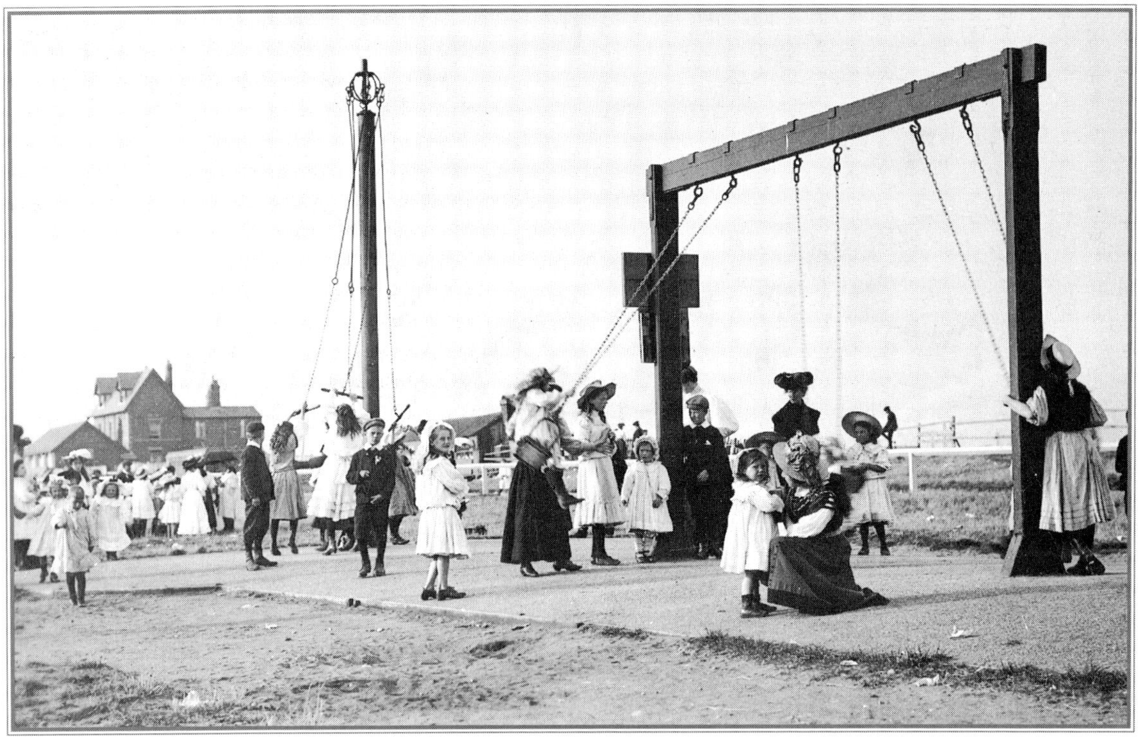

The children of Barrow-in-Furness were only a tram ride away from the Walney Island seaside with its swings and other delightful pastimes. At bank holidays the permanent fixtures were joined by other fairground entertainments from which our parents and grandparents extracted maximum enjoyment. Happy memories. (*E.C. of Blackpool*)

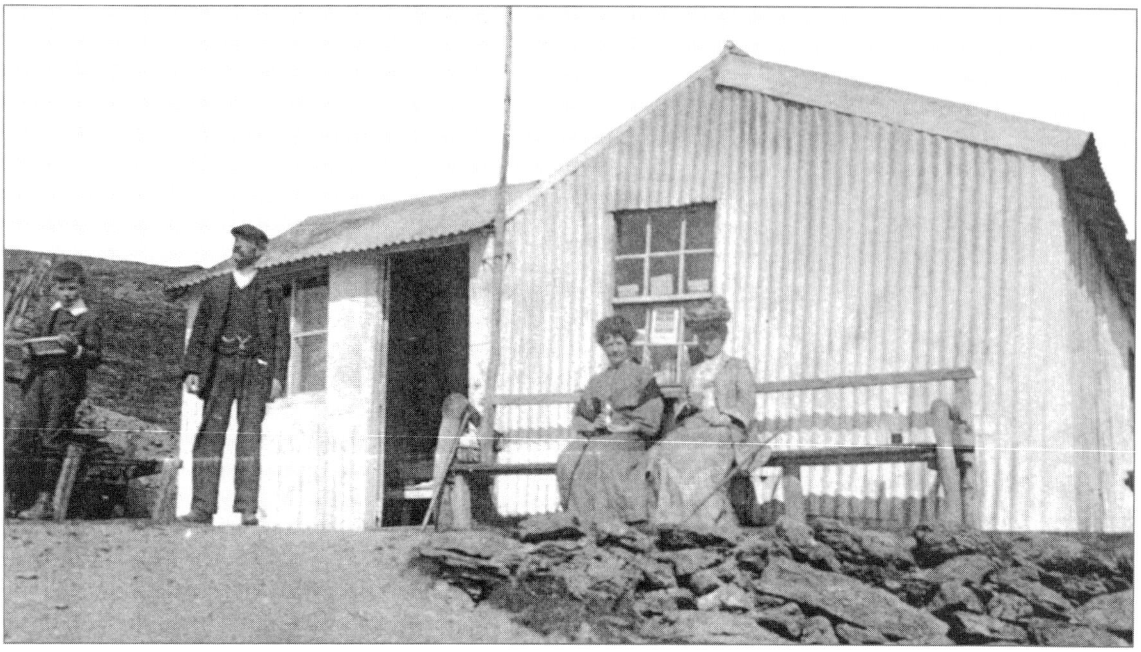

The hut on the footpath up Skiddaw from Keswick, *c.* 1905. Here the resolve of many would-be conquerors of the Skiddaw peak dissolved in a cup of tea, coffee, cocoa or lemonade and this was as far as many walkers got. The Skiddaw hut, unfortunately, gained a reputation for uncertain opening which precluded it ever being a destination in itself. The flag flying from the flagpost drew many up the fell but, by all accounts, some found it had just been left out from the previous day! One guidebook, in trying to explain the situation, said the hut was 'generally but not invariably open'. It no longer exists, alas. (*Maysons of Keswick*)

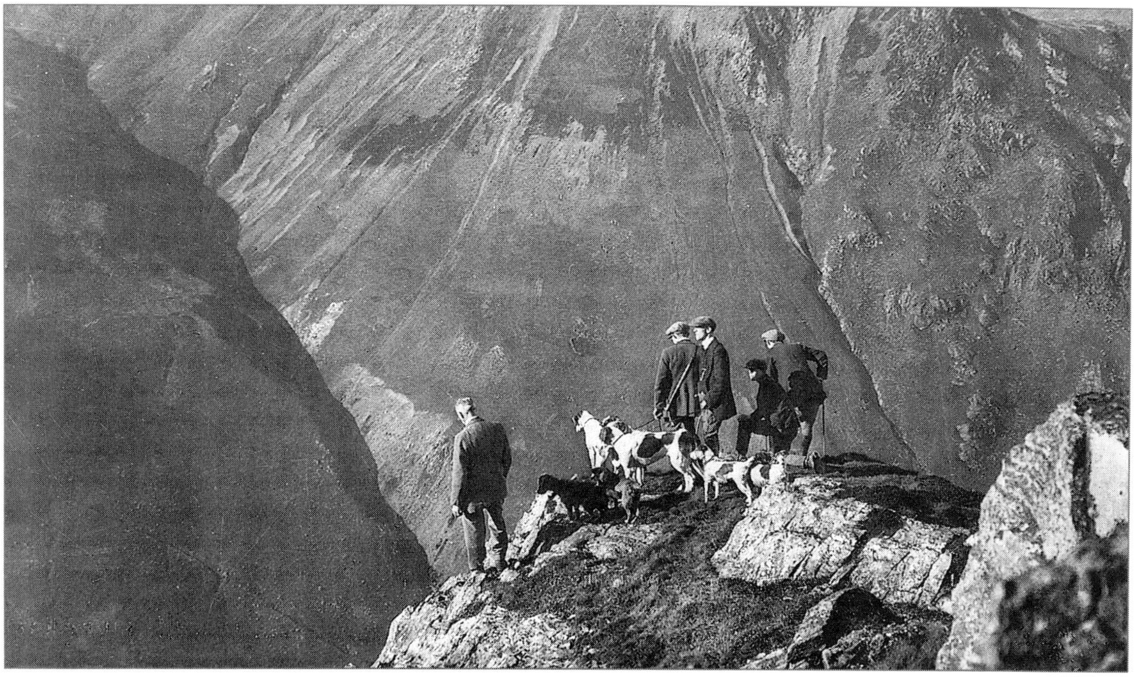

The Blencathra pack of foxhounds has kept the Keswick area fox population under control for many decades. For years the Speaker of the House of Commons, James William Lowther (MP for Penrith), was Master of this pack. Here Maysons pictured the pack and huntsmen in Newlands showing that the hunt was only for those who knew the Fells, and that the wisest hounds stayed with the huntsmen. (*Maysons of Keswick*)

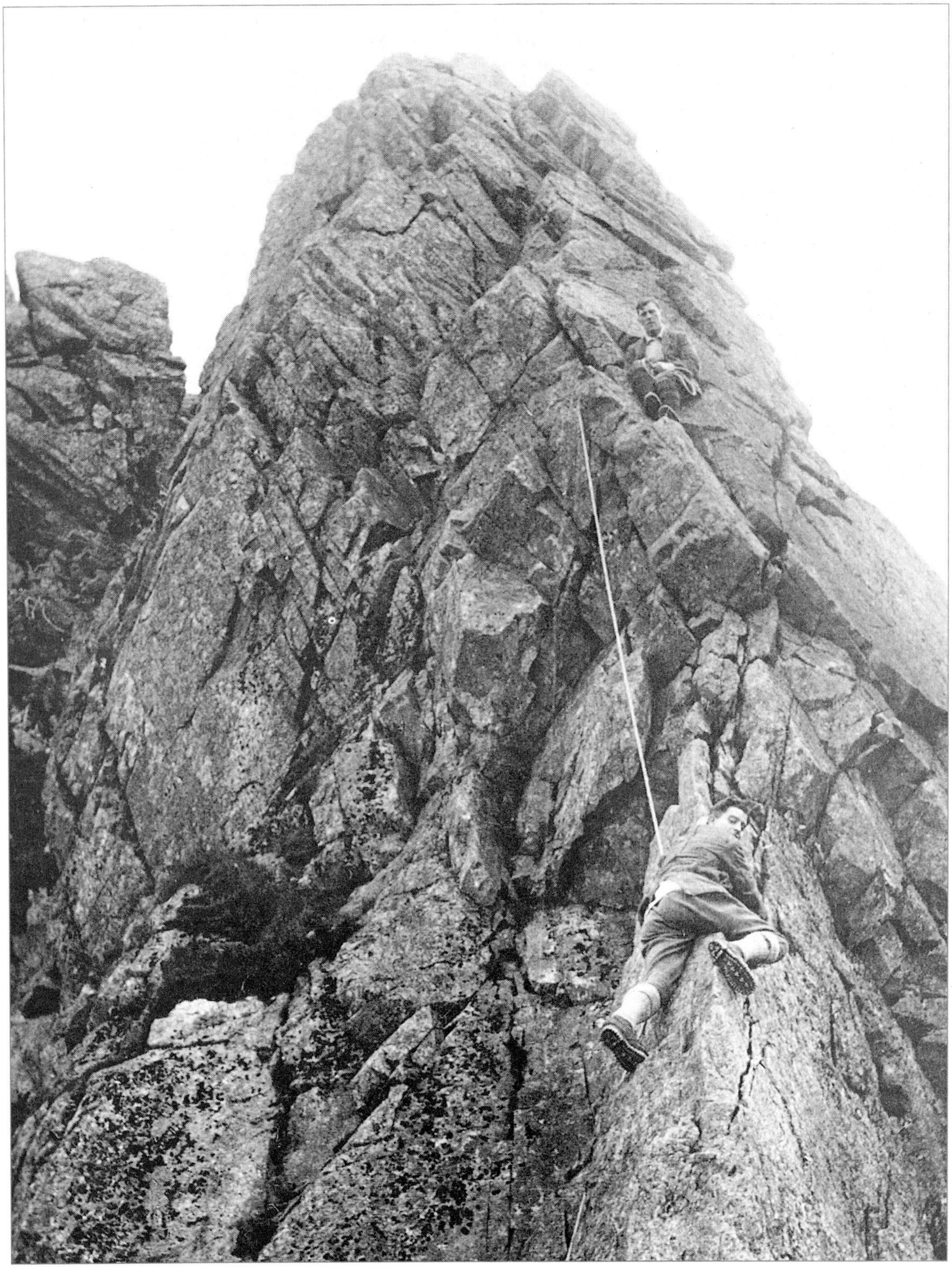

Atkinson & Pollitt's photographer followed in the footsteps of mountain photographers Abrahams, Maysons and Pettitts of Keswick when this photograph was taken on Scafell pinnacle in the 1920s. Mountaineering and photography were both increasing in popularity and the cameras were, by then, much smaller. (*Atkinson & Pollitt*)

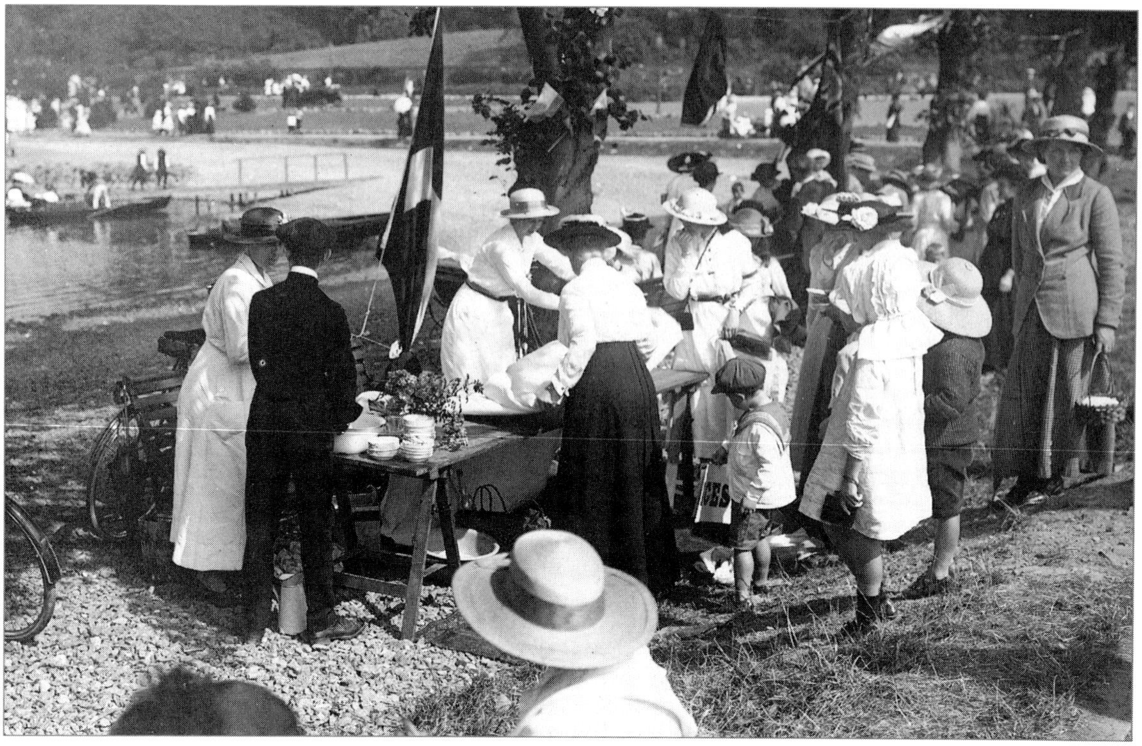

The crowds gather on the Glebe at Bowness-on-Windermere, round the charity stall run by the wife of the Bowness vicar, Canon Nurse, during the First World War. Mrs Nurse ran many events in the vicarage grounds and also supported the Calgarth hospital for wounded soldiers, entertaining many to tea at the vicarage. (*Herbert & Son, Windermere*)

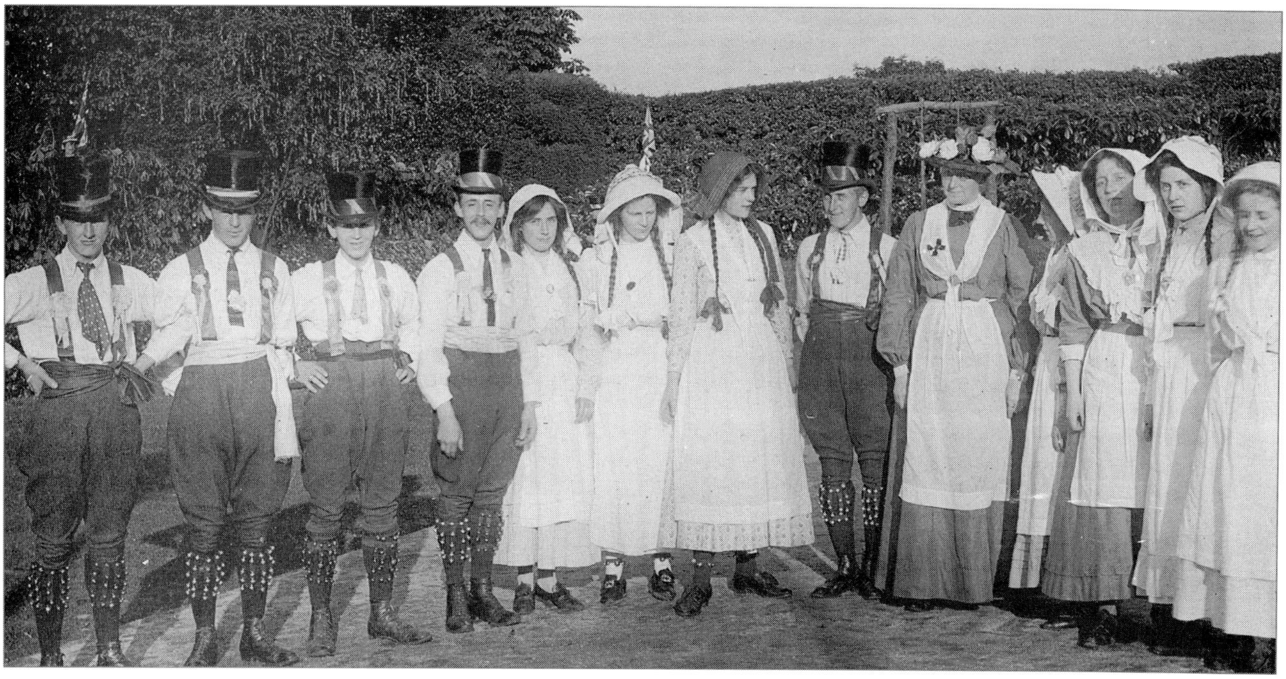

Beetham, near Milnthorpe, had a troupe of Morris dancers in the first decades of the twentieth century. Here they were photographed by Mrs Sutcliffe of Burton-in-Kendal at an appearance at a local garden fête. It is interesting to compare their Morris dancing dress with that seen today. (*Mrs Sutcliffe*)

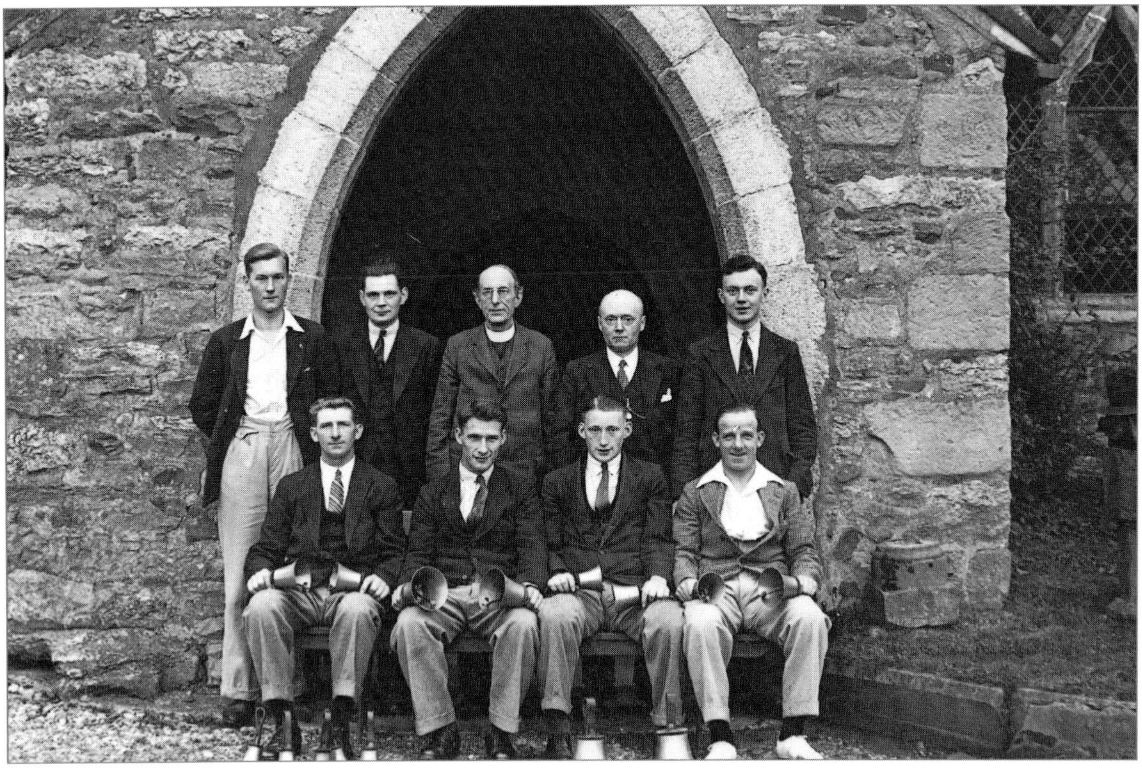

Burton-in-Kendal church has had a first-class peal of bells since 1804 and right up to the present day. In 1933 the bellringers had their photograph taken with the vicar, the Revd W.C. Ward, outside the church porch. (*John Marsh Collection*)

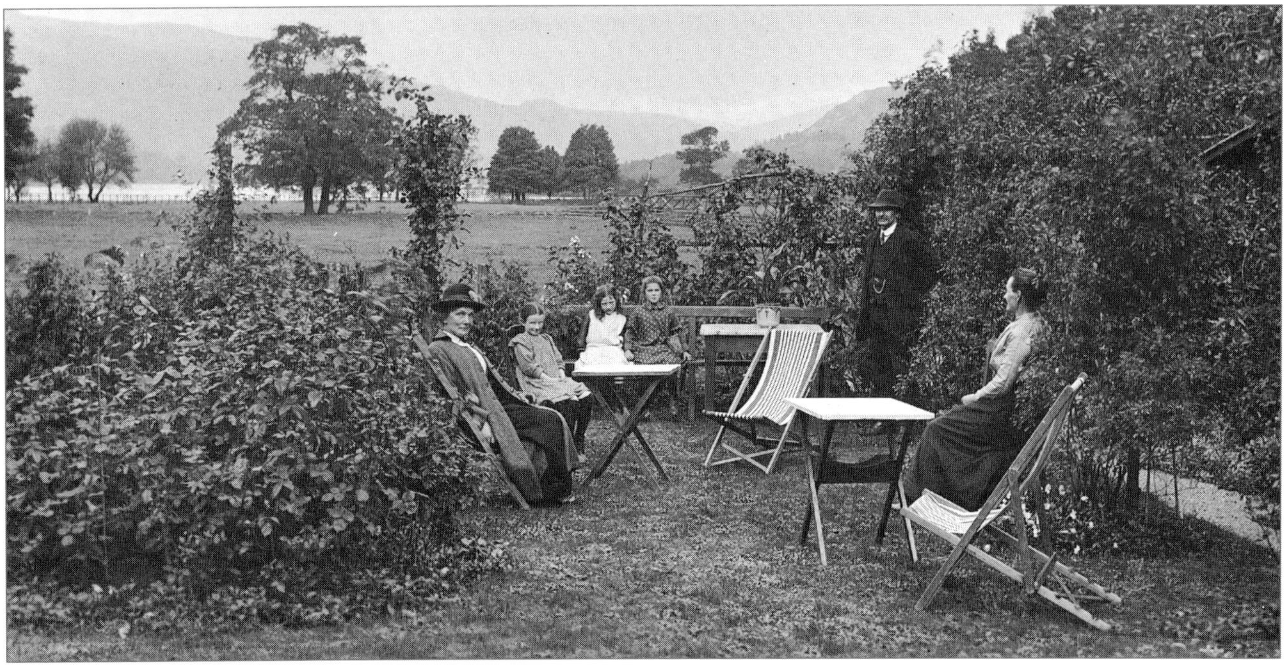

Kilner's Tea Gardens at Church View was visited by photographer Lowe of Patterdale. This outdoor refreshments garden was an extension of William Kilner's apartments business at Rose Cottage, Patterdale, with Thomas and Margaret Kilner taking over later from their Grisedale Bridge apartments. All now but a distant memory. (*Lowe of Patterdale*)

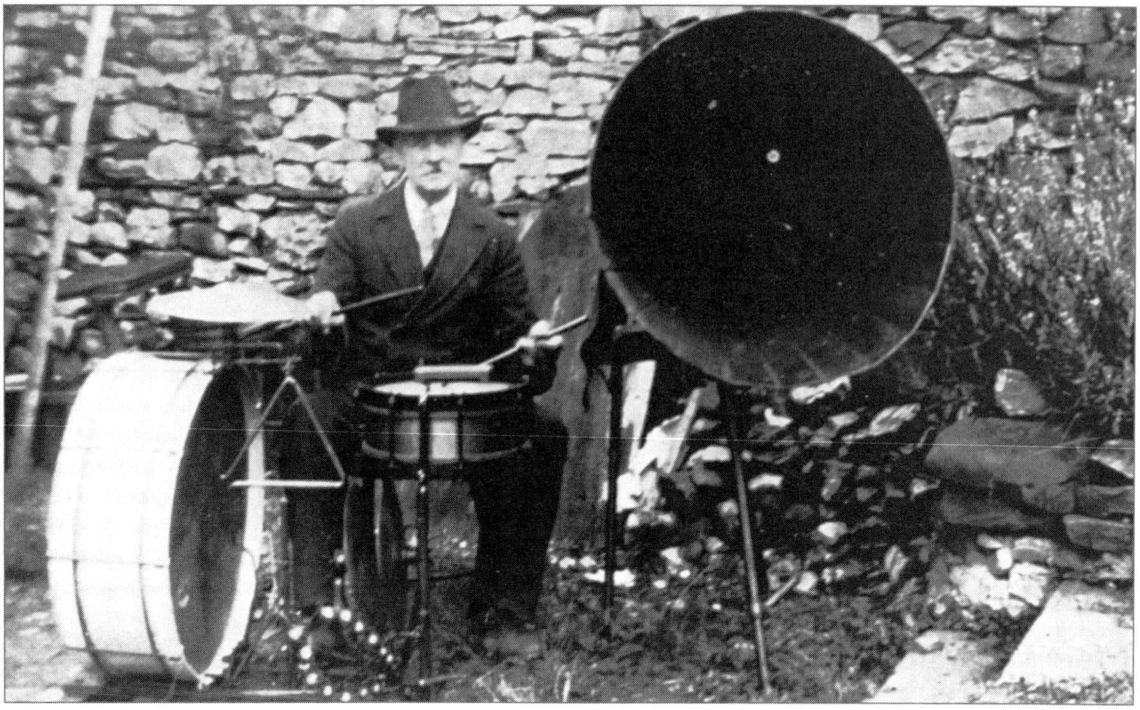

Milnthorpe Police's Sergeant Park must have thought himself a one man band many times before he retired and became one, but that time for the entertainment of the community he once policed. There can be no better expression of the community policing of the first half of the twentieth century which is now, unfortunately, just a memory. Nobody minded that this man knew everybody and everything that went on. (*John Marsh Collection*)

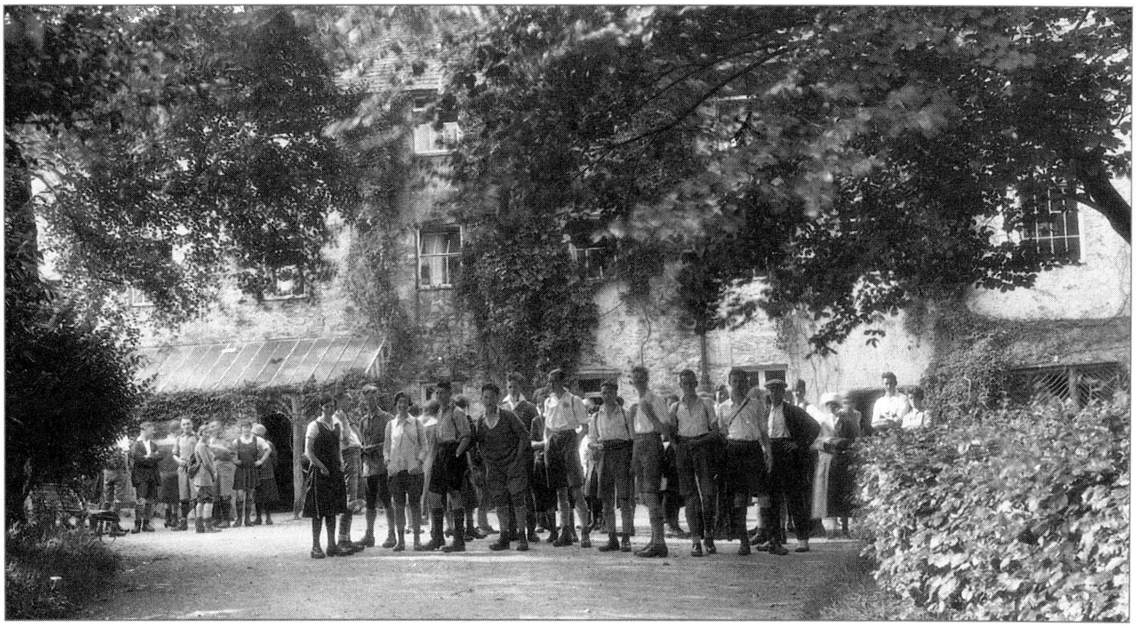

The Holiday Fellowship guesthouse at Stair in the Newlands Valley produced many happy memories from its opening just before the First World War. The growing demand for healthy outdoor holidays for workers and managers was being catered for and here, in August 1926, a happy holiday group on their outing to Grizedale were photographed before their departure. (*John Marsh Collection*)

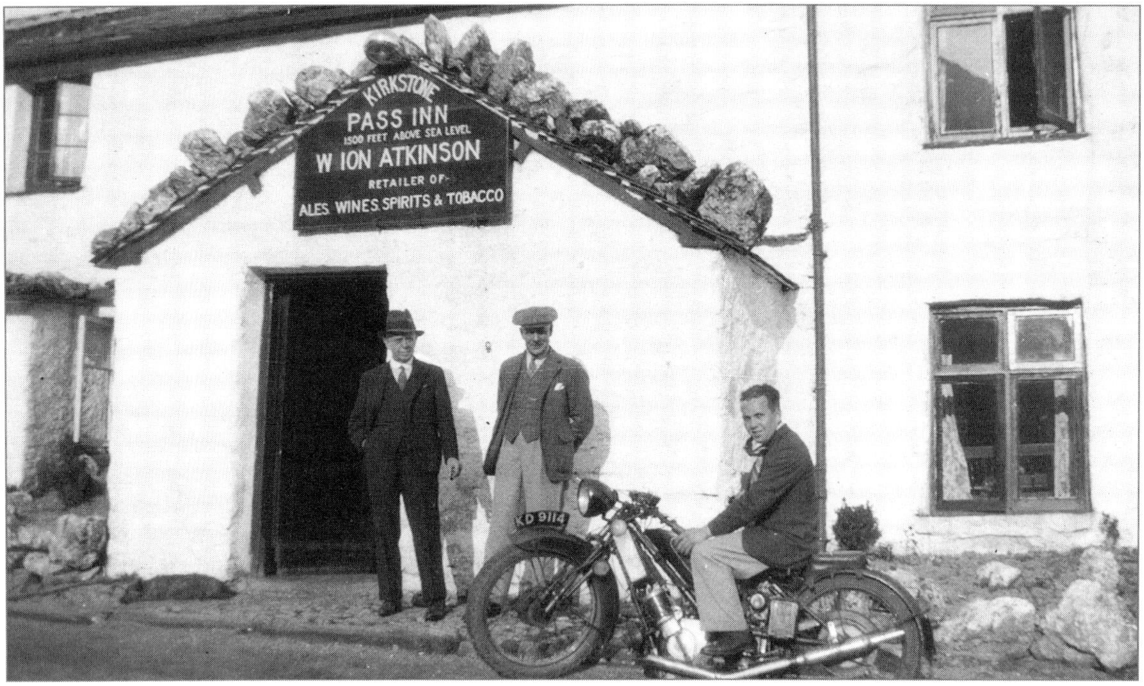

The Kirkstone Pass Inn was the trial venue for many motor cars and motor cycles up to the 1950s when this motor cyclist from Burton-in-Kendal was pictured at the inn on a machine nearly of 'vintage' class. (*John Marsh Collection*)

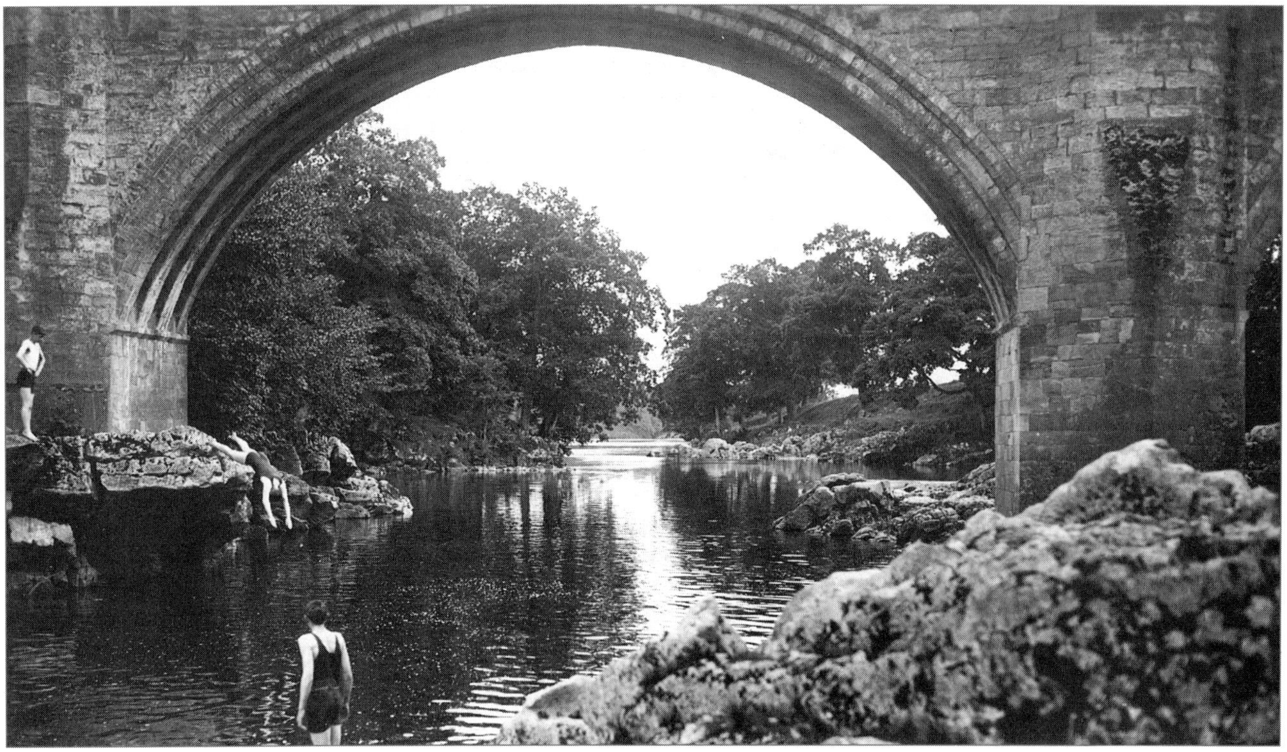

The bathing pool at Devil's Bridge, Kirkby Lonsdale, in the 1930s was where many young local men were to gain the courage needed for their forthcoming experiences in the Second World War. To dive from the bridge was a dare many did not wish to take up as diving from the rocks into the deep pool was enough. Atkinson & Pollitt photographed the scene under Westmorland's most ancient of bridges. (*Atkinson & Pollitt*)

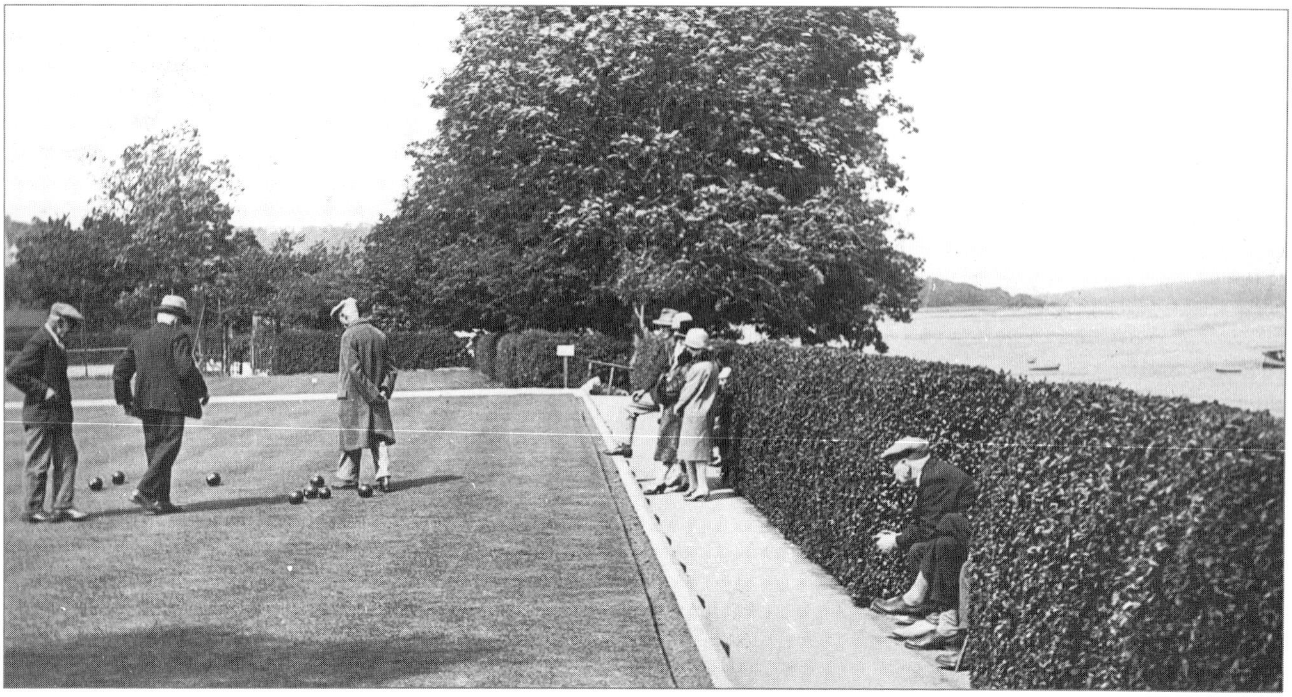

Grange-over-Sands promenade bowling green was visited in the 1930s by Atkinson & Pollitt's photographer who caught the scene between the railway line and the sea. How the loss of its own Urban District Council in 1974 was to change the pleasant town of Grange is only now becoming obvious but the bowling green is still here. (*Atkinson & Pollitt*)

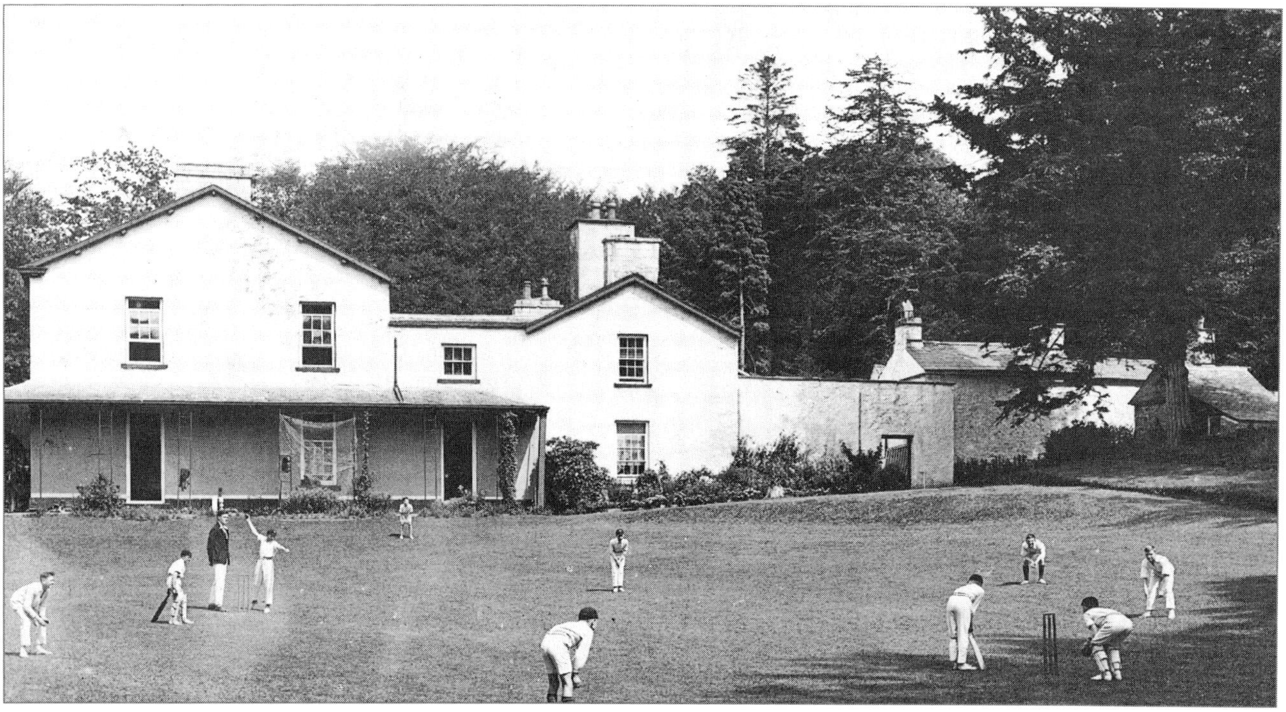

Across the estuary at Arnside, Earnseat Academy was a private school run by J.C. Barnes. Here, in 1925, cricket is being played on the lawn in a school photograph by Walter Scott of Bradford. When the school was closed in recent decades Mr Barnes presented the building, Ashmeadow, to that most ambiguous of bodies, the village, with the result that it has remained empty ever since as village groups and individuals argue about its use. (*Walter Scott of Bradford*)

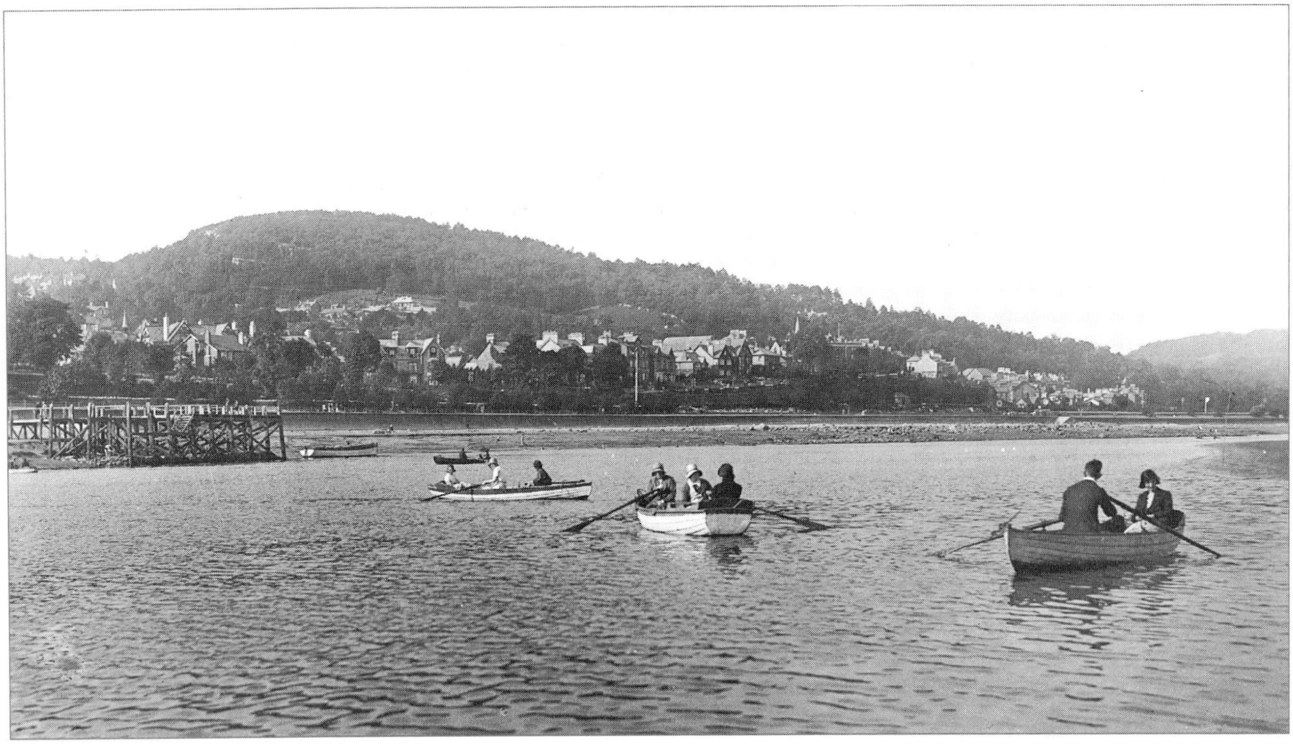

Grange-over-Sands in happier days can be seen in these two Atkinson & Pollitt pictures. The Clare House pier and boating on the estuary seen above are both no more and the superb 1930s lido, seen below when very new, has been abandoned for lots of reasons which should be resolved. The site deserves a better fate, one in keeping with the surrounding area. (*Atkinson & Pollitt*)

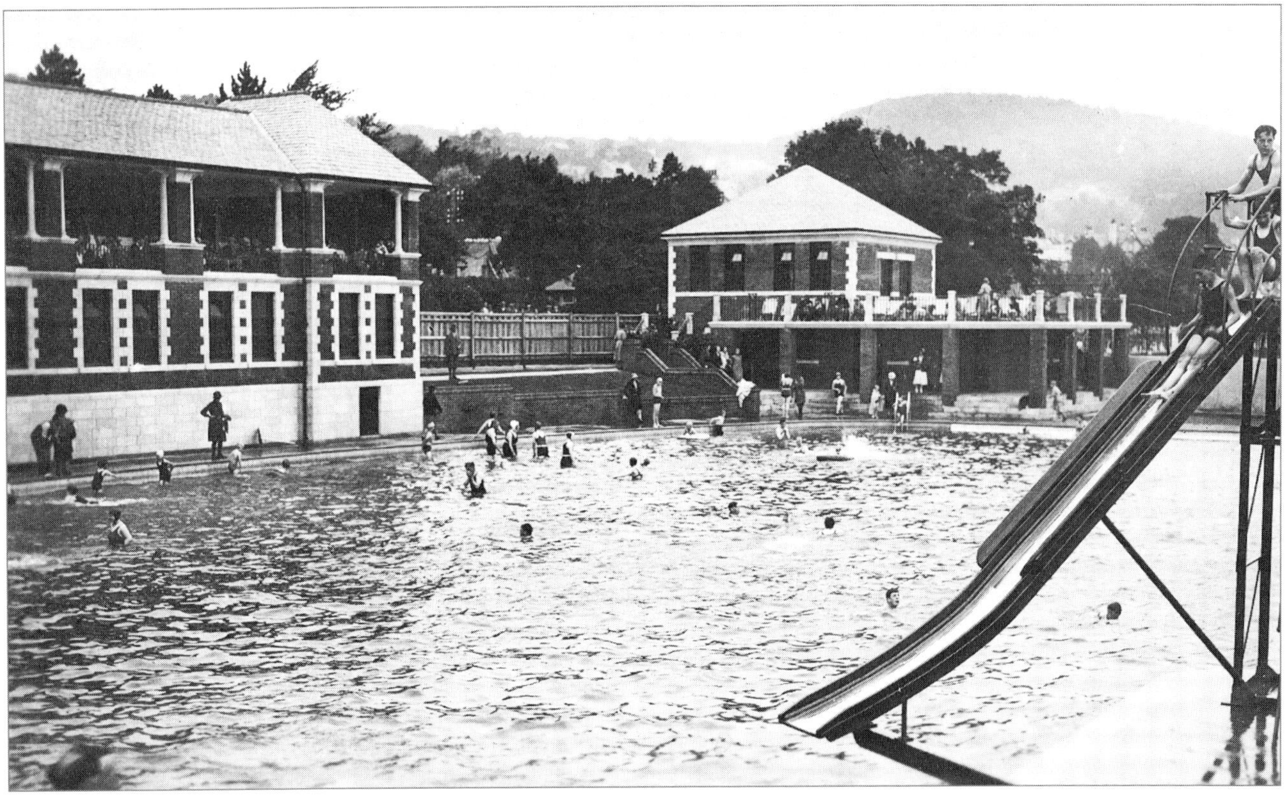

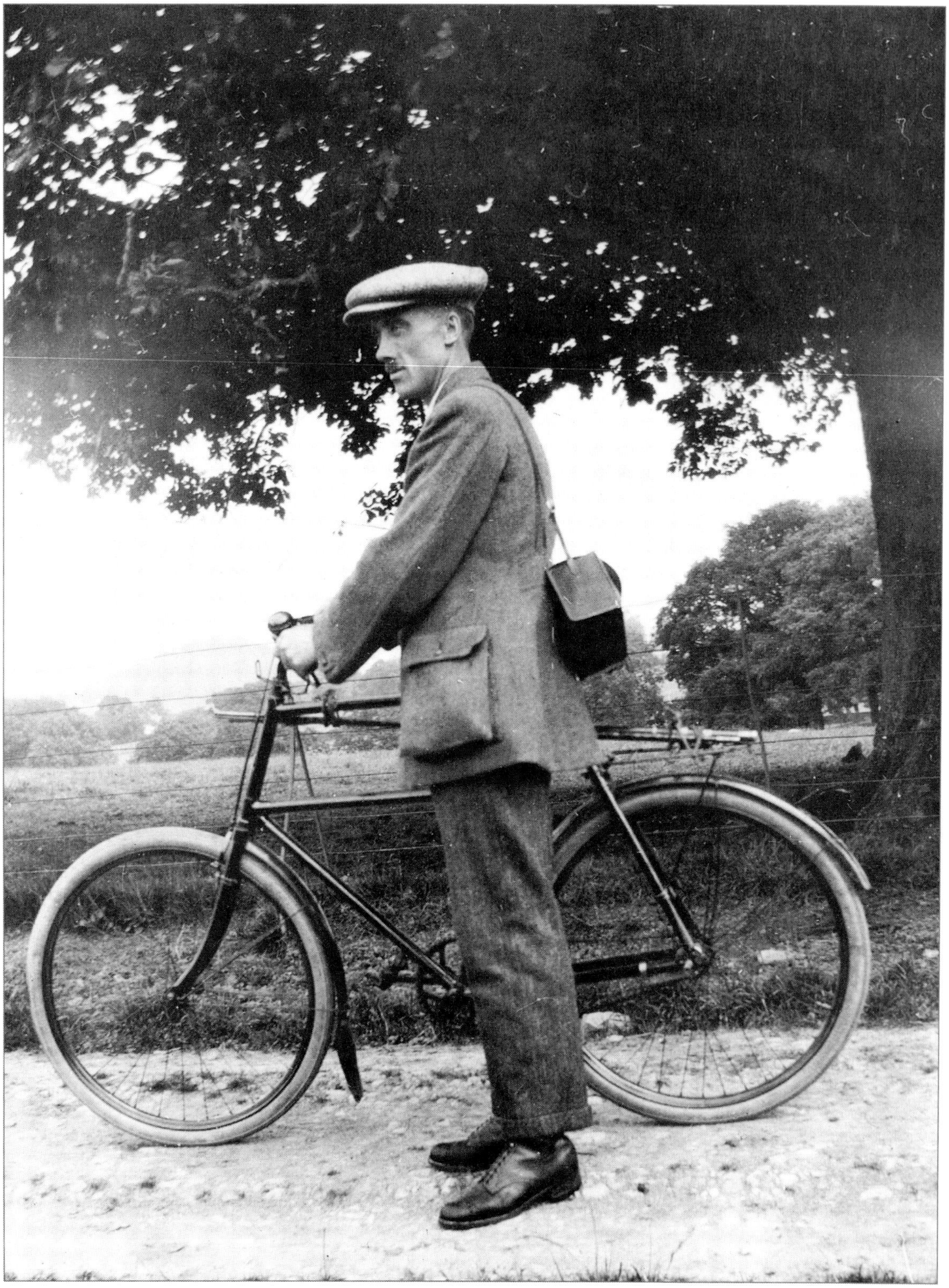

Off for a day's photography was this Burton-in-Kendal photographer in July 1922. Note the double cross-barred sit-up-and-beg bicycle and the box camera that, with roll film, allowed easy picture taking. (*John Marsh Collection*)

Places and Towns

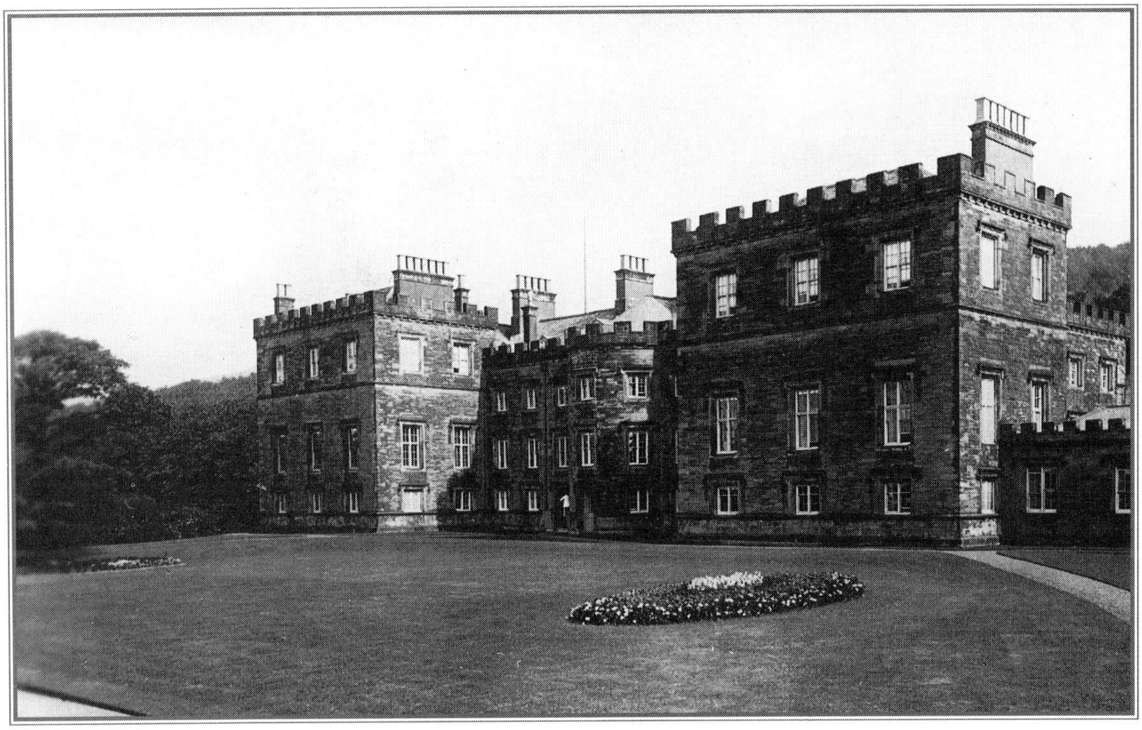

Whitehaven Castle was photographed by Brittain & Wright of Stockton-on-Tees just before the First World War when it was the town house of the Lowther family. The Flat, or Flatt Hall, was built in 1769 and was never a castle in the military sense. The building became Whitehaven hospital for many years and, after a period when it looked as though the fabric was doomed, is now being converted into flats, as its original name suggested. (*Brittain & Wright*)

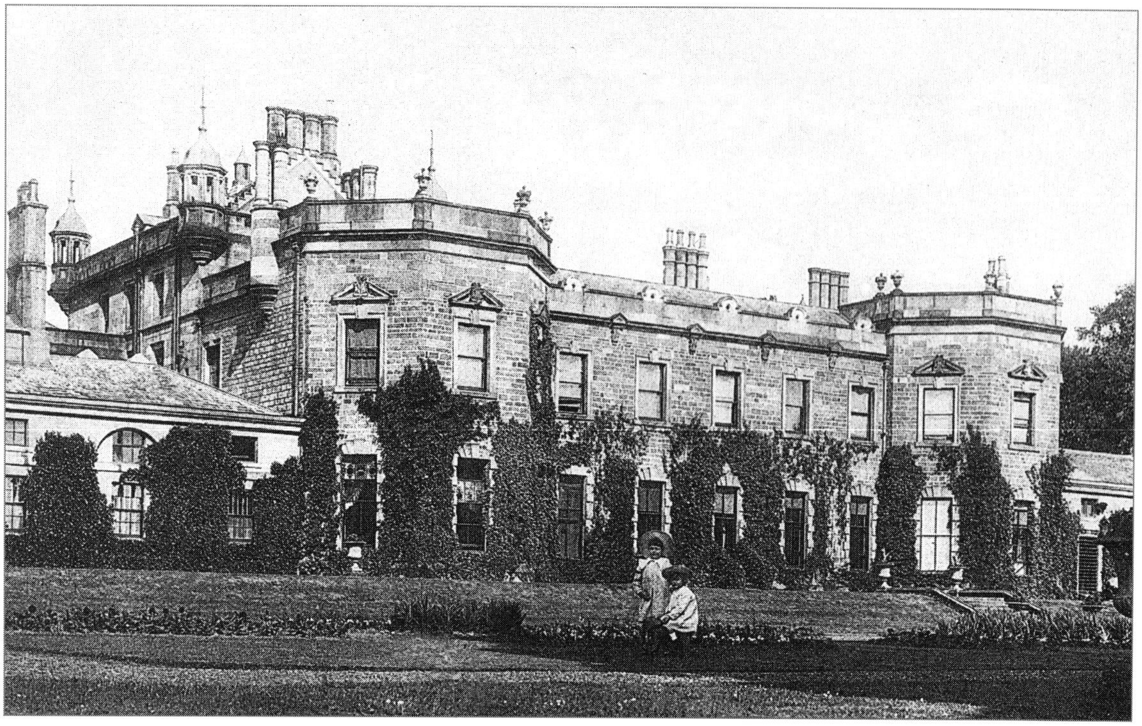

Netherby Hall near Longtown has long been the home of the Graham family. The hall looks Victorian but dates back to medieval times with many alterations over the centuries. (*John Marsh Collection*)

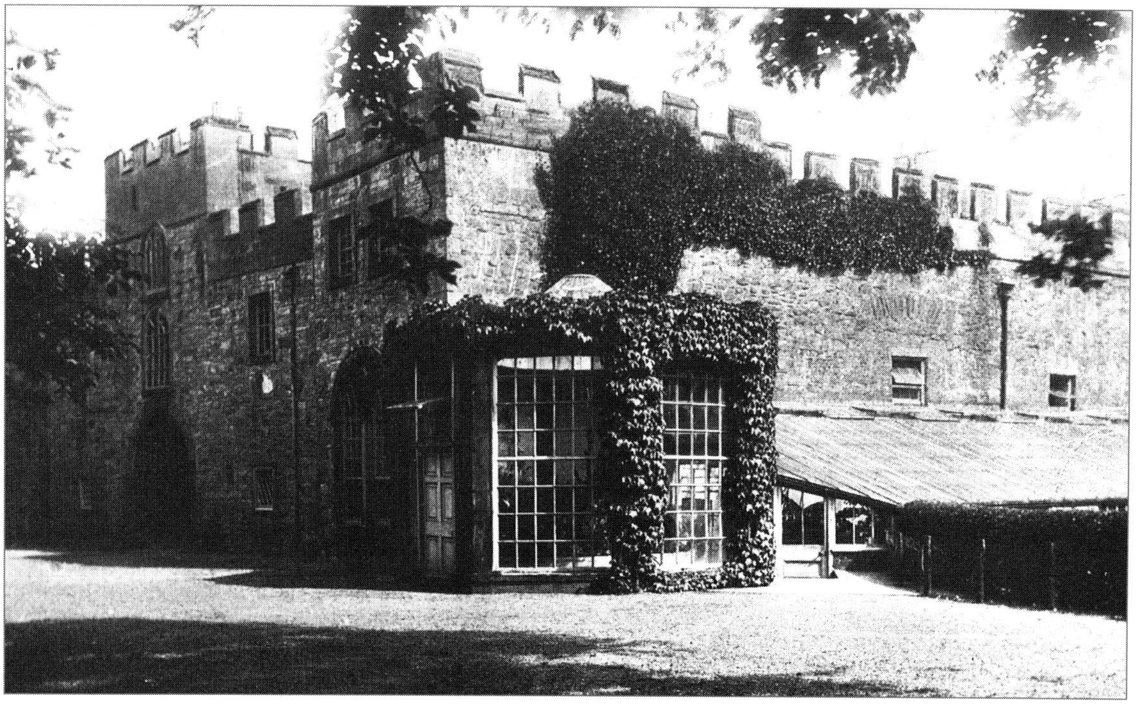

Workington Hall (see also pp. 66 and 149) when it was the home of the Curwen family. They left their ancient house to the local town, this time Workington, in the hope of it being preserved for posterity. The Borough Council did not have any idea what to do with it. After much political negativity it was pulled down to leave an architect-designed ruin in the middle of a municipal park. (*George Dawson Collection*)

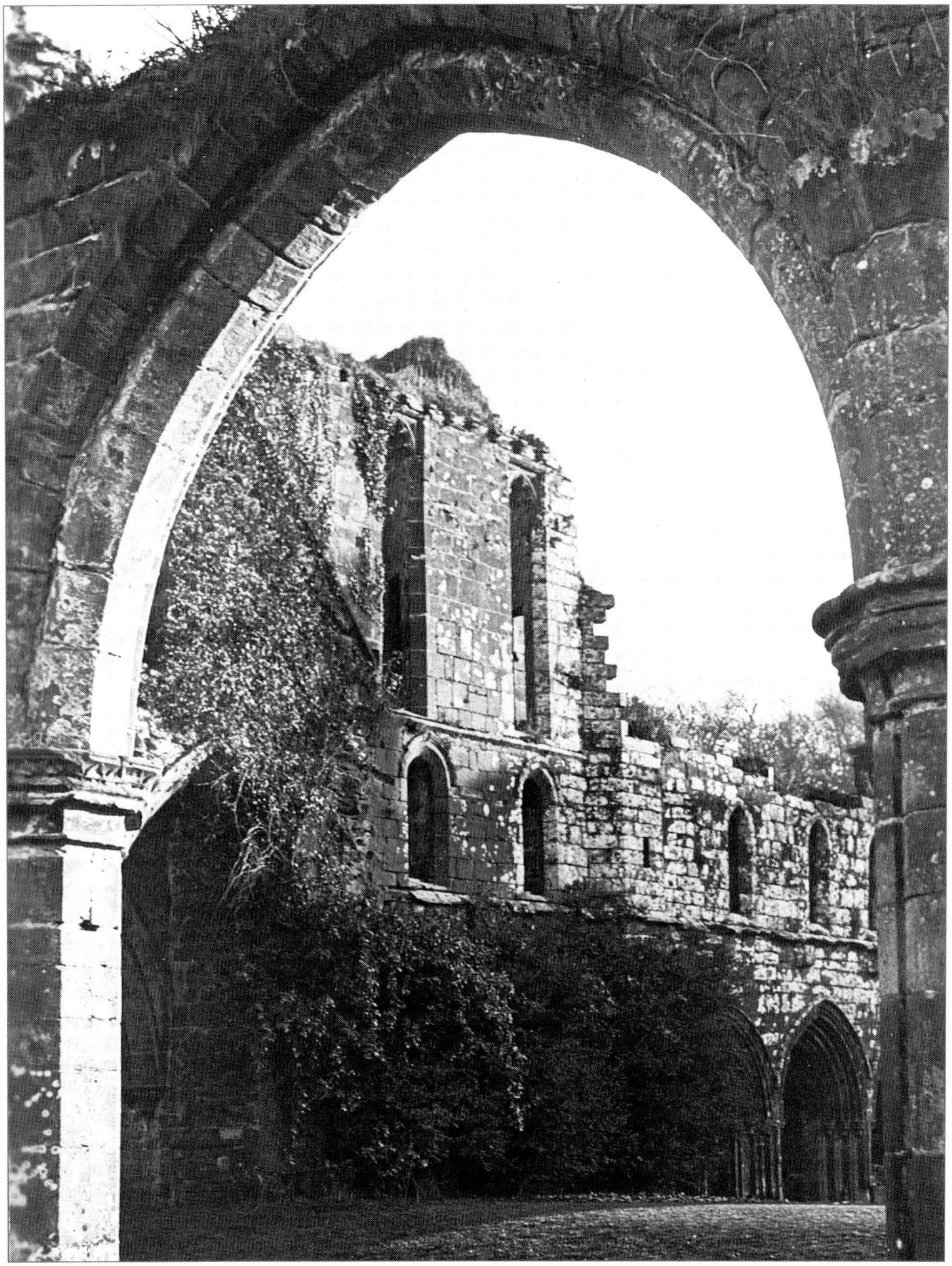

Calder Abbey was a Cistercian foundation until the Reformation. In the eighteenth century a house was built that included parts of the original abbey buildings. Many years of private ownership hardly preserved the abbey ruins, and only recently has government intervention allowed public access and hope of a conservation scheme. Here we see the cloister garth through an arch in the nave arcade in the 1920s. (*John Marsh Collection*)

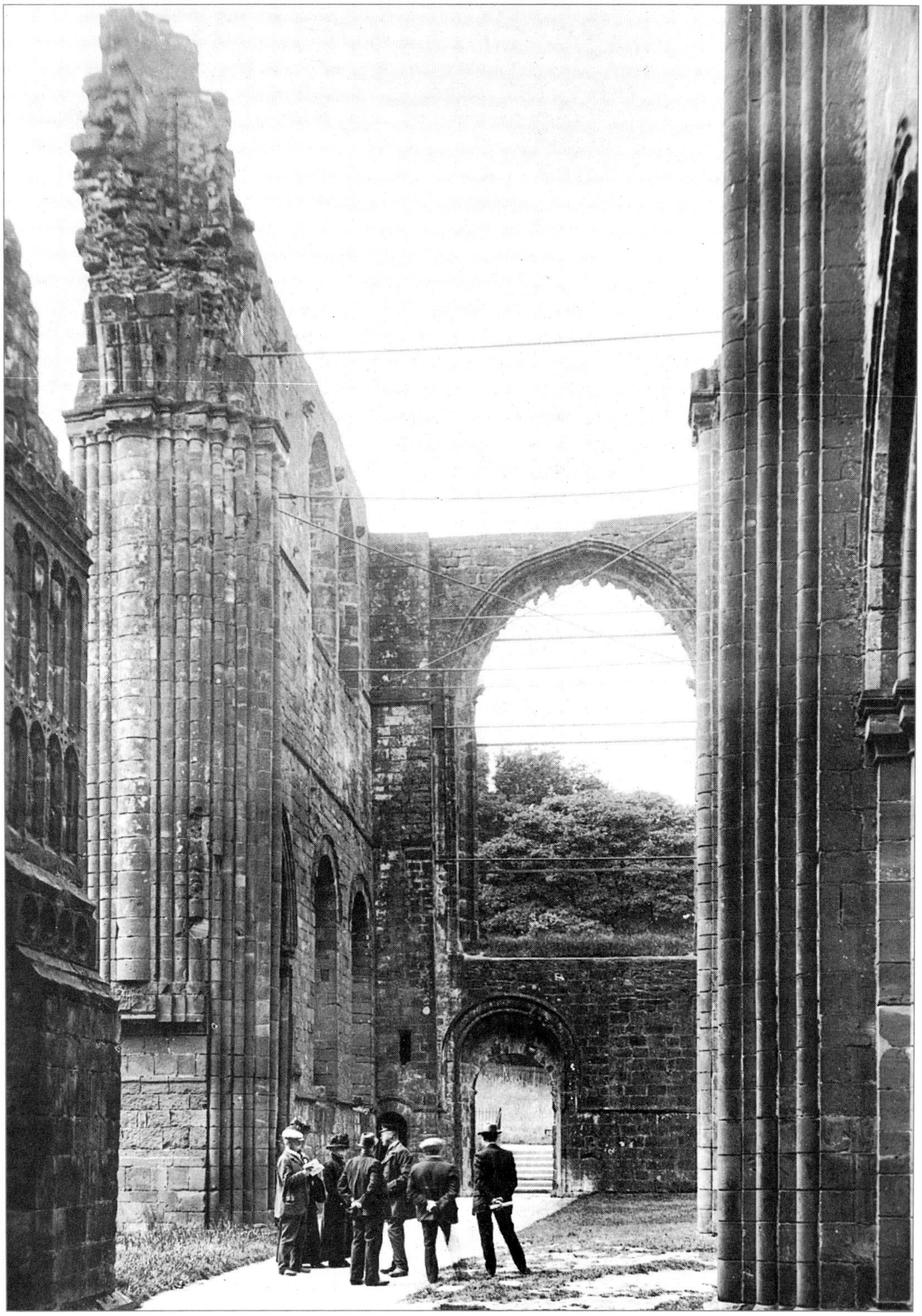

Furness Abbey was a Cistercian house until the Reformation. There has been much conservation work in the twentieth century. Note how the walls were kept standing with metal bars before the days of Ministry of Works conservation. Here the site guide in the early twentieth century talks to a group in the nave/transept crossing in a Furness Railway picture by Raphael Tuck. (*Raphael Tuck for Furness Railway*)

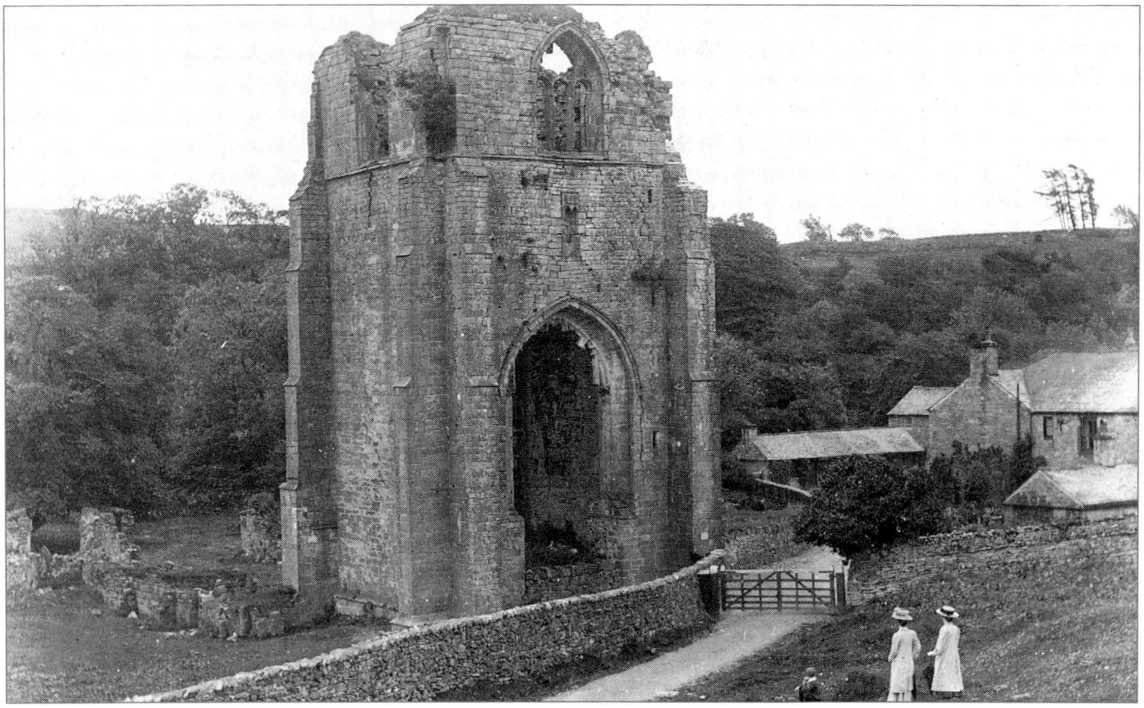

Shap Abbey was a safe house for travellers over the Shap Fells run by the Premonstratensians in medieval times and the old main road passed its doors. The ruins have been part of a farm for many years with the west tower still standing to nearly its full height. Lord Wharton (see p. 135) was given this abbey and lands by Henry VIII. (*John Marsh Collection*)

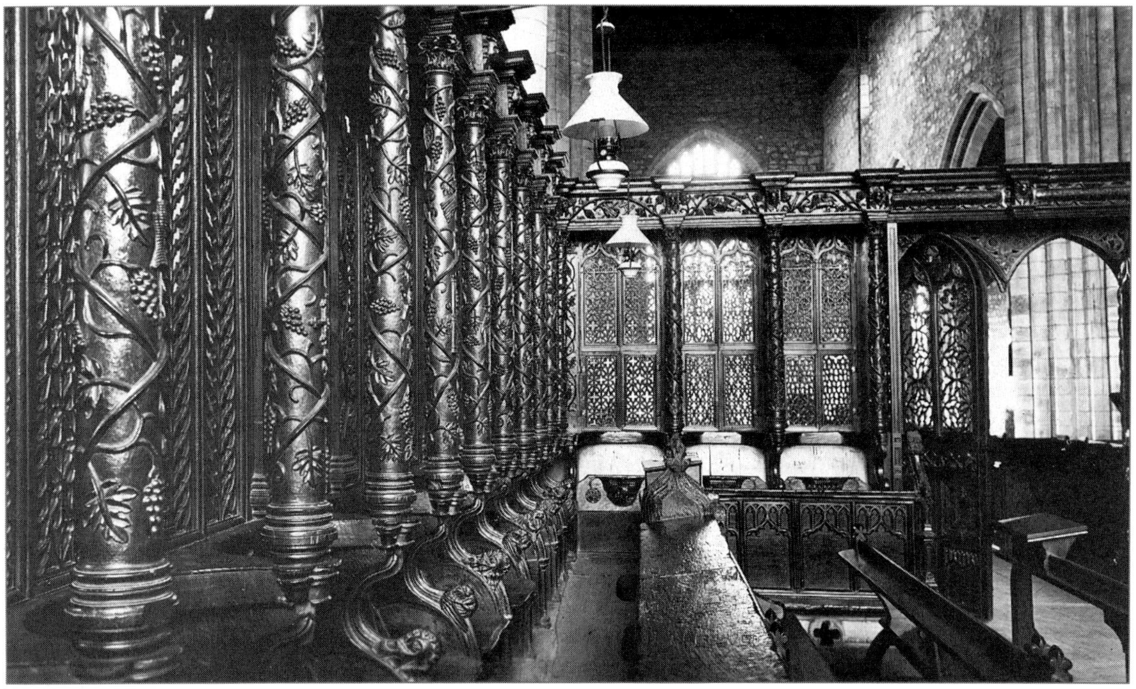

Cartmel Priory church was an Augustinian foundation and was taken into parish hands when the priory was closed. It continues to this day as the finest parish church in the south of the county. Here Atkinson & Pollitt pictured the seventeenth-century choir screen with oil lamps for the choir's use in the 1920s. (*Atkinson & Pollitt*)

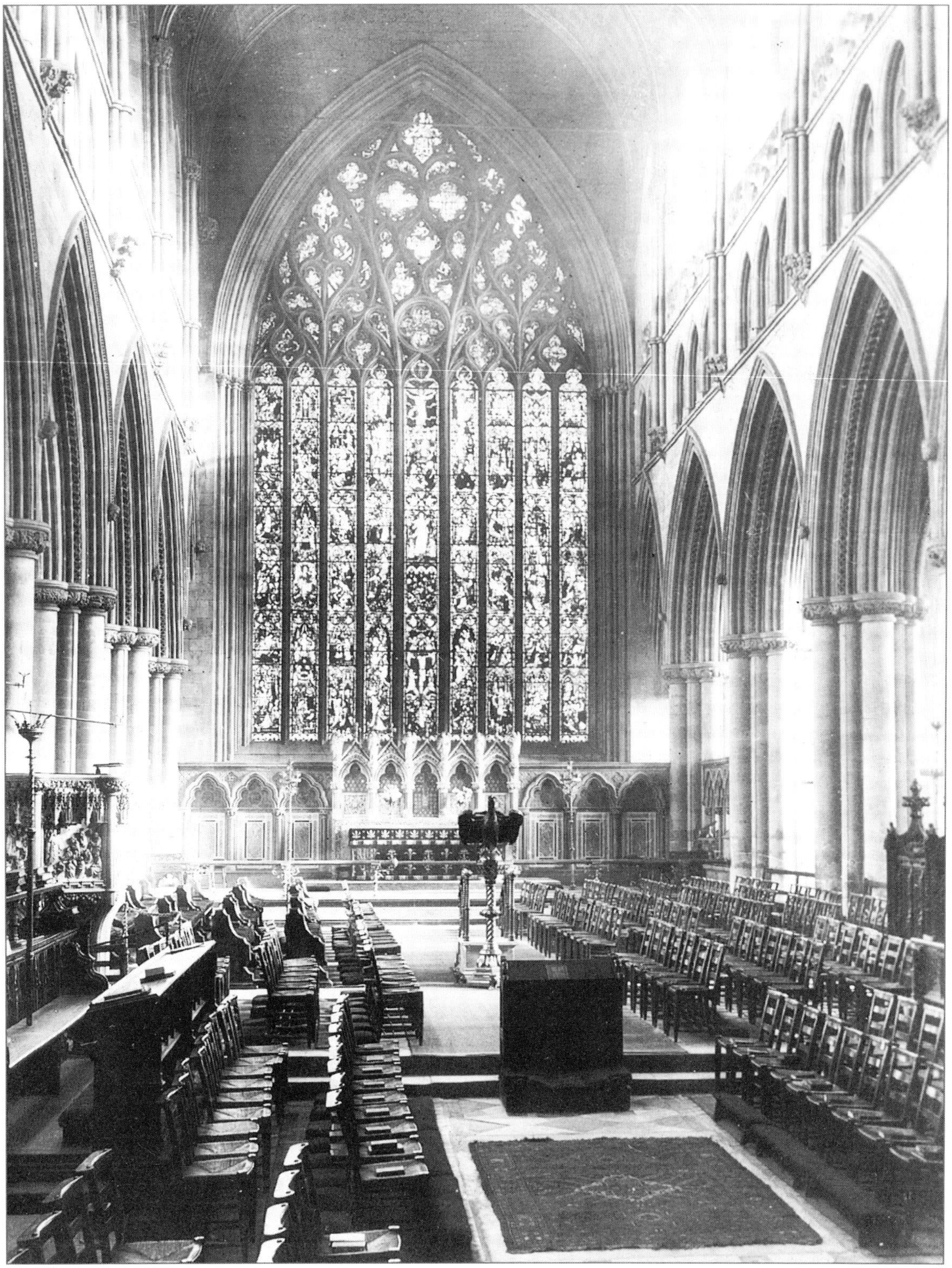

Carlisle Cathedral choir is seen in this 1916 photograph, which is amazing in the coverage of height and width. Like Cartmel this medieval survivor comes to our generation as an Augustinian foundation but also as a cathedral for a bishop, which it has been since its twelfth-century foundation. This is the only cathedral in Cumbria. (*John Marsh Collection*)

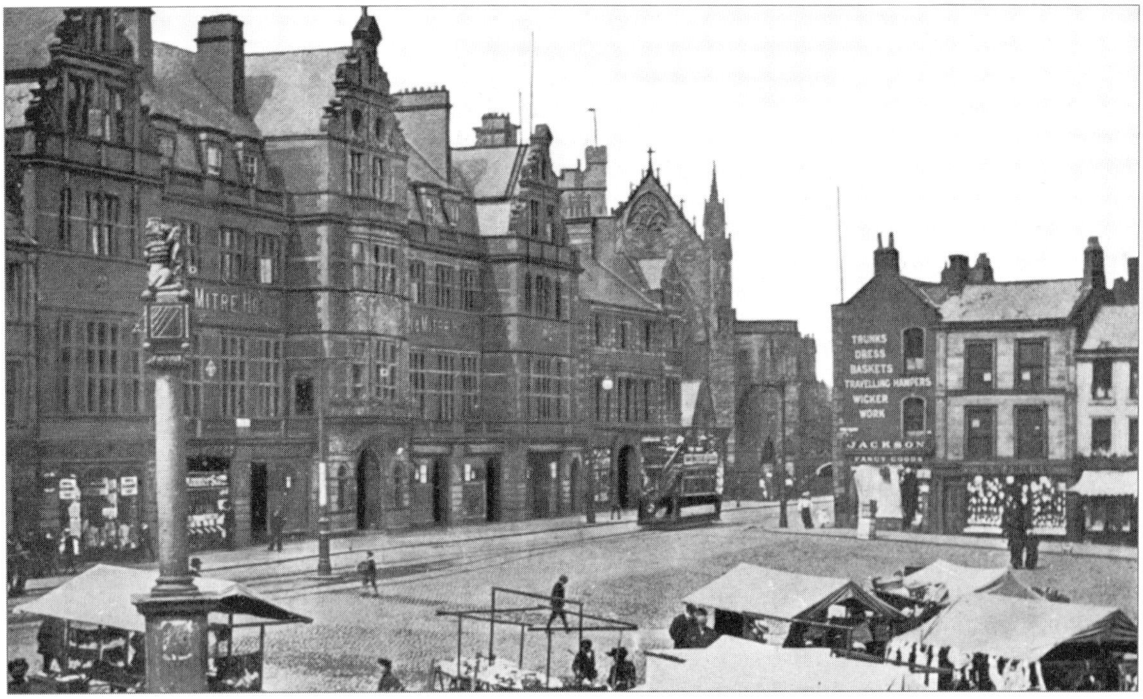

The Crown and Mitre Hotel in Carlisle was photographed across the market-place by Valentine's of Dundee in the first decade of the twentieth century. An electric tram can be seen travelling towards the cathedral and castle. Recent decades have made this area into as fine a city centre as any in the north as motorised traffic has generally been excluded, allowing civilised life to continue here as it has done since Roman times, with a brief fifty years or so of motorised madness in the twentieth century. (*Valentine's of Dundee*)

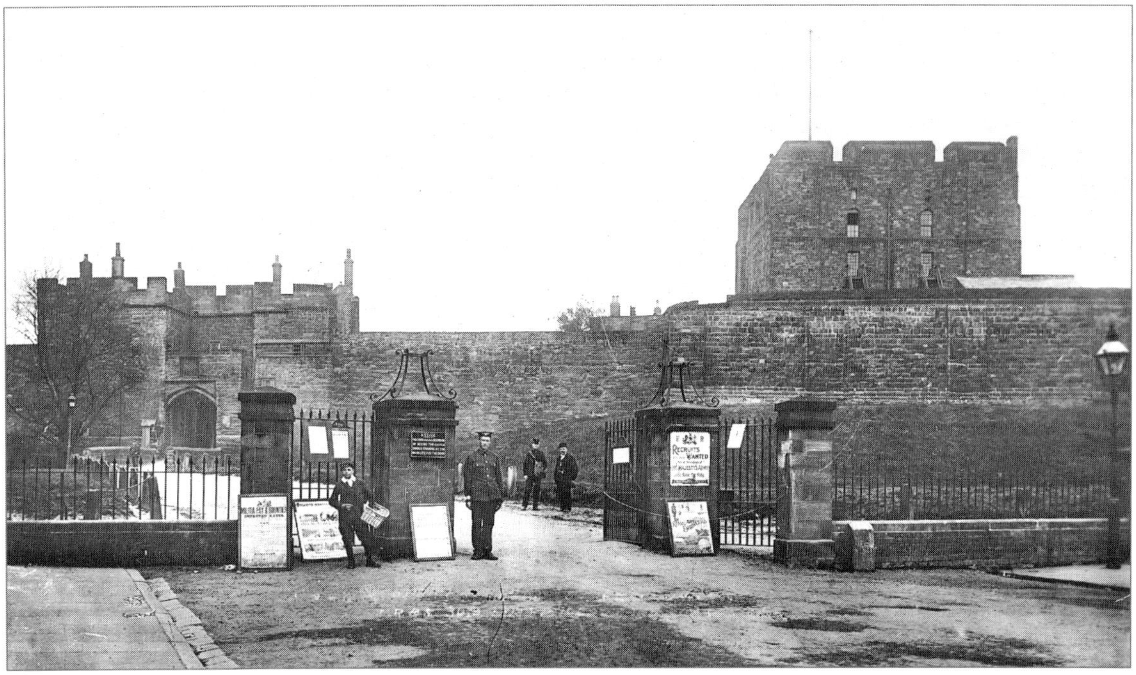

Carlisle Castle in about 1912 with recruiting posters surrounding the outer gates. The boy with a basket stands near a poster explaining the improved rates of Militia pay and bounties. A photograph of the gatehouse at the same period is to be seen on p. 84. (*Reliable Series*)

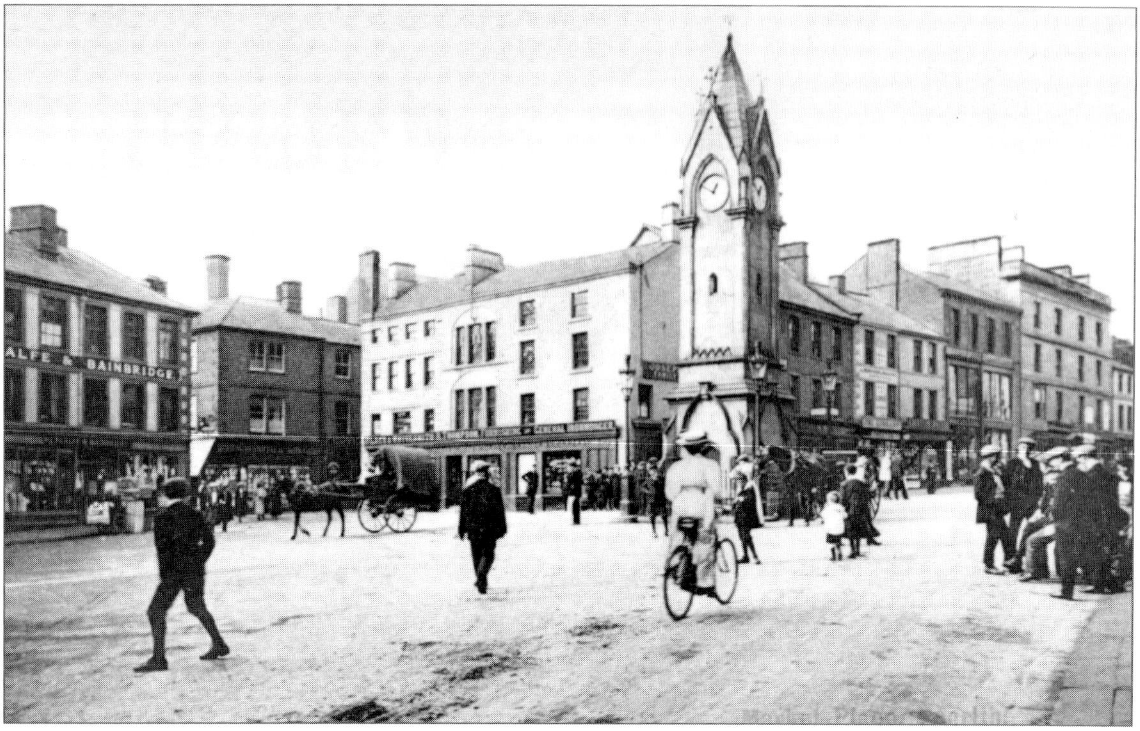

Penrith town centre had a more genteel quality in the days before the A6 road introduced its motorised pollution and virtually cut the town in two. Stengal and Company photographed most towns in the county prior to 1910. 'It is market day here', says Clara to Barbara at Witherslack in 1911, 'and everybody seems busy'. (*Stengal & Co.*)

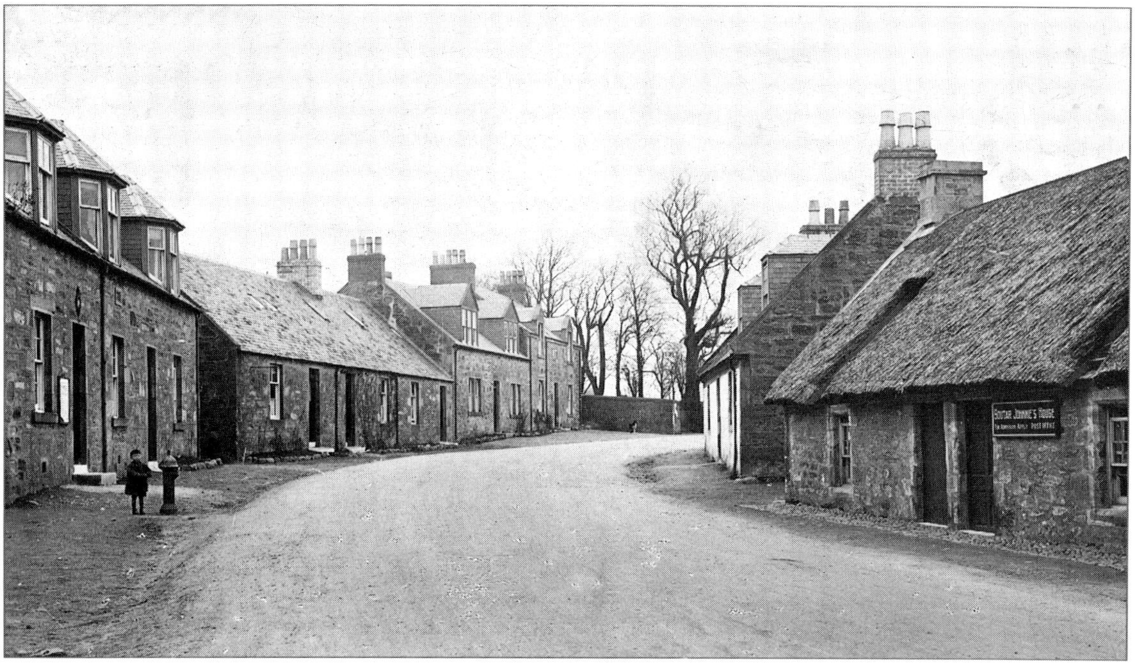

Kirkoswald main street photographed in the 1920s by Wm A. Templeton of the post office. The thatched cottage is that of 'Souter Jonnie' – key available at the post office, says the notice. This village has many memories for listeners to BBC Radio Children's Hour, as it was here that the ashes of the naturalist Romney were scattered. (*Wm A. Templeton*)

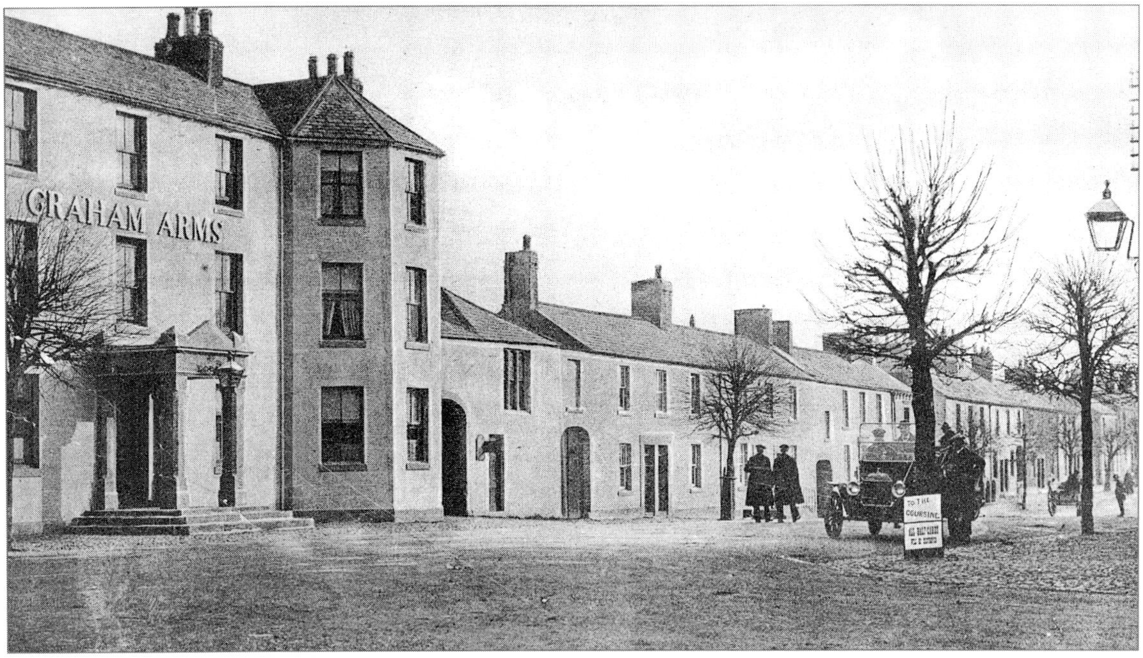

Two photographs by Nicholson & Cartner of Carlisle from the early decades of the twentieth century. Longtown, above, on the border with Scotland with a fine hotel named after the Grahams of Netherby (see p. 120), was always on the main western road from England to Edinburgh. Its market was described at one time as being a dangerous rival to Carlisle. In Brampton, below, the Wednesday market continued to attract local farmers long after the Longtown market had ceased to trade, as the photograph shows. It was in the Brampton area that the Earl of Carlisle laid the first railway in Cumbria in connection with his mining interests on his estates. (*Nicholson & Cartner of Carlisle*)

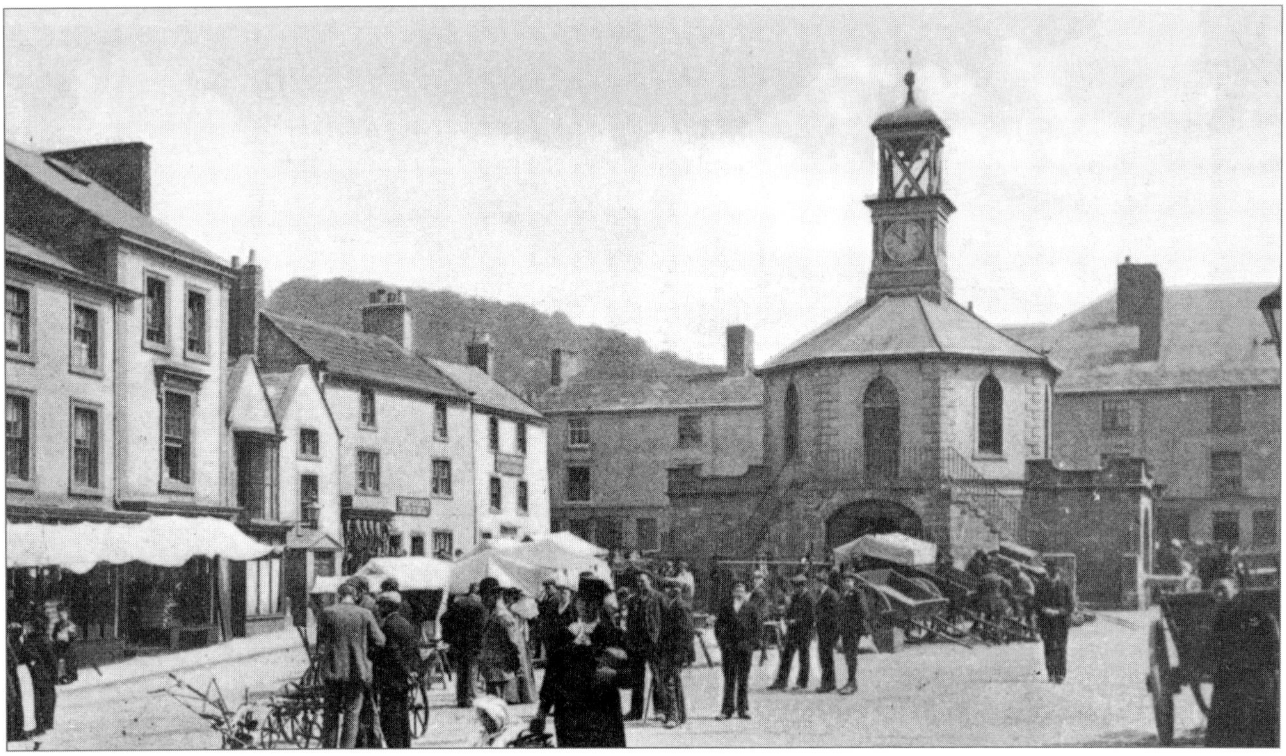

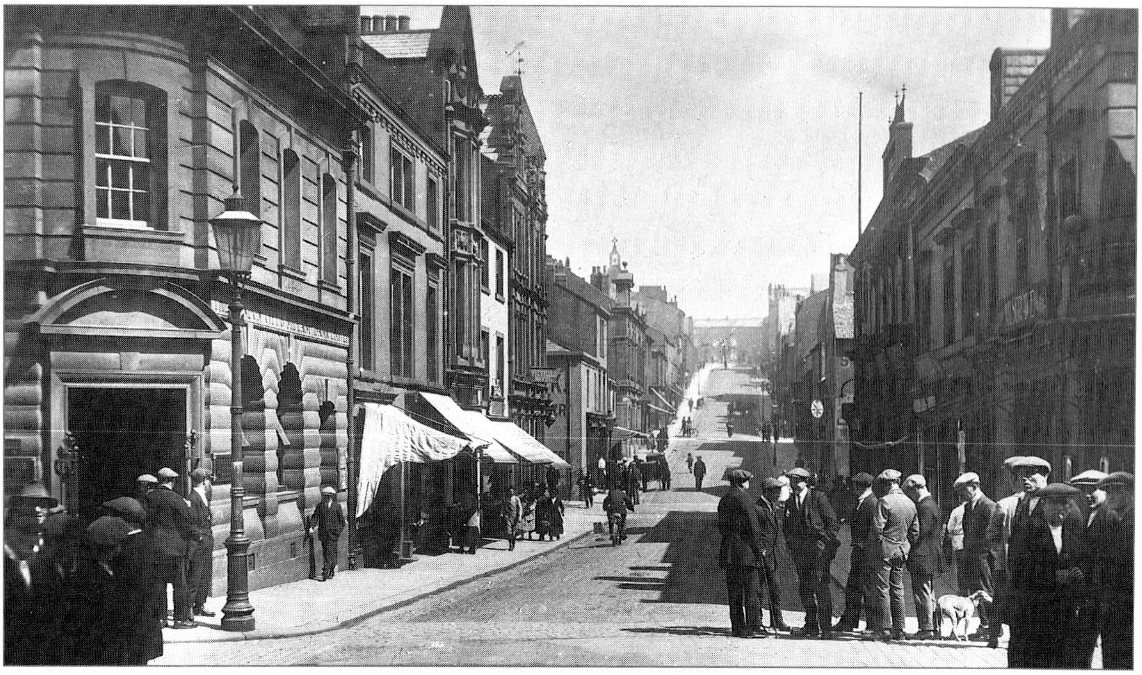

Crosby Street in Maryport, with groups of unemployed men, was photographed in the 1930s by Valentine and Co. to be sold by R. Adair, Stationer of Senhouse Street. Note the whippet which, together with racing pigeons, became a symbol of pastimes for unemployed workers throughout Cumbria in those dark uncaring years. (*Valentine's of Dundee*)

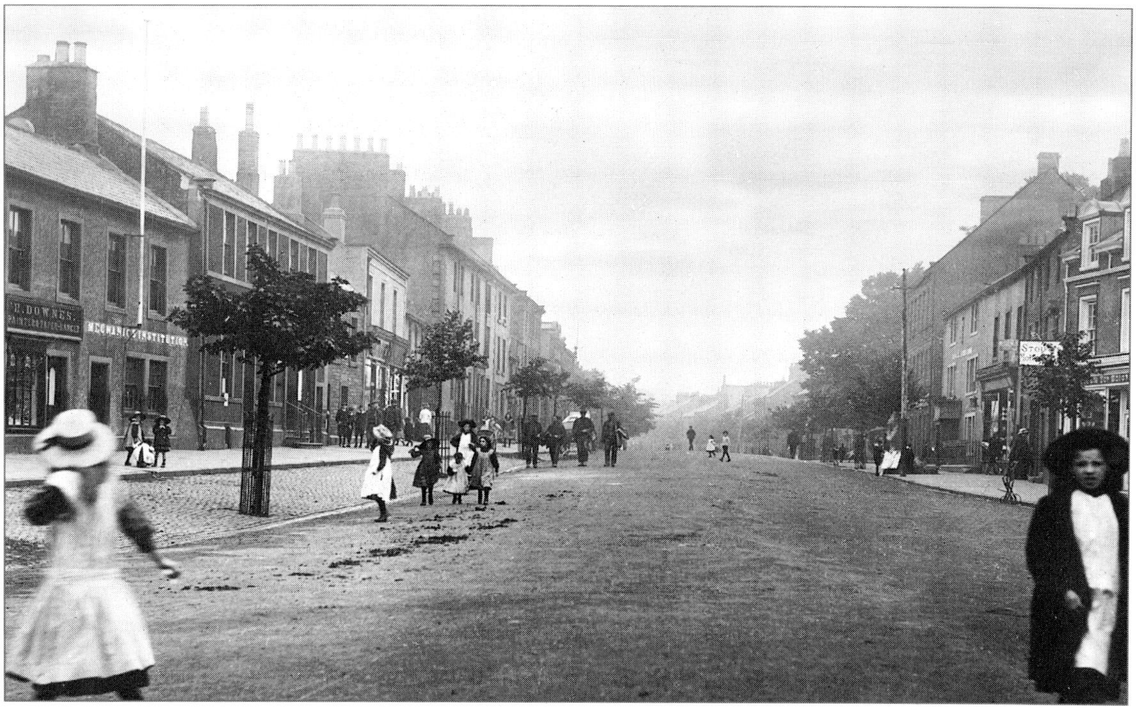

Main Street in Egremont was pictured by 'W. Bros' a decade or so earlier showing a street empty of traffic. In the centre, four miners look as though they are coming off shift from the iron mines and a group of boys and girls wait outside the Mechanics' Institute. The poor of Egremont could get refreshment at the soup kitchen in St Bridget's Lane on Tuesdays and Fridays even decades before the great depression. (*John Marsh Collection*)

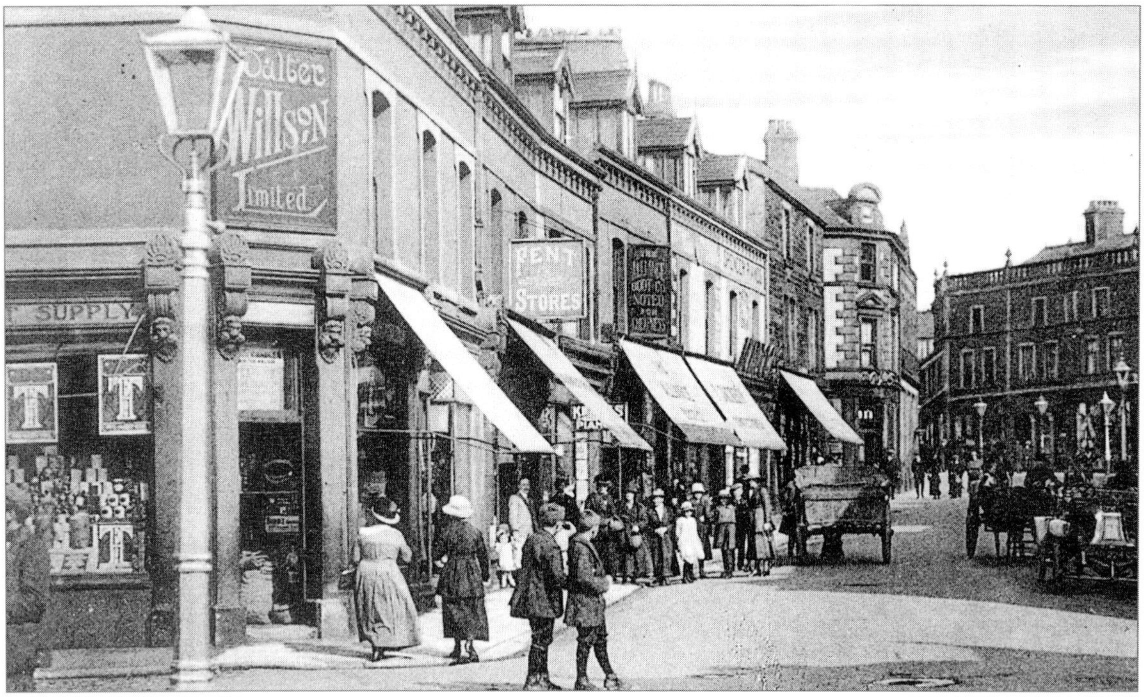

Fisher Street in Workington looks a prosperous place in spite of the depression years. Walter Willson's grocery shop was one of a series of branches in most Cumbrian towns, with a service that was typical of the days before supermarket shopping. The traffic in the picture, of two horse carts and one motor car, will also remind many of better town centre conditions. (*John Marsh Collection*)

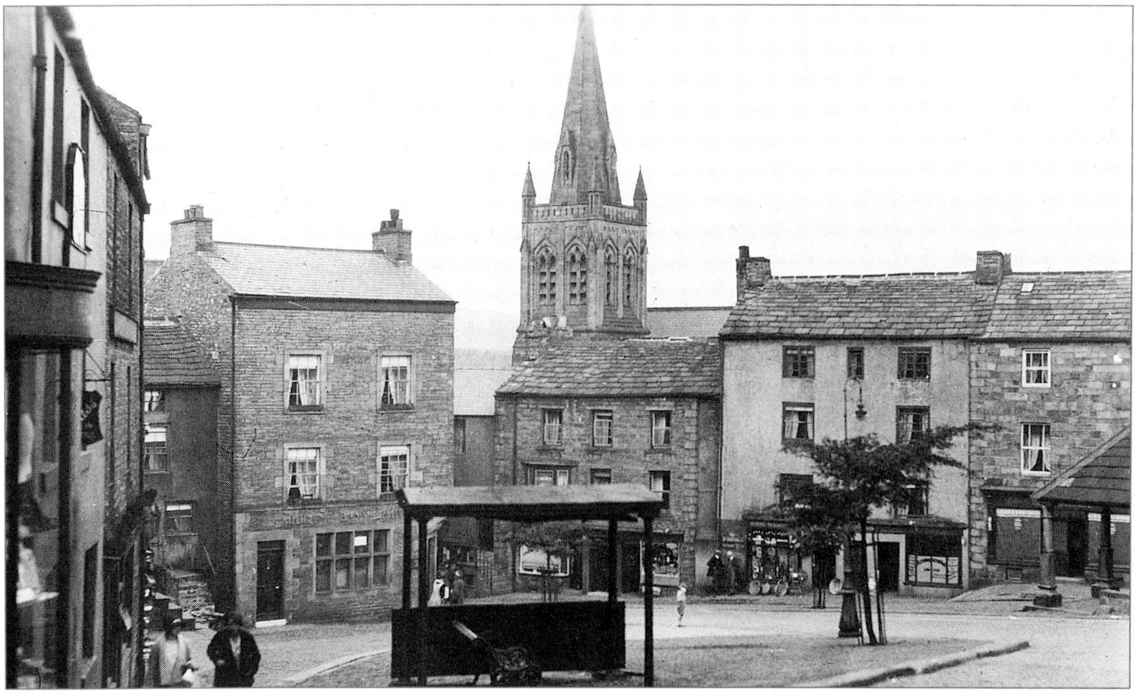

Alston Market Square, seen here in the 1930s, has recently been made famous in a most unlikely way – as a seaport in a TV drama based on Dickens's *Oliver Twist*. At 963 feet above sea level, it could not be more inland although in 1851 the Admiralty owned forty-eight lead mines hereabouts. (*P. Johnston of Gateshead*)

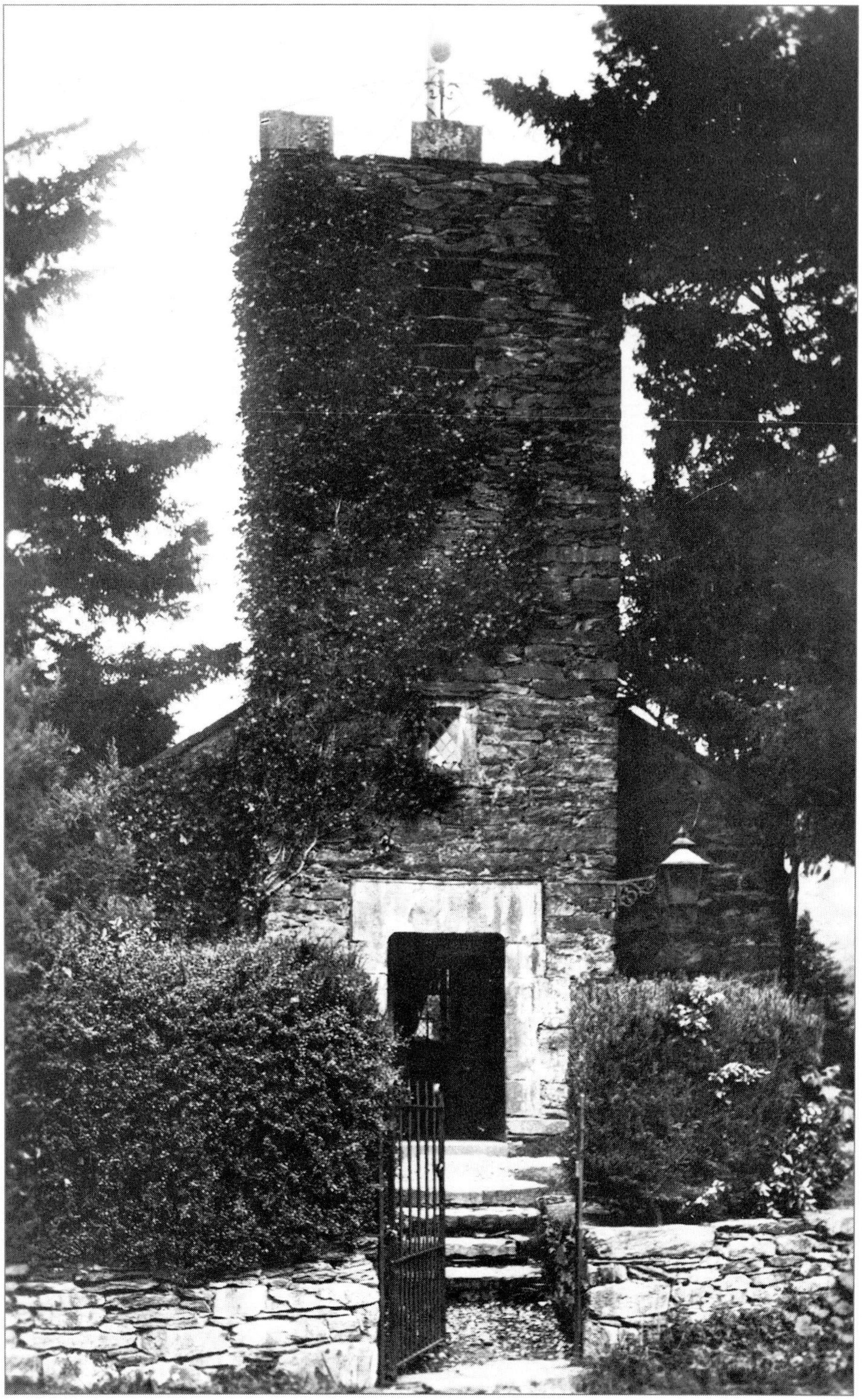

Mardale church was completely destroyed by the Manchester Corporation water engineers in the 1930s. On this page the west tower and main entrance door can be seen and the whole of the interior is shown opposite. Holy Trinity church was built in Mardale in about 1684 to accommodate fifty people. After demolition parts of the fabric were re-used elsewhere by Carlisle Diocese and the water engineers used many of the stones to construct a draw-off tower for their new reservoir. (*Atkinson & Pollitt*)

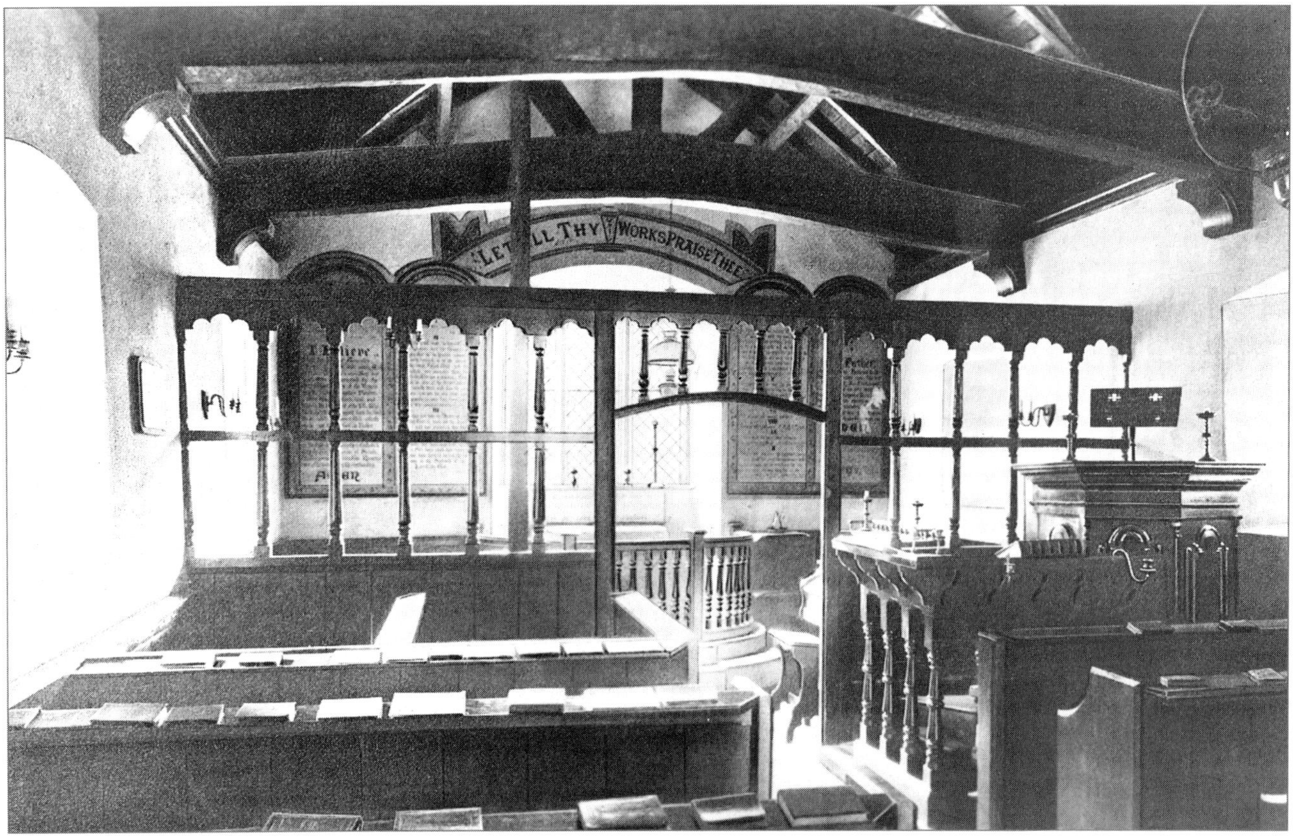
LET
THY WORKS PRAISE THEE

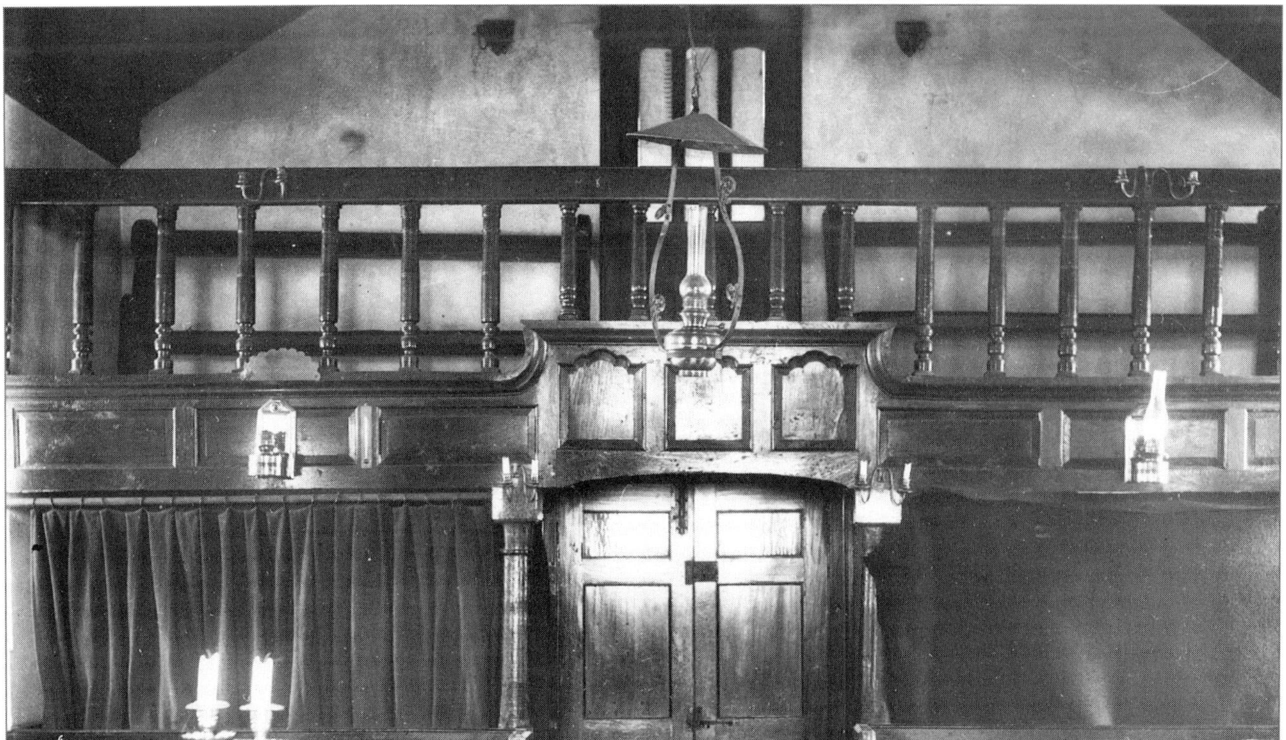

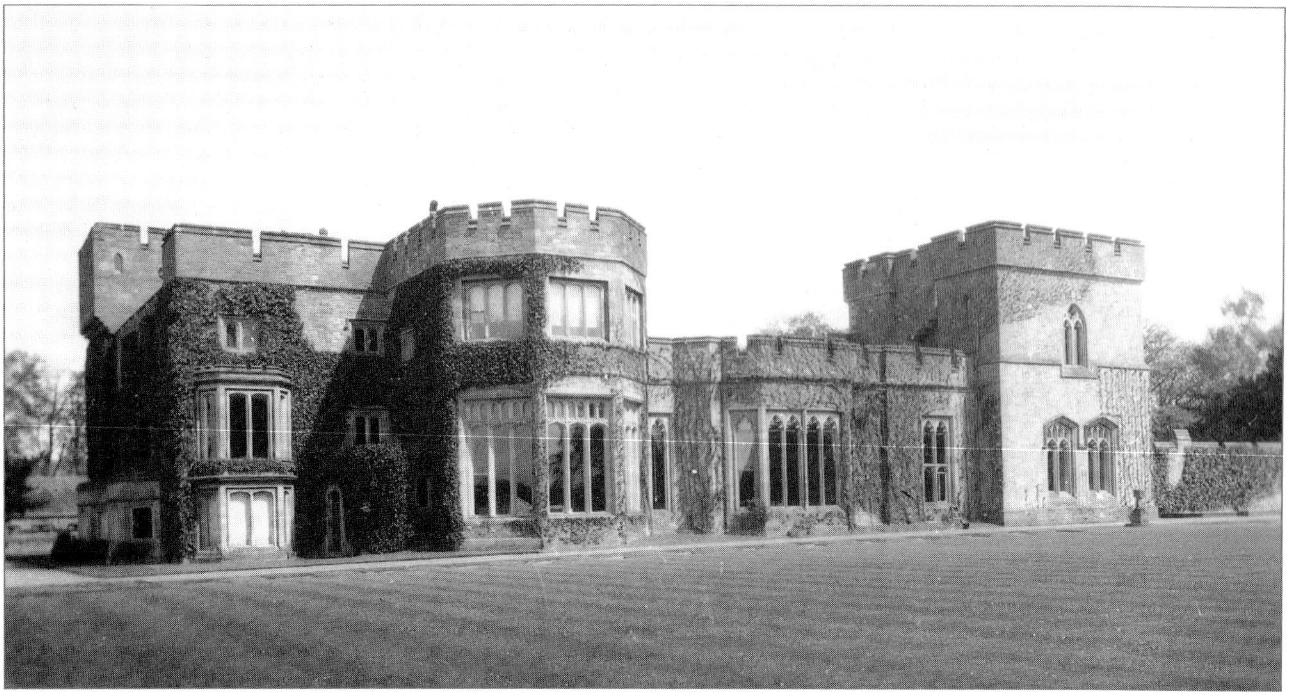

Brougham Hall near Penrith was on the Westmorland side of the River Eamont. It was called 'the Windsor of the North', and dated back to medieval times. When Lord Henry Brougham, who entertained the king in 1905 (see opposite page), died he was succeeded by Lord Victor Henry Peter Brougham who became famous as the man who broke the bank at Monte Carlo. He did it twice, but his gambling debts brought him and Brougham Hall to ruination. In the early 1930s the hall was sold to Geoffrey Carleton Cooper, an adjoining landowner, who set about its demolition in 1934. Very little of it now remains but there are plans for restoration and some ex-domestic buildings now house businesses. Above, the hall from the south garden. (*John Marsh Collection*) Below, the hall from the road to Eamont Bridge. (*E. Sankey of Barrow*)

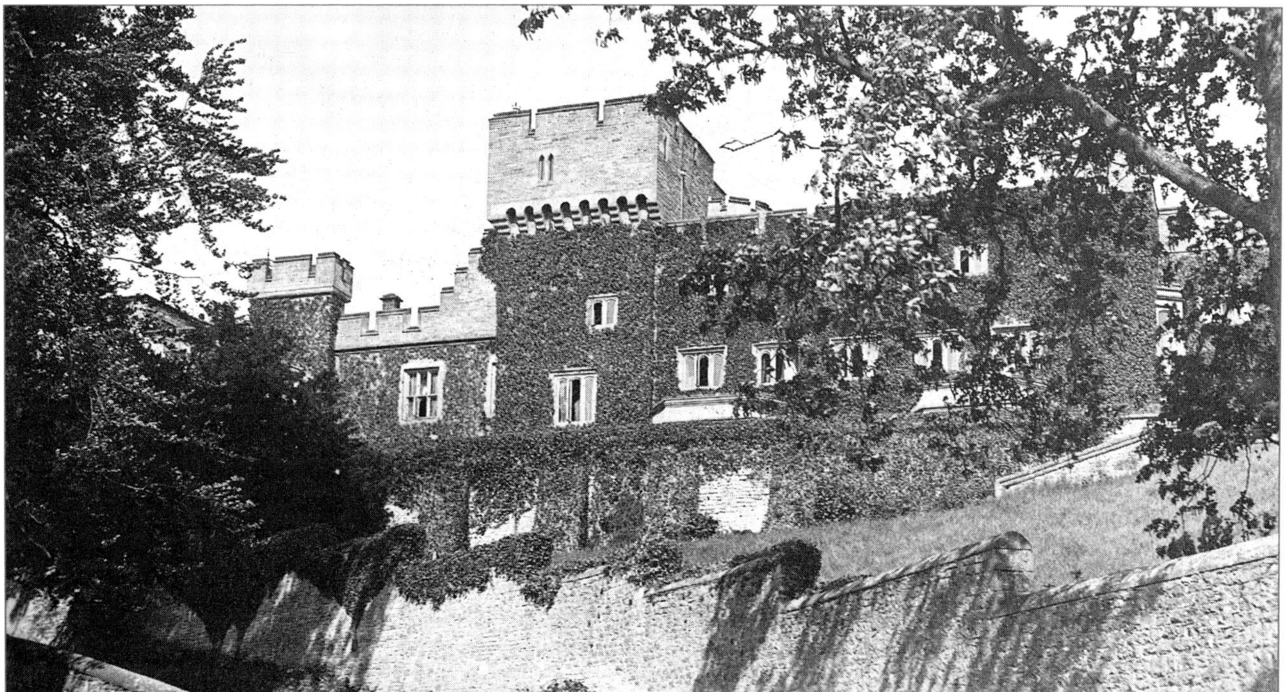

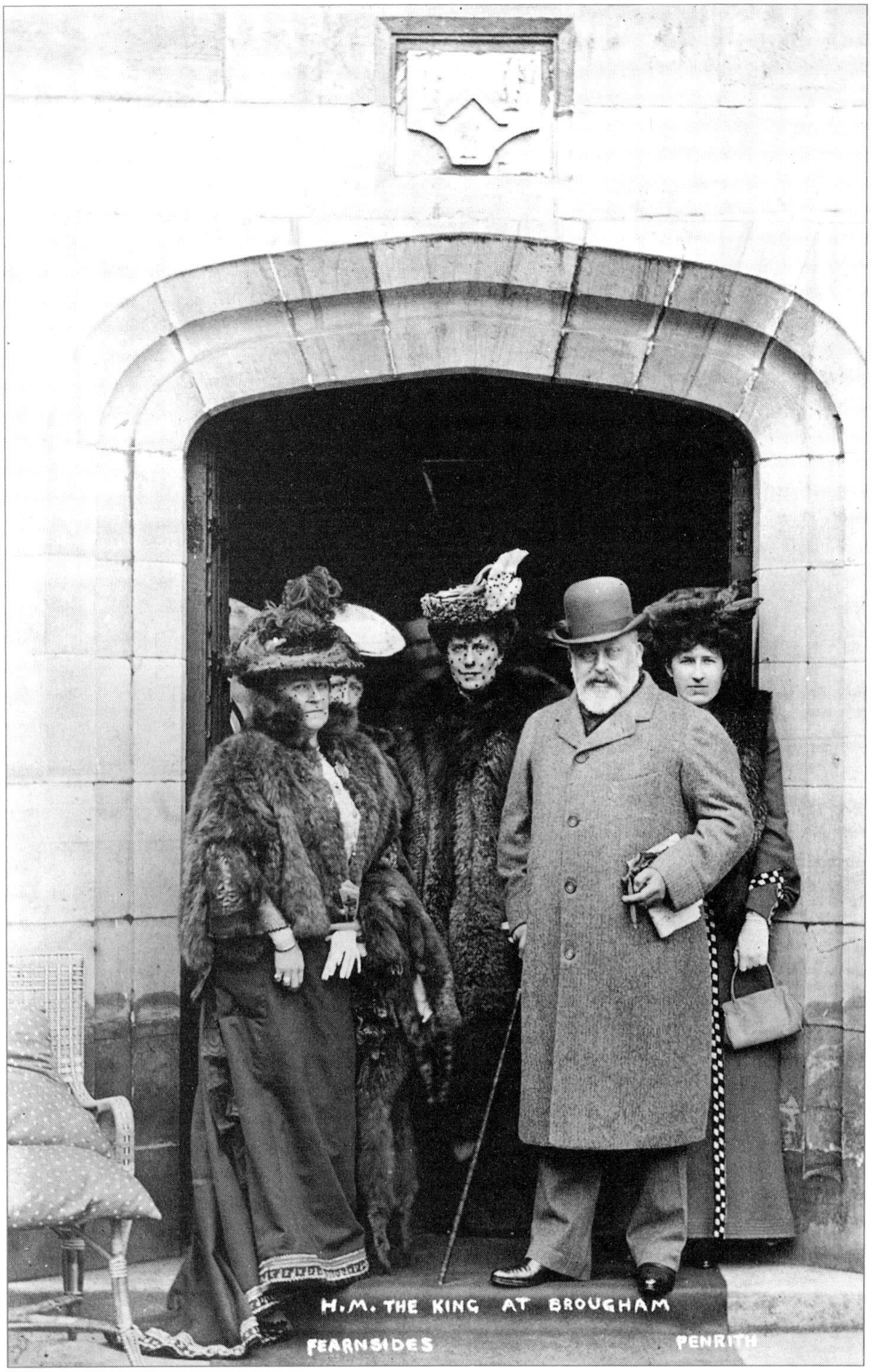

Brougham Hall, October 1905, when King Edward VII, seen with cigar, cane and mistress stayed for a week with Lord Brougham and Vaux. Mrs Alice Keppel is seen looking over the king's left shoulder. In press reports of the event she was named as 'The Honourable Mrs George Keppel'. This was the political time of the great Liberal revival which caused a constitutional crisis only a few years later when most of the Tory Lords refused to foot the bill to pay for the proposed reforms. Lord Henry Brougham was a leading Liberal. (*Fearnside of Penrith*)

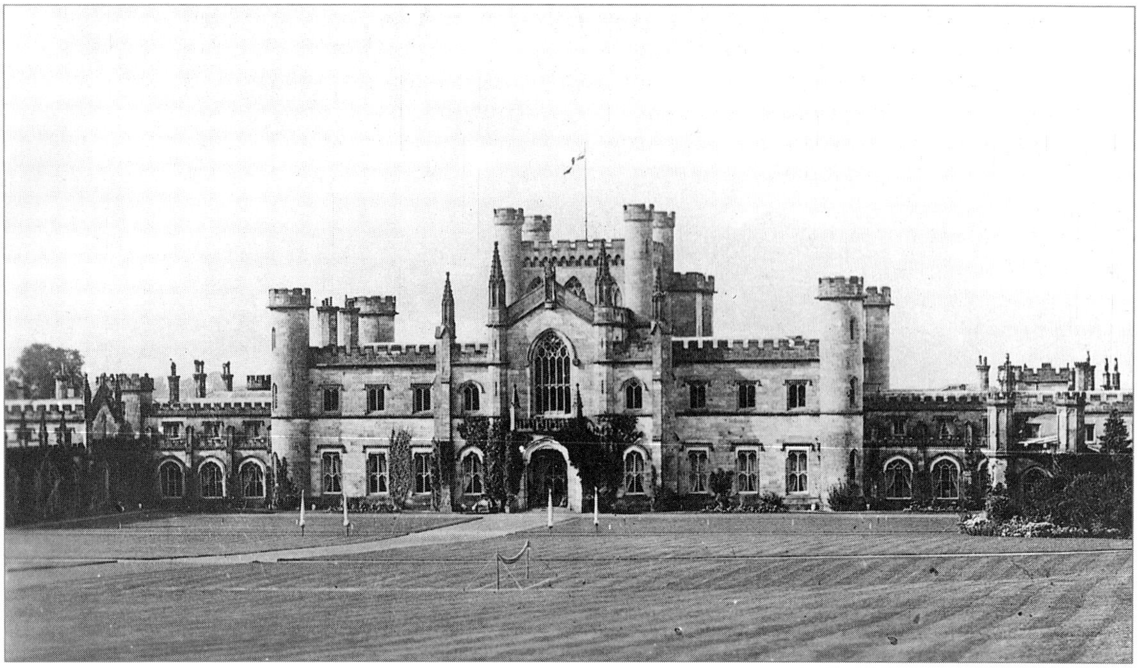

Lowther Castle was the home of the Lowther family, Earls of Lonsdale, but after the death of Lord Hugh (the Yellow Earl) in 1944 it was never used by the family again. Many people in the Penrith area will have memories of the 'sale of the century' in April, May and June 1947, when the valuable contents were sold – with little achieving the market value. The castle was the centre of a secret tank range during the war and suffered much from occupation by the military. Some years after the sale the building was reduced to a shell. (*Atkinson & Pollitt*)

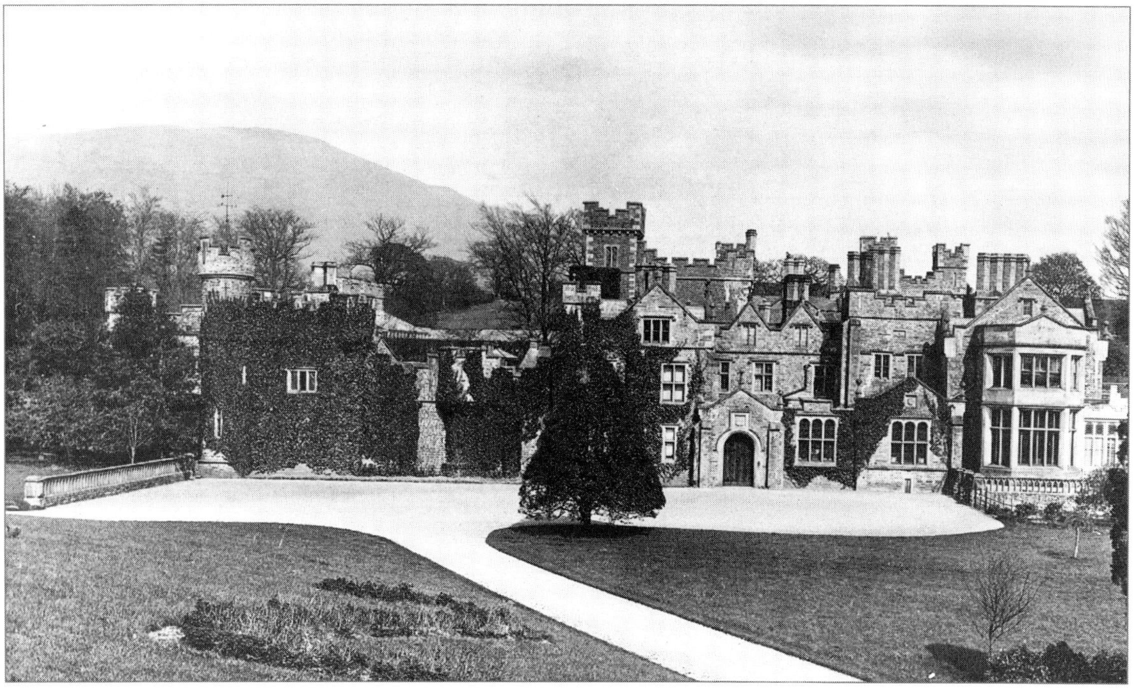

Ingmire Hall near Sedbergh was photographed by Valentine's of Dundee in the early years of the twentieth century when it was occupied by the Upton-Cottrel-Dormer family. Postwar years have not been kind to the ancient fabric which has suffered fire and partial demolition. (*Valentine's of Dundee*)

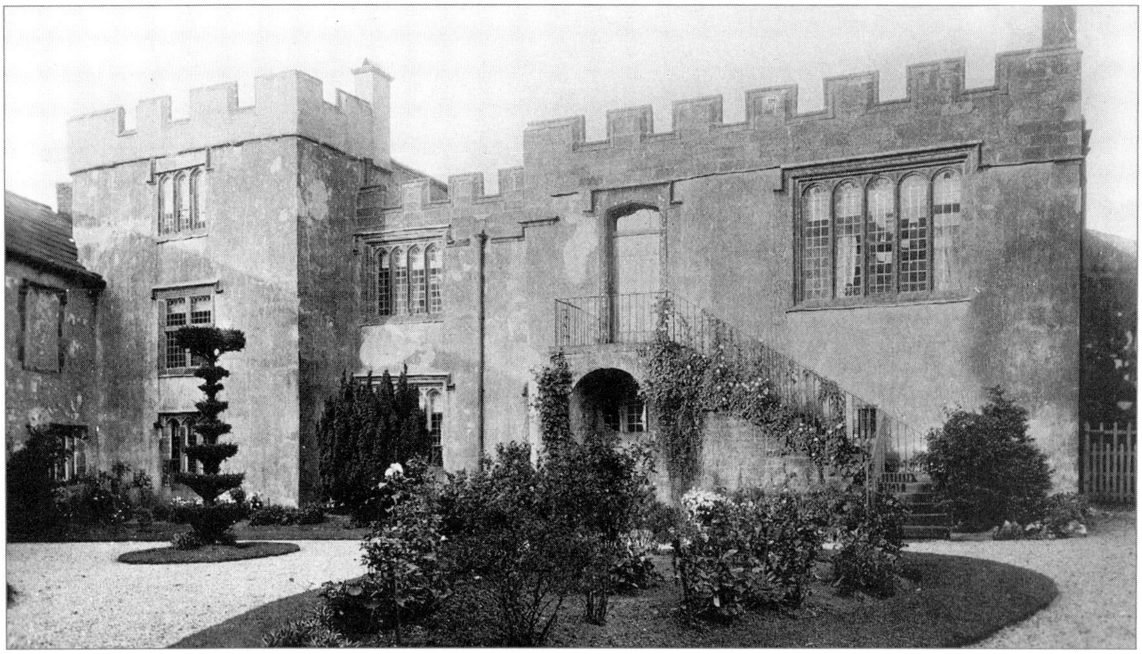

Wharton Hall near Kirkby Stephen is now a farmhouse, but as the home of the Wharton family from medieval times it became famous. Sir Thomas was knighted by Henry VIII and Lord Philip was a Parliamentary colonel under Oliver Cromwell. Lord Thomas, his son, was active in bringing William of Orange to the throne and he composed the famous 'Lillibullero' used by the Protestant cause (and the BBC World Service) until today. The last Lord Wharton died as a traitor in Spain in 1731. (*Close of Kirkby Stephen*)

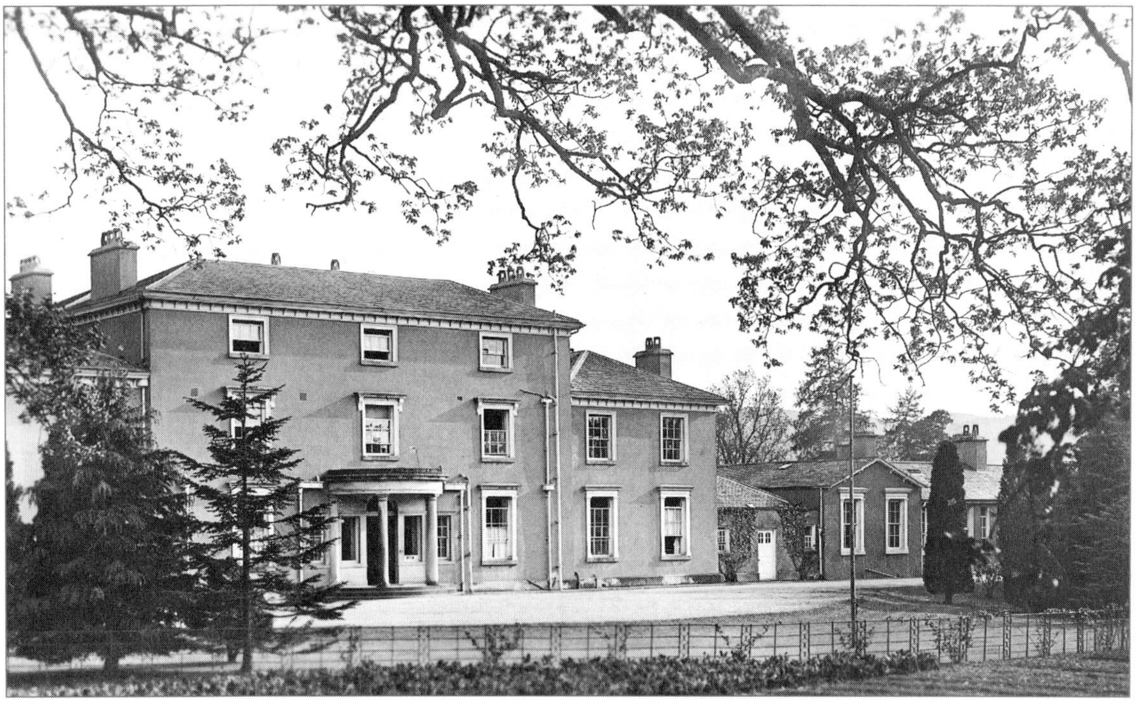

Calgarth Hall photographed by Atkinson & Pollitt in the 1930s when it was a hospital. The First World War saw this house occupied by the army as a hospital. Subsequently it became an orthopaedic hospital for children; this lasted until the 1970s when health reorganisation left it to be redeveloped as private retirement residential units. (*Atkinson & Pollitt*)

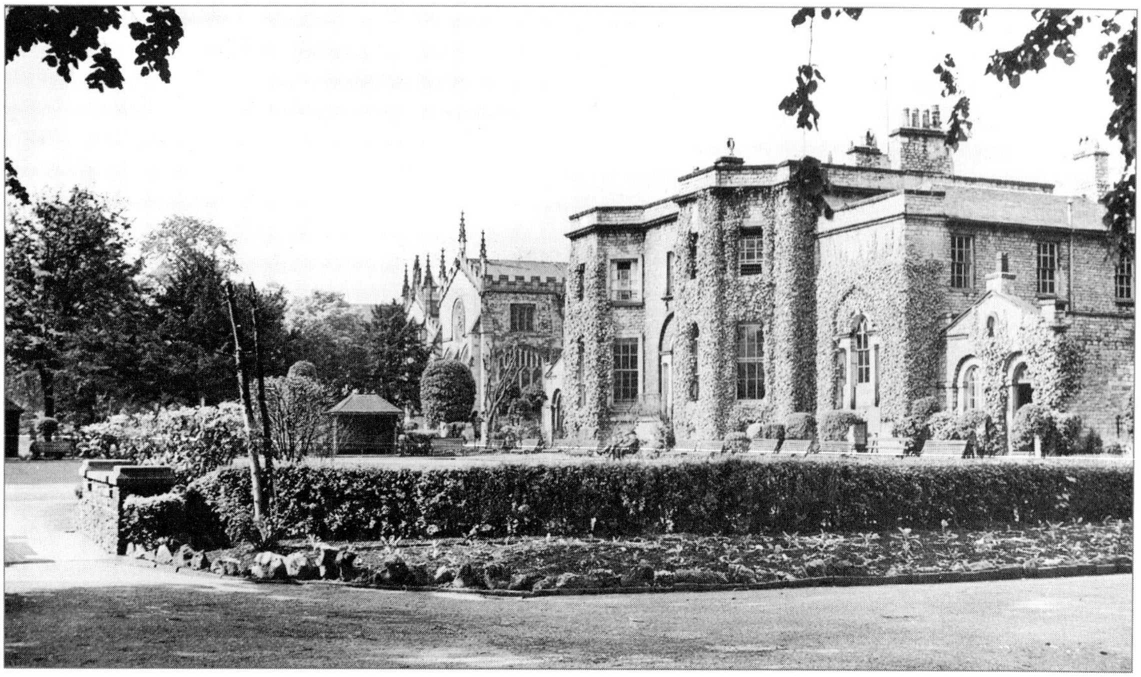

Abbot Hall, above, in the Kirkland area of Kendal as it was in the years when the then owner, Kendal Borough Council, was wondering what to do with the ancient mansion which had been gifted to them at the 1897 Jubilee. Its survival owes little to the council which seriously considered demolition, as was the vogue in the 1930s. Abbot Hall escaped the knock-it-down madness but a delightful 'old maids' hospital building, below, which the council acquired from the Dowker Charity at the entrance to Abbot Hall Park, was not so lucky. This Webster-designed treasure was swept away by the Borough Council to allow a new road to enter Highgate as part of the banal redevelopment of land acquired by the 1950s slum clearance of many of Kendal's ancient yards. Both views date from the 1930s. (*Atkinson & Pollitt*)

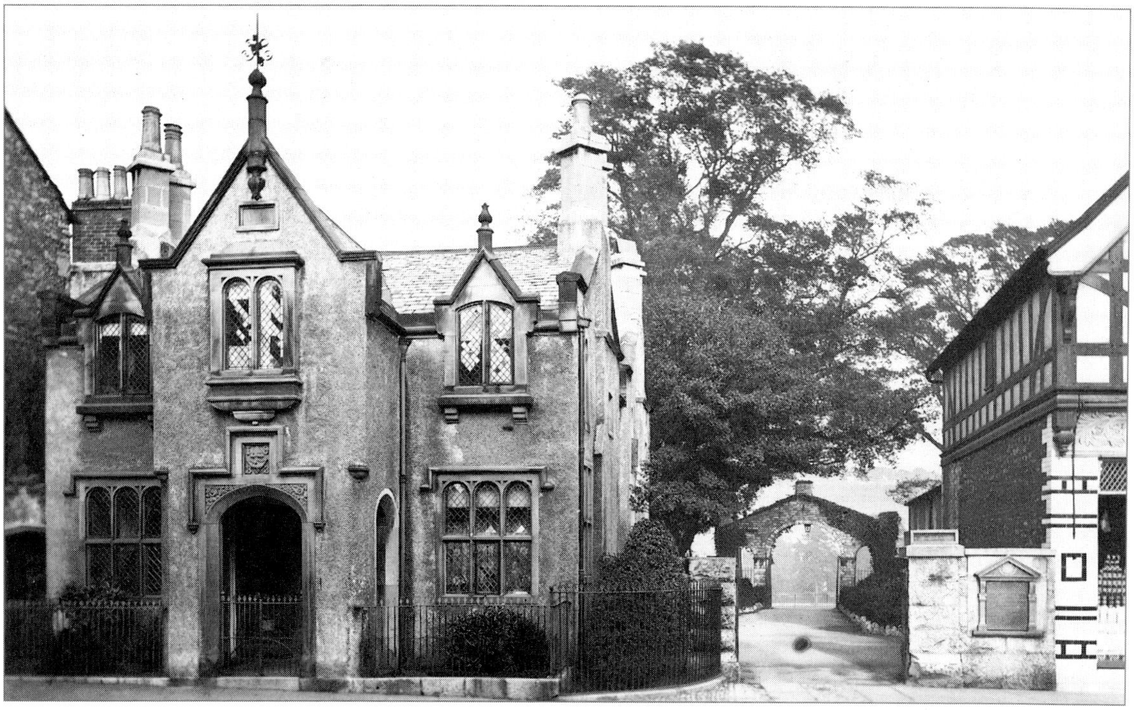

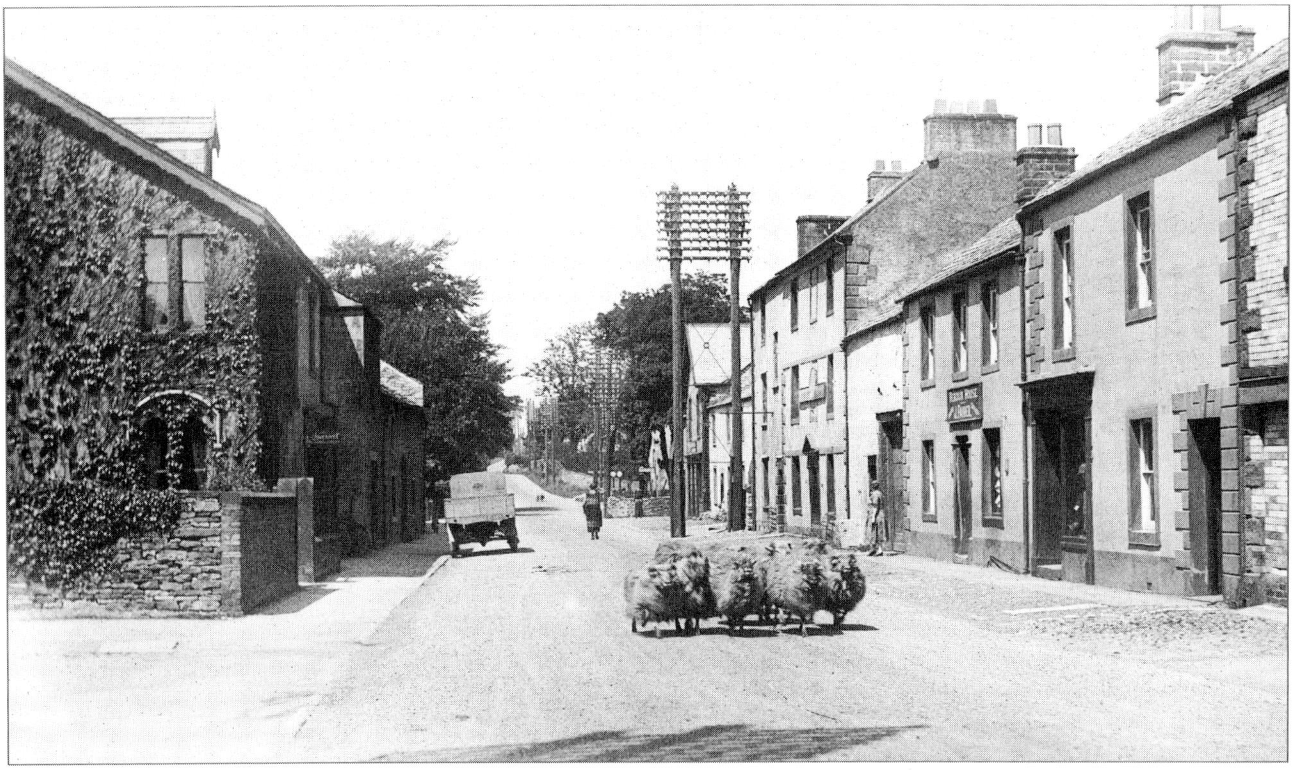

Shap main street in September 1925. A flock of sheep outside Fairer's shop and a small lorry offer memories of life on the A6 at the time. The main trunk telephone system followed the A6 for many miles and can be seen in the shape of the huge telegraph poles beside the road. (*Atkinson & Pollitt*)

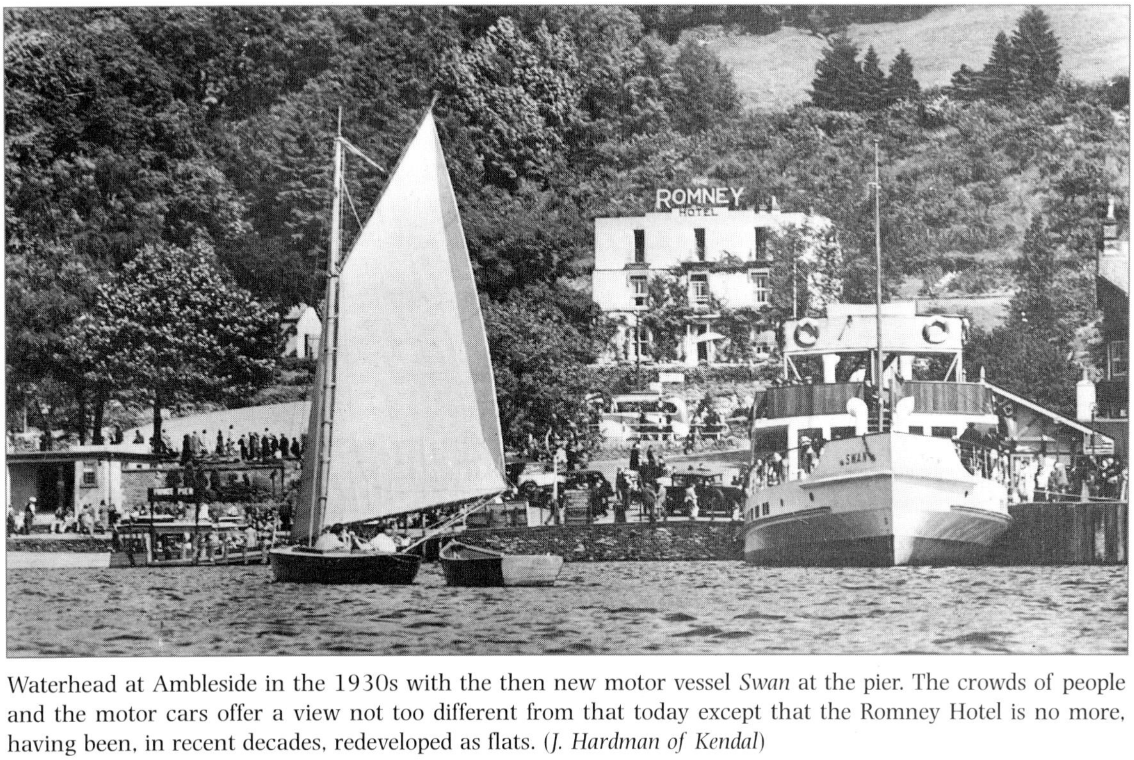

Waterhead at Ambleside in the 1930s with the then new motor vessel *Swan* at the pier. The crowds of people and the motor cars offer a view not too different from that today except that the Romney Hotel is no more, having been, in recent decades, redeveloped as flats. (*J. Hardman of Kendal*)

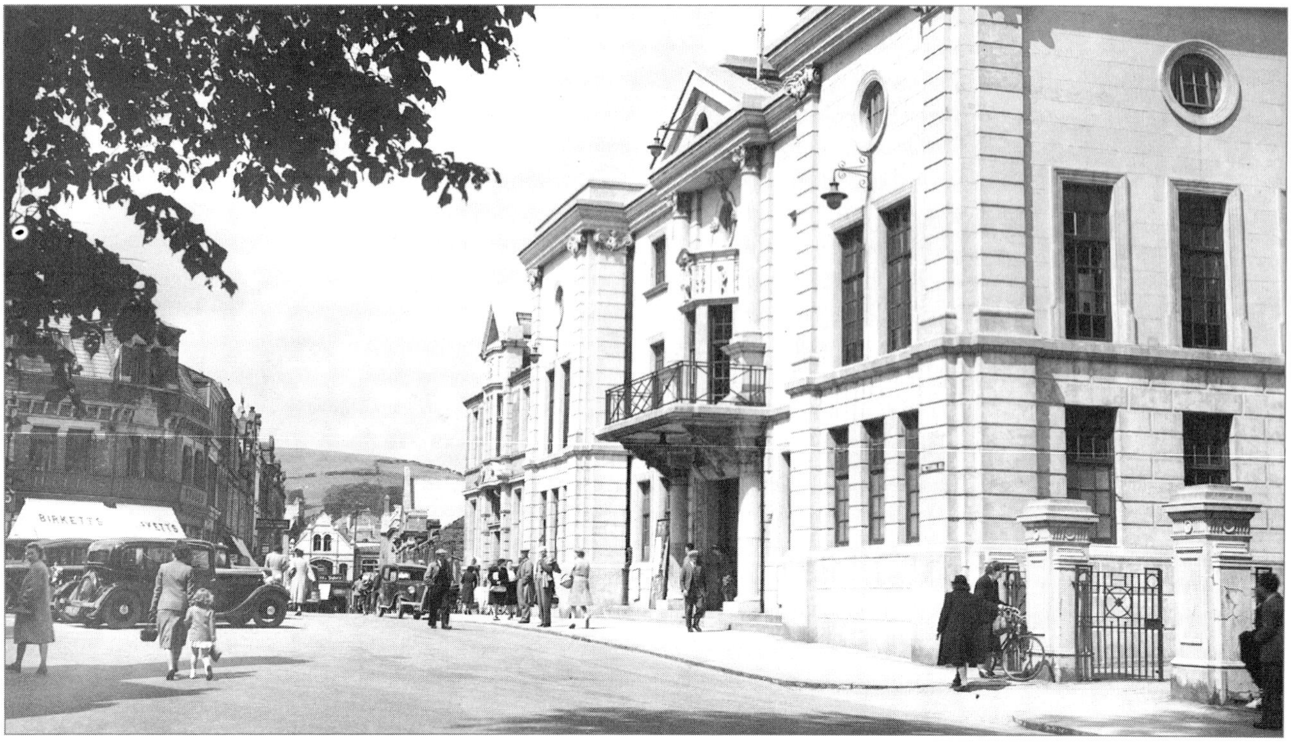

Ulverston in the 1930s: this is the town the authors grew up in. Above, the scene in County Square shows the nearly new Coronation Hall built in a style of municipal architecture soon to give way to the banal and functional. The Lancashire county policeman below is seen on point duty where the Market Street traffic (when there was any) merged with the main road. In those days the town had its own non-politicised Urban District Council and was in the Lancashire county area which offered many benefits: these were lost at the advent of Cumbria and the South Lakeland District Council. (*Atkinson & Pollitt*)

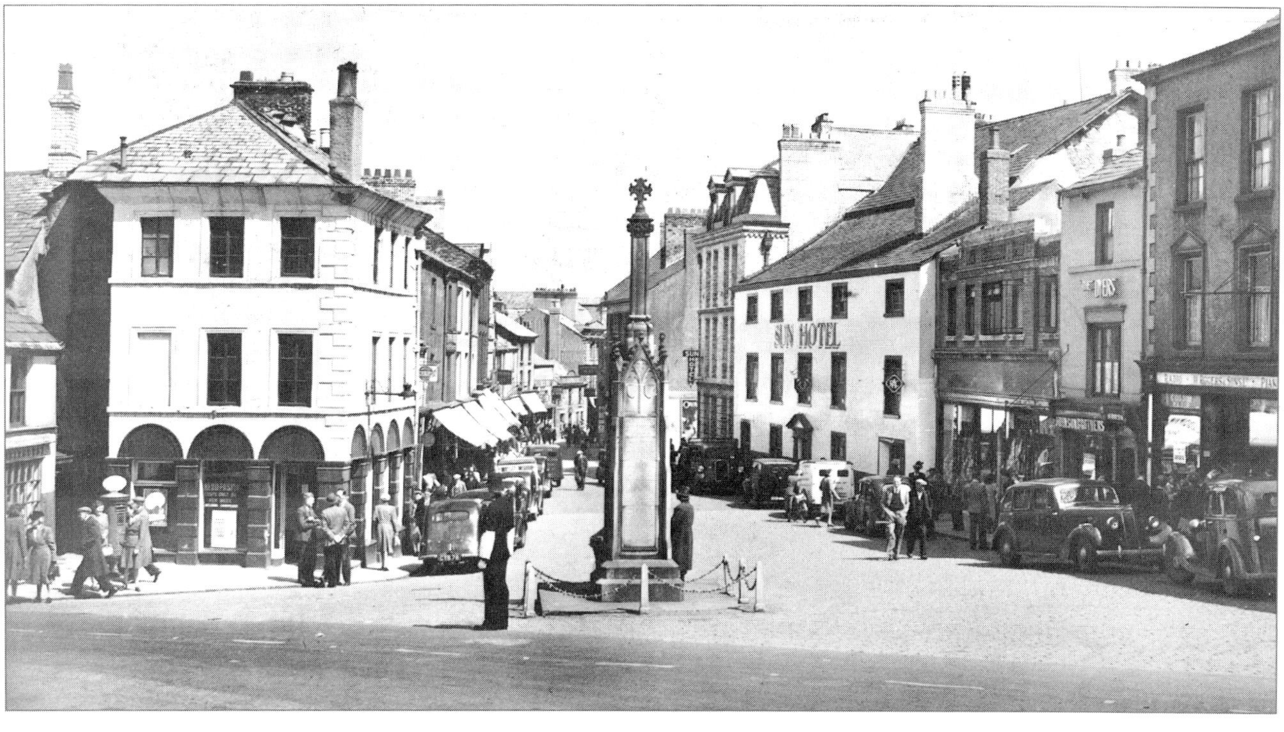

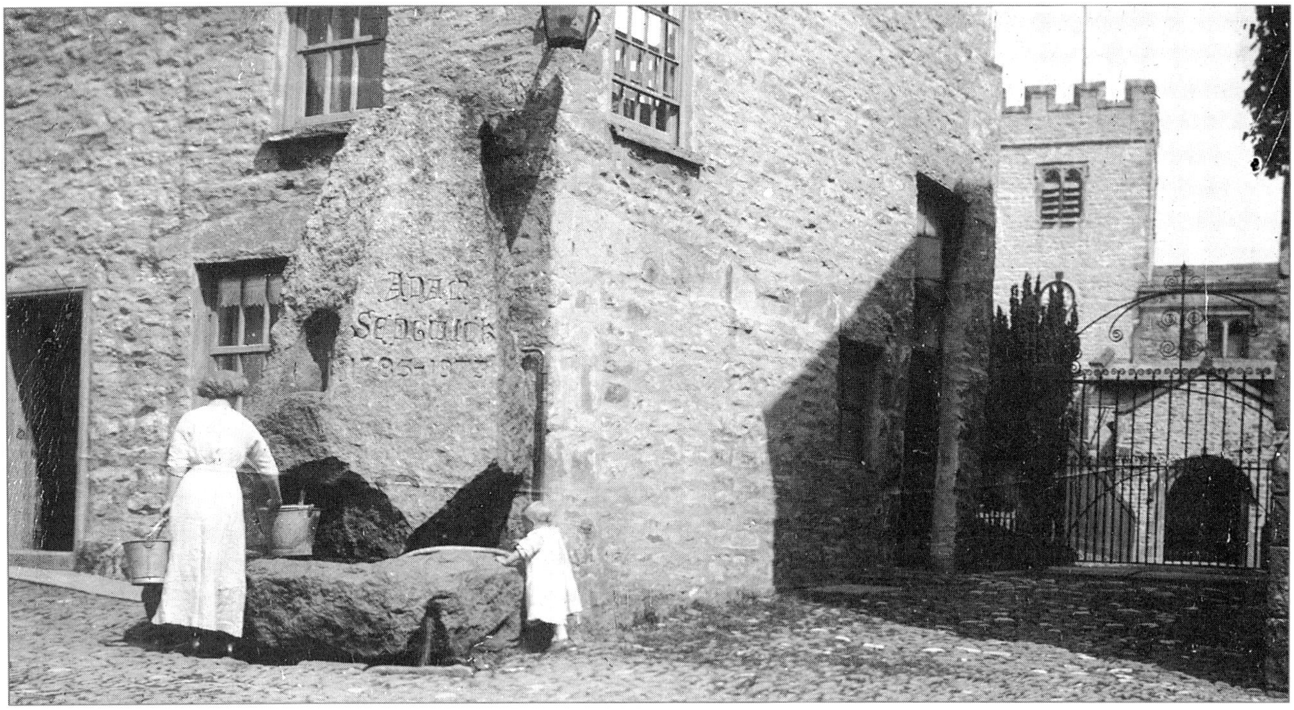

Dent was in the Yorkshire Dales until 1974 and is seen, above, when the water supply came through a fountain built into a granite block provided by Adam Sedgwick, Dentdale's famous son, as a memorial to himself. The fountain still exists but the village water supply is now piped to houses. (*M. Harper of Dent*) Below, the picture shows the Sportsman's Inn at the head of the dale. Nothing much has changed thereabouts. (*Atkinson & Pollitt*)

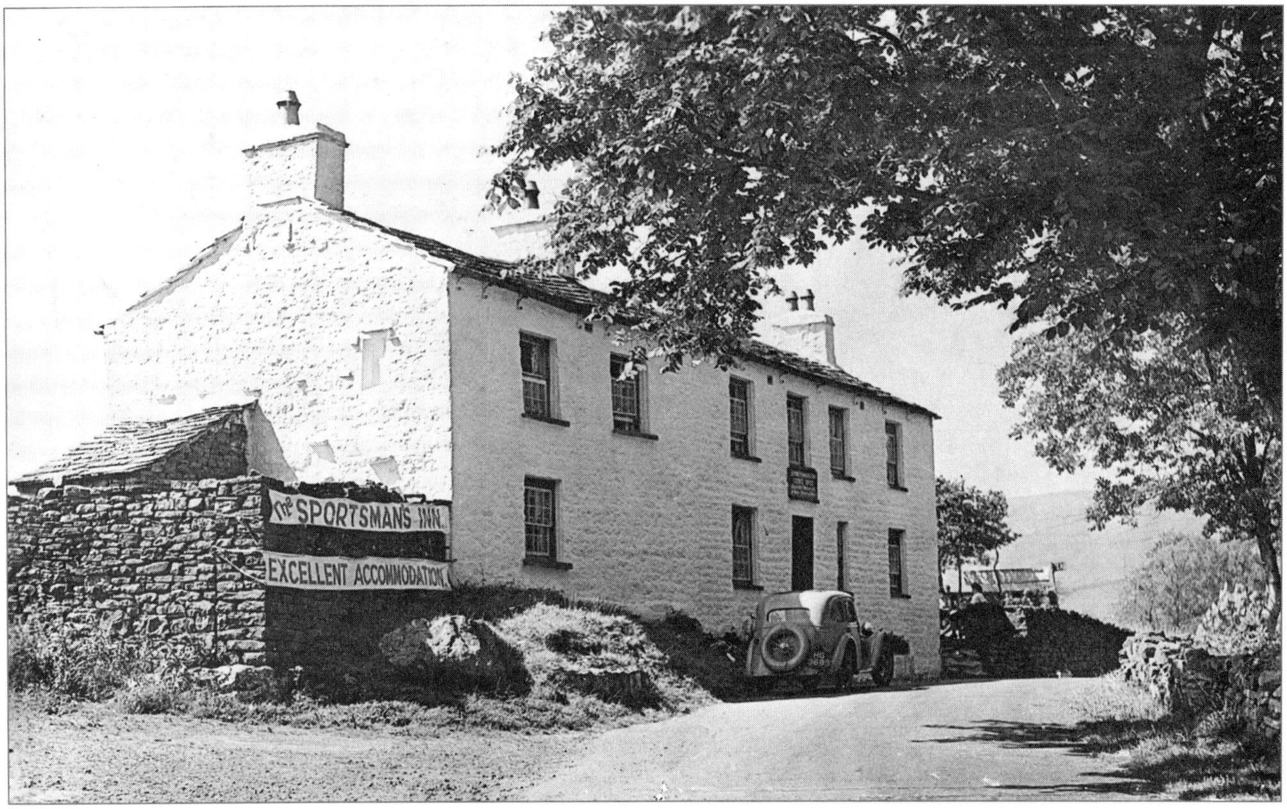

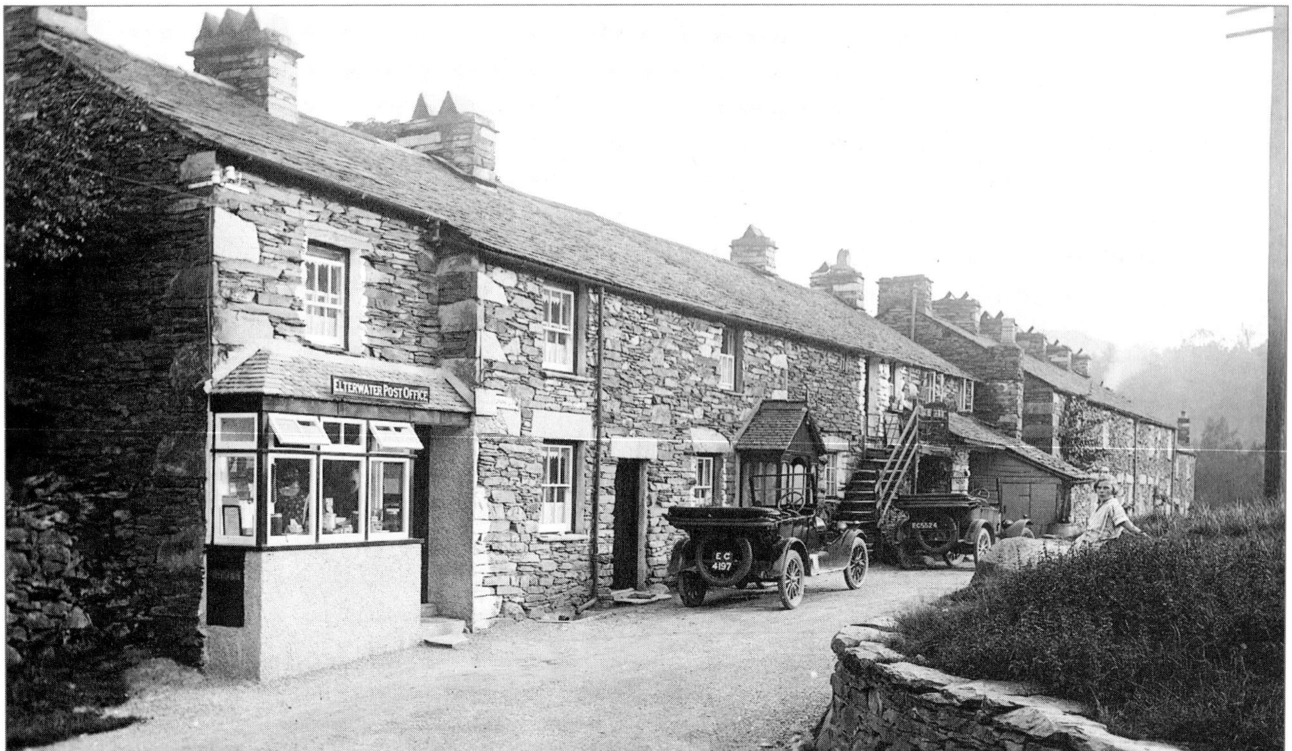

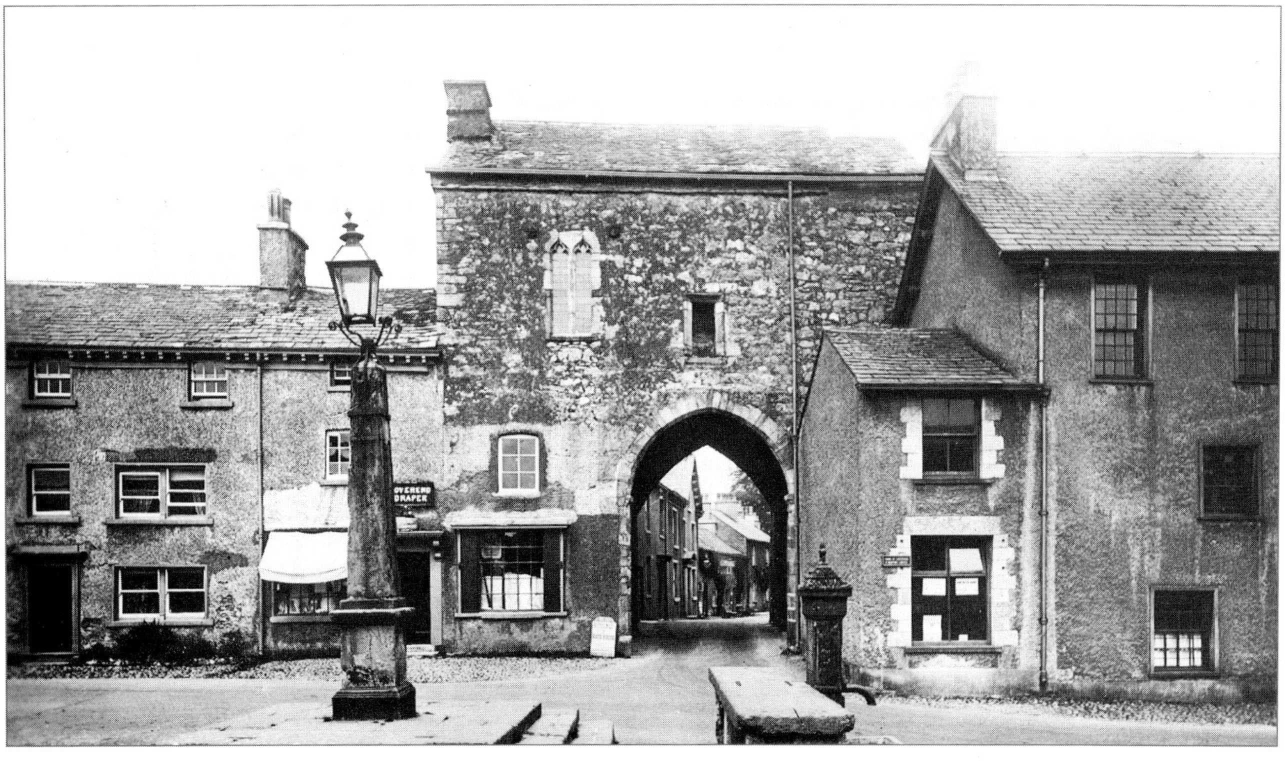

Elterwater with two Model T Fords and its post office built into one of the row of quarry workers' cottages, above, and Cartmel Square, below, when the village had a draper's shop. Both locations have now altered but still provide memories of quieter times. (*Atkinson & Pollitt*)

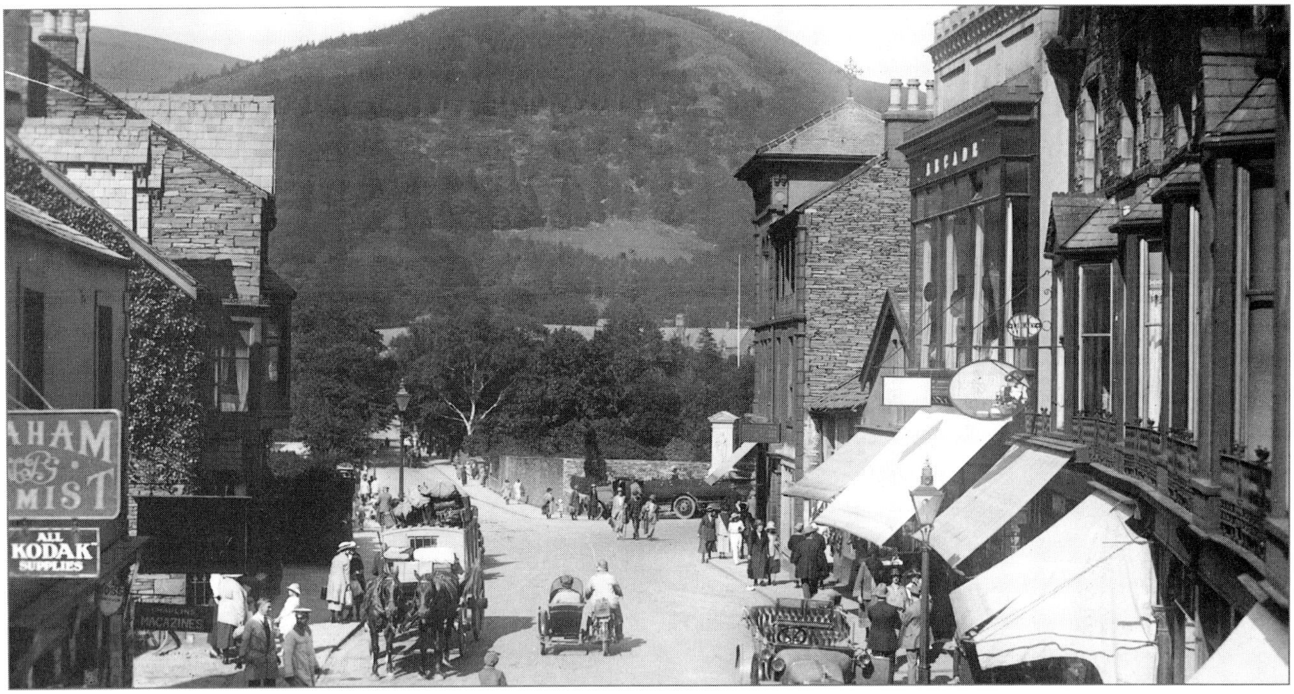

Keswick in the early days of the motor car. Station Street, above, was pictured when one of the hotels still had a horse-drawn bus to bring clients from the station, although there is a motor charabanc by the war memorial and other motor vehicles to be seen. (*G.P. Abraham*) There is an outdoor meeting by the Moot Hall, Main Street, below, and a farmer still has his horse and cart for transport. Note the cycles and motor cycles for hire on the right (see also pp. 32, 39 and 108, which show the changing face of this Lakeland market town). (*Alfred Pettitt*)

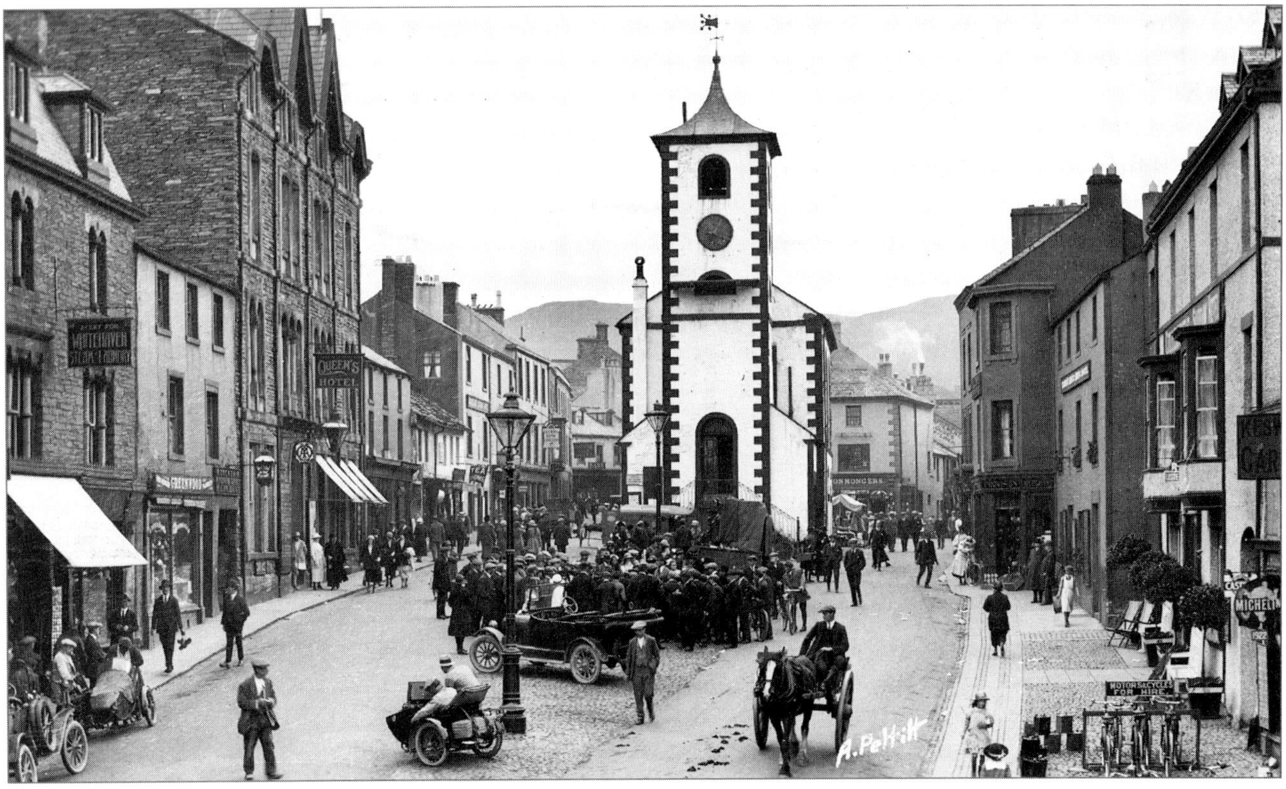

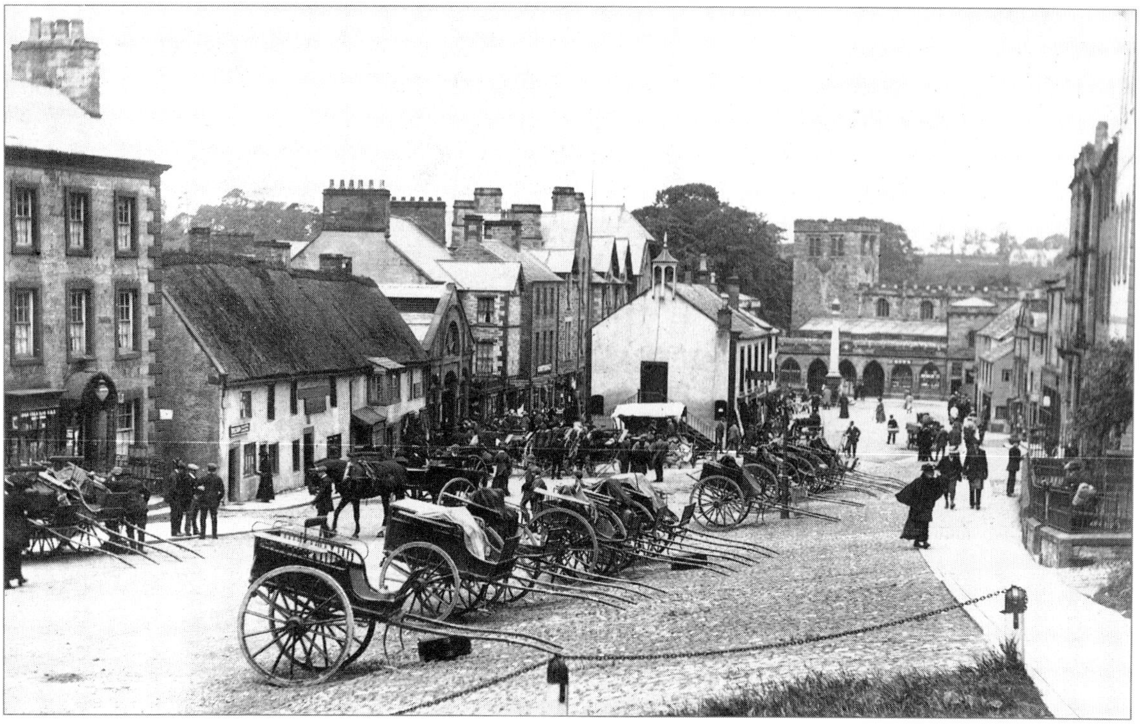

Appleby market day in about 1910. This photograph shows the neat parking of carriages and market-day business being carried on round the Moot Hall, with not a motor vehicle in sight. (*John Marsh Collection*)

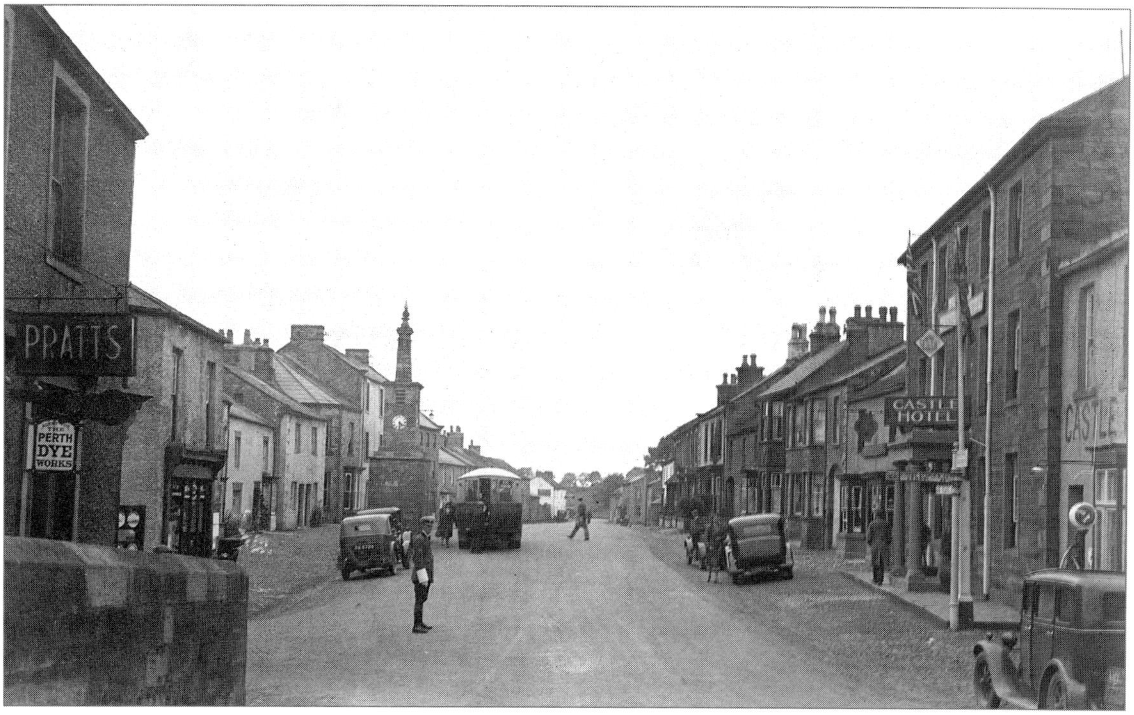

Brough, where the main A66 road traffic is in the care of an AA patrolman at the junction with the road to Kirkby Stephen. An early motorbus with rear exit is by the town clock before it was moved. This scene changed much as traffic increased to such an extent that a bypass was built through the centre of the village. (*Hayton of Carlisle*)

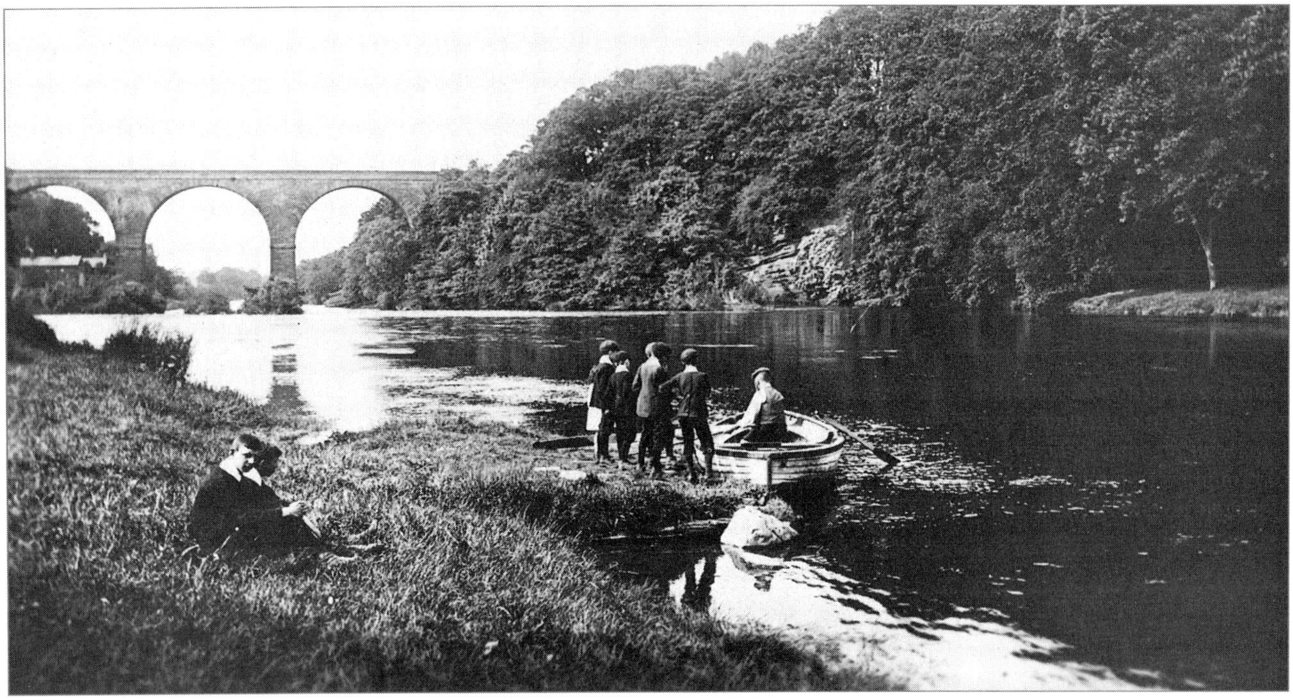

The River Eden at Wetheral, above, provided a good day out for youngsters especially when a rowing boat was available for a cruise on the river. Stepping stones existed throughout the county as ancient roads crossed streams and rivers. Below, Hart Publishing pictured them at Ambleside in about 1910 when they became an adventure for youngsters. Simple experiences such as these were the happy memories of many at about the time of the First World War. (*Above, John Marsh Collection; below, Hart Publishing*)

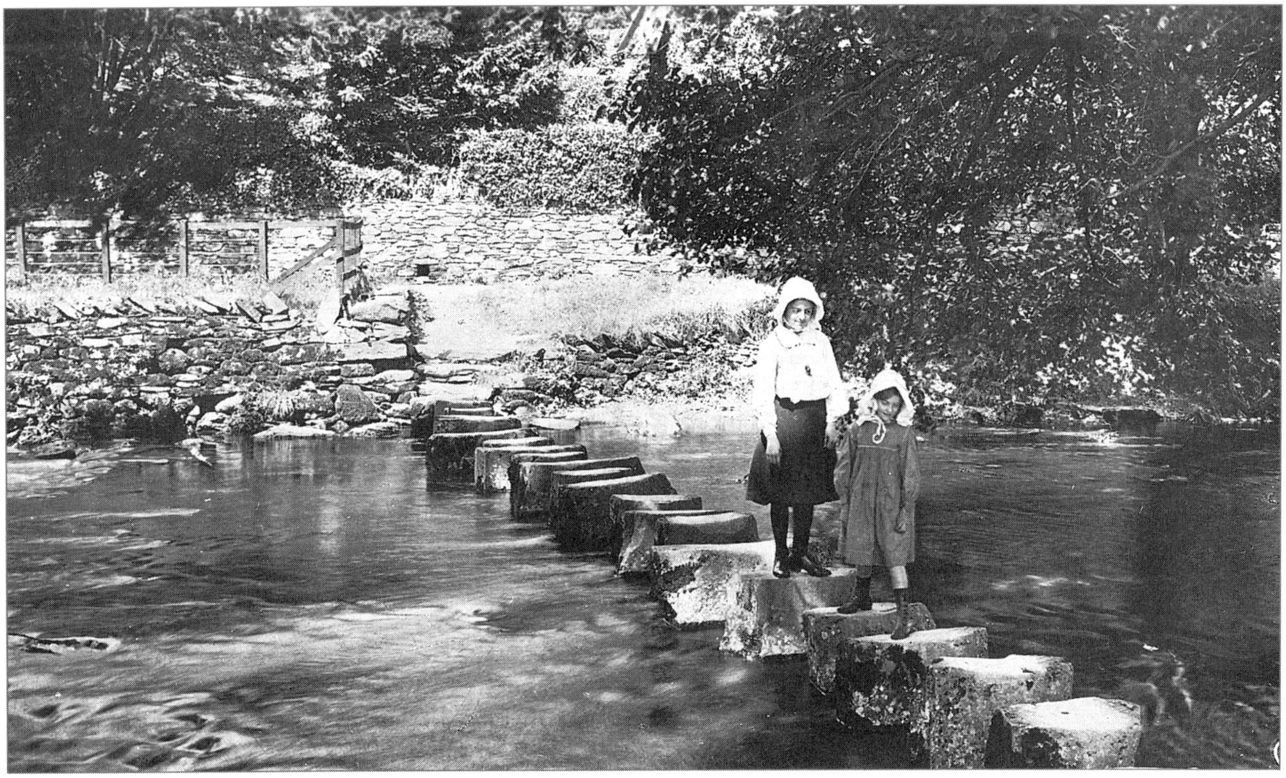

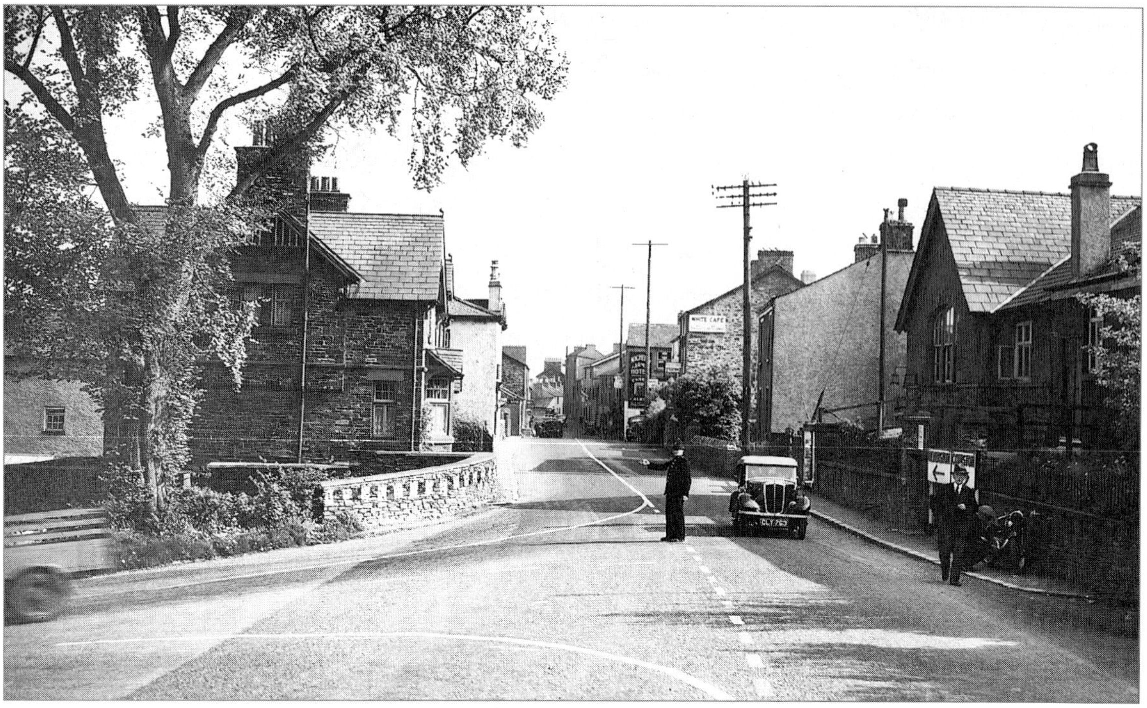

Greenodd main street just after the Second World War. Again a Lancashire county policeman is on point duty with hardly any traffic to control (see Grange on p. 57 and Ulverston on p. 138). (*Atkinson & Pollitt*)

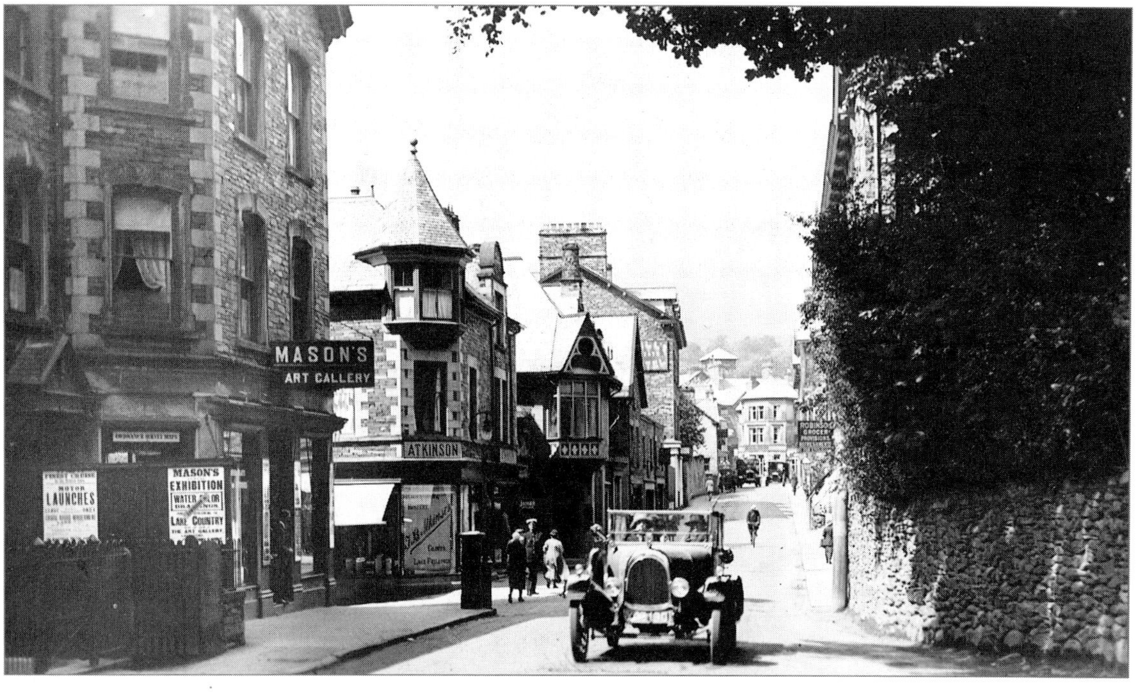

Lake Road, Ambleside, was pictured by Atkinson & Pollitt in this early 1920s photograph, which is taken from their postcard series which spanned four decades. Mason's Art Gallery building on the left has had many uses since that time. Lake Road was to take the brunt of the motor vehicle pollution which hit Ambleside when the railways were cut back. Even though a one-way system was introduced, like Kendal, nobody really knew what to do about all the motor vehicles which ruined this once quiet market town. (*Atkinson & Pollitt*)

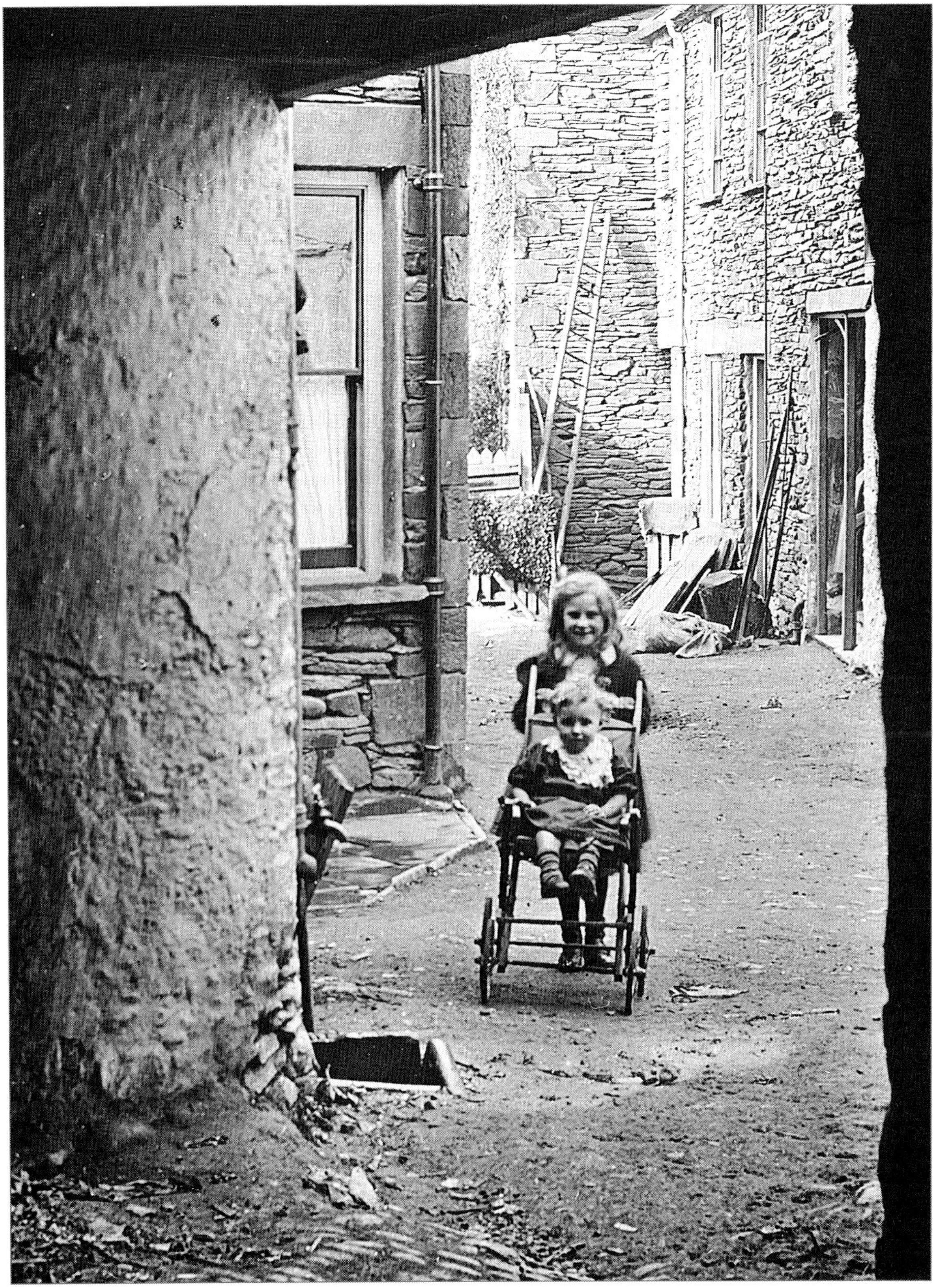

A magic memory of a yard in Ambleside: obviously not a place for tourists. Note the outside tap on the left – it possibly supplied all the premises in the yard. (*Lowe of Patterdale*)

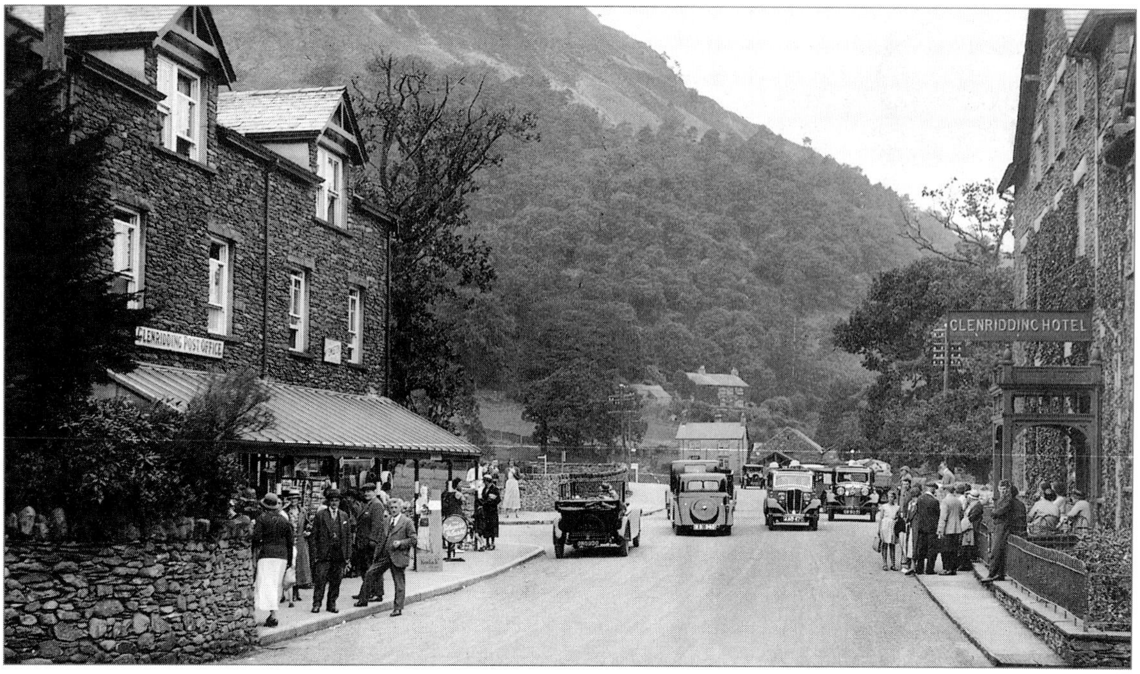

Glenridding main street, late 1930s. Ullswater holiday makers are to be seen in their motor cars, shopping at the post office and adjoining shops and waiting outside the Glenridding Hotel for their holiday transport. This scene will bring back holiday memories for many and, apart from fashions and the type of motor vehicle, has little changed today. (*John Marsh Collection*)

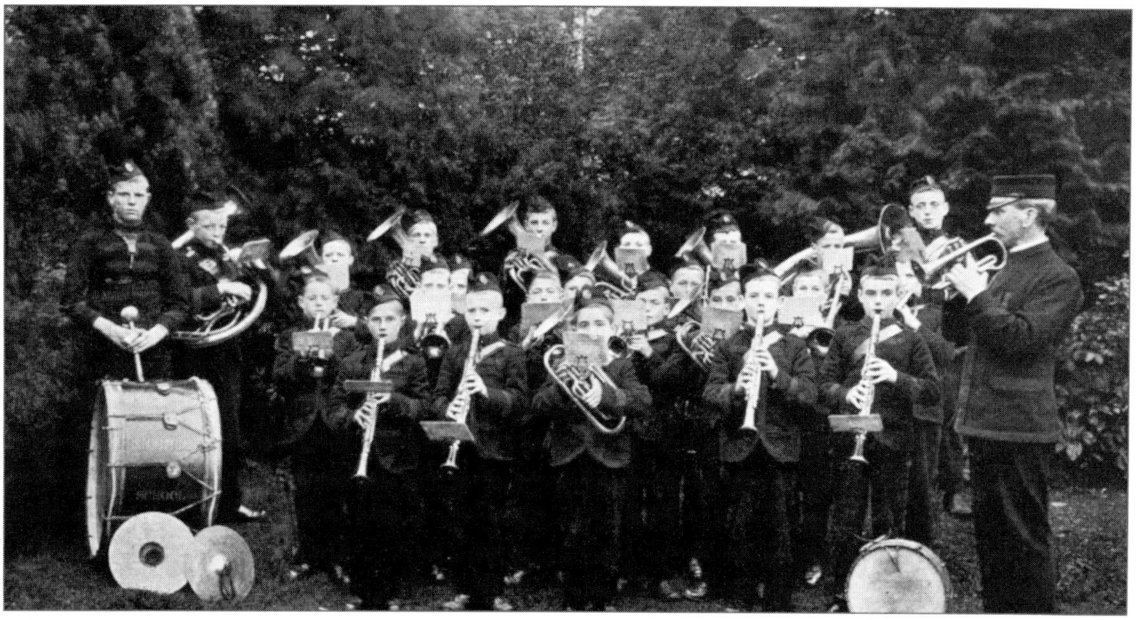

The Cockermouth Industrial School was opened in 1881 to accommodate 150 boys from the County of Cumberland 'to be trained to the habits of Industry and to be taught some handcraft or other by which they may afterwards earn an honest living'. It was government-aided and run by a committee of County Councillors. As the County Council for Cumberland was not formed until 1888 the school must have come to the council as a working institution, and is thus one of the earliest county schools in Cumberland and a replacement for the old Poor Law workhouse where some of the boys may have started life. A place in the band would, no doubt, open a bright future for those musically inclined. (*Beaty's of Carlisle*)

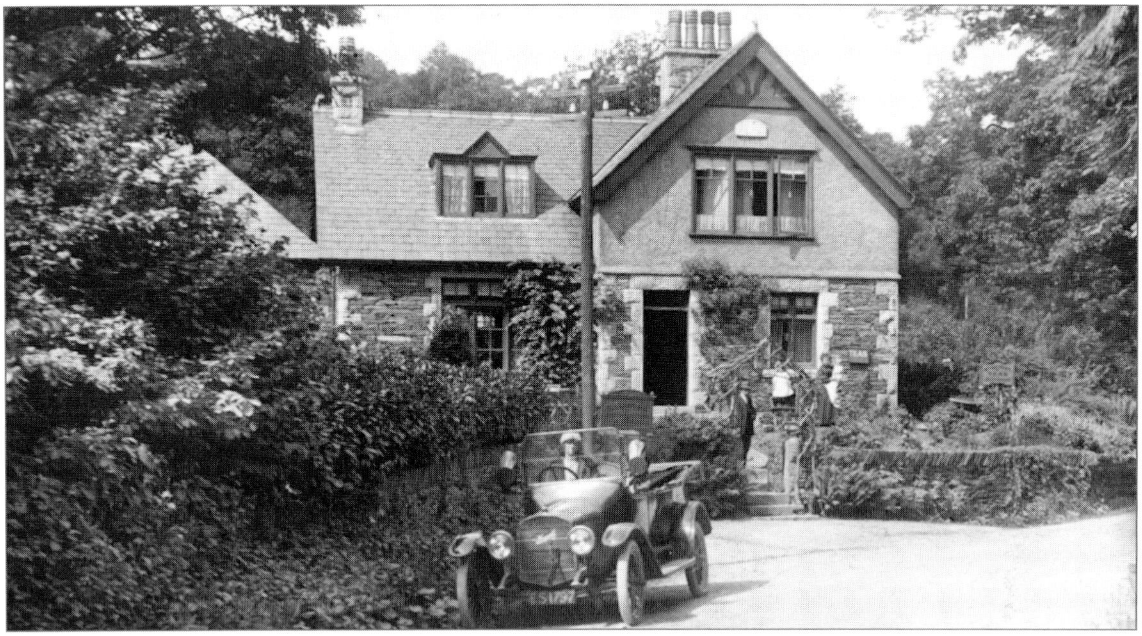

The Institute Refreshment Rooms at Lakeside were run by the Baythrop family for many years and they had this postcard taken by the photographic firm Lilywhite for their clients to buy. Many people coming ashore from the lake steamers found their way to the refreshment rooms before returning to Bowness or Ambleside. (*Lilywhite of Sowerby Bridge*)

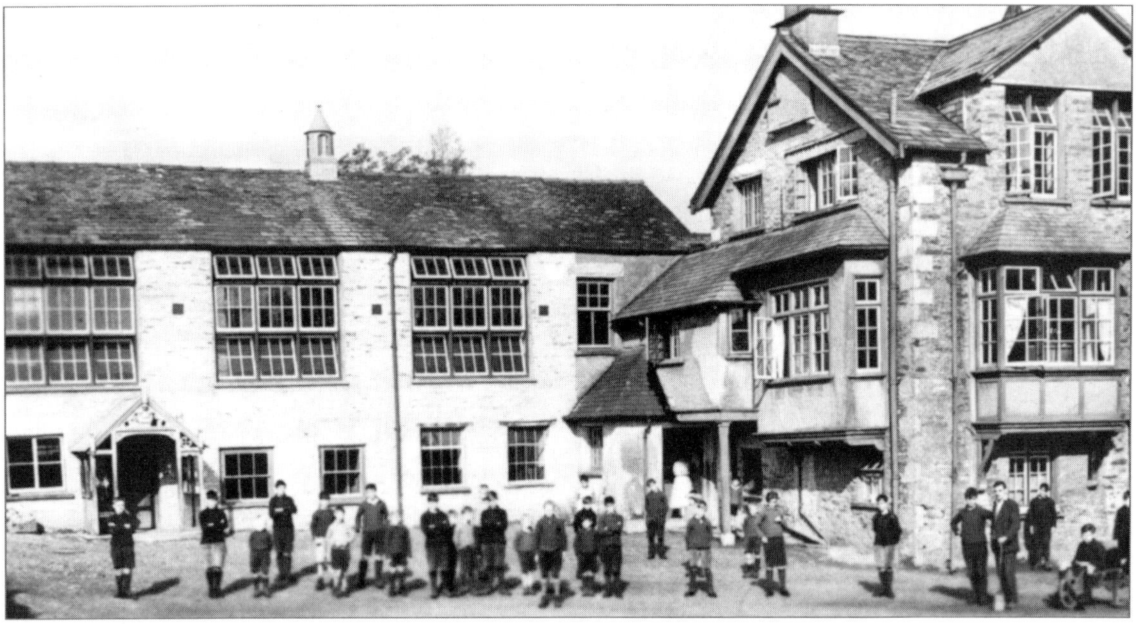

The Starnthwaite School near Crosthwaite was very different to the Cockermouth School opposite, being organised by the Christian Union for Social Service to 'take youths and men away from the listless apathy' of being epileptic in a workhouse. The photograph dates from the days of Miss Burford as matron in the early 1930s. The use of the buildings into our times shows very different reflections of a changing society. When the school for epileptics was closed owing to advances in medical science the school became one for delinquents. This offered boys from the cities of Lancashire and elsewhere a second chance. When a harder approach to delinquency was adopted the school buildings were sold for development into private houses and flats. (*Atkinson & Pollitt*)

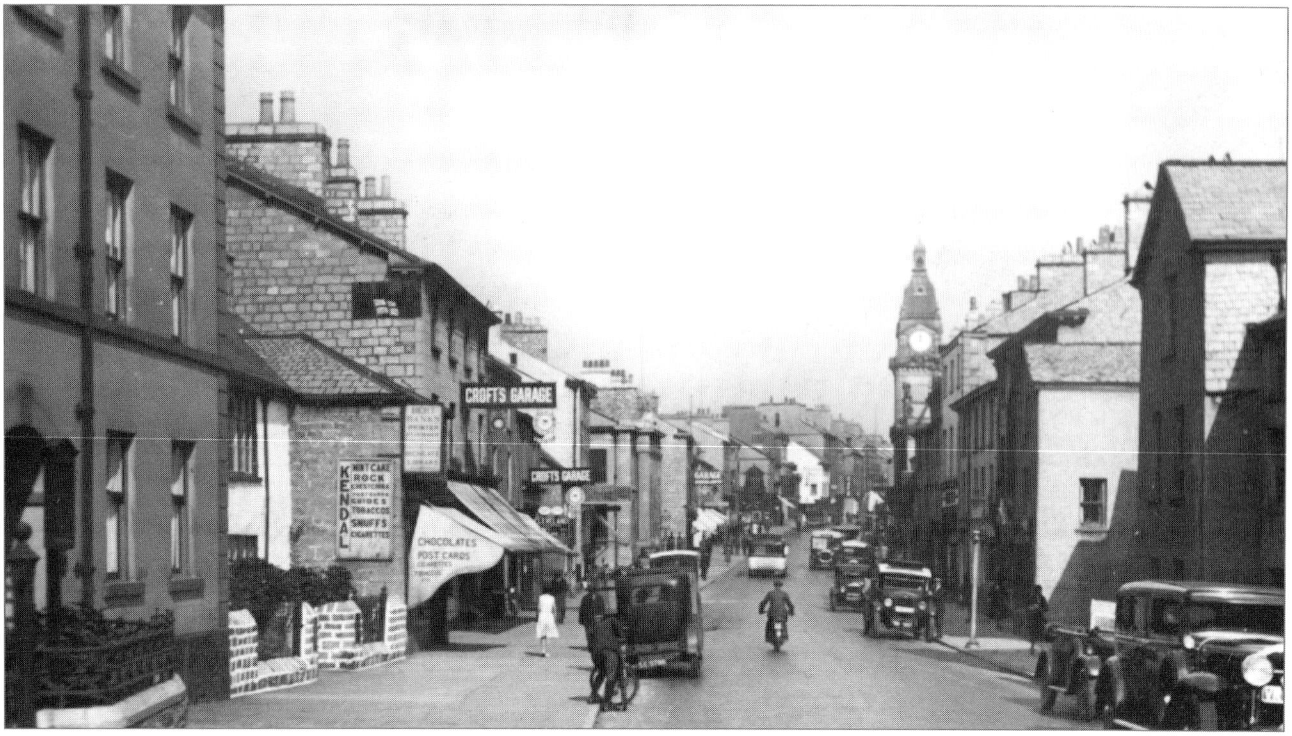

Kendal as seen in the 1930s. Above, Highgate, with a two-way traffic system, before the A6 produced the continuous traffic congestion that caused the road to be remade on a solid concrete underbase and the introduction of a one-way system that nobody now seems able to change, even though the M6 took away the main road traffic in 1970. Below, the Abbot Hall Park end of the Jennings footbridge and a railed-off public park with Colonel's Walk along the river. (*Atkinson & Pollitt*)

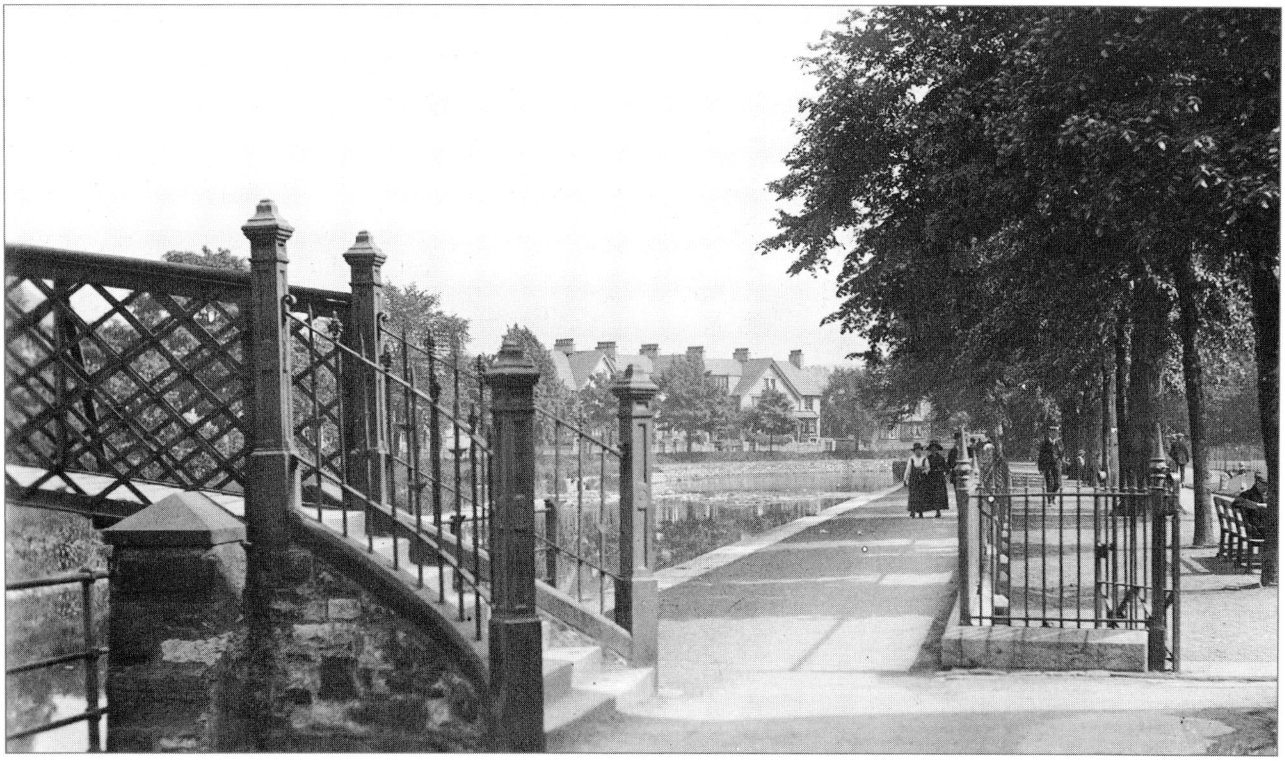

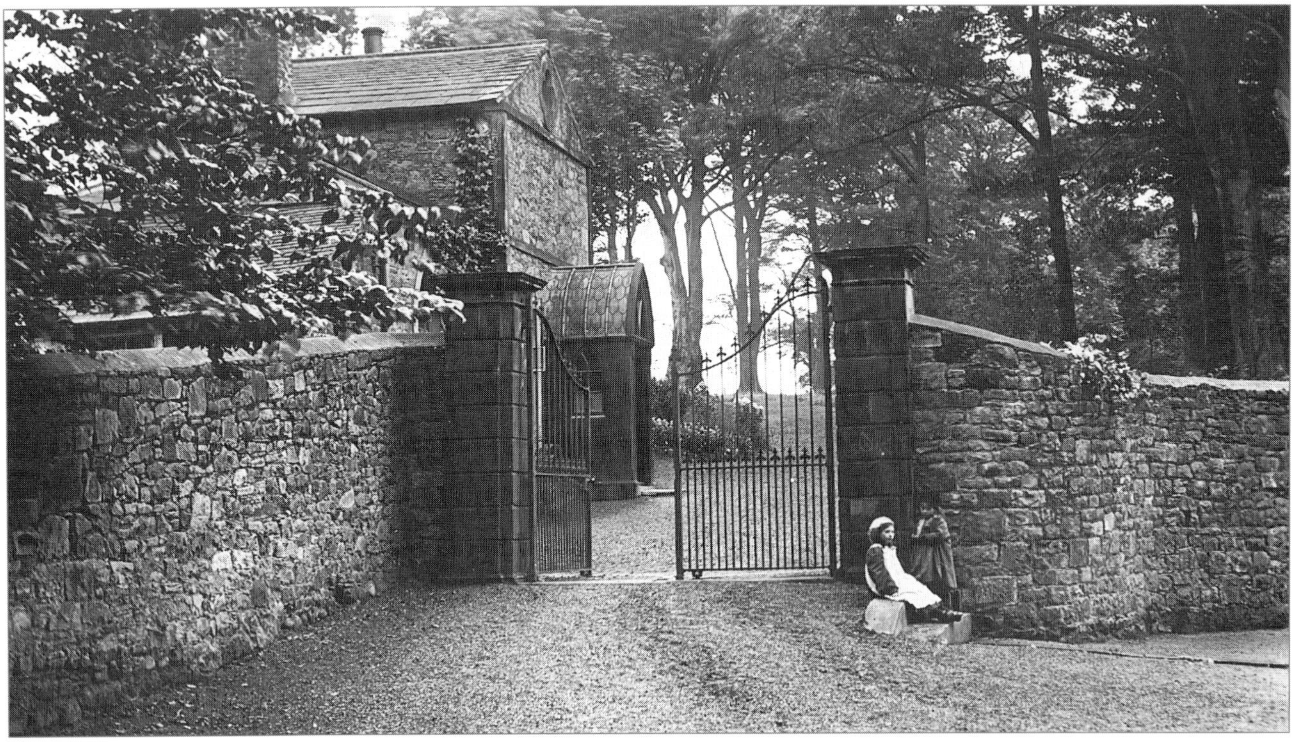

Workington Hall Lodge and gates near Cuckoo Arch at about the time of the First World War when a number of Workington folk were employed at the hall. The two children seem to be waiting for their mother to finish work. The hall was given to the local authority a number of decades later but municipal poverty and lack of imagination reduced the historic remains to ruins – a lesson in what not to do with an historic house. (*John Marsh Collection*)

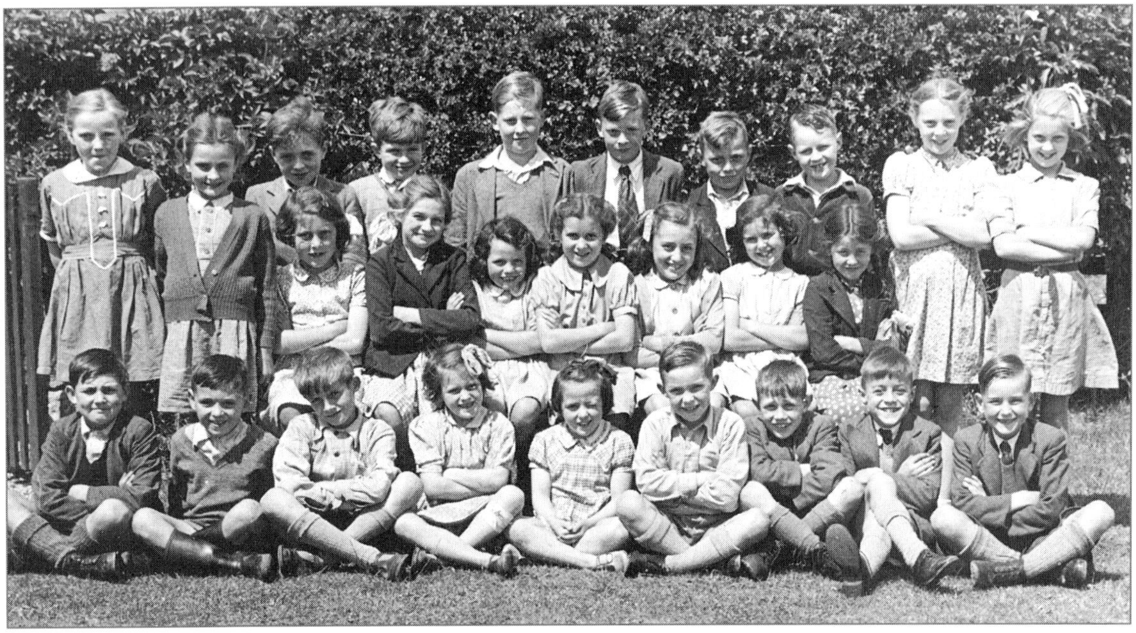

A school photograph for the seniors at Burton Morewood School, late 1940s. This picture captures well the high expectations and happiness of those postwar years. Many Cumbrians will remember the high hopes of those times. Kath Alderson poses with crossed arms in the centre of the middle row surrounded by her school pals. (*John Marsh Collection*)

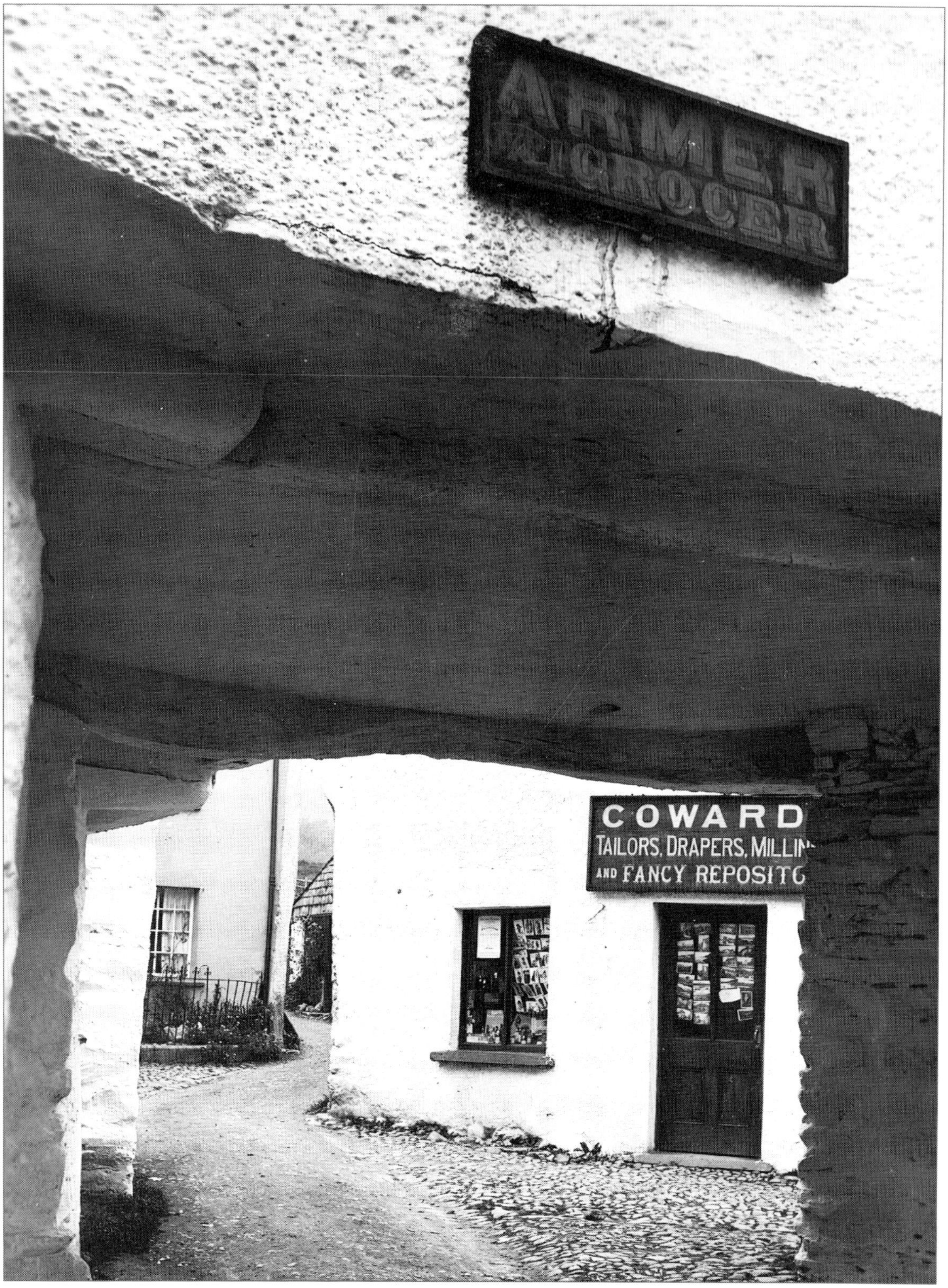

Hawkshead in the 1920s, with Coward's shop framed by one of the many arches in this quaint village: 'Tailors, Drapers, Milliners and Fancy Repository' with postcards for sale. Anything to make a penny in those far from affluent days well-remembered by many. (*Atkinson & Pollitt*)

Acknowledgements

The authors wish to acknowledge the help and assistance given by the following people in the preparation of this book. Most pictures are from our own collections of old photographs but we wish to express our thanks to the following who have permitted us to use photographs from their collections: Mr T. Allan of Cockermouth, Mrs A. Bonnett of Allithwaite, Mr George Dawson of Kendal, Mr Neville Stead of Whitley Bay, and Mr Preston Whiteley of Kendal. The photographs shown as by Atkinson & Pollitt appear by kind permission of the editor of the *Westmorland Gazette*, Kendal, and are copyright the *Westmorland Gazette*. The map of Cumbria was prepared by Mr Phillip Bonney.

Index